Constructive Guidance and Discipline

Preschool and Primary Education

FIFTH EDITION

Marjorie V. Fields
University of Alaska, Southeast

Nancy J. Perry
Arizona State University

Debby M. Fields

Foreword by Constance Kamii

Merrill
Boston Columbus Indianapolis New York San Francisco Upper Saddle River
Amsterdam Cape Town Dubai London Madrid Milan Munich Paris Montreal Toronto
Delhi Mexico City Sao Paulo Sydney Hong Kong Seoul Singapore Taipei Tokyo

Vice President and Editor in Chief: Jeffery W. Johnston
Acquisitions Editor: Julie Peters
Editorial Assistant: Tiffany Bitzel
Vice President, Director of Sales and Marketing: Quinn Perkson
Marketing Manager: Erica Deluca
Marketing Coordinator: Brian Mounts
Senior Managing Editor: Pamela D. Bennett
Project Manager: Kerry J. Rubadue
Senior Operations Supervisor: Matthew Ottenweller

Operations Specialist: Laura Messerly
Art Director: Diane Lorenzo
Cover Designer: Ali Mohrman
Cover Art: Banana Stock
Full-Service Project Management: S4Carlisle Publishing Services
Composition: S4Carlisle Publishing Services
Printer/Binder: Courier/Stoughton
Cover Printer: Courier/Stoughton
Text Font: Bookman 9.5/11.5

Credits and acknowledgments borrowed from other sources and reproduced, with permission, in this textbook appear on appropriate page within text (or on page 349).

All photos provided by the authors.

Every effort has been made to provide accurate and current Internet information in this book. However, the Internet and information posted on it are constantly changing, so it is inevitable that some of the Internet addresses listed in this textbook will change.

Library of Congress Cataloging-in-Publication Data

Fields, Marjorie V.
  Constructive guidance and discipline : preschool and primary education / Marjorie V. Fields, Nancy J. Perry, Debby Fields; foreword by Constance Kamii. – 5th ed.
    p. cm.
  ISBN-13: 978-0-13-603593-0
  ISBN-10: 0-13-603593-0
  1. School discipline.   2. Behavior modification.   3. Educational counseling.
4. Education, Preschool.   5. Education, Primary.   I. Fields, Debby.
II. Perry, Nancy, 1934–   III. Title.
  LB3012.F54 2010
  371.102′4–dc22   2009007135

10 9 8 7 6 5 4 3 2 1
ISBN-13: 978-0-13-603593-0
ISBN-10:   0-13-603593-0

*For the cause of
worldwide peace and harmony.
May it begin in the
hearts of children
and spread.
And may teachers be
sowers of the seeds
of peace and harmony.*

Foreword

This is a practical book with many examples and contrasts. It is not, however, a mere collection of recipes, but a book full of instructive examples based on sound, theoretical reasons. It also communicates a way of thinking about young children and attitudes of empathy.

The approach the authors recommend is good because it solves problems in positive ways and promotes the development of healthy personalities. In addition, though, the authors have a vision of autonomy as the aim of education that goes far beyond the development of healthy personalities. Since this vision may not have been articulated as forcefully as it could have been, I would like to take this opportunity to discuss autonomy as intended by Jean Piaget as the aim of education.

Autonomy, in Piaget's theory, means something different from its common meaning. Autonomy usually means the *right* to make decisions for oneself, and many people mistakenly think that it means the *right* to do whatever one pleases. In Piaget's theory, autonomy does not mean the right, but instead the *ability* to make decisions for oneself about right and wrong, independently of reward and punishment, by taking relevant factors into account. When one takes relevant factors into account, one is not free to lie, steal, break promises, disturb other people, or be irresponsible.

Parents and teachers have traditionally tried to teach right and wrong by using reward and/or punishment. Reward and punishment give the appearance of working, but the result, in the long run, is either blind conformity or susceptibility to manipulation through reward and/or punishment. The Watergate cover-up affair, for example, happened because the men under President Nixon expected to be rewarded for doing what they knew to be morally wrong. As far as the effects of punishment are concerned, we all know how the possibility of punishment leads to the calculation of risks.

A clear example of moral autonomy is Martin Luther King's struggle for civil rights. He took relevant factors into account, concluded that the laws discriminating against African Americans were unjust, and fought to put an end to these laws. Many people tried to stop him with incarceration, dogs, water hoses, and threats of assassination, but he could not be manipulated by reward or punishment.

The important question for parents and teachers is: How can we raise children to become morally autonomous adults who make decisions based on what is right, rather than on what is rewarded or punished? Piaget's answer to this question was that we foster the development of autonomy first by refraining from using reward and punishment. By giving stickers to children for completing worksheets, for example, we unwittingly teach them to become susceptible to manipulation by reward. If we punish children for lying, to cite another example, children can learn only to avoid being punished. Piaget would suggest that, instead of punishing a child for telling a lie, we might look him or her straight in the eye and say with affection and skepticism, "I can't believe what you are saying because . . . I want you to sit down and think about what you might do next time if you want me to believe you." This appeal to the human relationship between the child and the adult and to the direct consequence of the act has the effect of motivating the child to construct from within, over time, the value of honesty. Children who are thus supported in building their own convictions about the importance of honesty cannot tell lies, even for a president who might dangle rewards.

A discussion of specific techniques is beyond the scope of the present context, and the reader is urged to read this book. I also recommend *The Moral Judgment of the Child* (Chapters 2 and 3) by Piaget.

Today's children live with many serious potential problems, such as drug abuse, AIDS, teenage pregnancies, and guns in schools. Although each of these may look like separate problems, they collectively are actually symptoms of the inability to make decisions for oneself by taking relevant factors into account. Children who can take relevant factors into account do not take drugs, for example.

The belief that rules and values must be instilled in children from the outside through lectures, rewards, and punishment is outdated. Rules and values must be constructed (made) by children from the inside if they are to become the children's own. Only when children have convictions of their own do they have the moral courage to say "No" to drugs, sex, and violence. Children need the same strength of internal conviction Martin Luther King had when he stood up to the punishment heaped upon him.

The time to start fostering the development of autonomy is at an early age. Through building strong human relationships, exchanging points of view with children, and allowing them to learn from their own mistakes, we can help children develop the capacity to take relevant factors into account. Autonomy is a complicated goal, and I congratulate the authors for going beyond the perspective of what seems to work in the short run. What seems to work in the short run often defeats our long-range goal of turning out adults who can decide for themselves between right and wrong.

Constance Kamii
Birmingham, Alabama

About the Authors

Marjorie Fields   Dr. Marjorie Fields has recently retired after teaching in the field of early childhood education for over 30 years. She first taught kindergarten, then first grade, then began teaching teachers. Thanks to her own children, she also had experience in cooperative preschools and various types of child care.

Marjorie has a doctorate in early childhood education with research in parent involvement. She has been active in early childhood professional organizations at the national and local levels; she is currently president of the National Association of Early Childhood Teacher Educators (NAECTE) and has also served as vice-president of that association. She has served on the national governing board for the National Association for the Education of Young Children (NAEYC). She has published extensively in the field of emergent literacy, including the textbook *Let's Begin Reading Right* (Merrill/Prentice Hall), as well as in the field of child guidance.

This book is the outgrowth of over 25 years of reading and thinking in conjunction with developing and teaching early childhood discipline courses. Dr. Fields credits her two sons with initially helping her learn what is most important about child guidance and discipline. She now continues to learn from her grandchildren.

Nancy Perry   Dr. Nancy Perry is the Coordinator of Early Childhood Education in the College of Teacher Education and Leadership at Arizona State University. She is a former teacher and administrator with 20 years of classroom experience. Nancy has a Ph.D. in Curriculum and Instruction with an emphasis in early childhood education. She teaches both undergraduate and graduate courses in early childhood education. Nancy's research is focused on teachers' and parents' interpretations of curriculum policies and teachers' use of evidence-based guidance strategies.

Debby Fields   Debby Fields is a mental health counselor, currently working with adoptive parents. She is also a very involved mother of two young daughters. Debby has worked as an elementary school counselor and as a teen–parent counselor. Through her work and life, she has learned a great deal about child development. Early intervention and attachment were the focus of her work with teen parents. This work allowed her a window into the lives of young adults with attachment problems and the obstacles they face in raising their own children.

Debby has a master's degree in marriage, family, and child counseling. She presented her master's thesis on multicultural counseling at a national convention for the American Psychological Association. In addition to her training in attachment issues, she has focused on developing culturally sensitive practices and has a degree in anthropology. Debby previously worked in cooperative preschools with both of her children and now volunteers in their grade-school classrooms.

Preface

Constructive Guidance and Discipline: Preschool and Primary Education provides early childhood professionals with the best of approaches to help young children become happy, responsible, and productive people. We present guidance and discipline concepts within a framework of child development, developmentally appropriate practices, and constructivist education. Thus, only discipline approaches that are consistent with all three aspects of this framework are recommended here. We take a stand about what is best for young children, rather than merely presenting an impartial overview of various approaches. We are convinced that adults cannot effectively assist children's moral development through the coercive approaches of punishment or behavior modification.

We emphasize guidance for children ages 3 through 8, rather than 0 through 8, which is the entire scope of early childhood. Appropriate guidance and discipline must be tied to developmental level, and infant and toddler development is uniquely different from that of children in the preoperational years of 3 through 8. The approaches presented in this text require more emotional, social, and cognitive maturation than that attained by most toddlers. Clearly, the developmental level identified by Piaget as the preoperational stage presents its own set of guidance challenges. These challenges are our focus here.

MAJOR THEORETICAL INFLUENCES

The information and ideas presented in this text come from a number of respected sources. We see four theorists as having major influences on child guidance concepts in this century: Alfred Adler, Carl Rogers, B. F. Skinner, and Jean Piaget. Rudolf Dreikurs's recommendations of logical and natural consequences extended Adler's concepts; Thomas Gordon popularized Rogers's ideas through his Parent Effectiveness Training work; Skinner's work founded the widespread behavior modification techniques; and Piagetian scholars such as Constance Kamii and Rheta DeVries are spreading the word about Piaget's views on the development of morality. Although we reject Skinner's approach for the reasons explained in Chapter 9, we believe that the other three theorists have compatible views. Adler, Rogers, and Piaget all perceive the child as actively seeking understanding. This perspective contrasts the Skinnerian view, which sees education as something that happens to a child from outside sources. Adler and Rogers, as well as Piaget, respect the child's personal rate and style of developing social understanding. All three perceive the proper adult role as facilitating rather than controlling the child's gradual development into a constructive member of society. Piaget's theoretical framework is much broader than that of Rogers or Adler, including comprehensive moral as well as intellectual development. Thus, Adlerian and Rogerian concepts can be included as part of a Piagetian perspective, although the reverse is not true.

The research and writing of Jean Piaget and constructivist scholars regarding intellectual and moral autonomy are central to the message in this book. We have also adapted Thomas Gordon's recommendations for effective communication and interpreted Rudolf Dreikurs's concept of logical and natural consequences into our discussion of a constructivist approach to discipline. In addition, we have drawn on Erik Erikson's emotional development studies, referred to guidelines from the National Association for the Education of Young Children, and often quoted Rheta DeVries. Many other sources used in this book are listed at the end of the chapters.

We look at guidance and discipline as teaching activities; therefore, the principles of effective early childhood education apply as much to guidance and discipline as to academics. In addition, we discuss the ways in which effective early childhood education practices prevent or alleviate many common discipline problems.

Like any other aspect of teaching, guidance must acknowledge diversity among youngsters. In our recommendations, we have considered individual differences due to innate temperament or individual physical and intellectual capabilities. We also discuss the implications of culture, class, family problems, and gender.

We recognize that teachers must often deal with youngsters in crisis, creating major new challenges in guidance and discipline. Two chapters are devoted to providing background and support to teachers whose classrooms include youngsters with special needs or learning difficulties as well as those who have experienced difficult life situations that may make them more vulnerable to social or emotional difficulties.

ORGANIZATION OF THE TEXT

The first three chapters of the book constitute the foundations section, Part 1. Chapter 1 defines discipline as teaching autonomy and self-discipline while promoting self-esteem. Concepts introduced in Chapter 1 are more fully addressed throughout the book. Chapters 2 and 3 consider stages in children's physical, emotional, intellectual, and social development as they relate to discipline problems and solutions. We consider a clear definition of discipline and its goals, plus knowledge of child development, to be the basic understandings for a discussion of discipline.

Part 2 presents various approaches to discipline in descending order, from most positive to negative. This sequence can also be considered as an ascending order, from least intrusive to most intrusive. Chapter 4 discusses how to prevent behavior problems by creating an emotional and physical environment most supportive of children's healthy development. Chapter 5 explains the role of developmentally appropriate programs in preventing discipline problems. Chapters 6 and 7 emphasize both the prevention of problems and intervention when problems do occur. Chapter 6 explains how the examples shown by adults influence child behavior and shows how to help children use those examples during conflict situations. Chapter 7 presents effective ways to communicate with children both to prevent conflict and to address problems that arise and how to negotiate solutions to existing problems. Chapter 8 explains how early childhood professionals can help children to change unproductive behaviors by using related consequences to show children why certain behaviors are unacceptable. Chapter 9 analyzes behavior modification approaches, and explains why rewards and even praise are counterproductive to the goals of self-discipline. The dangers of punishment are presented in Chapter 10.

Chapters 11 through 15 constitute Part 3, which builds on the previous two parts. Child development knowledge from Part 1 is used to determine the cause of behavior problems. Then knowledge about guidance approaches from Part 2 is used to select an appropriate response. Part 3 analyzes typical causes of discipline problems and relates them to the approaches relevant to each. These chapters emphasize the necessity of dealing with the cause of problems rather than just the symptoms. Chapter 11 discusses the relationship between maturational level and acceptable behavior, and Chapter 12 looks at how unmet needs cause problem behavior. Chapters 13 and 14 explore serious problems with causes outside of the classroom and offer helpful suggestions for the teacher or caregiver. Chapter 15 presents an overview of possible causes of discipline problems and identifies which causes pertain to a particular situation. This chapter also provides a guide for matching the causes with the discipline approaches that are most likely to be effective for each.

PROVIDING EXAMPLES

Because we want to balance theoretical explanations with real-life examples, we use typical scenarios to illustrate ways to facilitate self-discipline and moral autonomy through positive approaches to discipline. This method is congruent with our message that teachers must not respond just to the behavior, but must consider the many factors that might relate to the cause of the behavior. These "stories" have proven extremely useful to college students trying to visualize the practical applications of text material but who struggle with abstract concepts.

Meet the cast of characters: Dennis, Maureen, Sheri, Nancy, and the rest of the staff of the Midway Children's Center, a composite of typical preschool/child-care centers in the suburbs, who provide examples of discipline with 3- and 4-year-olds. Moreover Mrs. Jensen, her first-grade students, and the staff of a typical city school demonstrate the same concepts with primary-grade children. Second-grade teacher Mr. Davis and his student teacher, Beth, teach at the same school, as does the kindergarten teacher, Mrs. Taylor. Mrs. Jensen and Mrs. Davis represent all the caring and effective public school teachers we have known.

Because contrasting desirable with undesirable practices often helps us define the desirable, we have also provided examples of common practices that we do not recommend. For this purpose, we have created two fictitious characters, preschool teacher Joanne and first-grade teacher Miss Wheeler, and described them in some very real situations. Miss Wheeler teaches at the same elementary school as Mrs. Jensen. Joanne teaches at the same children's center as Dennis, but she is in charge during the afternoon and Dennis is the lead teacher during the morning preschool session. Having Dennis and Joanne share the same students and support staff provides examples of how different approaches affect the same children. All teachers are fictional, but the good and bad situations described are real. We use first names for the child-care staff and last names for public school staff, not to imply more respect for the latter, but only as a reflection of common practice.

Examples from readers' own experience will be the most instructive. We believe that spending significant time with youngsters, preferably enough to establish authentic relationships with them, is necessary for internalizing theories about guidance and discipline. We believe that personal observation and experience are crucial to learning, whether in preschool or adulthood.

We use the term *teacher* throughout the book to refer to caregivers as well as other teachers. Any adults who guide children through their day are teaching them. We firmly believe that adults working with children in child care must be as knowledgeable about child development as any other teachers. Since youngsters are so profoundly influenced by the adults in their lives, it is essential that all teachers have a solid understanding of how to influence youngsters in positive directions.

CHANGES IN THE FIFTH EDITION

This edition is enhanced by the fresh voice of a new co-author Nancy Perry, who has made major contributions to the book. We continue our efforts to offer you a coherent analysis of relevant research and to provide guidelines for teacher decisions about appropriate guidance and discipline.

Content Changes

In addition to updating our sources, we added some new features that we think will make this text more useful. We added guiding questions to the beginning of each chapter to help students predict and track what they are reading. The beginning of each chapter also features a list of professional development standards from the National Association for the Education of Young Children (NAEYC); this should help faculty as well as students in relating reading to national ECE teacher accreditation standards. Additionally, this edition includes more tables and figures than previous editions because students report that these help them synthesize and remember key points in the text.

Some previous information has been expanded. Increased emphasis on observation as a way to discover the cause of behavior problems highlights a major theme of this text: that we cannot create a plan of action without an analysis of the problem. Finding the cause behind behaviors of individual children is also assisted by expanded discussions of temperament and emotion regulation, featuring an expanding research base in those areas. We've also added more information and examples about how to design a classroom environment and plan curriculum that prevents behaviors problems.

We have changed the emphasis in Chapters 13 and 14, renaming them *Diversity* and *Vulnerabilities*. We've used these chapters to strengthen our discussions about working effectively with children with special needs, second language learners, and children who have experienced difficult life situations due to abuse, poverty, illness, divorce, and/or the loss of a parent. There is also more emphasis on building respectful relationships with parents and including them as partners in their children's education. We have also introduced the importance of using a three-tiered approach when guiding children who display behaviors that teachers identify as most challenging. We believe that this approach will help teachers better understand how to integrate prevention strategies, intentional teaching, and individualized instruction to meet the needs of the diverse groups of children in today's classrooms.

Finally, this edition is enhanced by the inclusion of video vignettes that display many of the concepts presented throughout the text. You will find references to the videos within the text, as margin notes, and in the *For Further Thought* sections at the end of many of the chapters in this edition. The videos are hosted on Pearson's *MyEducationLab* Web site for easy access by both students and instructors.

This edition continues and strengthens the approach of the previous editions. We have continued to work at making the message of the book clear and understandable. Since behavior modification is so pervasive in our society, the recommendations in this book require most readers to radically alter their thinking. Assisting students in a major paradigm shift requires that principles be carefully documented and clearly explained. We have found that the examples of classroom practice are most effective in helping students understand the concepts; therefore, we have carefully reviewed the classroom vignettes, adding more and better examples. This edition works to better balance the preschool and primary-grade-level examples.

Expanded *Instructor's Manual, PowerPoint Slides,* and *Test Bank*

An expanded *Instructor's Manual* for this edition is located on the *Pearson Education Web site (www.pearsonhighered.com)*. It includes PowerPoint slides emphasizing the most important concepts in each chapter, a revised test bank, and teaching tips. Some of the instructor resources are from other college faculty who use this book to teach about guidance and discipline. In addition, we offer supplementary materials that your students may find useful. The test bank added to the fifth edition has been expanded to include a variety of question types and problem-solving situations. These are not test items requiring mere rote memory; they simulate actual classroom situations where problem solving is required for effective discipline. Even the multiple-choice questions require higher-level thinking. This approach to testing is congruent with a constructivist approach to education, allowing the college teacher to model the principles recommended.

Acknowledgments

I wish to thank Constance Kamii for her patience and guidance in my quest to better understand constructivism and moral autonomy. Thanks also to all the teachers whose classrooms I have visited and who have provided models of kind and constructive discipline. These include my sister, Deborah Hillstead, a wonderful early childhood teacher who keeps me in touch with classroom reality. I have learned the most from children themselves, however. All the youngsters in all the classrooms where I have spent time over the last two decades have helped me to understand child development and guidance. Raising my own two sons also taught me a lot, and I must thank them for being the subjects of my longitudinal research. Now I have five grandchildren, covering the entire early childhood age range of 0 through 8. They are teaching me even more about child development.

I have greatly appreciated Nancy Perry's clear insights and calm efficiency as a co-author. I am in awe of her talents and delighted to be working with her. It continues to be a joy to work with my daughter-in-law, Debby on this book. Our mutual interest in her children—my grandchildren—provided a personal perspective to our research. I am deeply indebted to the teachers at Sacajawea school in Seattle who allowed me to take photographs, and especially to Susan Rappleya, who assisted with parental permission forms. As always, I appreciate the guidance of our editor, Julie Peters, and I am grateful for the hard work of Kerry Rubadue, the project manager. Finally—as always—many, many thanks to my dear husband for his patience and help.

Marjorie Fields

I would like to thank my husband Chuck, son Bradley, and daughter Lauren for being so patient while I worked on this book. Without their love and support, my contribution to this book would not have been possible. I also acknowledge Elaine Surbeck, my mentor and friend who first introduced me to constructivism and helped me to gain a deeper understanding of Piagetian theory.

Special thanks goes out to the teachers and children of the Desert Heights Preschool in Glendale, Arizona, and the Polytechnic Elementary School in Mesa, Arizona, for welcoming me into their classrooms to videotape them while practicing many of the principles discussed in this book. Current and previous students from the College of Teacher Education and Leadership at Arizona State University also contributed this edition by sharing pictures of their classroom environments. I am grateful for their contributions.

Finally, I would like to thank Marjorie for offering me the opportunity to contribute to this edition. She is a wonderful mentor who encouraged me to stretch my thinking about children's social and emotional development and patiently guided me though the writing process.

Nancy Perry

I would like to thank Marjorie: my mentor, friend, babysitter, and mother-in-law. Without Marjorie, my contributions to this book would never have been possible. I am so grateful for her guidance and strong faith in me.

My work was also possible because of the support of my wonderful husband, Mike. He rushed home from many mountains to take care of our family. I am grateful for his generous and patient support.

I would also like to thank my children for all that they have taught me. They continue to be my inspiration.

Debby Fields

Thank you to the following reviewers:

Ann Aull Ivy Tech Community College
Katherine Yopp Collins Pitt Community College
Michael Glassman The Ohio State University
Carla Goble Tulsa Community College
Diana Nabors Sam Houston State University

Brief Contents

Contents

Contents

CHAPTER 7
Effective Discipline Through Effective Communication   154

PART 3
Matching Discipline Causes to Discipline Approaches   230

CHAPTER 11
Immaturity   231

CHAPTER 15
Analyzing Discipline Problems   321

Note: Every effort has been made to provide accurate and current Internet information in this book. However, the Internet and information posted on it are constantly changing, so it is inevitable that some of the Internet addresses listed in this textbook will change.

PART 1
Discipline Foundations

The first three chapters of this book provide the basic information necessary to study the topic of discipline. In Chapter 1, we describe discipline as discussed in this text, comparing the concept of constructivist discipline with authoritarian and permissive discipline. As part of this definition, we examine discipline in terms of the goals or outcomes desired. Chapter 1 also introduces the two basic premises of the book: working toward long-term discipline goals rather than only immediate concerns, and matching the discipline approach to the cause of the problem behavior.

Chapters 2 and 3 focus on child development issues that directly affect discipline in preschools and primary grades. Understanding how children grow, learn, and think helps adults to live more harmoniously with youngsters. This understanding not only creates more tolerance for normal childish behaviors, but also reduces inappropriate adult expectations. Adults who lack this understanding often unknowingly create discipline problems by putting children in situations where they are sure to have trouble. Adults who understand child development are able to use that knowledge to determine what skills are appropriate to expect of and teach children at various ages. We believe that effective discipline approaches must be based on knowledge of children's physical, emotional, intellectual, and social development and also on the individual characteristics of each child.

Chapter 1
Thinking About Guidance and Discipline

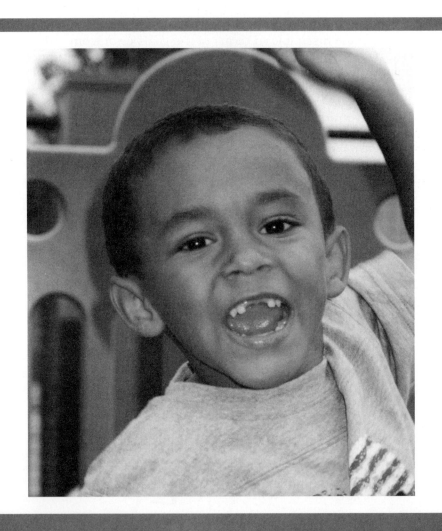

NAEYC Standards Addressed in This Chapter

Standard 3b: Observing, Documenting, and Assessing to Support Young Children and Families: Knowing about and using observation, documentation, and other appropriate assessment tools and approaches.

Standard 4a: Teaching and Learning, Connecting with Children and Families: Candidates know, understand, and use positive relationships and supportive interactions as the foundation for their work with young children.

Standard 4b: Teaching and Learning, Using Developmentally Effective Approaches: Candidates know, understand, and use a wide array of effective approaches, strategies, and tools to positively influence young children's development and learning.

Standard 5d: Becoming a Professional: Integrating knowledgeable, reflective, and critical perspectives on early education.

GUIDING QUESTIONS

- What is discipline?
- What is the long-term goal of discipline?
- How does a constructivist approach to discipline compare to other forms of discipline?
- How do teachers determine the causes of behavior problems?
- How do teachers work with parents who have different perspectives on discipline than they do?

Some books tell you they have the perfect formula to solve all your discipline problems; this one doesn't. This book says there is no one approach to discipline that will work for all problems, let alone for all children. Child guidance and discipline are incredibly complex, confusing, and frustrating. The many books and programs that offer simple solutions to discipline problems ignore the reality of individual differences, emotion-laden situations, and overburdened caregivers. In this book we do not offer any simple solutions, but instead acknowledge that effective child discipline is multifaceted, requiring a sophisticated set of understandings and skills. We try to provide the basics of the necessary understandings and skills, but, ultimately, what you get out of reading this book is determined by what you put into it.

This first chapter is intended to help you understand everything else in this book and give you our definitions for the terminology used throughout subsequent chapters. Ideally, as you read this chapter, you will have many questions and will use the book to help you find answers.

DEFINING DISCIPLINE

Notice that the title of this book includes both *guidance* and *discipline*. The term *guidance* is usually associated with helping youngsters deal with problems (as in guidance counselor), and the term *discipline* is too often associated with punishing children for doing things adults don't like. As you read, you will see that the term *discipline* is used broadly in this book, and that it includes what people generally think of as guidance, but it does not include punishment.

What do you think discipline is? Have you always thought of it as punishing a child for doing something wrong? Many people think that discipline is a smack on a child's bottom. You may have heard a (sick) joke that refers to a paddle as the "board of education." This book defines discipline differently: *helping children to learn personal responsibility for their behavior and to judge between right and wrong for themselves.* The emphasis is on teaching as we help youngsters learn responsible behaviors, rather than merely stopping unproductive actions. Did you know that the word *discipline* comes from the word *disciple*, which means "to lead and teach"? Teaching and leading are what adults should be doing when they discipline a child.

Instead of just enforcing rules about what not to do, we want to help children learn to make wise choices about what they should do. Note that learning to make wise choices for themselves is very different from just doing whatever they want. We are not advocating a lack of behavior controls or permissive approaches. Instead, we are advocating approaches that help children understand why certain behaviors are better than others, and that help children choose to act in a desirable manner, whether or not an adult is there to "catch" them at it.

This book is about how to support children in becoming responsible, kind, and productive citizens; it is not about forcing or otherwise coercing children to behave in certain ways. We will explain why we are convinced that external controls, such as reward and punishment, counteract the behavior and attitudes our society so desperately needs. We don't just tell you not to reward or punish children, we also explain better ways of reaching behavior goals.

A key element in the process is determining the cause of undesirable behaviors and working to eliminate that cause. Our approach to discipline is like diagnostic teaching: individualized to the needs and abilities of each child. This type of guidance and discipline requires extensive knowledge of child development and also of various guidance approaches. This book attempts to assist readers in obtaining the necessary knowledge in both areas; it then presents ways of using them together for child guidance.

∞ This book defines *discipline* as helping children to learn personal responsibility for their behavior and to judge between right and wrong for themselves.

Because we view discipline as teaching, not merely controlling, we recommend that school discipline be planned at least as carefully as other aspects of the curriculum. Schools long ago gave up punishing students for not knowing how to read or do a math problem (Butchart & McEwan, 1998). Instead of punishing children for missing skills and understandings, teachers now teach what is missing. This is the same process we advocate for helping children with missing social skills and for teaching them understandings related to behavior.

High Stakes

Can we afford to spend school time teaching social skills and caring attitudes? Evidence shows that we can't afford not to (Charney, 2002; Garrett, 2006). Although federal mandates have focused schools on academic testing, experienced teachers know that other areas of the curriculum won't get covered if discipline is not taught appropriately. But, more important, observers of human nature and human development researchers (Damon, Lerner, & Eisenberg, 2006; Hanish et al., 2007; Swick & Freeman, 2004) know that it doesn't really matter what else people learn if they don't learn to become caring, principled, and responsible; their lives will be lived in shambles. "Individuals do not develop into educated competent members of society by learning academic skills, absent of social skills" (Garrett, 2006, p. 154). In addition, it is becoming increasingly clear that schools must teach caring, communication, negotiation, and other violence-prevention lessons in an effort to make schools and neighborhoods safe.

Teachers report that classroom discipline is their biggest challenge. This challenge appears to be growing greater each year as more and more children arrive at school with unmet needs and insufficient social skills. Teachers struggle to create caring classroom communities with children who lack impulse control and have little ability to manage their frustration and anger (Brady, Forton, Porter, & Wood, 2003).

Teachers of young children need to spend time on discipline not only in self-defense, but because they have the children at the most opportune time. Brain research shows that the early years offer a critical window of opportunity for learning complex functions related to behavior, such as logical thinking and emotion regulation (National Scientific Council on the Developing Child, 2007; Shonkoff & Meisels, 2000). During the years from age 3 to age 10, the brain has more synapses connecting brain cells than at any other time. Brain imaging shows conclusively what early childhood teachers have said all along: the early years are the critical years for learning.

THE GOALS OF DISCIPLINE

Discipline approaches must be determined by our goals. Start by asking yourself, "What is the purpose of discipline?" It may be tempting to look at discipline merely as a means to keep control so you can teach other things, but children and society need so much more.

Long-Term Goals

Whenever you teach something, you need to start by clarifying your long-term educational goals. Teaching discipline or anything else without long-term goals is like trying to plan a trip route without knowing where you are headed. In order to examine long-term goals, you may find it useful to ask yourself what kind of people you value. Notice that the word is *people*, not *children*. Is there a difference? If you are thinking about children, you might be attracted to the goal *obedient*; however, you are not likely to choose that label for an adult characteristic. Keep in mind that early discipline influences character for a lifetime; therefore, it is essential to think about what kind of people function best in society rather than merely considering what kind of children are easiest to manage. What traits will make the best contribution to a democratic society?

Self-Concept and Self-Esteem

Many people list positive self-concept as a goal, but this seems to confuse the difference between self-concept and self-esteem. Self-concept is an understanding of who we are and what we can do; self-esteem is how we feel about that. A realistic self-concept is essential to mental health (Landy, 2002) and can provide the basis for developing good self-esteem.

There is general agreement that we want youngsters to grow up feeling good about themselves. Although almost everyone voices this goal, many still use discipline methods that damage self-esteem. Children are routinely treated with much less respect than adults are. They are lectured, ignored, bullied, and bribed in ways no adult would ever put up with. Children often aren't really listened to, either. Later chapters will discuss how punishment and other coercive tactics—even praise and other rewards—can damage a person's self-esteem.

Self-Discipline

Nearly everyone also agrees that self-discipline is a goal for children. Most approaches to discipline describe themselves as promoting self-discipline (Brooks & Goldstien, 2007; Charney, 2002). Disagreements center around what leads to this goal. Many believe that rewards for acceptable behavior, and punishments for unacceptable behavior, will lead to self-discipline. Such viewpoints do not recognize that being manipulated by reward and punishment is vastly different from learning about what is right and how to make wise, caring decisions (Kohn, 2005; Turiel, 2006). In contrast, this book is based on the view that children can't learn to regulate their own behavior as long as others are regulating it for them.

Moral Autonomy

A more sophisticated and little-known version of self-discipline is called *moral autonomy*. This is a concept presented in Jean Piaget's classic book *The Moral Judgment of the Child* (1932/1965), and elaborated for modern audiences by

Moral autonomy means having the ability to make decisions about right and wrong, regardless of any rewards or punishments, yet taking into consideration the rights and needs of all involved.

Piagetian scholars DeVries (e.g., DeVries, Hildebrandt, & Zan, 2000) and Kamii (e.g., Kamii & Ewing, 1996). According to these sources, *autonomy* means being governed and guided by your own beliefs and understandings. It is much more than merely "internalizing" a set of conduct rules and making yourself follow them. The morally autonomous person is kind to others out of personal feelings of respect for other human beings. The opposite is *heteronomy*, which means being governed or ruled by someone else. The heteronomous person would be kind to others only if that behavior would be rewarded, or if its absence would be caught and punished.

Some people misinterpret this concept and get worried when they hear about autonomy. They think that being governed by yourself means doing whatever you want. However, Kamii points out in the foreword to this book that Piaget's theory of autonomy doesn't mean just the right to make decisions for yourself, but also the "ability to make decisions for oneself about right and wrong, independent of reward or punishment, by taking relevant factors into account." If you think about the meaning of that statement, you see that a merely self-serving decision would be excluded because it wouldn't take into consideration the "relevant factors" of other people's needs. It is important to note that being governed internally also means that children are not so susceptible to peer pressure; therefore, morally autonomous persons would not join in inappropriate group activities in order to be accepted by their peers.

Thus, it is a person without moral autonomy who is likely to act irresponsibly when there are no external controls (Turiel, 2006). In fact, that description fits some young college students away from home for the first time. College dormitory life testifies to the fact that some well-meaning parents and teachers deny young people an adequate opportunity to develop inner controls. Inexperienced at self-regulating their work, play, and sleep, some first-year college students find themselves unable to achieve a workable balance. Some, whose behavior has been controlled through rewards and punishment, find themselves unable to make wise decisions when confronted with drugs and alcohol.

Autonomy does not mean lack of control; rather, it refers to the source of control. Autonomous people carry those controls within themselves. They are never without them, even when alone. Heteronomous people, by contrast, experience control only when someone else is present. They depend on an external judge to reward or punish their behavior. When you help youngsters develop moral autonomy, you affect how they behave, even when misbehavior isn't likely to be caught. Autonomous people don't need policing to keep them on the right path.

Long-Term versus Quick-Fix Solutions

Are teachers responsible for keeping children safe and orderly and also for helping them develop positive self-esteem, self-discipline, and moral autonomy? That's a tall order! Don't forget that teachers have to teach, too. Can they really be blamed if they have a hard time thinking about long-range discipline goals and are attracted to control for the moment? After all, teachers usually have a student for just one year.

Parents, however, are generally aware that they will be dealing with this child through the teen years and beyond. One mother reports that she was powerfully motivated to help her son Michael learn self-discipline when she thought about his getting a driver's license in 10 years. While Michael was little, she could protect him from harm by watching over him herself, but she doubted that she could ride along to make sure he was driving safely when he was 16. She knew that inner controls would stay with Michael long after she couldn't. Therefore, she focused on discipline approaches that fostered inner control rather than obedience. Nevertheless, even parents are sometimes tempted to ignore the future and concentrate on making their lives easier for now.

Teachers may be under the added pressure to present a "well-disciplined" class, in the old sense of appearing quiet and controlled. This can make a difference at evaluation time with principals who don't understand how young children learn best. As a result, discipline methods that boast quick, short-term results at the expense of children's self-esteem and autonomy remain popular. You will read about some of these methods in Chapter 9.

Fortunately, many teachers care too much about children to give in to temptation. They resist quick-fix approaches and work on positive alternatives. They know that helping children live together peacefully now and preparing them for the future can be compatible goals. Skillful teachers know how to work toward long-term discipline goals while maintaining a peaceful and productive learning environment. They know they don't have to make a choice between protecting children's self-esteem and keeping order. With the guidance of these knowledge-able and dedicated teachers, children can learn from experience to make wise decisions. In the process, they can also develop the positive self-esteem and moral autonomy necessary for becoming competent, caring, loving, and lovable people (Noddings, 2005).

DISCIPLINE MODELS COMPARED

Common approaches to discipline vary—from the very authoritarian, in which the adult makes all the rules and punishes any deviation, to the very permissive, in which the child makes all the decisions. Too many people think they have to choose one or the other of those models. One teacher says she plays the "heavy" until she can't stand herself; then she switches to the opposite until she can't stand the kids. Too few adults (teachers as well as parents) are even aware of any other options. We do not recommend trying to combine permissive and authoritarian styles in an attempt at a middle ground, but there are alternatives that balance the power of adult and child. You don't have to choose between either the adult or the child having all the power (Tzuo, 2007). A shared-power model best meets the needs of all. The needs and views of both the adult and the child can be accommodated when discipline is viewed as teaching.

Discipline Theory Terms

Many terms have been used to describe the different approaches to discipline. *Authoritarian* and *permissive* are commonly understood terms and concepts. Alternatives to these extremes have been harder to define and to understand. Baumerind (1967) wrote about authoritative discipline and explained how it differed from the authoritarian model through a focus on teaching rather than punishment. However, many people get confused by the similarities between the words *authoritarian* and *authoritative*.

Greenberg (1992) compares forms of discipline with forms of government. The *autocratic* holding of power by the adult is compared to a dictatorship, and *anarchy* is the label for the overly permissive style that grants too much power to the child. In contrast, Greenberg describes a shared-power approach that she labels *democratic*. This term may leave readers with the incorrect idea that behavior is decided by vote and the worry that the teacher will be outvoted.

DeVries and Zan (1994) use yet another way of explaining discipline styles. They contrast three classroom situations and label them: (1) the *boot camp*, (2) the *factory*, and (3) the *community*. The boot camp uses reward and punishment to enforce obedience. The factory model has the same controlling goals as the boot camp, relying heavily on reward and punishment, but with a kinder and gentler touch. The factory model describes the majority of elementary-grade or grade-school classrooms we have seen. The community model, in contrast, uses the constructivist approach to assist children's development of moral autonomy. Fortunately, few teachers are as harsh as those in the boot camp model, but, unfortunately, too few have the skills to create a true community of learners.

The following list categorizes the various models of teaching and guidance discussed in this chapter and shows their relations to one another.

Obedience Models	Respect Models	Passive Models
Authoritarian	Authoritative	Permissive
Behaviorist	Constructivist	Maturationist
Boot Camp	Community	
Autocratic	Democratic	Anarchist

FIGURE 1–1   Comparing Discipline Terminology

Because we view discipline as teaching, we believe it makes sense to base guidance and discipline on learning theory. Therefore, we compare the various approaches according to which learning theory they most closely reflect: behaviorist, maturationist, or constructivist (see Figure 1–1). The authoritarian style is consistent with the behaviorist philosophy of education, with its emphasis on molding behavior via reward and punishment. The permissive style is compatible with the maturationist philosophy of education, with its belief in time as the best teacher. The best alternative to these extremes of too much and too little adult intervention is the constructivist approach to education.

Constructivism does not reflect a "middle ground" between behaviorism and maturationism; rather, it is a whole different view of learning and of guidance and discipline. It is not a "nicer" way to get obedience; instead, it strives for much more than obedience. Constructivism helps children learn from their experiences and from reflecting on those experiences (DeVries, Zan, & Hildebrandt, 2002; Kamii & Ewing, 1996; Piaget, 1965). Through this process, the learner is assisted in gaining increasingly sophisticated levels of understanding. Thus, children gradually develop the ability to take many relevant factors into consideration when deciding what action is best for all concerned. The word "gradually" is important because it reflects the developmental basis for constructivist teaching. Constructivists recognize that teaching young children involves accepting immature thinking and requires working in conjunction with maturation to help children move to greater understanding.

Although creating community in a constructivist classroom is more similar to the authoritative and democratic models of discipline than to any obedience or passive models, it is not identical. Because constructivist learning theory is the basis for constructivist guidance and discipline, constructivist discipline has some unique traits. These traits are described throughout the book.

Discipline Goals Compared

In essence, each discipline style is based on the same motive: love and/or concern for the child. However, each has very different goals (see Figure 1–2). Obedience is the target behavior in the authoritarian model, which prefers unquestioning and immediate obedience (Dobson, 2007; Leman, 2005). The permissive model overemphasizes individual freedom (Baumerind, 1967),

Behaviorist	Molds behavior via rewards and punishment
Constructivist	Helps children learn from experience
Maturationist	Believes that time is the best teacher

FIGURE 1–2   Goals of Three Theories of Discipline

though it can also be a result of neglect. The constructivist model works toward moral autonomy: self-determined, responsible behavior, reflecting concern for the good of others and for oneself as well (Kamii, 1984; Kohn, 2005). Rewards and punishment are incompatible with these goals. The constructivist approach acknowledges the complexity of the ever-changing world; therefore, it teaches children to think for themselves about desirable or undesirable actions rather than telling them predetermined answers to current dilemmas. "Power assertive methods . . . fail to provide information that can be used to construct generalizable moral concepts" (Smetana, 2006).

Differences in Discipline Forms

Not surprisingly, each model uses very different forms of discipline (Bronson, 2000). Punishment and reward are used almost exclusively in the authoritarian model (Canter & Canter, 1992; Dobson, 2007). Lack of discipline is the distinguishing feature of the permissive model. In contrast to these two extremes, but definitely not a blend of them, the constructivist model offers a multifaceted set of discipline options that will be explained in this book.

These constructivist options focus on teaching and, like all good teaching, begin with good human relationships. Adults who are responsive, warm, and comforting are essential to children's healthy development (Gurian, 2001; Howes & Ritchie, 2002; Noddings, 2005). Good relationships between teachers and children do not mean the teacher tries to be a "pal," just one of the group. The constructivist teacher is still the adult in charge, responsible for setting necessary limits and keeping children safe. However, this is done in a caring and respectful way. Mutually caring and respectful relationships with adults and peers encourage youngsters to think about the effects of their behavior on other people. Teaching children to think critically is an essential aspect of constructivist teaching about discipline, and about other topics as well. Constructivist discipline strategies are aimed at helping children construct socially productive behavior rules and values for themselves. The approach is aimed at helping children become better able to reason, and thus become more reasonable human beings.

Differences in Results

What are the results of the different discipline models? We can never be certain about research findings concerning human beings because we cannot ethically control the variables in a person's life. Each person is a unique blend of genetics, family dynamics, societal influences, and individual experiences. However, certain trends occur frequently enough to suggest a relationship. The authoritarian model is associated with anger and depression, as well as low self-esteem and the

Mutual respect between teacher and child is an essential ingredient of effective discipline.

inability to make self-directed choices (e.g., Howes & Ritchie, 2002; Knafo & Plomin, 2006; Landy, 2002; Sigsgaard, 2005). "When we control kids excessively—for example, by offering the rewards and praise for doing what we want . . . they lose their ability to regulate themselves" (Kohn, 2005). Likewise, those people with an overly permissive background usually demonstrate low self-esteem and difficulty getting along with others. The constructivist or shared-power model results in high self-esteem, good social skills, general competence, and self-discipline (DeVries, 1999; Kohn, 2005; Tzuo, 2007).

Constructivist discipline approaches help most children quickly learn to negotiate solutions to problems, to resolve their own conflicts and to self-direct their learning activity (DeVries & Zan, 1994; Kohn, 2005). Teaching for moral autonomy has lasting results, including a morality of cooperation that results in a balanced understanding of justice (Lapsley, 2006).

Family Concern: Shouldn't They Learn to Obey?

Many people think in black-or-white terms; they think that you either make kids obey or they are "disobedient" and run wild. Some cultures emphasize obedience at home, enforced with punishment. Therefore, you may get worried questions about this guidance approach from your students' families. As in any situation, it is unwise to give advice unless it is asked for; but if it is, here are some suggestions you might offer to parents.

You need to help families understand that working for obedience is settling for much less than moral autonomy. Explain what you have learned about long-term versus short-term goals. Point out that obedience without understanding requires external enforcement of some sort, a reward or punishment (DeVries et al., 2002; Kohn, 2005). Teachers can introduce parents to the research provided in

Chapters 9 and 10, which describe the negative effects of reward and punishment. A lending library of relevant books, such as Kohn's (2005) *Unconditional Parenting: Moving from Praise and Rewards to Love and Reason*, would be helpful. Be sure to warn families about one of the most common and most devastating reward/punishment approaches: making parental love and approval conditional on obedience. However, remember to listen to what families want for their children and to be respectful of differing views.

Teaching for Moral Autonomy: The Constructivist Approach

Certain basic ideas are central to a constructivist approach to discipline:

1. A relationship of mutual respect between adult and child is the foundation for development of moral autonomy (Kamii, 1982). *Mutual respect* means that it is just as important for you to treat the child with respect as it is for the child to treat you with respect.
2. Constructivist teachers always strive to help children understand why a behavior is desirable or undesirable.
3. Providing age-appropriate choices for youngsters and supporting them in solving their own problems is a way of showing respect for children and also a way of teaching thinking and assisting understanding.
4. When undesirable behavior occurs, your discipline efforts must address the cause of the behavior for effective teaching to take place.

Now let's examine these concepts in more detail.

Mutual Respect

Constructive discipline involves respect and affection for the child. The quality of the relationship between child and adult is crucial to the success of any discipline approach. Unless a child knows you care about him or her, and unless that child is concerned about maintaining a relationship with you, there is really no reason for the child to pay attention to what you ask. Having a relationship with a child requires investing time in getting to know children as individuals and attempting to understand them. If you are going to be effective during a behavior crisis, you need to first build a relationship by spending time on pleasant interaction. Spending time with a youngster and listening to that child not only helps an adult understand the child, but also demonstrates respect. Too often adults expect youngsters to listen to them but don't reciprocate. Respecting children and their viewpoints helps them to respect our viewpoints (Kamii, 1984). According to DeVries and Zan (1994), "Children do not develop respect for others unless they are respected" (p. 76).

Mutual respect is an essential ingredient of effective discipline. Any discipline response can turn into punishment if accompanied by put-downs, which, of course, are inherently disrespectful. For instance, to call a child "sloppy" for spilling something, or "mean" for knocking down some blocks, would destroy the educational value of your discipline teaching. The child would focus on self-defense rather than on the problem behavior. It is also important to be aware of how your attitude is projected. Anger or disgust in your tone of voice can override even the most carefully chosen words. Listen to yourself as you talk to the children in your care: Are your words something they would want to listen to? Or are you teaching children to tune you out by relaying a steady stream of commands and criticism?

Helping Children Understand

Like other people, children are more inclined to do as they are asked if they understand the reason behind the request. Often it seems obvious to an adult why a certain behavior is appropriate or inappropriate, but young children have little experience in the world and don't automatically know all that seems obvious to you. Therefore, you need to help youngsters learn the reasons behind rules and requests. Sometimes words are helpful teaching tools, but usually young children need experiences to help them understand the explanations. You can teach without punishing by asking Aaron, for example, to mop up the puddle he made when he splashed water on the floor during exuberant water play. Similarly, you can help Kenji learn a better way of showing he wants to play than by knocking over other children's buildings. The teacher's role in developing moral autonomy is to help children figure out why their behavior is causing a problem and provide them with the opportunity to help resolve the problem.

∾ Mrs. Jensen discovered one day that she had not helped Lesa to understand why she was asked to leave group time: Lesa came up to Mrs. Jensen after the group meeting and said, "I'm sorry. I won't do it again." Mrs. Jensen asked her, "Won't do what again?" She was astounded at the child's honest reply, "I don't know." Too often, youngsters learn to mouth meaningless words of apology or appreciation with no idea about what they mean or why they would be appropriate. ∾

Perhaps the most crucial understanding for young children is that other people have needs and wishes different from their own. Dennis's approach to the following doll bed dilemma was aimed at helping Sara and Sophie each begin to think about a viewpoint other than her own. Learning to consider the viewpoints of others in making decisions is part of learning moral autonomy. According to Piaget, we also teach moral autonomy and the necessary understanding of others' views when we help children realize the effects of their behavior rather than merely punishing it. Following is an example of this principle in action.

∾ When preschoolers Sarah and Sophie were tugging on the same doll bed, each screaming, "I had it first!" Dennis, their teacher, resisted coming over and immediately taking the toy away, although it might have been simple to say, "If you can't play nicely, I'll have to put this away." Nor did he start the usual inquisition trying to determine which child had it first so that he could make the fairest decision. Those approaches are common when the teacher's goal is simply to solve the problem for now and when the discipline approach is authoritarian.

Because Dennis's goals are long-term, he wanted to help the children learn to think about their behavior and to develop skills for solving their own conflicts. His discipline approach is constructivist. Therefore, he facilitated decision making on the part of the children instead of making the decisions himself. He helped the girls to clarify the problem by stating what it appeared to be: "You both want a bed for your dolls." He further identified the dilemma: "There's only one of these beds and two sleepy babies." Then Dennis asked them what they thought they could do to solve their problem. In this way, he helped the girls learn to think about fairness for both sides. ∞

Problem solving takes practice, just as other complex skills do. It is also dependent on levels of maturity. Young children have limited reasoning ability, but they become more capable when encouraged to discuss their different views. The teacher works with children at their levels of maturation, demonstrating ways of expressing their feelings and suggesting possible approaches to solutions. The teacher may ask questions, such as, "Where else could a baby doll sleep in this house?" This method still leaves the children in charge of a search for alternatives. Even if they aren't immediately successful, Dennis doesn't take over. However, if the children's frustration and anger appear to be getting beyond their ability to control, he might resort to taking the doll bed and putting it out of reach until they cool down. He then would assure the girls that they could have it as soon as they come up with a solution.

Guiding Choices

Constructive discipline encourages children to make as many of their own decisions and choices as possible. This helps children to learn from their mistakes as well as their successes. In other words, your job is to help children

Help children to analyze their mistakes so they learn to manage their own behavior.

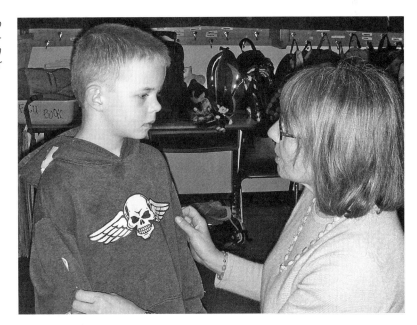

learn how to make wise choices, not to make all the choices for them. In the process of learning to regulate their own behavior, children make both good and bad choices for themselves. It is hard, but necessary, to let youngsters make some poor choices as well as good ones. No matter what their age, people tend to learn best the lessons learned through their own experience—especially from analyzing their mistakes. Think about your own mistakes: Probably someone older and wiser warned you, but you had to find out for yourself, didn't you?

Of course, adults must monitor the choices; not all choices are safe or appropriate. For instance, children don't have the choice of putting their fingers in an electrical socket to experience a shock. But they do have the choice of not eating their snack and getting a little hungry, or the choice of not cooperating in play and subsequently being rejected by peers. Teachers whose goal is helping children learn to think for themselves don't help by thinking and acting for their students. They do not instantly step in and solve conflicts for youngsters. Instead, conflicts and problems are seen as potential learning situations and opportunities to offer meaningful teaching (Bronson, 2000). The children work at problem solving. The teacher's job is to facilitate the process as needed.

Treating the Cause Rather than the Symptom

No amount of respect, teaching, or choice will make discipline effective *unless your approach deals with the reasons why the behavior occurred.* If you only stop the behavior without treating the cause, the behavior problem will probably continue to be repeated (Kaiser & Rasminsky, 2006). Discipline is like weeding a garden: If you don't get the roots out with the weeds, the weeds will be back in a few days. Effective approaches to discipline work to get at the root of the problem. Yet, very few discipline/guidance approaches involve considering the cause of a behavior problem before deciding on an intervention. A main focus of this text is matching guidance and discipline approaches to the causes of behavior problems.

It isn't easy to figure out why children do the things they do. You certainly can't determine the cause simply by seeing the behavior. For instance, there could be several reasons why Aaron might have spilled water during water play:

- Perhaps he was just having such a good time that he didn't think about where the water was going.
- It is also possible that he spilled because of immature coordination, which made it hard for him to pour the water where he intended.
- Then again, maybe he knew what he was doing and did it on purpose. He might have spilled to get attention or to alleviate boredom.

A useful way to think about the cause of undesirable behavior is to think about what the child needs in order to act in more appropriate ways. You may find it useful to reflect on the causes of behavior problems by using an observation form similar to the one shown in Figure 1–3. Each different cause of behavior problems points to the need for a different solution. Yet, there are many teachers and caregivers who have one solution for any and all infractions of the rules.

Use the following questions as a guide toward discovering the causes of a behavior problem. Record your observations and thoughts in the boxes next to each question (there may be several "right" answers).

Is the environment meeting this child's needs?	
Enough movement? Enough privacy? Enough space? Sufficient materials?	
Is the curriculum meeting this child's needs?	
Appropriate challenge? Personal interest? Meaningful?	
Are the behavioral expectations appropriate for the child?	
Developmentally? Culturally? Temperamentally?	
Does the child have unmet physical needs?	
Hungry? Tired?	
Does the child have unmet emotional needs?	
Friendship? Trust? Personal power? Self-esteem? Attention?	
Is the child missing some social skill?	
Perspective taking? Entering play?	

FIGURE 1–3 Discovering Causes of Behavior Problems

Does the child need help with communication skills?	
I messages? Negotiation?	
Is the behavior the result of inappropriate role models?	
Media? Admired adults? Admired peers?	
Does the child understand why the behavior is important?	
No experience with outcomes?	
Has the child learned negative ways of getting needs met?	
Received attention for inappropriate behavior?	

FIGURE 1–3   (*continued*)

Think about how the commonly used time-out bench would affect Aaron in the case of each suggested cause for the spilled water:

- How would the time-out bench affect his feelings about preschool fun if the spill was caused by his eagerness to explore?
- How would time-out affect his feelings about himself if the spill was caused by poor coordination?
- If attention-getting or boredom was the cause, would time-out keep Aaron from spilling water again?

As you read later chapters, you will find suggestions of appropriate responses to each of these and other causes of undesirable behavior.

Observing to Discover the Cause

The best way to determine the cause of a child's behavior is to observe the child carefully and record your observations (Jablon, Dombro, & Dichtelmiller, 2007). You need to know a lot about a child to plan effective discipline. You need to note whether this is usual or unusual behavior, and also under what circumstances it occurs. Are certain activities likely to trigger it? Is there a pattern of when, where, or with whom behavior problems are most likely? What do you know about the child's home routine, health, or family situation that might provide some clues? Communicating with parents and keeping careful records of child behavior are both indispensable parts of determining the cause of problems. You assess the child's social learning needs through this process of finding causes for behavior problems. This assessment is an essential guide for effective teaching.

Never overlook the possibility that you may have caused a discipline problem. Chapters 2 and 3 illustrate how teacher expectations that don't reflect child development, temperament, or culture cause discipline problems. Chapters 4 and 5 discuss how inappropriate school environments often cause behavior problems. Chapters 6 and 7 raise the issue of undesirable adult examples and communication styles as sources of undesirable child behavior. Chapters 9 and 10 explain how coercive and punitive discipline approaches backfire and create worse behavior problems. Chapters 11 and 12 examine various situations, demonstrating the process of finding the cause and matching it to an appropriate response. Chapters 13 and 14 explore causes outside the realm of the classroom. Chapter 15 helps you keep it all together.

Targeting the cause of a behavior problem is a difficult task, compounded by the fact that there are usually multiple and interactive causes. The information presented in Chapters 2 through 6 is especially crucial to determining the causes for undesirable behavior.

As you read this text, you will be guided to match probable causes of behavior with appropriate approaches to discipline. Selecting the right approach requires that you understand many different approaches, as well as understand children and the many different reasons for their actions. This text presents a set of guidance/discipline strategies, each related to a specific cause. These are explained throughout the text as we explore various causes of behavior problems.

CONCLUSION

This chapter has attempted to stimulate your thinking about your values as they relate to guidance and discipline. Our comparison of discipline approaches resulted in the recommendation of constructivist discipline, rather than an authoritarian or a permissive approach. We began an introduction to ways of implementing constructivist approaches to discipline, with more complete explanations to come in the following chapters.

This chapter offers an overview of ideas presented in the rest of the book. If you can't visualize how all this works yet, don't worry; that's what the rest of the chapters are for. We hope that you will supplement what you read here with further reading from the recommended reading list at the end of the chapter. We also hope that you will spend significant time with young children, proving guidance and discipline concepts to yourself through your own observation and experience.

If you haven't read the foreword and preface to this book, we suggest you do so. Constance Kamii's discussion of moral autonomy in the foreword should help you better understand the idea. The preface should provide further explanation about the theory base and intent of the book. The preface also gives an overview of the three-part organization of the text: (1) discipline foundations, (2) discipline approaches, and (3) matching discipline causes to discipline approaches. Be sure to also read the introductions to each section of the text; they will help you understand what you are reading about. We hope you will also read and think about the dedication at the front of the book.

As you continue to read and think, remember that going to school represents the child's entry into our society (Feeney, Christensen, & Moravick, 2006). For the first time, young children may be encountering the necessities of following basic rules and respecting the rights of others. The skills of problem solving, predicting consequences, and planning ahead are vital for children to escape the culture of violence (Swick & Freeman, 2004).

If you are now saying to yourself, "But don't kids need limits?" or "I know people who grew up with complete freedom and they felt their parents didn't care," then go back and re-read the chapter. If these are new ideas for you, it will take careful reading and thought to understand that there are helpful alternatives to forcing obedience. The choice isn't just between power-tripping children or letting them run wild.

As you begin to implement the ideas presented here, you should be prepared for less-than-instant success. Understanding complex ideas involves hard work accompanied by trial and error. Changing established ways of interacting with children is also very difficult, requiring time and commitment. At first, you may even find that your discipline efforts seem less effective than before. As they are learning new approaches, some people report feeling "paralyzed" by indecisiveness about what to do. Just as we urge you to be accepting of children's gradual learning processes, we urge you to accept your own gradual progress. When, inevitably, you forget your new plans and don't live up to your expectations, just try again. That's what we do.

∞ *FOR FURTHER THOUGHT*

1. Create your list of desirable goals for discipline. Compare your list with those of others. Select the three characteristics you would most want to encourage through child guidance. Explain your choices and compare them with a friend's.

2. Think about your own parents' approach to child rearing. What characteristics do you think they most valued? How did those values influence your own childhood? Do your choices reflect those of your parents, or are they different?

3. How would you rate yourself on a continuum from heteronomy to autonomy? How does this rating reflect the discipline approaches of your parents and teachers? If you are heteronomous, can you help children become autonomous?

4. A problem to solve: Carlos is using the playhouse broom. Betsy wants it and grabs it away. Carlos hits Betsy, and the battle is on.

   a. Describe a response that solves the problem but does not teach autonomy or self-discipline.

   b. Describe a response that solves the problem and does teach autonomy and self-discipline.

∞ RECOMMENDED READINGS

DeVries, R., & Zan, B. (1994). *Moral classrooms, moral children.* New York: Teachers College Press.

Garrett, J. (2006). Educating the whole child. *Kappa Delta Pi Record, 42*(4), 154–155.

Jablon, J., Dombro, A., & Dichtelmiller, M. (2007). *The power of observation.* Washington, DC: National Association for the Education of Young Children.

Kamii, C. (1982). Autonomy as the aim of education: Implications of Piaget's theory. In C. Kamii (Ed.), *Number in preschool and kindergarten* (pp. 73–87). Washington, DC: National Association for the Education of Young Children.

Kohn, A. (2005). *Unconditional parenting: Moving from rewards to love and reason.* New York: Atria Books.

Noddings, N. (2005). *The challenge to care in schools: An alternative approach to education.* (2nd ed.). New York: Teacher's College Press.

Piaget, J. (1965). *The moral judgment of the child.* New York: Free Press. (Originally published in 1932.)

Tzuo, F. (2007). The tension between teacher control and child freedom in a child-centered classroom: Resolving the practical dilemma through a closer look at related theories. *Early Childhood Education Journal, 35*(1) 33–39.

∞ *Chapter* **2** ∞
Physical and Emotional Development Affect Child Behavior

NAEYC Standards Addressed in This Chapter

Standard 1: Promoting Child Development and Learning.

Standard 3: Observing, Documenting, and Assessing to Support Young Children and Families.

Standard 4b: Teaching and Learning: Using Developmentally Effective Approaches.

Standard 4c: Teaching and Learning: Connecting with Children and Families.

GUIDING QUESTIONS

- How do children's physical immaturity and developmental needs affect their behavior?
- How do adult responses to children's temperaments influence teacher–child interactions?
- How do children develop emotional regulation, and how does children's understanding of emotions affect their behavior?
- What is attachment, and how might teachers support children with attachment problems?

Each stage of child development brings its own set of needs, abilities, and perspectives. Your knowledge of children's physical, emotional, intellectual, and social development will help you guard against adult-caused behavior problems. In this chapter we will examine physical and emotional development; Chapter 3 looks at intellectual and social development.

Teaching is much easier when you are knowledgeable about child development. As we will repeat many times in this book, effective discipline addresses the causes of behavior problems. When you know more about child development, you can determine if immature development may be the cause of a behavior problem. Then, it will be easier to find an effective solution. You can eliminate many discipline problems by matching your expectations of children to their individual maturation levels. In other words, you will not expect children to be successful at tasks beyond their developmental level. Nor will you blame children for behavior that is a result of maturational level.

Effective child guidance and discipline require knowledge of factors that affect emotional development: Temperament strongly contributes to children's unique paths of emotional development. Attachment is also a key factor in emotional development. Children have basic human needs that must be met for healthy growth and development. If these needs are not met, children will have difficulty developing emotional regulation. To develop effective discipline interventions, we must understand how temperament, attachment, and basic needs impact a child's emotional development.

In this chapter, we will examine how temperament, developmental stage, attachment, and basic human needs affect children's emotional competence and how they are related to discipline issues. We will revisit these developmental issues again in Part 3 (Chapters 11–15) as we look for the cause of and possible solutions to real-world classroom issues. Chapters 2 and 3 are not intended to be a comprehensive coverage of child development. Please refer to the recommended readings at the end of each chapter for more comprehensive sources.

RELATED PHYSICAL DEVELOPMENT ISSUES

It is obvious that young children's physical needs and abilities are different from those of adults. We know that young children are often unable to handle new tasks when their needs for adequate rest and nourishment are not met. Also, children repeatedly demonstrate that they are not able to sit still for very long. However, teachers sometimes forget this last fact and cause trouble for themselves and their students.

Need to Move Around

∞ Devon and several of his classmates in Miss Wheeler's first-grade class routinely upset their teacher's day. They simply won't sit still and listen during group time. They are always getting up and wandering around when they are supposed to be working in their seats. Miss Wheeler constantly reminds them to sit still or to go back to their seats. She just doesn't understand that most young children have difficulty sitting still for very long.

Next door, in Mrs. Jensen's first-grade room, children are free to move around between learning centers. There is very little enforced sitting in that room, and very little need for the teacher to reprimand anyone. In addition to movement indoors, lessons often include outdoor activity. Sometimes, a parent helper and Mrs. Jensen take the class outdoors for a gardening session on the school grounds, allowing physical movement as well as some hands-on lessons about plant life.

Miss Wheeler feels like a police officer instead of a teacher, but she thinks it is the children who are at fault. Matching her expectations of the children with their level of development would make her life much easier, as well as eliminate a lot of needless tension for her students. ∞

Children need to move, not only for their physical development, but also for their intellectual development. Brain research shows that physical movement stimulates the myelinization process critical to development of neural pathways in the brain. The process of myelinization allows young children to gain control over their muscles and their sensory abilities; it also facilitates their cognitive processes (Berger, 2007). Physical movement also increases blood flow to the brain, optimizing its performance, and helps children build social skills and peer relationships. Taking turns being the leader in a game assists in social-emotional development. Games that require children to watch movements and mimic them with their own bodies help with the development of sensory integration. Sensory integration is important for the development of reading and writing skills (Gartrell & Sonsteng, 2008). After game playing or other physical movement, the ability to concentrate is greater for most children. An assessment of how girls and boys learn differently points out that movement may be even more important for boys and their reduction of emotional stress (Gurian, 2001). Physical activity has short-term as well as long-term benefits. Physically active children are healthier and eventually grow up to be more active, healthy adults. Increased physical activity is needed to counteract the problem of childhood obesity in the United States (Jelalian & Steele, 2008). In addition, physically competent children tend to have higher self-esteem than less-competent peers. Competence in performing motor skills boosts children's confidence. Success and enjoyment associated with physical activity affect how children feel about themselves and how they interact with peers. Having good agility, balance, coordination, power, and speed can promote social interaction and peer acceptance. Children with physical disabilities that affect their gross motor development often share their classmates' interest in physical activities. Therefore, playgrounds and outdoor equipment should be accessible for children with disabilities (NAEYC, 2008).

Small-Muscle Coordination Takes Time

Not only do young children have a need to exercise their large muscles regularly, but they also need practice with small-muscle skills. Young children typically are not very adept at small-muscle work (NAEYC, 2008). Both the need for large-muscle activity and the lack of small-muscle ability create problems in classrooms where children are expected to sit at their seats and do paperwork much of the day. Such a schedule focuses on the children's areas of weakness, and therefore, puts a huge pressure on them.

Individual differences and gender play a role in the development of dexterity. Girls tend to be more advanced than boys in fine motor skills and in gross motor skills requiring precision, such as hopping and skipping. Boys generally excel in skills that require force and power, such as running and jumping (Berk, 2007). For most children, it is a fact of physical development that fine motor coordination lags behind gross motor coordination. Nate, who is a fast runner and a great climber, may not be able to tie his shoes yet; and Margo, the best rope jumper in kindergarten, may not be able to make a pencil do her bidding. Placing pressure on these children to perform above their current level of development will result in frustration and feelings of failure. Negative behaviors will surely follow. Matching your expectations to children's abilities will avert some potential discipline struggles.

Although you want to be careful not to push fine motor tasks too early, fine motor development can be encouraged appropriately. Ample opportunities for

Snack time offers many opportunities for children to use fine motor skills.

practice, appropriate tools (scissors that actually cut, for instance), and adult support assist children's fine motor dexterity. Children with certain kinds of identified disabilities may require adaptations or assistive technologies for activities such as writing and drawing. By the time they enter the primary grades, children are usually much more capable of fine motor work than when they were preschool age, when it often generates neurological fatigue.

Needs for Food and Rest

Young children also have a need for nutritious food and rest in order to work and play cooperatively at school. Many children today are "misnourished," with a large amount of their calories coming from non-nutritive foods (Bhattacharya & Currie, 2001). Eating too many non-nutritive foods contributes to our ever-growing rate of childhood obesity, and affects children's behavior (Jelalian & Steele, 2008). Too much sugar or a lack of protein or complex carbohydrates can lead to a sugar crash. This crash may affect individual children differently. You may know a child who loses all self-control if he or she has too much sugar or gets too hungry. Some may become impulsive, while others may become withdrawn or distracted. Allowing for snack time, with healthy, low-sugar snacks, may prevent discipline problems. When schools don't provide snacks, asking for healthy snack donations from businesses or other parents can also help build community.

Sometimes Kayla cannot seem to focus on any of the morning classroom activities, and Dennis, her teacher, figures that she didn't eat much breakfast that day. When this happens, he allows her to have her mid-morning snack a little early. Dennis is taking into consideration Kayla's individual needs as well as the group's needs. The standard practice of snack time acknowledges the fact that children in general can't eat much at one time and can't go as long between meals as older people can.

Scheduled rest time at the preschool level also acknowledges a physical need at that age, but formal rest periods tend to disappear once children enter kindergarten or first grade.

∞ Zoe attends the before- and after-school care program at Lincoln Elementary. She gets to school at 7:30 in the morning and doesn't go home until 5:30 in the evening. Sometimes she gets crabby and picks a fight or bursts into tears for no apparent reason. Fortunately, her teacher understands that when Zoe acts that way, she needs a break, not a punishment for being difficult. Mrs. Jensen sees Zoe's need and encourages her to find a comfortable pillow and a good book in the secluded classroom book nook. After a short rest, Zoe is able to participate with the group again. ∞

Mrs. Jensen is trying to teach Zoe and others with similar needs how to take a break when they need it, rather than push themselves beyond their limits. Her classroom offers several soft, secluded spots, and her schedule offers the flexibility to use them.

EMOTIONAL DEVELOPMENT AND GUIDANCE

Go to MyEducationLab and select the topic "Families and Communities" and watch the video "Parental Involvement in the Emotional Development of Toddlers."

Each child experiences the world in different ways. Children's relationships with family members and others, their cultural context, and their brain development are just some of the factors that affect their unique path of emotional development. Temperament, gender, and individual strengths and weaknesses also affect emotional development (Denham, 2007). In the following pages, we specifically explore some of these factors and how they may play into discipline issues in the classroom. Meeting children's basic emotional needs is essential to creating a peaceful learning environment. Meeting their needs is also essential to children's overall success in school and life beyond.

Temperament

The definition of *temperament* continues to evolve as we gain understanding about children and their individual differences. Temperament is a component of personality. It is, in part, determined by our genetics, but is also influenced by how we are nurtured (Eisenberg, Eggum, & Vaughan-Edwards, in press). Our individual temperament determines how we react to stimuli and how we regulate these reactions (Rothbart & Bates, 2006). Some children quickly enter new settings or

When children are provided with opportunities to be independent, they come to trust their own abilities.

readily meet new people. Some children watch carefully and for a long time before trying something new. Some children experience very intense anger and joy, while others are more mellow. Some children quickly recover when they become upset, while others may need a long time to calm down. Some children are easily distracted while others cannot be deterred from their focus. These are all examples of different temperaments. The development of emotion regulation is largely dependent on temperament (Macklem, 2008). Learning appropriate ways to express emotions and acceptable reactions to stimuli will be easier for some children than it will be for others, based on each child's individual temperament. A child who quickly approaches new settings and is not highly sensitive to stimuli will have an easier time adjusting to a school setting. A child who has strong intensity of reactions or struggles with transitions will have a harder time adjusting to any setting. It is important to remember that the way the child reacts is not his or her fault, but rather a combination of temperament and life experiences.

Temperament not only determines how the child reacts, but also how others react to the child. The challenge for the caring adult is to respond positively to the more difficult child. Some children adapt easily to change, have a pleasant mood, and their emotions are easy to read, making them a joy for caregivers and teachers. However, some children who are born with a high energy level, a short attention span, difficulty with change, or a negative outlook, are often in trouble with their teachers. While these children can be difficult, they need your help and understanding because their difficult temperaments are making life more difficult for them, too. These individual differences in temperament influence children's social interactions throughout their lifetime and can have long-term effects on their mental health.

When Annelie cries at the drop of a hat, her friends tease her, calling her a "crybaby." Children like Annelie will need significant support with social skills and emotion regulation to prevent them from developing low self-esteem, or other emotional or behavioral problems. Caregivers must focus their interests on adapting the environment and teaching styles to accommodate the needs of the children involved. This is part of making the school fit the child, as opposed to trying to make the child fit the school. Helping children develop emotional competence can be done through emotion coaching, which is discussed at the end of this chapter. Emotion coaching in the classroom not only helps children develop life-long skills, but also helps prevent discipline problems.

When teachers assess the cause of a discipline problem to determine the best action to take with a child, temperament is often a consideration.

∞ Annelie and Jack are attempting to build a road system together, each with her and his own idea of where the road should go. When Dennis sees that Annelie's frustration level is beginning to rise, he knows from prior experience that she may need some help calming herself down. Dennis calmly approaches Annelie before she rises completely out of control, and invites her to continue building her road in the sand at the sensory table. Dennis knows that the sand play and some time alone will help to calm Annelie. Dennis does not attempt any negotiation between Annelie and Jack when he knows that her intensity of emotion is too high for this to be effective. Chapter 12 further discusses temperament issues as a potential cause of behavioral problems. ∞

Developmental Stages

Though individual differences play a significant role, children nonetheless progress through various predictable developmental stages in their emotional development. Children build upon what they learn in one stage to progress onto the next, and as they do so they lay the foundation for their mental health throughout their lives. It is important to note, however, that one developmental stage is not completed, like a closed book, when the child moves on to another stage. All stages will be continually revisited and built upon as the child grows and continues developing for the rest of his or her life. Erikson's (1963) theory of personality encompasses the entire lifespan and attempts to explain patterns of behavior throughout every stage of life.

According to Erikson's widely respected theory, each of these stages has a particular focus, or developmental task, that influences the child's responses at this time. In his explanation of these stages, Erikson addresses the emergence of emotional development (Eisenberg, 2004). We find Erikson's explanation of emotional development especially relevant to discipline issues. Understanding child behavior in terms of the stages that Erikson describes can help us prevent discipline problems; this understanding also can be used to guide intervention when problems do occur. We will discuss only the stages relevant to early childhood, although Erikson's stage theory continues through adolescence, adulthood, and old age (see Figure 2–1).

Trust vs. Mistrust	Babies learn whether the world around them is safe and nurturing.
Autonomy vs. Shame	Toddlers learn to define themselves as individuals or feel shame about their independent urges.
Initiative vs. Guilt	Children learn to test their individual powers and abilities or feel guilty about making mistakes.
Industry vs. Inferiority	Children extend their ideas of themselves as successful workers or learn to feel inferior and incapable.

FIGURE 2–1 Erikson's Stages of Child Development

These stages are roughly correlated to ages, but individual differences and diversity of experiences create variations from this norm. As mentioned, as children proceed along their developmental path, they are continually building upon and continuing their growth in previous stages of emotional development. Teachers and parents also may notice a child who is in an emotionally stressful situation at home regressing to a previous developmental stage. Some serious problems, such as family crises and how they affect learning, will be discussed in Chapter 14.

Trust versus Mistrust Even if you never plan to work with babies, you need to know about the trust versus mistrust stage of development, which Erikson relates to infancy. Erikson explains that infants' early interactions with their parents form the basis for the development of emotional regulation (Eisenberg, 2004). When babies are making their first discoveries about what kind of a world they have entered, they are forming the foundation of emotional health for the rest of their lives. Many are welcomed into homes where they are the center of attention, and their slightest protest is met with efforts to alleviate distress. These babies begin early to trust that they are important and that someone cares for them enough to meet their needs. For these babies, the world is a safe and friendly place. Some babies aren't so lucky, however. Their parents may be overwhelmed with personal problems, and a baby is just one more worry, or their caregivers may be overworked and untrained. These babies may continually cry from hunger or other discomfort without any response. What a different image of themselves and their world these babies get!

Children's early efforts to communicate their needs deserve a response. Responsive adults are setting the stage for children to build trusting, cooperative relationships throughout their lifetime. When a child's needs are unmet, the child feels insecure and does not trust in others to care for him or her. Trust develops along with attachment to a significant adult. Later in this chapter we will talk more about attachment as a basic human need and a foundation for healthy emotional development.

Children continue to actively work on developing trust during preschool and in the early school years, especially if they had a problem with it earlier. They are looking for evidence that they can count on people in their larger world. Some have had negative experiences in their past that lead them to expect continued disappointments from everyone they encounter (Watson, 2003). You may see some of these children constantly checking to see if someone is still their friend. They may also frequently seek the reassurance of the teacher's attention. Others just expect rejection, as in the following example:

∽ September 29th was the first child's birthday in her class. However, Mrs. Jensen didn't see Noah's mother put party invitations into six of the children's cubbies. As the first child discovered hers, a mad rush of others hopefully checked their cubbies. There were a few shouts of delight and many disappointed faces. "Oh dear," Mrs. Jensen thought. "I should have made it clear that party invitations should not be distributed at school unless all children are included." Mrs. Jensen noticed that Cody didn't even bother looking. He didn't expect to be invited, just as he couldn't believe that other children would let him join in their play.

Cody's life hadn't made him feel secure or wanted. He had been in four foster homes in 2 years. Mrs. Jensen wondered what his birthdays had been like. Mrs. Jensen reached for her circle time basket and removed the story she'd planned to read, replacing it with A. A. Milne's *The World of Pooh.* She put her bookmark on page 70, "In which Eeyore has a birthday party and gets two presents." She also changed her plans for the topic of the group discussion, deciding to discuss feelings of being left out.

Mrs. Jensen begins group time by sharing a short, humorous, but sad, personal story of a time she remembers feeling left out as a child. Two children share similar experiences. When Mrs. Jensen reads the part of the story where Piglet wishes Eeyore "Many happy returns of the day" and Eeyore can hardly believe that his friends remembered his birthday and even gave him presents, Cody giggles especially loudly.

After the story, the group discusses how Eeyore felt and they come up with a list of ways to help him trust his friends next year. Mrs. Jensen then points out how she put paper candles on her calendar to mark all the children's birthdays. She ends with an explanation about most homes not being big enough to invite a whole class, so they will have birthday celebrations in the classroom for everyone. (Class parties are acceptable this year because she doesn't have any children in her class from families who don't celebrate birthdays or holidays.) She mentions the birthdays coming up during the next few months, and Cody beams as she ends with, "and December 6th we'll celebrate Cody's birthday!" ∽

If a child's experiences repeatedly lead to a lesson in mistrust rather than trust, that child's whole life can be affected. Future friendships, and even marriages, may suffer from this lack of trust. It first appears as insecurity with friends and excessive demands on teachers. Later in life, an inability to trust co-workers and the suspicion of spouses can undermine relationships. As relationships fail to withstand the pressure, a vicious cycle of self-fulfilling prophecy is perpetuated. We have all known children and adults who fit this pattern: They expect others to reject them, so they behave in ways that invite rejection. Your challenge is to help children have experiences that will reverse this cycle and help them begin to develop trust in caring adults.

Autonomy versus Shame   Erikson's autonomy stage is the period when young-sters work at defining themselves as separate from the adults they have, until now, completely depended on. (Erikson's use of the term *autonomy* to describe emotional development is different from Piaget's concepts of intellectual and moral autonomy, which were discussed in Chapter 1.) The toddler years are the time for development of autonomy, as Erikson defines it. As infants, children are so dependent that they actually consider themselves a part of their parents or caregivers. But toddlers suddenly begin to see that they are separate people, with ideas and wills of their own. They need to test this new revelation to make sure it is true and to convince themselves of their independence. While it is often a mis-nomer, this period is known to some as the "terrible twos." This stage may not be-gin until age 3, but it can create serious discipline problems for the unwary adult. The formerly docile child suddenly responds with an emphatic "No!" to all sug-gestions and tests the limits that are set.

∞ Georgia is so caught up in her ability to say "No!" that she sometimes says "No!" to things she really wants. Dennis asks her to join the group at the snack table when she is in a particularly assertive mood. "No," says Georgia proudly, en-joying her moment of control. Dennis knows that Georgia is asserting her power to say "Yes" or "No," but she is likely to want some snack when the other children start eating theirs. When Georgia inevitably changes her mind and does decide to join the group at the snack table, Dennis doesn't lecture her about the fact that saying "No" means she doesn't get any. Instead, he subtly looks the other way when she comes to the table for snack, allowing her to join in without feeling embarrassed. He then cheerfully gives her the option to choose apples or raisins, encouraging her budding independence by allowing her to make decisions for herself. ∞

Dennis allows the children in his preschool room as many opportunities as pos-sible to make decisions and choices. These opportunities not only help children feel proud of their increasing independence, but also may help them cooperate during times when there is no choice. Children who routinely have a chance to exercise their personal power are often more able to accept times when adults must make the decisions. Nancy offered choices to Ava to encourage her cooper-ation at the end of her day in the early care and education center, as shown in the following example.

∞ It seemed that Ava was asserting herself by refusing to cooperate when getting ready to go home, antagonizing her tired and hurried father. Nancy didn't give any attention to the undesirable behavior by wheedling and bribing her to get her boots and coat on, nor did she take away Ava's independence by forcing her to put them on. Instead, Nancy gave Ava some choices about how to get ready. "Do you want to put on your boots first or your coat first?" asked Nancy. "Would you like me or your daddy to help you with your zipper?" was the next question. "Can you put on your own boots, or would you like help?" was an-other. In no time at all, Ava was ready to go and feeling proud of herself. ∞

Erikson's theory says that when children do not develop emotional auton-omy, they develop a sense of shame instead. Shame can be caused by their ex-periences with adults who don't understand what is happening when children assert themselves; these adults think that their job is to stamp out "naughti-ness." Unfortunately, they may only be successful at making children believe they are being bad, when really the children are just working at being grown-up. As a result, the children develop feelings of shame about the natural urges of independence.

Initiative versus Guilt   Erikson's next stage of development is called initiative versus guilt. Most preschool and many kindergarten children are in this stage. You will see them further testing their individual powers and abilities. As their physical and intellectual abilities increase rapidly, they try out new and more challenging skills. This stage is like a bridge that children may continually move back and forth across, trying out being a "big kid" and then moving back into the security of their dependency on caregivers (Koplow, 2002). Children in this stage want to feel involved and powerful as they try out new tasks. They may be competitive and want to be the best at everything they do. Likewise, they may be intimidated and fear failure when tasks are too difficult for them. It is helpful to offer children appropriate opportunities to feel successful, as in the following examples.

∞ Megan is always right there when it is time to prepare the morning snack. She takes great satisfaction in setting the table or spreading peanut butter on celery sticks. She practices small motor coordination, and even math skills, as she meticulously places five raisins on each celery stick. Her feelings of accomplishment and confidence are also growing.

Megan and her classmates are invited to assist with many necessary jobs in the morning session of preschool. They care for the guinea pig, cleaning her cage and feeding her. They water the plants, sweep up under the sand table, and organize the dress-up clothes on hooks. They take pride in this work be-cause their teacher, Dennis, communicates his belief in the children's abilities. The teacher accepts the children's ability levels and doesn't make a fuss if a job isn't done perfectly, or if a little something is spilled in the process.

Whenever the morning staff thinks about developing a new learning center, they first discuss the plan with the students. Dennis knows from his classes in early childhood education, as Nancy knows from raising four children, that children will learn much from the planning process and that their involvement will help ensure that the new materials are used appropriately. After a field trip to a bank, the children want to play bank in the pretend play area. Instead of looking all weekend for materials, Dennis and his assistant Nancy invite chil-dren to bring things from home that could be used in a bank. The weekly newsletter explains the plan to parents and asks them to contribute. On Mon-day, the children arrive with old checkbooks, deposit slips, canceled checks, a real cash box, and play money. Aaron's mom works in a bank, so she con-tributes a pad of loan application forms.

As the interested children work to arrange these materials in a way mean-ingful to them, they cooperate in problem solving and planning. They are will-ing to invest effort to resolve disagreements in their bank. Before long, things are set up to their satisfaction, and several youngsters are busily scribbling on the checks, making important banking transactions. These children are feeling good about the work they have done, and it shows in their behavior.

When teachers save all the work for themselves, no one "wins."

In the afternoon session at Midway Children's Center, the teacher makes the snack in advance and pours juice for each child. Joanne, the teacher, discourages the children's offers to help, telling them that they will only spill if they try to pour their own juice. Joanne spends long hours after school and on weekends preparing materials and rearranging the classroom. She prides herself on always having everything ready for her students when they arrive. She wouldn't dream of using class time to set up a new activity; everything is strictly preplanned and scheduled. She doesn't have pets in her class because she doesn't have time to care for them, and the children "are too young to do it properly." Everything is under control: hers. In spite of all her careful planning, Joanne has many more discipline problems than the morning staff does. The students often seem disinterested in what Joanne has planned for them. They frequently "misuse" the materials, pursuing their own ideas instead of copying the model at the art table. When the children don't follow Joanne's plans, she tells them how disappointed she is.

When children feel successful their behavior mirrors their good feelings about themselves.

Andre and his friends feel ashamed when they disappoint their teacher. They don't understand that it is their healthy curiosity and energy that is getting them into trouble. They only know that what they are interested in doing is "bad." They assume that they are bad children. Because Joanne's training is with older children, she isn't familiar with this stage of child development. Thus, she often misinterprets the children's actions. ∽

What a different kind of experience this teacher and her young students would have if Joanne only knew how to harness their constructive energy into activities that would develop their sense of initiative.

Industry versus Inferiority   School-age children are working through an emotional development stage that builds on the preschool stage of initiative versus guilt. Erikson calls this next stage industry versus inferiority. During this phase, children are extending their ideas of themselves as workers and contributing members of society. If they feel successful, their behavior mirrors their good feelings about themselves; negative behaviors go along with negative feelings about themselves. Their tasks now focus on earning recognition by producing things and mastering the tools to do so. In a subsistence society, this stage means learning to hunt, fish, cure skins, gather berries, and preserve food. For today's mainstream society, it means learning to read, write, think quantitatively, and work cooperatively. Feeling successful at this age means seeing yourself as a capable person. Once again, children need to have opportunities for real work that is meaningful to them and that they are allowed to do on their own.

∽ Mrs. Jensen's first graders were planting seeds this afternoon as part of their study to learn how things grow. They had read about what plants need to grow and now they were reading the specific directions on the seed packets. They had a variety of fast-growing seeds available: beans, radishes, lettuce, and alfalfa. They also had access to a variety of planting materials and containers.

Some were interested in the idea of watching bean sprouts grow in a jar of water. Others liked the idea of growing an alfalfa crop in a paper cup filled with dirt. The prospect of actually growing a radish to eat was attractive to many. The students had the opportunity to explore as many of the options as they wished. They also had the freedom to do their planting in their own way. The parent helper was worried because some of the seeds weren't being planted at the recommended depth. Mrs. Jensen reassured him that the variety of planting approaches and the varying results were an educational experience. The children certainly weren't worried. They felt very important to know that they were starting the process of making something grow.

When the seeds were planted, the youngsters began making journals for recording the growth of their plants. The children made the books themselves, counting out the agreed-on number of pages, choosing a cover color, and then folding and stapling the pages into booklet form. The parent helper noticed that the children could not keep the pages lined up as they stapled. He offered to help with folding and stapling. Mrs. Jensen explained to the well-meaning father that the children took pride in doing this work themselves. Sure enough, the children all loved their books, crooked and crumpled as they were. Everyone felt like a success. ∽

Too many children are labeled as failures at this stage. You certainly have seen the devastating consequences for the child who fails to begin reading on society's schedule. This is the child whom others shun for being dumb. This is the child who disrupts class out of frustration and anger. This is the child the teachers are eager to send off to the reading specialist. Many students who eventually become school dropouts begin dropping out in first grade (Denham, 2007). Lifelong inferiority complexes begin early. The children in the following examples were spared.

∞ Emily had a narrow escape. She came home in tears, saying, "I'm dumb now." Her teacher had said she wanted Emily to go to the reading specialist for help on her phonics skills. Fortunately, this step couldn't be taken without a parent conference. Miss Wheeler explained to Emily's mom that Emily didn't seem able to do the daily phonics worksheets; therefore, she obviously needed special help. Emily's mother was puzzled by this report, because her daughter was already reading at home and wrote wonderful stories, too. Her teacher was surprised to hear about Emily's success at home. She couldn't figure out how a child could read and write but not be able to do phonics sheets. Miss Wheeler was new to first grade after teaching in the upper grades and wasn't knowledgeable about beginning reading. She didn't realize that phonics sheets are much more abstract than actual writing is, and that most children learn phonics through meaningful writing experiences. Miss Wheeler listened to the child's mother, however, and did not further damage Emily's belief in herself as a learner.

Austin not only couldn't do worksheets, but also really wasn't interested in writing when he was a first grader. Mrs. Jensen met with his parents and decided that Austin just wasn't ready yet. They knew he was a bright child and would become a reader and writer in time. They made sure that he had plenty of opportunities to experience books and many purposes for writing, but they made no demands for a certain level of performance from him. Most of all, they made sure that he never felt like a failure. If Austin couldn't read in the first grade, it was not the end of the world. However, feeling like a failure could endanger his self-esteem and his future ability to learn. This child was supported as he negotiated the industry versus inferiority stage in his own time. ∞

Families and Attachment

A secure attachment is the foundation for healthy progression through all the stages of emotional development. Secure attachment is a loving relationship with special people; interacting with these people is pleasurable and their nearness is comforting in times of stress (Berk, 2007). Very young children need to be supported, accepted, and comforted as they begin to learn about the world. When a parent provides this type of environment for a child, the child forms a secure attachment with his or her parent (Ainsworth, Blehar, Waters, & Wall, 1978). Developing a secure attachment includes giving a child room to explore while also being aware of and sensitive to the child's needs (Landy, 2002). This is the beginning of trust development, as mentioned when we discussed Erikson's stage of trust versus mistrust (Erikson, 1963).

Some of the most difficult children you will encounter as a teacher come from family situations where their attachment experience has been stressful,

A secure attachment is the foundation for healthy emotional development.

dysfunctional, or even dangerous (Gurian, 2001). Children with attachment issues may not be able to express their own feelings; they may be aggressive toward or reject others. They may be whiny, impulsive, needy, or disorganized and unpredictable. Typically they are not well-liked due to their behavior (Riley, San Juan, Klinkner, & Ramminger, 2008).

For instance, Tomas may be very successful at pushing other people away when they try to engage him. He may act quite nasty to others and appear unworthy of affection and attention. If Tomas was abandoned, neglected, or abused, his behavior is understandable. If he could not trust in a caregiver to consistently respond to and protect him, his repulsive behavior is only a protective mechanism. He is attempting to protect himself from what he believes will ultimately be rejection from everyone he encounters.

Teachers and Attachment

Fortunately, during the preschool and early school years it is not too late to intervene in the lives of children with attachment problems. When a child enters a school or early education setting without the foundation of a secure attachment, the most important task for the teacher is to focus on building a positive, consistent, and trusting relationship with that child. Children who are more securely attached to their teachers get along better with other children and have fewer behavior problems (Riley et al., 2008). Even if Tomas doesn't have a consistently available adult at home, a secure relationship with his teacher can help. His caring teacher can disprove his expectation of rejection. He can learn to trust his teacher. Rather than reinforcing Tomas's belief that he is unworthy of love and caring, your task is to provide Tomas with a predictable and safe environment, consistently respond to his needs, and show positive feelings toward him. He can learn valuable relationship skills from you that will help him succeed in all areas of his life.

∞ In the following example, we see how Sheri built a caring relationship with Tristan. From Sheri, Tristan is learning how to build his own caring relationships with others. Tristan's behavior had become increasingly aggressive since his arrival at the early care and education center last fall, and Sheri was very concerned. In fact, things were getting out of control. Last week, when she had to remove Tristan from the block area where he was hitting other children with blocks, he had hit and kicked her uncontrollably. She tried to hold him soothingly, but his outburst didn't stop until he was exhausted. He refused to be comforted by her.

Tristan had some pretty harsh words for Sheri. No matter what he said to her, Sheri told him repeatedly, "I'm sorry you feel that way, Tristan, but I still like you." Although Tristan was often doing something he wasn't supposed to be doing, Sheri looked for every opportunity to make a positive comment to Tristan. When he used the green crayon, Sheri commented, "I see you chose to use a green crayon; green is such a beautiful color." She also complimented him as often as she could, saying, for example, "I saw you running fast on the playground today; you are building some strong muscles." Sheri told Tristan that she planned a project that would be perfect for his strong muscles. The class was making lemonade and he could use his strong muscles to push down hard on the lemons to squeeze the juice out. As she had hoped, Tristan liked squeezing the lemons and felt proud of his ability to squeeze out lots of juice. Since Tristan had been the first to start making lemonade, the other children allowed him to tell them how to do it. Tristan had a great time, and even cheerfully helped with the cleanup. Sheri told him, "I enjoyed working with you today, you really know a lot about making lemonade." Tristan was feeling so good about himself; he was friendly and cooperative at story time and saved the teacher a place to sit next to him at snack time, giving her a hug as she did so. ∞

Notice that Tristan is beginning to bond with Sheri as well as to feel proud of himself. Of course, one day doesn't undo years of problems, but each step toward meeting a child's emotional needs is a step in the right direction.

Human Needs

Forming a secure attachment is a basic need for healthy emotional development. Beyond attachment, there are other emotional needs that all humans continue to have throughout life. Adler (1917) proposed that power, attention, and acceptance are basic human needs required for individuals to feel personal significance and a sense of belonging. When these needs are met, people feel good about themselves and tend to interact with others in positive ways. This creates a cycle of positive interaction that further convinces them that they are significant in their world. When these needs are not met, the reverse is true: Human nature leads people who feel insignificant to behave in ways that further alienate them from the acceptance and approval they desire. These needs apply to adults as well as children.

Power   A need for being in charge of your own actions, also known as personal power, is central to feeling significant (Adler, 1917). Children and adults who experience too much external control over their behaviors have unmet power needs. This may make them bossy and controlling of others, or it may overwhelm them to frustration and anger. Sometimes temper tantrums are a result of feeling powerless. You may have seen situations when children began screaming and crying when told they had to do something that seemed insignificant.

If you have spent much time with young children, you will recognize these statements as common: "I don't have to!" "My mom said!" "You're not the boss of me!" These are clear evidence of children's attempts to get personal power. This need for power is often evident when watching children play. Themes of invincibility and control are very attractive to kids. Unfortunately, this play is often violent and may reflect the violence that children have seen in their homes, communities, or the news. The children most likely to play out these violent themes are those who feel the most powerless and vulnerable (Levin, 2004).

Young children are especially vulnerable to unmet power needs because they are able to make so few actual decisions for themselves. This is another reason why it is important to give them choices as often as possible and to say "No" to them as seldom as possible. Children whose power needs are met are definitely easier to get along with.

Attention   A major indicator of significance and social recognition is having other people pay attention to you. Being ignored is painful because it makes you feel unimportant. Having someone listen to what you have to say, or be interested in what you are doing, is incredibly validating. Unfortunately, many adults unwittingly teach children to misbehave in order to get the attention they crave. They pay no attention to children who are getting along well or who are working productively; they only give attention when there is a problem. This means that many children have no idea how to get attention in positive ways; therefore, they strive to get it in negative ways. Interestingly, the drive for attention is so strong that people would rather have others mad at them than ignoring them.

෴ Max has been sitting in group time waving his hand wildly, hoping to get a turn answering a question. He knows all the answers, but never gets a chance to show it. He is getting very disgusted at listening to other kids who don't know the right answer. Why won't Miss Wheeler call on him? He could tell her the right answer. Max decides not to wait to be called on anymore; he yells out the answer to the next question. Miss Wheeler instantly reprimands him for breaking the rule about raising his hand and sends him to the time-out bench. As he sits there all alone, he sees the plants that the class planted last week. Some are starting to sprout. Max breaks the tender shoots off the plants. ෴

Acceptance Being accepted by others, having friends and playmates, is another essential human need. Some people behave in ways that makes others want to be with them, and others do the opposite. Young children generally lack understanding of others' feelings; this often causes them to act in ways that result in rejection. Teachers of young children see variations of the following situation over and over again. Social skill problems such as this will be discussed in Chapter 3.

∞ Adam wanted to play with Shaun, an older, admired playmate, so he ran up to him and exuberantly banged into him. Shaun didn't see this as a friendly gesture, so he shoved Adam away—hard. Adam fell against the wall and cried brokenheartedly, not just from the bump but also from the rejection. ∞

Motives of Misbehavior

Dreikurs (1964) expanded on Adler's theory of basic human needs to specifically discuss children's behavior. Dreikurs proposed that children will often misbehave in an unconscious attempt to have their basic needs met. Specifically, behavior problems may be the result of a need for power, attention, revenge, or an attempt to avoid failure. "Avoidance of failure" means a child has totally quit trying. This is the result of experiencing too many failures in the quest to fulfill personal needs, becoming convinced there is no hope of success. Children may also have behavior problems when they cannot regulate their emotions. When children do not understand their emotions and do not have the skills to express them in a socially acceptable way, behavior problems are often the result.

As children's brains and nervous system mature, they can better control their emotions.

Emotion Regulation

Emotion regulation refers to our ability to control our internal reactions and outward expressions of our emotions (Landy, 2002). When children develop emotion regulation they can identify their feelings and verbalize them to others, they can cope with emotional highs and lows appropriately, and they can refrain from acting on their impulses when needed. Children also learn to delay gratification and motivate themselves into action as they develop emotion regulation skills. Emotional competence expands upon emotion regulation. Emotionally competent children are aware of their own emotions and the emotions of others. Emotionally competent children can also read social cues and show empathy to others (Gottman, 2004; Hyson, 2004).

Developing emotional competency takes time; there is much for children to learn. How to deal with frustration, cope with fear and anxiety, and express pleasure in an appropriate way are just parts of developing emotion regulation. Unfortunately, some people never master these skills, even throughout their adult years. You probably know at least one adult who cannot control his or her anger, or you may have a friend who is overwhelmed by his or her fear and anxiety. We develop the ability to regulate our emotions in several ways. Our genetic makeup, brain development, temperament, and attachment affect our ability to regulate emotions (Macklem, 2008). This means that our ability to regulate our emotions does not depend only on our environment. Each individual comes into the world with some natural emotional strengths and challenges. Our individual temperaments play a major role in the development of emotional competency. If negative mood and an intense reaction style are elements of Nicole's temperament, then learning to regulate her emotions will be a more difficult task for Nicole than for a more even-tempered child.

In addition to temperament, developing a secure attachment with a caregiver may be one of the most important contributors to developing emotional competency. Through the foundation of secure, trusting relationships with consistent caregivers, children begin to understand their emotions and the emotions of those around them. As we discussed earlier, a secure attachment involves a responsive adult who acknowledges a child's emotions and provides comfort when needed. In this way, a child experiences empathy from the caregiver and begins to learn how to express empathy for others, a critical element in developing emotion regulation (Landy, 2002).

∞ At the preschool there are four trikes the children can ride when they go outside to play. When the doors open, Sadie runs to the trikes just in time to see four other children hop on them and ride off. She immediately begins to cry. Maureen recognizes this situation as a teaching moment. Maureen kneels beside Sadie and says, "You are feeling sad because you didn't get the first turn on one of the trikes." Sadie agrees with her and cries more. Maureen explains that she feels sad sometimes too. She gives Sadie a hug and sits with her for a moment. Sadie's crying begins to slow down and Maureen knows this is the time to help her learn some problem-solving skills. Maureen asks, "Would you like to wait here for a turn on one of the trikes, or do you want to find something else to do while you wait?" Sadie looks around and then runs to grab some sidewalk chalk to use while she waits for a turn on a trike. She asks Maureen to draw with her while she waits. ∽

In addition to teaching emotion regulation skills, caregivers also serve as models for emotional competency. Children learn to identify their feelings and put them into words by watching those around them.

Many studies show that academic success is linked to learning emotion regulation skills (Elias & Arnold, 2006; Flook, Repetti, & Ullman, 2005; Fonagy, Twemlow, Vernberg, Sacco, & Little, 2005). When we are under stress it is more difficult to remember and understand what we learn. Therefore, children who can manage their emotions are more able to concentrate on learning new skills. With emotional competence, children are better problem solvers and can be better friends to their peers. Children who can soothe themselves emotionally have fewer behavior problems and are less likely to commit acts of violence (Gottman, 1997). When schools focus on helping children develop their emotional competence, academic achievement increases, quality of relationships with peers and teachers improves, and behavior problems decrease (Macklem, 2008).

Helping Children Develop Emotional Competence

With adult assistance, children become more able to behave in socially acceptable ways as they mature. We have already mentioned that attachment is crucial to developing emotional competence. Therefore, forming a positive and supportive relationship with children in your classes is the first and possibly most important step in assisting in their emotional development. If kids trust you, they will be able to express their emotions to you much more easily. For children who have not experienced a secure attachment, learning to express their emotions in an acceptable and healthy way may not come easily. If you work on developing your relationship with them as the first step, their emotional competence will gradually begin to grow as well. Relationship building is discussed further in Chapter 4.

There are many other proactive ways to help children develop emotion regulation skills. Teaching children to be aware of their emotions and how to handle them in healthy ways is called *emotion coaching* (Gottman, 2004). Teachers are some of the best emotion coaches. Being aware of your own emotions and taking care of your own emotional health is the foundation for emotion coaching. Remind yourself and your class that all emotions are acceptable, but all behaviors are not. Have discussions with the class about ways we express our emotions, and set clear limits on behavior in the classroom. As a class, identify the emotions of characters in books and stories, and allow children to express their emotions in role-plays with puppets or figures. You can place visual cues in the classroom with emotion words and/or facial expressions. Allowing children to draw pictures or make up their own metaphors to represent feelings can be helpful, particularly for children with limited language abilities. Talk about children's emotions during conflicts between peers, asking about or pointing out the facial expression of the other child, and help them to name the feelings they are expressing. These coaching techniques will help children learn to read the emotions of others and develop empathy.

- Build positive, respectful relationships with each individual child.
- Integrate discussions about emotions into the curriculum.
- Acknowledge children's feelings (don't minimize or ignore emotions).
- Help children put their feelings into words they understand.
- Model appropriate expressions of your own feelings.

FIGURE 2–2 Helping Children Develop Emotion Regulation

When a child is distressed, there are simple emotion coaching steps you can follow to help a child develop emotional competency. These steps are essentially the same ones used in conflict resolution, which is discussed in Chapter 7. Begin by listening to the child's feelings without judgment or criticism. After hearing the child, help him or her put feelings into words. This helps the child develop an emotion vocabulary for the future. When children feel heard and have a label for how they feel, they are often able to move beyond their distress. If a child is still distressed, you have a great opportunity to help him or her identify appropriate solutions to the problem. Likewise, acknowledge your own emotions to your students and model techniques for calming yourself, such as taking deep breaths or taking your own quiet time. Figure 2–2 shows some of the strategies you can use to teach emotion regulation. How to accept children's emotions and model appropriate expressions is discussed further in Chapter 6.

Acknowledging and accepting children's emotions can go a long way. Many times our anger is more manageable after we have expressed it to someone who understands. Instead of minimizing, criticizing, or denying children's emotions, allow them a time and place to feel all of their emotions. Continually communicate the message that no emotions are prohibited, only certain behaviors are off limits. You can enforce limits of behavior, but acknowledge the child's emotion as valid. Listen to children's verbal and nonverbal expression of emotions, and help them put their emotions into accurate words.

∞ Sarah and Sophie are playing house. Sarah is being "the mommy" and pushing her baby in the buggy, when Sophie decides she is ready for her turn. She grabs the buggy away, knocking Sarah over in the process. As Dennis approaches, Sarah is crying as she tells him, "I hate Sophie. She is mean." Dennis sits beside her, putting an arm around her, and says, "I can see you are really angry with Sophie for taking your baby buggy. I feel angry too when someone takes away something I really want. I'll go with you while you tell Sophie that you will finish your turn with the buggy and then she may have her turn after you." ∞

Dennis also acknowledges Sophie's feelings, "I can tell you are sad that you don't have that baby buggy right now. Sometimes it is hard to wait, and it's okay to be sad. It isn't okay to grab toys from our friends. Next time I know you'll ask or wait your turn."

As children develop emotion regulation, they learn not to cry at minor disappointments and how to comfort themselves when upset. They also gain the ability to control impulsive behavior. Impulse control is needed for a social skill such as taking turns, which requires that a child be able to postpone the immediate gratification of desires. When Molly puts her thumb in her mouth instead of crying after her mother drops her off, she demonstrates the ability to soothe herself. When Dylan is able to wait his turn on the slide, he shows that he can delay gratification. Min Ho's nonexpressive style is evidence that he has learned his family's cultural standards for emotion regulation.

CONCLUSION

Children's physical and emotional needs affect their behavior. Understanding child development is necessary for dealing with discipline issues. Many factors contribute to emotional development in children; temperament and attachment play a major role in the development of emotional competence. Children have parents and teachers who help them develop trust in others and belief in their own abilities. Knowledgeable adults meet these children's basic needs and support them in developing emotional competence. Guidance by knowledgeable and supportive caregivers is necessary for children's healthy emotional development.

⌘ FOR FURTHER THOUGHT

1. Observe an early childhood setting, watching for examples of young children's inability to sit still for very long. What problems do you see when adults forget this aspect of child development?
2. As you observe young children, try to identify different temperaments as described in this chapter. What is the difference between a person's current mood and that person's temperament?
3. Think about people you know well. Do any of them exhibit signs of an insecure attachment as described in this chapter? How does that problem affect their social interactions?
4. Observe toddlers, watching for expressions of developing emotional autonomy as described in this chapter. How do adults respond? Do you recommend any different

responses based on your understanding of this aspect of emotional development?
5. Observe preschoolers, watching for expressions of their desire for real work. Does their environment meet this need? What changes could be made to assist their development of initiative?
6. Observe your own emotions, put a name to a feeling, and talk about it with someone.
7. A problem to solve: Jeremy isn't working on his writing assignment. He is fooling around and bothering others instead.
   a. What are some possible causes of this behavior?
   b. How would you address the various causes?
   c. How might the problem have been avoided?

∽ RECOMMENDED READINGS

Erikson, E. (1963). *Childhood and society* (2nd ed.). New York: Norton.

Gottman, J. M. (2004). *What am I feeling?* Seattle WA: Parenting Press.

Lantieri, L., & Goleman, D. (2008). *Building emotional intelligence: Techniques to cultivate inner strength in children.* Boulder, CO: Sounds True Inc.

Macklem, G. L. (2008). *Practitioner's guide to emotion regulation in school-aged children.* New York: Springer Science.

Riley, D., San Juan, R., Klinkner, J., & Ramminger, A. (2008). *Social and emotional development: Connecting science and practice in early childhood settings.* St. Paul, MN: Redleaf Press.

✂ Chapter **3** ✂
Intellectual and Social Development Affect Discipline

NAEYC Standards Addressed in This Chapter

Standard 1a: Promoting Child Development and Learning: Knowing and understanding young children's characteristics and needs.

Standard 1b: Promoting Child Development and Learning: Knowing and understanding the multiple influences on development and learning.

Standard 1c: Promoting Child Development and Learning: Using developmental knowledge to create healthy, respectful, supportive, and challenging learning environments.

Standard 2c: Building Family and Community Relationships: Involving families and communities in their children's development and learning.

Standard 4b: Teaching and Learning, Using Developmentally Effective Approaches: Candidates know, understand, and use a wide array of effective approaches, strategies, and tools to positively influence young children's development and learning.

Standard 4c: Teaching and Learning, Understanding Content Knowledge in Early Education: Candidates understand the importance of each content area in young children's' learning. They know the essential concepts, inquiry tools, and structure of content areas including academic subjects and can identify resources to deepen their understanding.

GUIDING QUESTIONS

- How is young children's thinking different from adult thinking?
- How does young children's thinking affect their behavior?
- How does egocentricity affect children's ability to form relationships with peers?
- How can teachers help children develop the skills and understanding required for positive social interaction?
- How do cultural, socioeconomic, and gender differences affect children's behavior?

Young children are not miniature adults. That idea is central to early childhood education and basic to the constructivist view of learning. It reminds us that children have unique needs that must be considered in their care and education. The statement also cautions us against adult egocentricity in assuming that children's thinking is the same as ours.

In this chapter we examine some ways in which children's ways of thinking influence their behavior and affect your discipline decisions. Information about young children's intellectual and social development will not only help you immeasurably in the areas of guidance and discipline, but will also help you be a more effective teacher in general. This information builds on the discussion of emotional development from Chapter 2; intellectual and social development are intertwined with emotional development.

INTELLECTUAL DEVELOPMENT AND BEHAVIOR

Lev Vygotsky and Jean Piaget, both born in 1896, are two major contributors to the understanding of intellectual development. They are both considered *constructivists* because they emphasized that knowledge is actively constructed by the learner rather than passively received from others (Bodrova & Leong, 2007; Pass, 2004). However, neither suggested that input from others is not necessary; both writers acknowledged the essential role of social interaction for the development of understanding. Vygotsky wrote convincingly of social experience shaping how people think and interpret their world (Gredler & Shields, 2008). Piaget's work frequently discusses the role of social interaction with adults and with peers, as learners exchange viewpoints to construct understanding. Piaget (1965) explained that social interactions between children are necessary for the development of intelligence, morality, and personality.

Both Piaget and Vygotsky also described processes of organizing information as central to learning. Vygotsky's work (1962, 1978) describes young children moving from randomly categorizing information in "heaps" to an increasingly more sophisticated classification system based on analysis of the relationship between pieces of information. Piaget's work focused extensively on the significance of individually created logico-mathematical frameworks for classifying relationships between ideas and information (Wadsworth, 2004).

What is commonly known about the work of either Piaget or Vygotsky is only the tip of the iceberg, and their most significant contributions are widely ignored due to their complexity. Both Piaget and Vygotsky are best known for the one aspect of their work that is easiest to understand: Vygotsky is best known for the idea of the *zone of proximal development* (Gredler & Shields, 2008), which will be discussed later in this chapter. Piaget is known for his *stage theory*, indicating a sequence of maturation in understanding and thinking. Vygotsky agreed with Piaget that young children's thinking differs from that of older children, and that abstract thought is a later development (Berk, 2001). Due to Piaget's life and career lasting much longer than Vygotsky's, Piaget and his associate researchers at the Geneva Institute were able to amass huge quantities of research data about the learning process. Because children were the subjects of the studies, they provided excellent views of children's thinking.

Young Children's Thinking Is Different

The work of Piaget and his colleagues clearly shows that a child's view of the world and reality is different from an adult's. Children's limited reasoning ability, coupled with their limited experience, often brings them to conclusions inconsistent with adult logic. This situation often gets children into trouble. Teachers and parents get angry at youngsters for what adults perceive as disobeying rules, telling lies, being selfish or inconsiderate, and behaving in totally irrational ways. To make matters worse, the children don't realize that they have done anything wrong. For a parent or teacher who doesn't understand what Piaget (1964) has explained about intellectual development, this behavior can be totally infuriating. However, it is often just normal behavior for a young child.

Breaking Rules

Part of Piaget's (1965) famous and extensive studies of children's thinking involved their understanding of rules in games. He focused on rules in the game of marbles, finding out that children's views of rules differ with age. The younger children weren't able to follow the rules but believed that they were quite sacred because they were imposed by adults. Piaget pointed out that these youngsters nevertheless seemed unconcerned about following the rules. Older children felt free to change the rules by mutual consent, and only then felt bound to play by them. Piaget related this concept to the difference between guidelines for life that are imposed by others (heteronomous rules) and those that children reason for themselves (autonomous rules). The latter situation is related to self-regulation.

The way children deal with the rules of a game can help adults understand how children deal with societal rules and expectations (Piaget, 1965). As you watch youngsters playing games, you can see for yourself that their ideas about rules vary with their ages.

Dennis is amused at how his 3-year-old students think about rules for their games. When they play hide-and-seek, they tend to yell out, "Here I am! Come find me!" If some adult sets up a race, the children don't wait for "ready, set, go." After the race, if someone asks who won, they all say with conviction, "I won! I won!" It is clear that young children respond according to their perceptions of what is important, not according to adult rules.

Most preschool youngsters don't understand, or can't cope with, the competitive aspect of games. The first time Dennis set up a game of musical chairs with 4-year-olds, he quickly learned a better way of structuring the game. He was faced with torrents of tears when youngsters were "out" after not finding a chair. Dennis immediately changed the rules so that there was a chair for everyone; the challenge was simply to find a seat quickly when the music stopped. The important thing was that no one was forced out of the game.

Primary-grade children become concerned about rules and about winning. The desire to win often colors the interpretation of rules, and each child wants to change the rules in his or her favor. Mrs. Jensen values the arguments and discussions that are an inevitable part of board games among her first graders. She recognizes that learning to resolve their own disputes about rules helps children learn to reason. She appreciates that young children can learn about cooperation from these opportunities to consider each other's position (e.g., DeVries & Zan, 2006; Siccone & Lopez, 2000). By learning to consider the viewpoint of others, children learn about behaving in ways that are compatible with the needs of others. This lesson takes time and careful adult assistance, but it is an important part of the long-term goals of discipline.

It is important for adults to realize that children who break rules, whether in play or in the classroom, may not understand that they have done so. Much of what adults take for granted is unknown to children. Piaget's (1965) studies of moral development indicate that young children are not capable of understanding why certain behaviors are acceptable or unacceptable; therefore, many behavior problems are caused by a lack of understanding, and the child truly has no idea of wrongdoing. One way to alleviate "rule breaking" in the classroom is by offering children the opportunity to contribute to the creation of classroom rules.

A child can learn to be generous only when sharing is a real choice and not forced.

Being Selfish

Parents and teachers tend to get very cross at young children who don't share; however, intellectual maturation plays a big role in learning to share. It is normal for young children to see things only from their own viewpoint. This aspect of their intellectual development affects their interactions with others. They are not necessarily being inconsiderate when they overlook a playmate's feelings; a very young child is often not even aware that someone else has feelings (DeVries & Zan, 2006). It's not surprising, then, that young children have many conflicts and that their teachers spend a great deal of time dealing with those conflicts. Teachers who understand child development don't get upset at these normal misunderstandings. Instead, they use the situation as a teachable moment, as Dennis does in this next example.

∞ Eli is playing by himself in the sandbox, carefully filling a dump truck with sand and emptying it, creating a hill. Caroline is playing next to him with a toy bulldozer. She suddenly drives her bulldozer over Eli's hill to flatten it out for a road. Eli immediately starts to cry and to hit Caroline.

Dennis arrives on the scene and comforts both children. He has observed enough from across the room to say to Eli, "I don't think Caroline knows why you are upset; can you use your words and tell her?" But Eli is too upset to talk yet, and so Dennis gives him more time by rephrasing the question. By then, Eli is able to say that he didn't want Caroline to touch his hill.

Dennis realizes that neither child had considered the intentions of the other. Eli thought Caroline was being mean, and Caroline was shocked that he was mad at her. Having encouraged Eli to express his view, Dennis then asks Caroline to explain what she was doing. It turns out that she was trying to be helpful in building a road, not understanding what Eli was doing. With help from Dennis, Eli is able to say, "I don't want a road, I'm making a hill." With this information, Caroline is happy to work on her road in another part of the sandbox and all is peaceful, for the moment. ∞

Conflict is an opportunity for an alert teacher to help youngsters tune in to the feelings and viewpoints of their playmates (Riley, San Juan, Klinkner, & Ramminger, 2008). Knowledgeable teachers do not blame the children or make anyone feel guilty for being thoughtless of others; they understand that this behavior is normal for young children.

Mrs. Jensen also works at helping her young students grow beyond their ego-centricity by encouraging them to tell one another how they feel. Often she needs to help children find the words to express themselves; they learn from her example as she walks them through the process of communicating their feelings in a constructive way. (Effective communication of these useful "I messages" is discussed further in Chapter 7.) This is part of effective guidance, which teaches life-long interpersonal skills. As children's intellectual ability to understand the views of others develops, their social development is enhanced as well. Learning to think about how others feel, called perspective taking, is discussed further in the Social Skills section of this chapter.

The goal is voluntary unselfishness, but many adults force children to share instead. Few adults would be as generous with their prized possessions as parents and teachers often insist youngsters must be. Would you turn your new car over to someone you barely know because "she doesn't have one"? Why should Rosa let Samantha ride her new bike? Rosa's right of ownership and right to decide whether or not to share must first be respected in order to prepare her to voluntarily share. Children often think that sharing means giving something away permanently (Landy, 2002); their generosity may be increased by reassurance of getting the object back again.

Only when sharing is a real choice and not coerced can a child make the choice to be generous. Even with classroom materials not owned by any individual, the rights of possession must be respected.

Lying and Stealing

Our society takes lying and stealing seriously; they are moral as well as legal issues. Adults without child development knowledge usually believe their role is to punish children for lying and stealing, not realizing those behaviors are linked to maturation (Landy, 2002). As a child, seeing things from your own viewpoint may mean that something is true because you want it to be true and that something is yours because you want it. These beliefs cause children to tell "lies" that they genuinely consider truths and guiltlessly take things that don't belong to them. An adult who understands how children think can help a youngster learn from these situations.

When Sophie tells her teacher that she is going with Olivia to Disneyland next week, Dennis understands and is able to respond with empathy: "You really wish you could go to Disneyland." This response helps Sophie separate her wishes from reality without making her feel bad about herself. The following example presents an actual problem of disappearing preschool materials.

∞ Madeline was in her favorite dress-up outfit from the playhouse. She announced to Sheri that the outfit she was wearing was her own and that she was going to wear it home and even to bed. Sheri said, "Dressing up is one of your favorite things to do at school, isn't it?" Madeline agreed and then repeated that the outfit was hers.

Sheri tried again, "I recognize those clothes as preschool dress-up clothes. It sounds like you wish they were your very own. You want to be able to take them home with you." Madeline held her ground, and Sheri tried explaining, "If everyone took their favorite clothes home, we wouldn't have any dress-up clothes to play with at school." Finally, Madeline seemed to be listening.

Yet Madeline still insisted that the clothes were hers, but she was very attentive as Sheri continued to discuss the problem. "I remember a few times when you went home with the dress-up clothes you were wearing. When I found out, I felt bad. I was worried that there would not be enough dress-up clothes at preschool anymore."

After listening carefully, Madeline put her arms around Sheri's neck and whispered in her ear, "Sheri, I know they are preschooler clothes." Then she smiled and danced away. ∞

Madeline's struggle with fact and fantasy is not unusual. Piaget (1965) found that young children really do not understand the nature of a lie. Even 6-year-olds in his study could not differentiate between an honest mistake and a purposeful mistruth. Additionally, they tended to judge how bad it was to tell a mistruth in relation to how likely it was to be found out and therefore punished. Thus, with this line of reasoning, a believable lie is acceptable, yet a lie that stretches the truth too far is bad. Piaget's research about children's thinking should help teachers and parents understand why explaining their adult logic to youngsters doesn't work. Instead, children need to experience the problems that come from deceiving others. As they get older, they can be helped to realize the impact of untruths on relationships. They can also be helped to understand that taking something from others makes the others sad. For these lessons to be effective, children must have caring relationships with others (Noddings, 2005; Riley et al., 2008).

Schoolwork Problems

Intellectual development stages determine what kinds of materials and activities best help children learn. If you don't match the experiences and materials to the children, you are sure to have behavior problems as well as academic problems (Noddings, 2005). Piaget's (1960) work explains the importance of young children having real experiences with real materials to construct their knowledge about

Teachers who understand how young children learn have fewer problems with child behavior because they provide age-appropriate learning activities.

the world. The term *concrete* is often used to describe the type of materials children need for productive explorations. Concrete materials include the water in the water table, the manipulatives in the math center, and magnifying glasses in the science center.

Some teachers present abstract lessons to children who cannot yet make sense of them—for example, asking kindergarten children to complete addition problems before they've mastered number sense. This type of developmentally inappropriate instruction can create discipline problems. When children are not capable of doing what they are asked to do, they are likely to behave in ways adults dislike. Certainly they are not likely to complete the work on schedule. Often, youngsters who are frustrated and discouraged by school tasks that are beyond them are then punished for not doing the work. It is common to see these children sitting dejectedly at their desks during recess, still confused by what they are being asked to do. Is it any wonder that they are tempted to be less than cooperative or even to lash out in anger?

Some people get confused and think that plastic magnet letters or wooden letters that fit into puzzles are concrete. These letters can be touched and moved around, but they are still only *representational symbols*. Some representational materials are more easily recognized than letters or numbers are. For instance, a doll is more recognizable as a symbol for a baby than are the letters in the word *baby*. Pictures of real things are not concrete either, but they may be useful symbolic representations.

Sometimes teachers are striving for developmentally appropriate education but don't realize that their teaching materials are not concrete. Not everything that a child can touch and manipulate is concrete. Clocks and quarters are examples of apparently concrete materials that are actually representational rather than concrete. Young children can't construct knowledge of time or money through manipulation or observation of clocks or coins. No wonder lessons in telling time and making change are such difficult activities for young children. They involve both *symbolic representation* and arbitrary *social knowledge*. (Social knowledge is explained in Chapter 5 as one of three kinds of knowledge.) As such, they cannot be learned through an exploration of materials.

Teachers who understand how young children learn have fewer problems with child behavior because they provide age-appropriate learning activities and materials for children. They provide many materials that lend themselves to real-life experiences and multiple opportunities for children to show their knowledge. A classroom that offers children a choice of materials and learning opportunities meets children's needs. Mrs. Jensen's first grade has a wide assortment of concrete and representational materials accessible on open shelves for children to make selections. Miss Wheeler, next door, keeps everything but the worksheets in closed cupboards and rarely brings out anything else. She doesn't realize that the worksheets are entirely representational and meaningless to many of the children in her classroom.

∞ Dylan was in Mrs. Jensen's room, and his identical twin brother, Devon, was in Miss Wheeler's class; both were learning addition of single-digit numbers. Mrs. Jensen told the children addition stories and encouraged children to solve the story problems using manipulatives. She then asked the children to discuss the strategies they used to solve their problems with one another. In Miss Wheeler's class, the children were given worksheets filled with addition problems and told to keep quiet so they didn't disturb the work of their classmates. Dylan shared his addition stories with Devon when they were at home.

The next day during math time, Devon took matters into his own hands and got out an armload of special things from the teacher's cupboard, and began using them to create his own addition stories. But Miss Wheeler didn't appreciate his efforts. She was upset that he would dare to get into the cupboard without permission. How sad that she missed the important message Devon was sending about his learning needs. ∞

SOCIAL SKILLS AND GUIDANCE

Missing social skills is the single most common cause of discipline problems. Children's squabbles over materials and their unskilled efforts to make friends cause frequent disruptions to both preschool and primary classrooms. Social skills are discussed last because we see them as an outgrowth of the previously discussed aspects of development. Physical abilities, emotional development, and levels of intellectual understanding all combine to determine current levels of social skill and understanding.

Teachers of young children have a big responsibility because the early years are crucial for social development. Youngsters who do not develop social competence in the early childhood years typically continue to experience difficulty with peer acceptance throughout the school years (Howes & Ritchie, 2002; Johnson, Ironsmith, Snow, & Poteat, 2000). Not surprisingly, these children are at risk as adults for social and emotional problems (Denham et al., 2001; Yanghee, 2003). Helping youngsters learn how to make a friend and be a friend is crucial to their life-long happiness. It's also a big help to teacher happiness when children learn how to get along.

Constructing Knowledge for Social Skills

Children construct knowledge as a result of reflecting on their experiences. As they experiment with blocks, for instance, they observe the results of trying to stack, balance, and bridge structures. Thinking about the results helps children revise erroneous ideas. This process helps them construct understanding about such concepts as gravity, balance, and measurement. Children construct their theories of how social interactions work using the same sort of trial-and-error analysis (Kemple, 2004).

As youngsters experiment with different ways of interacting with others, they observe the results of various approaches. Reflecting on the results of their social overtures can help children figure out how to play with others successfully and how to make friends. We have remarked previously on the value of peer conflicts as teaching situations. You may be surprised to hear that children's fights are useful teaching tools. Conflicts tend to challenge children's assumptions and encourage an exchange of viewpoints. They help youngsters realize that not everyone sees things their way. Thus, conflicts provide the necessary experience for learning, as well as teachable moments. Helping children deal with their disputes gives the teacher an opportunity to guide children's thinking about the experience. The adult role varies, depending on the child's individual levels of emotional, intellectual, and social development.

Teaching children to think critically about their behavior and to use reasoning abilities to learn to solve interpersonal problems is consistent with current recommended approaches to teaching other subjects. National guidelines in every area of the curriculum urge teaching for critical thinking and problem solving instead of old approaches of memorized learning (Noddings, 2008). Some adults think it is enough to simply tell children how they are expected to behave and then punish them if they do not. That approach would be the same as a teacher merely demanding mastery of mathematics without instruction, assessment, and re-teaching.

Adults who are focused only on immediate outcomes will use punishment to get desired behaviors, believing that the teaching approach is too slow. Keeping long-term goals in mind is especially important and difficult when dealing with behaviors linked to maturation. True, you won't get 4-year-olds (or even 5-year-olds) to truly understand the feelings of the child they just hit; but that doesn't mean you stop working toward your goals. If you resort to coercive tactics, you will make it more difficult for the child to eventually become considerate of others (Kohn, 2005; Russell, Hart, Robinson, & Olsen, 2003).

Have you noticed that we are not talking about social skills as learning to say *please, thank you,* and *I'm sorry*? These are polite ways of speaking, but they are only superficial behaviors and do not necessarily reflect true feelings (Flicker & Hoffman, 2002). Some adults and children confuse these memorized phrases with the understanding needed for true social competence. You have certainly seen children who are caught doing something wrong and who automatically say, "I'm sorry," yet show no signs of remorse. These children have merely learned the magic words for getting out of punishment. Too many adults focus on teaching socially acceptable words instead of helping children understand others and develop caring feelings.

∳ Mrs. Jensen realized the uselessness of teaching words instead of understanding several years ago when she rescued Isabel from Jason's physical aggression. Jason was angry with Isabel and was gripping her wrists very hard, hurting her. After Mrs. Jensen pried his hands off Isabel and helped Isabel to tell Jason how she felt, she asked Jason what he could do to make Isabel feel better.

Jason said "Thank you," and Mrs. Jensen asked Isabel if that made her feel better. Isabel replied in a disdainful voice, "No. Jason, you have to say 'sorry.'" So Jason said, "Sorry." However, Mrs. Jensen could tell that one platitude was as meaningless as the next. ∳

How Children Develop Social Competence

What is social competence? It refers to a set of skills that allow people to have satisfying interactions with others and maintain positive relationships over time, while balancing personal needs with those of others (Kemple, 2004).

However, we should always keep in mind that ways of having satisfying interactions and relationships may vary from culture to culture (Lillard & Curenton, 1999). Research-based definitions of social competence include the ability to play cooperatively, to take turns and share, to initiate friendly contact, and to respond positively to friendly contact from others (Kemple, 2004). Many skills and understandings are prerequisite to these abilities.

As in other teaching topics, we need to start with the "basics" when we teach social skills. Like any other learning, the ability to successfully master social skills requires that children's physical and emotional needs are met. A child who lacks security and confidence has difficulty working on anything else. Children are most likely to be secure, confident, and socially competent if their parents are warm and attentive and also help them understand limits (e.g., Kohn, 2005; Landy, 2002). If these needs cannot be met adequately at home, schools must try to fill the gaps (Koplow, 2002; Noddings, 2005).

We need to think about a child's motivation for prosocial behaviors, such as sharing or otherwise compromising. You have surely seen youngsters who don't care one bit whether they hurt other children or make them mad. These are usually the children who feel rejected by others, and who reject others in return. If a child doesn't care about others, you aren't going to have much luck with lessons about getting along. Being able to consider another person's feelings is a different issue than wanting to do so. It really isn't until children have something to lose, such as a playmate, that they have reason to consider how their actions affect others (Riley et al., 2008). You have probably noticed that as children develop the idea of friendship, they often use the "friendship threat" ("I won't be your friend!") in an effort to get their way (Wheeler, 2004).

Therefore, a "basic" for learning social skills is having friends, which for children means having playmates. In order to have playmates, children must be able to successfully enter into play with others, which may be the most "basic" part of developing social skills. The process of playing with others not only provides motivation for learning social skills, it also provides excellent practice (Riley et al., 2008). Because play is so essential to children's social, emotional, and intellectual development, and because this is not widely understood, teachers must work to protect and defend playtime in school (Ashiabi, 2007; Hanish et al., 2007). Play provides many opportunities for conflict and negotiation, which helps children learn to consider the needs and feelings of others. Considering the needs and feelings of others is called *perspective taking,* and is also basic to developing social skills (Eisenberg & Eggum, 2007).

Guiding children's attempts to enter play will increase their social competence.

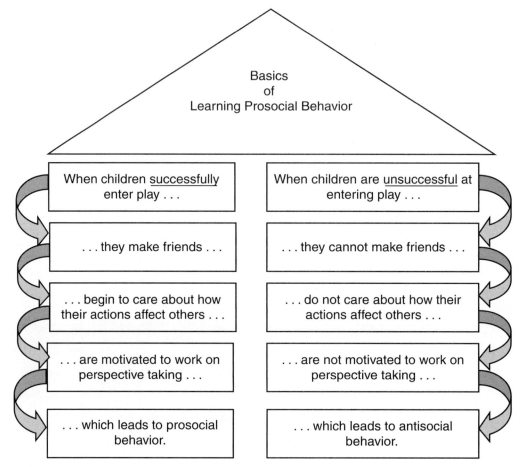

FIGURE 3–1   Basics of Prosocial Behavior

Figure 3–1 shows how each component of developing social competence influences the other. We see a necessary initial sequence to the components of learning social competence: first comes the ability to enter play successfully, which creates feelings of being accepted by others, which leads to friendships and to caring about others. These relationships make youngsters more willing to consider the perspective of others instead of just their own. When these pieces are in place, a child is generally open to teacher assistance with social skills and behaves in a fairly socially acceptable manner. Let's look now at how to help get these pieces into place.

Learning How to Enter Play

How many times have you seen a child crying because of not being allowed into a play situation? Research indicates that approximately 60% of attempts to enter ongoing play are rejected (Landy, 2002). Asking "Can I play?" is often ineffective and can even invite rejection because it offers the power to say "no." Instead, children can be helped to learn more productive strategies for being accepted as a playmate.

PEARSON
myeducationlab

To see an example of how teachers facilitate friendships by teaching children's names, go to MyEducationLab and select the topic "Guiding Children." Under Activities and Applications, watch the video "Facilitating Friendships: A Tisket A Tasket."

than about those of other people (Corso, 2003), thereby encouraging them to practice perspective taking. By early elementary school, many children have established a best friend. These relationships are important because they offer the best opportunities for developing the interpersonal understandings needed for socialized behavior. "Since friends want to maintain the relationship, they are motivated to learn social skills such as sharing, negotiation, cooperation, and conflict resolution (Riley et al., 2008, p. 44).

Learning Perspective Taking

Because children want to stay on good terms with their friends, they have more reason for trying to understand another child's viewpoint in a conflict. This isn't to say that friends will have fewer disagreements, but rather that they are more likely to try to work them out than nonfriends. Working out their differences provides valuable practice that enhances children's intellectual ability to understand another's point of view (Kempel, 2004), increases their desire to value another person's feelings, and develops conflict management skills (Riley et al., 2008).

The ability to see things from another's viewpoint, *perspective taking*, is essential to social competence, but requires intellectual ability to think about another person's feelings. Without this ability, youngsters remain self-centered and unable to relate to the interests, needs, and rights of others. "The root developmental achievement that underlies every domain of social cognitive development is perspective taking" (Lapsley, 2006). Until children can take into consideration the viewpoint of another person, they cannot make progress in reasoning about fairness. When they can only see their own views, their idea of justice consists of that which they desire for themselves. Obviously, this perception will not endear them to playmates.

There is considerable difference of opinion about how young children are able to understand another person's thoughts and feelings. Some people get confused by research on empathy and young children (e.g., Valiente et al., 2004), thinking that empathy is the same as perspective taking. Although frequently discussed together, empathy is not the same thing as perspective taking. Empathy and sympathy are tied to emotional development, while perspective taking is tied to cognitive development (Spinrad & Eisenberg, 2008). There are levels of empathy that have nothing to do with understanding how another person feels, such as the contagious crying of babies in a room together (deWaal, 2008). We agree that certain forms of empathy appear early, such as sympathizing with another child who is sad. However, true perspective taking, the ability to take another person's view into consideration even when it conflicts with your own, is another matter. A 3-year-old who gives a cookie to a hungry child when there are plenty of cookies is not likely to do so when there is only one cookie, especially if that 3-year-old wants the cookie for himself or herself. Though very young children have been observed sharing and helping others, it is not clear that these are demonstrations of true perspective taking. Positive social behaviors may be motivated from other sources.

Learning to consider another person's needs and feelings is a huge task—especially if those needs and feelings are in opposition to your own.

Awareness develops gradually from an egocentric perspective to the ability to respond to and even predict how others will feel (e.g., Bloom, 2007; Hyson, 2004; Lapsley, 2006). Anyone working with young children is aware of their egocentricity (Flicker & Hoffman, 2002). According to researchers (DeVries, Hildebrandt, & Zan, 2000; Selman, 1980), with experience and guidance, people move through five levels of perspective taking as follows: Level 0, not recognizing that others have feelings or ideas different from your own, is common during preschool. During the primary grades, most children operate at level 1. At this point, young children realize that others have their own feelings, but can't consider someone else's feelings while thinking about their own. Our observation shows that this is particularly true when their own feelings are in opposition to the other person's. As they move into upper elementary school, level 2 thinking is more common. This brings the ability to consider another person's views as well as their own. Levels 3 and 4 bring increasing decentering and the ability to coordinate mutual perspectives. However, these generally do not emerge until adolescence and adulthood. Theory of mind research points out the role of maturation as children develop understanding of their own and others' thinking (Flavell & Hartman, 2004).

This information about children's thinking should help you to be more accepting of how they behave. You will respond differently when you realize that young children probably aren't being mean when they disregard another child's feelings; they're just being young. This information about levels of intellectual development also offers essential guidance for helping children move to higher levels. The message is not to just accept the child's lack of perspective taking, but to aim your teaching one level higher than what the child is doing (DeVries et al., 2000).

Working with young children, you will often see situations like the following.

∾ Jessie is working on a drawing, using the only yellow marker at the table. Jack reaches over and grabs the marker out of Jessie's hand. He seems somewhat startled when Jessie yells at him and tries to grab the marker back. Soon the two are in a tug-of-war, with both sides claiming they need the marker.

    Dennis stops the struggle and calms the children with his gentle presence. He works at getting each child to explain his or her feelings, trying to get them to use the "I messages" he consistently models. (See Chapter 7 for more detail on "I messages.") Then Dennis shows Jack where he can get another yellow marker. ∾

When Jack grabbed Jessie's marker, he demonstrated that his perspective taking was at level 0. He took the marker simply because he wanted it, with no thought about Jessie. Therefore, Dennis aimed at helping Jack realize that Jessie has wishes and feelings, too. Notice that Dennis tried to get the children to explain their viewpoints to one another; he doesn't do the talking for children unless he absolutely has to. Instead he supports and encourages them to do their own talking. Hearing about how another child feels directly from that child, while looking at that child's face, presents a more powerful, concrete message than hearing it from the teacher. Although Dennis encouraged the children to exchange viewpoints, he understood that it probably wouldn't be worthwhile to try to teach higher-level cooperative negotiation to Jack because it would be too far above his level of understanding at that time.

Children can make better-than-normal progress through these levels of understanding with the support of understanding teachers (DeVries & Zan, 2006). And, as Vygotsky (1962) reminds us, children can perform at higher levels with assistance than they can alone. Vygotsky's writings about the *zone of proximal development* and *scaffolding* refer to how adults help children to do things, and thus teach them to perform independently. Teachers often use puppets, role-playing, and storybooks to guide children to think about the feelings of others. Through story and drama, teachers can ask children to put themselves in another person's place and imagine their feelings without calling attention to any "misdeed" that has taken place in the classroom.

Learning Conflict Resolution

Children who have some perspective-taking ability can be helped to learn conflict resolution skills. The ability to avoid and resolve conflicts constitutes another essential aspect of social competence. It involves the ability to communicate personal needs and to listen to others expressing theirs. It also involves willingness to compromise as well as the capacity to manage aggression (Siccone & Lopez, 2000). All of these aspects of negotiation require the child to take into consideration the viewpoint of others. These sophisticated abilities require significant practice.

∾ "You dummy!" yells Megan as Sam pours rice onto the toys Megan is playing with at the rice table. Her teacher calmly walks over and asks Megan, "You don't like something Sam is doing? Tell Sam that you don't like it when he pours rice on your work." Then the teacher guides Megan's words from merely expressing anger to clear communication of what is upsetting her. Sam needs help hearing this message and deciding what to do about it. The teacher is there to make this a valuable learning experience for both children. ∾

To see how a teacher might help children talk through their problems, go to My EducationLab and select the topic Guiding Children. Watch the video, "Managing Challenging Behavior: Dealing with Conflict."

As mentioned in Chapter 1, children do not get this practice if adults solve problems for them. Instead, adults must guide youngsters in age-appropriate ways and help them to resolve their own differences. For very young children with limited language ability, the teacher may do the talking for both parties in reflecting the two viewpoints. As children mature, they can gradually take a more active role in the expression of their different views. The goal is for the teacher or parent to intervene as little as possible, allowing children a chance to resolve differences on their own (Riley et al., 2008). In the following example, Stephen seems to have learned a lot.

∞ Kyle had grabbed a truck from Stephen and wouldn't give it back. Then he took a larger truck and hit Stephen with it. The first impulse of the teacher, Maureen, was to go to Stephen and see if he was all right. But the chain of events that happened next kept her out of it.

Stephen stood up, looked at Kyle with an angry face, and said, "What's my face telling you? I'm mad, and if you hit me again or won't play nice I'm going someplace else to play!" Then Stephen sat down and began to play again. Kyle looked surprised, gave back the truck, and they were off playing together again. Maureen caught Stephen's eye, smiled, and winked a congratulatory message. She felt wonderful to see the results of the teaching she had been doing. ∞

The Teacher as Coach

Various teaching methods are useful in helping children develop social competence. The teacher who respectfully considers children's viewpoints is teaching by

When children have disputes, the teacher can be a coach for problem solving: recommending useful approaches, providing encouragement, and critiquing performance.

example. When children are involved in a dispute, the teacher's appropriate role might be more of a coach, providing encouragement, critiquing the performance, and recommending strategies for improvement. Sometimes the most helpful adult role is to stand back and let children experience the social consequence of their actions. Kyle might need to learn from experience that other kids don't want to play with him when he grabs things from them.

Although it is important not to intervene more than necessary, it is also important to be there as needed, both for safety and support. Therefore, when Dennis sends Colette over to the playhouse with a suggestion for joining in play there, he also tells her to come back and talk to him if it doesn't work. Dennis helps Colette to watch what Kelsey and Megan are playing and to think of how she can help. He helps her plan her entry into the play activity, and stays nearby to lend her confidence while she carries out the plan. Dennis could simply tell Kelsey and Megan they have to let Colette play, but that wouldn't teach Colette useful social skills. It certainly wouldn't make her more popular with her peers, either.

The playground at recess definitely offers the richest opportunity to help children learn social skills. Yet, in most schools, teachers are given recess time as part of their preparation time, leaving playground supervision to aides. The problems with this situation are many: the ratio of children to adults is likely to be at least 100 to 1, making it impossible to do any teaching. Even mere crowd control is a challenge with those numbers. Even if the numbers were appropriate, the aides can't know the children well enough to provide guidance aimed at the needs of individuals. In addition, very few aides have adequate background and training to provide the kind of guidance that will be beneficial. No wonder kids just get sent to the principal when a fight breaks out. The opportunity for on-the-spot problem solving is lost. For this reason, more and more teachers are choosing to go out to recess with their students. They report that they are able to observe natural peer dynamics and diagnose the causes of many social problems as a result.

Working with Families

Your success in enhancing the social skills of your students will be greater if you can bring the child's family into the process. Research shows that the type of discipline techniques used by both teachers and parents relates to children's development of social skills (e.g., Haskett & Willoughby, 2007; Landy, 2002). Therefore, it is important to share your goals for children's social competence with families. Parents may not know that children who are helped to understand the harmful effects of their behavior on others exhibit more positive social behaviors (Dunn, 2006; Smetana, 2006). Children who are aggressive to others are generally rejected, but those who show consideration for others are sought-after playmates. Therefore, it will be helpful for you to tell parents that one of your teaching goals is to teach children why certain behaviors are acceptable or not, instead of just punishing undesirable behavior, so that they will develop better social skills and stronger relationships with peers.

Parents may be anxious because their preschool child doesn't share toys and grabs from others. Young children are not maturationally capable of functioning at high levels of interpersonal understanding (Bloom, 2007; Selman & Schultz, 1990), but they can grow toward higher levels with adult assistance. Providing parents with information about maturation can help families support the developmental process, rather than worry about it. As Vygotsky says, "The only good kind of instruction is that which marches ahead of development and leads it" (1962, p. 104). This can be compared to how we help babies learn to talk: Just because they can't talk yet doesn't mean we don't talk to them. Similarly, just because children's early efforts aren't very good doesn't mean we don't respond and encourage further effort. Families effectively teach oral language by talking to their infants long before they can respond with language. Similarly, adults at home and school can effectively teach higher levels of thinking about interpersonal relationships by modeling and scaffolding conflict resolution skills, aiming just a little above the level the child is capable of independently.

ACCOMMODATING INDIVIDUAL DIFFERENCES

There are some basic developmental accomplishments that apparently transcend cultural differences. These include learning how to make friends, learning language, learning to organize and integrate perceptions, and learning how to think, imagine, and create. But how these accomplishments occur varies according to the cultural context in which they occur (Lillard & Curenton, 1999). Therefore, it is important to remember that appropriate social behavior varies from group to group. Family expectations for children vary according to the child's culture, family background, economic status, and gender. The teacher who holds all children to one standard of behavior is actually being unfair to some.

Cultural Differences

Culture is not skin color or ethnic origin; it is the context within which we view the world. We don't assume that all people of European ancestry are the same, nor can we say that all Latinos or African Americans are the same. Culture is the product of multiple sources—not just race, language, ethnicity, and religion, but also experiences, educational level, socioeconomic status, gender, age, lifestyle, political orientation, geography, and temperament (Kaiser & Rasminsky, 2003). Each of us has a culture, but generally we are not aware of it until we experience a conflict with someone else's. This lack of awareness creates interpersonal misunderstandings, between teachers and children as well as between teachers and families (Kemple, 2004). When a teacher finds a child's behavior unacceptable, one question in discovering the cause must be whether it is the result of a cultural mismatch. Teachers who hold all youngsters to one standard inadvertently cause some to fail socially and academically. As Gonzales Mena (2008) says, "if you continue to follow just your own ideas about what's good and right for children and their families, even if those ideas are a result of your training, you may be doing a disservice to children whose parents disagree with you" (p. 6).

The culture of school reflects the dominant culture of the setting. Those children whose homes and family expectations are most similar to those of the school have the least adjustment to make. Increasingly, schools host children from

Culture is not skin color or ethnic origin; it is the context within which we view the world. Teacher expectations of children must reflect the world view of each child's family.

multiple cultures, making the teacher's role immensely complex and the children's adjustments equally complex. Cultural differences affect all expectations and interactions. Communication can be hampered due to differing ideas about such things as when and how speech is used, what body language means, whether a direct question is rude, and whether it is polite to look directly at the speaker. Cultural differences affect relationships, too. Different groups hold varying ideas about the proper relationship between children and adults, acceptable styles of peer interaction, and about whether it is better for children to be cooperative or competitive. Differing expectations of children at home and school cause confusion and mistrust. For instance, Western European culture expects children to be independent, but interdependence is valued in most of the world's cultures. There are enormous implications for different behaviors based on this one set of expectations (Kaiser & Rasminsky, 2003). Following are examples of some of the kinds of cross-cultural misunderstandings that can cause problems.

∞ Rabia's teacher is upset because Rabia is not able to put on her own coat or shoes for going outside. Her teacher discovers that Rabia's parents dress her at home and also carry her to and from the car at school.

Ahmed gets into trouble because he won't stay on his mat at rest time. His teacher discovers that he has never slept alone but always with his parents.

Miriam doesn't talk at school and she doesn't say when she needs help with her assignments. Her teacher discovers that Miriam relies on nonverbal cues to relay her needs.

Phuong smiles when the teacher reprimands her for talking during morning worktime, making the teacher think Phuong doesn't care about the reprimand. Her teacher later discovers that smiling is a polite, respectful response to such reprimands in Phuong's family. ∞

For some people, fitting in with their own culture and succeeding in the dominant culture are not compatible. Too often, efforts to help children become bilingual and bicultural end up with children who lose their home language and home culture or who don't fit into either culture (Gonzales-Mena, 2008). An additional problem is that learning a new set of expectations can be very stressful for young children who are still learning their home expectations. Sensitive teachers will help by eliciting information from families and by being accepting and respectful of children's home values. They will also help children bridge the culture gap by being explicit about their expectations, instead of assuming that everyone knows what is expected and being upset when some don't conform. Teachers who respect all cultures will also educate themselves about their students' cultures and modify expectations to assist all children in feeling comfortable (Barrera & Corso, 2003). The NAEYC Code of Ethical Conduct (2005) says it is the ethical responsibility of teachers: "to respect the dignity and preferences of each family and to make an effort to learn about its structure, culture, language, customs, and beliefs" (p. 119).

Socioeconomic Differences

Cultural differences based on family income, jobs, and educational background also result in different behavioral goals and patterns. These variations may cause children from different backgrounds to be less comfortable with each other, causing social interaction problems (Gonzales-Mena, 2008; Ramsey, 1991). Adults, too, are often less comfortable with those from different backgrounds (Kaiser & Rasminsky, 2003). This discomfort can inhibit the flow of communication between home and school and disadvantage the child. The topic of discipline may reveal major differences of opinion between adults from middle-class and low-income backgrounds. Families from low-income families typically strive to help their children become tough to face an uncertain future, and oftentimes use authoritarian discipline styles. This approach is at odds with teachers, many of whom are middle-class, who use authoritative discipline practices with the aim of helping children to see the world as a safe and welcoming place. Therefore, it is important to recognize that children can become confused by differences in home–school behavioral expectations and in teaching methods used by parents and teachers, resulting in them forgetting how to behave in one place or the other.

Disturbingly, research has shown that some preservice teachers have an unfounded bias about children from poorer families. Pettit and Sugawara (2002) found this bias among the group of teacher education students they studied. The future teachers rated children from lower socioeconomic backgrounds as less competent socially and cognitively than peers from families of higher socioeconomic status. These ratings occurred despite the fact that the children actually had similar competencies.

Teachers who remember that "different" is neither better nor worse will help more children succeed in school. The youngsters whose background values are different from their teachers' are most at risk for school failure and dropping out. As Ramsey (1991) says, "We must be sure that we do not exacerbate economic disadvantage by undermining the social skills and styles that children have developed, even though they may be less compatible with the current structure of the classroom" (p. 61).

Gender and Brain Development

The fact that a child is a boy or a girl also affects behavior. Although we acknowledge that sex-role stereotyping contributes to behavior differences between boys and girls, brain research explains why our efforts at gender neutrality have failed (Gurian, 2001). Buying dolls for boys and trucks for girls has had limited success.

The differences begin early prenatally, as soon as gender is determined. The parts of the brain develop differently, different chemicals and hormones dominate, and developmental rates are different. Female brains develop more quickly than male brains; this is especially evident in the rate at which girls develop verbal skills. This gives girls an edge in resolving disputes through negotiation, while boys tend to rely on nonverbal communication. Male brains secrete less of the chemical serotonin, making boys more impulsive and more fidgety than girls. The chemical oxytocin is more constantly stimulated in females, making girls more empathic. Male brains deal with emotion more in the brainstem (where fight-or-flight responses are stored), while female brains move emotion to the upper brain, where complex thought occurs (Gurian, 2001). Of course, boys have more of the testosterone hormone, making them more aggressive; the female growth hormone, progesterone, is considered the bonding hormone. Given this information, it is no wonder that teachers often complain when they have more boys than girls in their classes.

Teacher complaints about too many boys are related to viewing typical "boy behavior" as problem behavior (King & Gartrell, 2003). Boys tend to be developmentally younger than the girls in their class, and they need more physical activity than girls. Girls fit better into a quiet and controlled school environment. As a result, normally active little boys may be mislabeled as having attention deficit hyperactive disorder (ADHD). Instead of drugs, these children need more physical activity in their daily agenda. Block play, woodworking activities, outdoor learning, and large-motor opportunities will help little boys be more cooperative. Teachers who understand and accommodate for normal gender differences are better able to appreciate the social competencies of boys (Pettit & Sugawara, 2002).

Although boys and girls don't often choose to play together (Hoffman & Powlishta, 2001), they may benefit from interacting with one another. Children with at least one playmate of the opposite sex demonstrate higher levels of social competence (Howes, 1988). Interacting with male friends may help girls become more independent and assertive (Powlishta, 1995), and interacting with girls may help boys become more caring, cooperative, and less aggressive. Therefore, you may want to do something to minimize gender segregation. Group projects that interest both boys and girls can encourage cooperative interaction between them. In contrast, organizing games as "girls against boys" emphasizes gender distinctions. On the other hand, there is significant discussion about the value of segregating boys and girls for academic instruction, pointing out the different learning styles and interests (Wall, 2008).

CONCLUSION

This chapter and Chapter 2 examine some aspects of child development only as they directly pertain to discipline issues. Knowledge about children's thinking can help you distinguish between immature thinking and purposeful misbehavior. Information about the development of social competency will help you intervene in children's social conflicts in more productive ways. Realization of how behavior is affected by differences such as culture, socioeconomic status, and gender will give you more realistic expectations of children. When teachers understand child development and match their expectations to what individual children can comfortably do, teachers are happier with their work and they have more cooperative students. Matching your expectations to child development can make the difference between dreading to go to school and looking forward to each new day. Following the guidelines in this chapter is not an easy task; be patient with yourself as you strive toward the goals presented.

Social development tends to be the primary content for teaching discipline. Children who have trouble getting along with peers and cooperating in a group create common discipline problems. Therefore, the topic of social development leads us into our next section, which discusses approaches to discipline. See the sources in the Recommended Readings at the end of the chapter for more comprehensive coverage of the topics introduced in this chapter.

∞ *FOR FURTHER THOUGHT*

1. Observe young children playing games. What evidence do you see of their unique perception of rules?
2. As you interact with young children, watch for examples of their inability to think about another person's viewpoint. Try to help youngsters learn to express their views and to hear those of another child. Analyze this experience and discuss with your peers how you might improve your approach.
3. Listen to young children. Do you hear them confusing personal fantasy with fact? What is the best adult response?
4. Do you know a youngster who has difficulty being accepted into play with other children? Practice the coaching techniques described in this chapter. What are the results? What did you learn?
5. Have you or someone you know experienced difficulty in school because of a mismatch with the culture of the school? How did you or your friend respond? What were the long-term effects?
6. A problem to solve: Conrad accidentally spilled the paint at the easel, but he denies that he did it.
   a. What is the probable cause of this "lie"?
   b. What is the best adult response to the situation?

7. A problem to solve: Mason grabbed the illustration Stephano just added to his story and ran away with it, laughing. Stephano dissolves into tears and the teacher comes to help. Her efforts to get Stephano to tell Mason how he feels are unsuccessful, as has been typical with Stephano. The teacher is concerned about teaching Stephano to stand up for himself and contacts the family to discuss those concerns. The response from Stephano's mother implies that the teacher's expectations are not appropriate.
   a. What might cause this difference of opinion between Stephano's mother and his teacher?
   b. What is the best solution for the problem?

∽ RECOMMENDED READINGS

Barrera, I., & Corso, R. M., with D. Macpherson. (2003). *Skilled dialogue: Strategies for responding to cultural diversity in early childhood.* Baltimore: Paul H. Brookes.

Corso, W. A. (2003). *We're friends, right? Inside kids' culture.* Washington, DC: Joseph Henry Press.

Derman-Sparks, L., & Ramsey, P. (2006). *What if all the kids are white? Anti-bias multicultural education with young children and families.* New York: Teacher's College Press.

Johnson, C., Ironsmith, M., Snow, C. W., & Poteat, G. M. (2000). Peer acceptance and social adjustment in preschool and kindergarten. *Early Childhood Education Journal, 27*(4), 207–212.

Kaiser, B., & Rasminsky, J. S. (2003). Opening the culture door. *Young Children, 58*(4), 53–56.

Kemple, K. M. (2004). *Let's be friends: Peer competence and social inclusion in early childhood programs.* Upper Saddle River, NJ: Merrill/Prentice Hall.

Piaget, J. (1965). *The moral judgement of the child.* New York: Free Press. (Originally published in 1932.)

Ramsey, P. G. (1991). *Making friends in school: Promoting peer relationships in early childhood.* New York: Teachers College Press.

Riley, D., San Juan, R., Klinkner, J., & Ramminger, A. (2008). Social and emotional development: Connecting science to practice in early childhood settings. St. Paul, MN: Redleaf Press.

PART 2
Discipline Approaches

Chapters 4 through 10 present an overview of approaches to discipline. We present these approaches in sequence, from most to least positive; this presentation also moves in sequence from least intrusive to most intrusive.

Chapters 4 and 5 examine ways to prevent discipline problems from occurring—the most pleasant discipline option. Chapter 4 looks at the physical design of the classroom as well as the interpersonal climate. Chapter 5 explores prevention of behavior problems by establishing consistent routines and rituals and by involving children in a well-organized, engaging curriculum. Chapter 6 shows how adults model desired behaviors through example and the use of carefully designed curricular experiences. Chapter 7 explains how to teach communication and negotiation skills so that youngsters can manage potential behavior problems for themselves. Chapter 8 presents ways to enforce limits while helping children learn why certain behaviors are more desirable than others are. Chapter 9 discusses the use of behavior modification programs to externally control behavior, an approach we do not recommend but that is widely used. In Chapter 10, we explain the negative consequences of using punishment to control behavior and why is it damaging to the discipline goals of most people in society.

We do not believe that any one discipline approach holds all the answers for all children at all times. As discussed in Chapter 1, determining the cause of the behavior is essential to selecting the appropriate discipline approach. We have confidence that teachers with a good understanding of children's social development and a wide variety of positive discipline approaches from which to choose will respond to children's misbehavior with sensitivity and skill.

∽ Chapter 4 ∽
Creating Environments That Prevent Discipline Problems

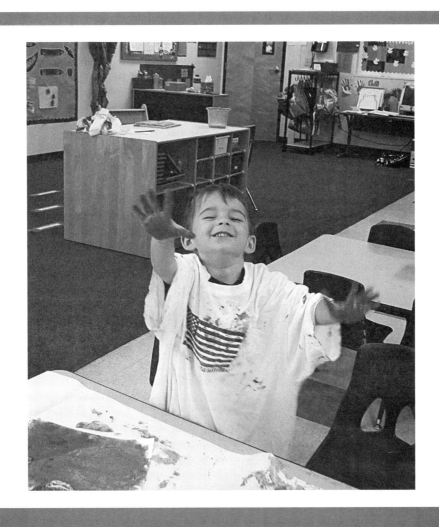

NAEYC Standards Addressed in This Chapter

Standard 1c: Promoting Child Development and Learning: Using developmental knowledge to create healthy, respectful, supportive, and challenging learning environments.

Standard 4a: Teaching and Learning, Connecting with Children and Families

Standard 4b: Teaching and Learning, Using Developmentally Effective Approaches

GUIDING QUESTIONS

- How do a well-organized learning environment and strong interpersonal relationships between teachers and children prevent behavior problems?
- How can teachers organize classroom spaces so that children have opportunities to work in groups and alone?
- How do teachers build relationships with students?
- How do teachers establish a community in the classroom?
- How can teachers promote children's initiative, perspective taking, and sense of belonging?

Some people think of discipline as a reactive process, addressing misbehavior as it occurs. We advocate a proactive approach to discipline that starts before children arrive in your classroom. You may have visited a classroom where things went so smoothly that you envied the teacher for having such a well-behaved group of students. Chances are that the children were normal, but the teacher was very skilled at creating an environment that fostered cooperation and positive interactions. Designing a classroom environment that promotes children's autonomy and prevents behavioral problems is a much more sophisticated approach to discipline than simply reacting to misbehavior as it occurs. In this chapter we will look at ways you can prevent the cause of many behavior problems by creating a physical environment and interpersonal climate in the classroom that provides children with multiple opportunities to build positive relationships, show initiative, practice perspective taking, and learn self-regulation or autonomous behavior.

THE PHYSICAL ENVIRONMENT

We all know how important our surroundings can be. Consciously and unconsciously, our environment affects our moods and influences our behavior. The way we design our classroom has a profound effect on students' motivation, sense of well-being, behavior, and learning. Recent findings in brain research, cognitive studies, and learning theory have done more than change our approach to instruction, they have changed the way our classrooms look and feel (Greenman, 2005).

The physical arrangement of the classroom affects how children learn and the manner in which they relate to one another. A well-organized classroom can facilitate learning and positive social interactions, while a poorly designed classroom can discourage learning and children's self-esteem (Maxwell & Chmielewski, 2008). The organization of the early childhood classroom is designed to encourage independence, foster responsibility, and help students develop the skills necessary to live and learn in collaboration with others. Creating a comfortable environment that nurtures learning and supports prosocial interactions does not happen by chance. It requires significant planning on the part of teachers.

PEARSON
myeducationlab

To see an example of a well organized classroom environment, go to MyEducationLab and select the topic Early Environments *and watch the video "Room Arrangement Preschool".*

When planning the layout of their classrooms, prekindergarten and primary-grade teachers consider the following factors:

- How to organize the space to accommodate whole-group, small-group, and individual instructions.
- What types of learning centers or interest areas will be most beneficial to children of a given age level.
- Where to set up learning centers, taking into consideration the types of activities that will occur in the center (e.g., small group/individual; child directed/teacher directed; active/quiet, etc.), the location of needed resources (e.g., electricity for the computers), and how traffic patterns might minimize or increase distractions in the area.
- How to organize materials in learning centers to encourage independent access and cleanup.
- Whether materials in the classroom reflect the cultures of the children.
- How to provide children with personal spaces for privacy and their belongings.
- Where to display instructional materials and children's work.

Spaces for Instruction and Learning

In the past, many thought that education depended mainly on children's attention to the teacher. Research now underscores the fact that students not only learn from interactions with their teachers, but also from interactions with peers and direct involvement with the materials necessary for learning (Bransford, Brown, & Cocking, 2000). These findings have greatly expanded our ideas about what teaching and learning look like in classrooms. Early childhood teachers use a wide variety of instructional approaches, from student-initiated learning and collaborative group projects to teacher-directed lessons. Because teachers in constructivist classrooms use multiple teaching methods to facilitate learning, the physical environment must incorporate enough variety and flexibility to embrace varied learning opportunities (Brumbaugh, 2008).

Large-Group Areas   Most early childhood classrooms have a meeting area that is large enough to accommodate group meetings, whole-group lessons, group games, and/or music and movement activities. This area of the classroom is usually located near a bulletin or white board so teachers can use visual aids to enhance instruction. Depending on the size of your classroom, the large-group area may serve two purposes. For example, in a prekindergarten or kindergarten classroom, the group meeting space may be in the block area when it is not in use. In a primary classroom, the group area may also serve as a space for reader's theater activities. However, children often experience confusion when the behavioral expectations associated with a particular space change to accommodate different learning activities. In these situations, it is the teacher's responsibility to help children manage the contradictions they feel as a result of the changing expectations.

∞ As she called the children to story time with the xylophone, Joanne dreaded the inevitable power struggle that was sure to follow. Story time just wasn't working for her. The block shelves surrounded the only space big enough for story time, and the children just couldn't keep their hands off the blocks as Joanne read. It was impossible to keep their attention. Because the shelves were on wheels, she tried pushing them as far back as she could, but the children just inched their circle back to get to them. She repeatedly reminded them that it was time for a story, not for block play. Still, it was like trying to keep bees from flowers! ∞

Joanne's story time arrangement sent a mixed message to the children. She carefully arranged the blocks in a way that attracted children's attention and invited them to play. Asking the children not to play with the blocks while she read a story conflicted with the message sent by the environmental arrangement and behavioral expectations during other times of the day. Although the size of your classroom might make this type of room arrangement unavoidable, placing children in a conflicting situation and then scolding them for not paying attention is a recipe for unnecessary teacher–child conflict. To avoid such conflict, you might Velcro® curtains on the block shelves that can be opened when it is time for block play and closed during other group activities. If the blocks are out of sight during story time, children will be less enticed to want to play with them. If you explain to children that you need their help telling the story and provide them with props to use during the reading, they will have a reason to stay actively engaged. If children still cannot focus on the large-group activity, they many need a retreat from the stimulation of being in a large group (Maxwell, 2007).

Individual Areas   Have you ever experienced strong antisocial feelings after extended periods of interacting with other people? Spending a full day in school, especially when combined with before- and after-school care, can be extremely wearing psychologically. You may notice that youngsters get crabby as the school day wears on. They are more than just tired, they are struggling to keep up with the demands placed on them when learning to interact in a group setting. It is quite possible that their crabbiness is an indication that they need some alone time, away from the stimulation, sights, and sounds of being in a group.

Children thrive in environments that are respectful of their need for privacy (Maxwell, 2007). Research on emotional development tells us that children should

Spaces where children can play alone or with one other peer provide a respite from the bustling activity of early childhood classrooms.

be allowed to move freely between group and individual activities (Maxwell, 2007). Many classrooms feature special, cozy places for being alone or visiting with one other person. Mrs. Jensen created a small space between two file cabinets and furnished it with cushions, books, and a reading lamp. Dennis found a spot under a stairway in the preschool that was perfect for one or two children. It too has been cozily fitted with pillows and decorated with pictures of children's families. When the demand for the private spots becomes too great, children can either sign up on a waiting list or create their own spaces. Some children will take refuge under a desk or table. Others will simply lie down on the floor, away from the activity.

In fact, children might need a bit of privacy before they feel up to serious work. In the story time situation described earlier, Joanne might have told the child who couldn't remain focused on the story to go to the classroom private space to read a book on her own.

Small-Group Areas   Children learn best in small groups (Downer, Rimm-Kaufman, & Pianta, 2007). A small-group area should contain storage space for materials as well as a surface area (i.e., table or floor space) for children to work collaboratively. Teachers may use the small-group area to bring together a group of children to work on a specific literacy or math activity. They may also choose to work with small groups of children on activities that require extra supervision for safety reasons. For example, it is much easier to monitor safety procedures

Children learn best in small group settings that are inviting and comfortable.

during a cooking or science experiment when working with 4 or 5 children than it is with a group of 20 children.

Children may use the small-group area to work on collaborative projects, such as creating an airplane to put in the dramatic play area, playing board games, or creating costumes for a play or reader's theater activity. In these types of small-group activities, children engage in work without direct guidance from the teacher. Providing spaces where children work collaboratively without the direct involvement of the teacher facilitates perspective taking, negotiation skills, and problem solving (Wasik, 2008). When children share ideas while working together to achieve a common goal, they soon learn that several heads are better than one! The same benefit is derived from children's interaction in learning centers.

Learning Centers

The space and materials in a developmentally appropriate classroom are arranged in learning or activity centers that highlight domains of learning or single subject areas. Activity centers that are well defined, with specific boundaries, content-related materials, and surfaces for work or play, promote engagement in learning and positive interactions among young children (Kantrowitz & Evans, 2004). Shelves, rugs, or tables might serve as borders for learning centers. Prekindergarten classrooms typically contain centers for dramatic play, art, blocks or construction, manipulatives, writing, science or discovery, a reading/library area, and a computer center. Primary-grade classrooms are typically divided by subject area, such as science, mathematics, arts, social studies, and reading. In both cases, centers are designed to support students' diverse learning modalities and to provide them with direct access to learning materials. The location of learning centers can invite investigation, curriculum integration, and feelings of competence, or can be a source of distraction and an invitation for trouble (Maxwell, 2007).

The arrangement of learning centers should offer opportunities for single-subject investigations, while promoting cross-curricular integration. For example, you might put the block area and the dramatic play area near one another so children can see the possibility of using the blocks to create a bed for a baby or a couch for the living room. Similarly, the science area may be located near the sand and water table to enhance opportunities for sensory exploration. The math and science areas might be located near one another so that children have easy access to mathematical tools (e.g., rulers, Unifix cubes, etc.) that might be used to collect data during science experiments. By placing the writing area near the computer area, children can easily transition from writing to publishing final drafts of their stories without distracting others.

When teachers don't consider how the location of their centers will influence traffic patterns and child–child interactions, disputes are sure to occur. If children have to walk across the classroom to wash their hands after a painting activity, someone is sure to get dirty. If a center is crowded, children will surely complain about their right for space to learn. Teachers work hard at planning their room arrangement and must continuously reflect upon how it is meeting children's needs throughout the year. Adjustments are made to the environment based on how well the children function in the spaces provided.

    ∞ It had been a rough day in Ashley's first-grade classroom. Aaron's screeching as he defended his space on the reading couch had given Sheri a headache—again. Ashley liked the idea of having a couch in her library, but didn't like the disputes centered around the use of the seating area. She talked with her colleagues and tried to figure out a solution. They agreed that the couch took up too much space in the library and decided that the library area needed to be rearranged to make it large enough to accommodate the couch as well as floor space for reading. One last piece of advice provided by Ashley's colleagues was to include the children in planning the changes to the center.

    The next day, Ashley asked the children if they had noticed there were problems with people finding a cozy place to sit during independent reading. They had. So the first graders and their teacher brainstormed ways they could rearrange their classroom to make things better. The children thought of ways to use space and materials in the classroom that their teacher hadn't. They suggested enlarging the reading area and moving the pillows from the couch to the floor so that children could have several soft places to sit. ∞

After school that day, Ashley was busy! She implemented the changes agreed on by the group and ended up with a more comfortable library area. Modifying the environment to meet the needs of the children in this group solved the disputes caused by the crowded conditions in the reading area. See Figure 4–1 for an example of a primary classroom layout.

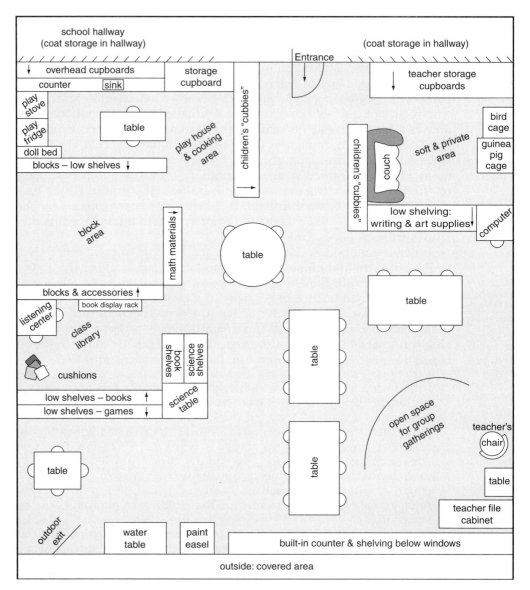

FIGURE 4–1 A sample primary-grade classroom arrangement. This classroom layout provides spaces for large-group, small-group, and individual work. The centers in the classroom are clearly defined and organized in a way that provides for student interaction while reducing distraction. This room arrangement could be adapted for younger children.

Materials

Have you ever heard the old adage, "there is a place for everything and everything is in its place"? Walk into most early childhood classrooms and you'll see this axiom in action. Teachers model organization by systematically arranging materials in learning centers. For example, all of the art materials that children use are stored in one area. Materials might be further organized through the use of clear plastic storage bins that allow children to view materials without having to remove bins from the shelf. Arranging materials on low shelves and applying labels to shelves and storage containers will help children independently locate the materials they need for activities. For emergent readers, adding a picture of an item to the container in which it belongs provides an additional organizational guide. Organizing materials in a clear, predictable pattern helps build children's independence and memory capacity (Barry, 2006). As children come to remember where materials are stored, they are more likely to participate in cleanup routines without assistance from adults.

Honoring Diversity   Materials selected for the classroom should also reflect the culture of the children. For example, you might add food boxes from different types of cultural foods into a dramatic play area and literature that provides children with authentic representations of people from their cultural groups. It is also important to make the classroom feel home-like through the addition of rugs, plants, lamps, artwork, family photos, and soft places to sit and relax.

Children with special needs should have access to all materials available in the classroom. There are many inexpensive ways to adapt classroom materials to meet the needs of young children with special needs. For example, you might apply knobs to puzzle pieces, or add Velcro® to charts, attendance forms, or sign-up sheets for children with fine motor delays. You might widen the pathways throughout the room to accommodate a child-size wheelchair for children with physical disabilities. For children who are easily overstimulated, such as those with autism or ADHD, you may choose a solid-colored carpet for your circle area rather than one covered with designs. You might also limit the amount of materials displayed in any area and instead rotate your materials frequently.

Displays   What children see around them influences their approach to learning (Seefeldt, 2002). Providing children with opportunities to personalize the classroom environment promotes a sense of belonging in the classroom, which in turn promotes prosocial behaviors and attitudes (Maxwell & Chmielewski, 2008). Displaying images of children and their families as well as artifacts that represent children's cultural heritage enhances a sense of connectedness among classmates (Maxwell & Chmielewski, 2008). Having children collect and exhibit artifacts of their work together promotes thinking and talking about individual and collective accomplishments. Displays of children's work serve not only to document learning, they offer children multiple opportunities for communication and encourage relationship building through sharing ideas. Classroom displays also facilitate communication between families and teachers (Brumbaugh, 2008).

The physical environment of your classroom sends a powerful message to children about who the classroom is for, the teacher or the student, and how people are expected to behave in the setting. When children enter a classroom designed around their interests and needs, they sense that they are being invited to be involved, cooperative learners.

THE EMOTIONAL ENVIRONMENT

The adults set the tone in school and determine whether it is a caring community or a "dog-eat-dog" society. "Achieving a sense of community entails that children understand that they are part of a larger group and that being thoughtful and cooperative with others benefits both themselves and the entire group" (Howes & Ritchie, 2002). As part of a caring community, children acquire the judgment, sensitivity, self-control, and skills to be able to treat others well. Although classroom communities support academic learning, teaching children caring and kindness may be the most important mission of our schools (Noddings, 2005).

Relationships

Relationships provide the foundation for building community and for effective teaching in general (Downer et al., 2007). Classrooms include multiple types of relationships: between teachers and children, between children, and between the teacher and the child's family. All of these relationships play an important role in building community and creating an environment that supports children's social, emotional, and intellectual development.

Teacher–Child Relationships   Teacher–child relationships are a critical part of teaching, whether teaching science or social skills (Downer et al., 2007). Teachers need to build positive relationships with children in order to influence their behavior and thought. The same teaching approaches that develop good relationships with children also create harmonious classrooms conducive to learning. In addition, supportive relationships with the teacher are important for children's self-esteem, confidence, and feelings of security (Downer et al., 2007). Children need to know you care about them, will keep them safe, and can help them succeed. When they know these things, children have fewer behavior problems.

How do you establish good relationships with children? First, you get to know them. There are many ways to do this: You can follow a child's lead in play, listen to children talk about their interests and experiences, give hugs and high-fives, hold a child's hand, have a conversation over snack or lunch, and greet each one individually. Make sure to acknowledge children's absences and be sure to tell them how much they were missed when they return to school. This practice will let children know that you care about their well-being and that they are important members of the classroom group. Make sure to discuss any difficulties, academic or social, that occurred during the school hours with children before they leave for the day so the residue of unpleasant experiences doesn't interfere with interactions outside of school (Lehman & Repetti, 2007).

Building relationships with children has much in common with making friends of your own age. Relationships are based on sharing, caring, attention, and trust. Sharing some of your own personal life with children also helps build relationships: show pictures of your children or pets, talk about your weekend activities, and share your related experiences during conversations about children's experiences. In other words, be a "real" person, not detached and remote. Children can tell whether adults want to be with them; therefore it is necessary that teachers of young children actually like them and accept their immature behaviors (LoCasle-Crouch et al., 2007). Children can also tell if you are not really paying attention to them; being physically present is not the same as being mentally present. Too often teachers get busy and only pretend to be paying attention. We know that pretense and other deceit damage relationships, but adults are often guilty of not being truthful with children. Usually this is an effort to protect children by making light of their fears and concerns. However, denying children's observations and feelings is counterproductive. Sometimes children have bad experiences with other adults; they need to have someone they can trust to listen and care. Other times, the problems are among peers. In the following example, acknowledging Max's feelings is the teacher's first step in working with him to try to solve his problem.

∾ Max comes crying to Sheri, telling her that the other kids don't like him. Sheri's first thought is to reassure him by telling him "Of course they do!" But she has seen Max being rejected and knows he has a reason for his feelings.

So she says, "It makes you feel bad when Zach won't let you sit by him, doesn't it?" ∾

Children's Relationships with Peers   If children aren't getting along, learning is disrupted and so is the sense of community. Children who have difficulty with peers, either through aggression or withdrawal, are lonely and become victims of

Having friends is essential to children's healthy social and emotional development. Children who have difficulty making friends need the teacher's help.

other children's aggression. When they are preoccupied with social problems, children lack motivation for learning (Lehman, 2007). Helping children learn social skills is crucial to creating a harmonious learning environment. As a teacher who has good relationships with children, you are in the perfect position to assist children with their peer relationships.

Two additional ingredients are needed for effectively promoting peer relationships: knowledge of child development and freedom to focus energy on the task. Child development knowledge is essential to understanding age-appropriate behavioral expectations and to accurately diagnosing the causes of peer relationship issues. Spending time on promoting children's social competence with peers is essential, especially in the early years. However, pressures to increase academic achievement leaves teachers with little time or incentive to focus on the long-term goal of children's social development (e.g., the No Child Left Behind Act of 2001). It would be wise for all to remember that a focus on academic performance at the expense of building relationships is counterproductive (Hansen & Zambo, 2007), since academic achievement is linked to healthy relationships (Downer et al., 2007).

How do you help children build positive relationships with their classmates? First, you must ensure that children have time to interact with one another. Teacher-directed classes often keep children so busy responding to teacher-assigned tasks that there is little time for peer interaction or for social problem solving. Open-ended and collaborative activities, and play time or recess, are not only important for children's learning, they also offer opportunity for in-depth interaction between children. Observing peer interaction during these types of activities provides teachers with necessary information about individual children's social abilities and about group dynamics. Teachers use this information to plan intentional interactions and assignments that will build children's social competence.

Family–School Relationships   Supportive relationships with children's families are also essential to an effective early education program. Young children are tightly linked to their families, and their families are the main source of information about the child's life so far. Teachers who know students' families are much better able to build relationships with the children and to help them learn.

How do you build relationships with families? Home visits are a start. Home visits have been routine for Head Start teachers for years. Other preschool teachers, and even elementary teachers, have begun to adopt this valuable approach for getting to know their students. A home visit is a good chance to learn from parents. You can find out what the parents want from their child's educational experiences, and you can learn special information about the child. For instance, knowing the child's pet name at home and something about his or her favorite family activities will help you relate more personally to the child. You might also want to ask parents to bring family photos to school for their child to share. Families could help make "All About Me" books with their children. You could find out if a child has a favorite book and then read it to the class.

This kind of planning is difficult when the family and teacher do not share a language. A translator can help bridge the gap; a community volunteer, a professional translator, or a friend of the family could provide needed assistance.

A translator should be available to families for formal teacher conferences and also for times of informal communication.

Inviting family members to school and to school events or outings is another way to connect with them. Evening events allow working parents to be involved. Potluck dinners are a great way to involve families in evening events and also are a great way to build community among families. No matter where you meet, the key to establishing relationships is being respectful of what the other person knows, wants, and believes.

Mutual Respect

A caring classroom community requires a teacher who is kind and respectful to children, but who is nevertheless clear about his or her authority. As DeVries and Zan (1994) note, "Children do not develop respect for others unless they are respected" (p. 76). Children are also more likely to go along with what you want if you are willing to go along with what they want sometimes. In other words, you encourage children to respect your wishes by showing respect for theirs (Miller & Pedro, 2006).

Most adults are pretty clear about why they want kids to respect adults, but perhaps you haven't thought about adults showing respect for children. Your model of respect will spread and encourage respect between youngsters. Your model will also come back to you as respect from children. Learning to respect the needs and rights of others is basic to treating others well. Treating others well is central to what our society views as acceptable behavior. The construction of moral values is widely believed to be based on learning respect for others (DeVries, Hildebrandt, & Zan, 2000).

Respectful Communication   What does it mean to respect children? An obvious indicator of respect is how we talk to children (Miller & Pedro, 2006). Too often adults speak to children in ways they would never consider speaking to an adult. Respecting children also involves accepting them for who they are instead of trying to make them into what you want. Many adults have trouble accepting children's reasoning because they don't understand how children develop negotiation skills or perspective taking. These adults try to get youngsters to parrot adult reasoning without regard for their lack of mature reasoning abilities. Respectful interaction between adults and children involves listening to children to understand their viewpoints (Miller & Padro, 2006) and asking them honest questions about their thinking.

How does an honest question differ from a "dishonest" one? An honest question is one you don't already know the answer to. "What color is your dress/shirt?" is a dishonest and patronizing question from any adult who is not color blind. "Why do you think that happened?" is an honest question unless you have a preconceived "right" answer in mind. If we ask others what they think, we need to accept their answer. What they think may not be what you think but, certainly, it correctly describes their thinking.

Respecting Children's Needs   Adults demonstrate respect for children by providing for their emotional, intellectual, and physical needs. For instance, young children may need transitional objects such as a teddy bear from home to help them feel safe at school (Hansen & Zambo, 2007). Respect for youngsters means accepting that although they are still small children, they have a strong need to be seen as "big" important, successful, and contributing members of the group. Endless shouts of "Watch me!" demonstrate how important it is to be big when you are small.

The human need to be significant is one reason why respect for children involves letting them have choices and be decision makers. In Chapter 1, we discuss choice as crucial to the development of moral and intellectual autonomy, as described by Piaget. In Chapter 2, we discuss the role of choice in the emotional autonomy stage, as described by Erikson, and in the need for power, as described by Adler. Choices are essential for feeling good about life and about your position in it (DeVries, Hildebrandt, & Zan, 2000).

Teachers who make all the decisions in their classrooms have more rebellious students. Teachers who involve children in deciding how best to accomplish goals have a much easier time. Occasionally, even the most enlightened teachers find themselves in a power struggle. Power struggles occur when you give an ultimatum and a child decides not to go along with it.

∞ Dennis learned a lesson on the day he said, "No one eats lunch until your mess is cleaned up." Amy flatly refused to pick up the dress-up clothes she had been trying on. Now what? Dennis didn't really intend to deprive anyone of lunch; his remark had just been thoughtless. But the other children had picked up on it and were telling Amy she wasn't going to get any lunch. Amy was wailing hysterically over the thought of missing lunch, but she was not picking up any dress-up clothes.

Would the children ever believe him again if he let Amy have lunch without picking up? He couldn't in good conscience actually deny her food. What could he do?

He decided that he could teach a really valuable lesson to his young students. He could demonstrate how to admit an error graciously and to remedy it. This social skill is pertinent to the lives of preschoolers as they work at getting along. Dennis congratulated himself on modeling something much better than the "might makes right" concept, which his threat of missing lunch had perpetuated. So he went over to Amy and gently touched her shoulder to get her attention. He sat down on the floor beside her and explained that he had spoken without thinking. He assured Amy that she would not miss lunch.

Feeling calmer, Amy was able to listen as Dennis clarified his intent: to get the playthings out of the way so there would be space for eating lunch. With the ultimatum removed, Amy was able to problem-solve and reason. She proposed to move her dress-up clothes out of the way for now and finish putting them away after lunch when she wasn't so terribly hungry. Dennis was pleased to accept the compromise, realizing that it was not only logical but also a mutually face-saving solution.

Later, as he thought about the incident, Dennis examined the issue of saving face as it relates to power struggles. He acknowledged that his own pride was involved and he thought about children's pride. He decided that if he got himself into a similar situation again, he would not hesitate to back off. He analyzed his reasons for going against the common assumption that adults must not lose in a battle of wills with a child. Dennis's conclusion was that losing such a battle meant damaged pride, and therefore damaged self-esteem. Were his own pride and self-esteem more important than the child's? Because enhancing children's self-esteem was one of his major educational goals, Dennis was clear about the answer. He didn't want to make himself feel important at the expense of a little child. His was a respectful solution and one that took courage on his part. ∞

Respecting Differences

Feeling good about yourself requires that you be accepted for who you are. A caring community honors the diversity of the group. Classrooms that accept and honor cultural differences meet the needs of minority students while teaching all children the concepts of cultural pluralism (Copple, 2003; Long, Volk, & Gregory, 2007). In respecting the cultural background of the child, it is also important to see the child as an individual and not just as a member of a certain group. Seeing children as individuals helps guard against stereotyping them according to their culture. The teacher's attitudes can affect the attitudes of children and may counteract prejudiced ideas (Derman-Sparks & Ramsey, 2006).

Most teachers find that they have a lot to learn to avoid common, well-intentioned, but generally counterproductive efforts toward multiculturalism. Long et al. (2007) share explanations of the mistaken and limited assumptions about diversity demonstrated by most teachers. Teachers find that learning how to achieve true cultural plurality, as opposed to "pseudo-multiculturalism," requires significant study.

∞ Mrs. Jensen is working within her school to help her colleagues move away from pseudo-multiculturalism. Her school as a whole is very proud of its annual Multicultural Fair. For this event, each grade level represents a different country or culture. Each group makes costumes to wear and learns songs and dances to perform. They form a huge parade, winding through the school and into the multipurpose room for the songs and dances. Though this is quite spectacular, Mrs. Jensen is convinced that the way it is done teaches nothing helpful and probably creates stereotypical thinking.

What do the kindergartners think or understand as they are instructed in making "mukluks" from paper bags as part of their Eskimo costumes? Do they realize that mukluks are made from animal skins, not paper bags? Do they understand why people living in cold climates, without access to shoe stores, would make and wear mukluks? Do they realize that their classmate Mollie, who wears Velcro-fastened sneakers, is half Eskimo? When they join the school parade right behind the Chinese dragon created by the third graders, what connections do they make between dragons and mukluks? ∞

Remember, young children are not capable of understanding abstract issues involving different time periods and faraway places. They create their theories based on what they see and experience.

Cultural stereotyping is not limited to minority groups. One of the common misconceptions is that all white children are from a common culture, a perception that overlooks different backgrounds among them. As explained in Chapter 3, no matter what skin color or ethnicity a child has, family patterns, religious beliefs, and class differences create unique cultural backgrounds for each. In addition, Caucasian children may be recent immigrants from a variety of countries: Russia, Romania, and Croatia are represented in Mrs. Jensen's school in addition to children with Asian, Native American, and Latino backgrounds.

Each child comes to school with a unique set of prior experiences that includes a set of family values (Kirmani, 2007). Many of these values relate to guidance issues. Remember that different families have different ideas about acceptable and unacceptable behavior; they also have different ideas about how to teach children to be better behaved. Understanding these differences is another reason for teachers to get acquainted with parents. Getting acquainted is also essential for dialogue about how to deal with differing expectations between home and school.

An increasing number of children arrive at school with a primary language other than English. Not only does a language difference complicate communication between teacher and child, it puts the child at great risk for social isolation. Lack of a mutual language certainly gets in the way of play and other interaction with peers, often leading to frustration and/or withdrawal for the child unfamiliar with the dominant language. Tabors (1998) points out that these children are caught in a "double bind of second language learning: To learn a new language, you have to be socially accepted by those who speak the language; but to be socially accepted you have to be able to speak the new language" (Tabors, 1998, p. 22). Group play that requires little verbalization is essential for counteracting the social isolation that inhibits language learning. Mrs. Jensen notices that block play offers an ideal opportunity for second language learning. Other helpful teacher strategies include having a predictable schedule and using repetitious songs and rhymes; these strategies help preschool and primary-grade children learning English as a second language just as they help younger children learning English as their first language.

Language and cultural differences are not the only things that make individual children unique. Different temperaments and individual histories cause children to respond differently to new experiences and school routines. Teachers who respect such differences respond to each child in ways appropriate for that child's needs.

Including Children with Special Needs   Children with special needs who are included in regular classrooms add another dimension of diversity. The teacher's example will help counteract children's fears of this and other kinds of differences. When you focus on the child and not the disability, you will more easily integrate the child with special needs into your group (Fox & Lentini, 2006). You can help your other students become comfortable with a wheelchair, prosthesis, or whatever special assistance a child requires. Then your students, too, can focus on the child as a person. Children with special needs often are rejected by peers because they are different (Dyson, 2005). Sensitive teachers can help with this problem by modeling acceptance and honoring the strengths of all children (Dyson, 2005). The mother of a child with Down syndrome spoke with tears of joy about the friends her son had found after he was included in a first-grade classroom with a helpful teacher. The little boy just couldn't stop talking about his friends.

All people have needs for friendship, success in worthwhile endeavors, and recognition for their efforts. A classroom community does not exclude any members due to a disability. It is the teacher's responsibility to make sure such exclusion does not occur (Fox & Lentini, 2006). Children spend a large part of their day in the school setting and must be able to find friends, success, and recognition at school. It is essential that a teacher understand these needs and know how to provide for them.

Children's Emotional Needs

Fostering the emotional well-being of young children requires that teachers, administrators, aides, and guidance counselors learn about emotional development and commit to supporting children's emotional health (Sink, Edwards, & Weir, 2007). A classroom that nurtures children's good feelings will encourage "good" behavior (Wilson, Pianta, & Stuhlman, 2007). Conversely, damage to pride or self-esteem generally is expressed in some undesirable behavior. In fact, bad feelings of any kind are likely to show up as "bad" actions. Helping children in your classroom feel good about themselves and their school experience is an important part of effective classroom management, community building, and harmonious group dynamics.

Friendship   Classrooms and child-care centers where friendship and socializing are encouraged tend to be happy and harmonious places (Honig, 2004). Important social studies lessons occur constantly as the teacher assists youngsters in their efforts to work cooperatively. Disagreements are viewed as teaching opportunities instead of reasons to keep kids apart. These classrooms are places where the teacher isn't continually telling children to be quiet. The teacher's energy is directed into more useful ways of helping children use their time productively.

With building community as a goal, the children's energy isn't wasted by trying not to talk to one another. Teachers who understand the need for friendship and the value of peer interaction don't go around being mad at kids for doing what comes naturally. And kids don't end up feeling bad about wanting to communicate with their peers. Happier teachers and children create a friendly, relaxed atmosphere more conducive to learning of all kinds.

In fact, schools truly committed to building caring communities schedule time for children to enjoy one another in a relaxed atmosphere (Watson & Battistich, 2006). Mrs. Jensen's school encourages teachers to take their students on a two-day overnight outing to a nearby camp that offers cottages for sleeping and a lodge for group gatherings. She schedules this event for early in the school year to maximize its benefit. Many parents go along, helping to supervise the children, but also creating bonds among parents and between parents and the teacher. We also know teachers who schedule Saturday family hikes for their classes, contributing their own time to the important goal of building community.

Such events help children make individual friends as well as create group camaraderie. As we have stated before, having friends is essential to children's healthy social and emotional development. Children who have difficulty making a friend need the teacher's assistance. Friendship skills include sharing, turn taking, contributing to play, giving and receiving help, paying compliments, and coping with teasing or bullying (Honig, 2004). Sometimes missing skills are the problem, and other times it is a lack of contact due to shyness. You can encourage the interaction of shy children by setting up small groups for cooperative learning activities (Arbeau & Coplan, 2007).

In spite of the importance of having a friend, you probably have seen situations when best friends have been separated in school so that they will not disturb one another's work. This well-intentioned intervention ignores the importance of friendship for the child's intellectual and emotional development. Youngsters learn a great deal as they strive to get along with a friend: They learn to think about another person's views, they learn much about compromise and problem solving, and they learn about caring and being cared for. They also practice emotion regulation. These things don't happen with just any peers; they require someone who is special to the child. As we have said before, a child must care enough about another child to be willing to examine egocentric views and work out disagreements.

∞ Mrs. Jensen works to ensure that children in her first-grade classroom find friends. She doesn't have a seating chart at first. Instead, she encourages youngsters to try different places for a couple of weeks. After they have had a chance to get acquainted, the children are asked to choose a place to sit for a while; Mrs. Jensen puts their names at those places for the time being. There is always an opportunity to make new choices as new relationships blossom. Mrs. Jensen says, "The most important thing you can do for some kids in a school year is to make sure they have friends."

Some teachers are not tuned in to friendship as a legitimate need and overlook its educational value. Miss Wheeler is not only unaware of the importance of friendship, but she also doesn't know that children need to interact with their peers as a part of learning. She spends much of her energy each day in futile efforts to keep children from socializing. Her attempts to enforce an unnatural quiet in her classroom are counterproductive to academic and emotional development.

Mrs. Jensen, however, enjoys the busy hum of children sharing ideas and discussing experiences. In this environment, the several children who came to her class speaking a language other than English are fast becoming fluent in English. The interactive learning style of this classroom is perfect for their language-learning needs. Sometimes individual children need to be reminded to talk more softly, but they are not told to be silent in Mrs. Jensen's classroom. She notices that adults talk while they work and wonders why so many try to impose silence on children. ∞

Recognition   When they come to school, children enter a big new world and have the task of finding some way not to be lost in the crowd (Sink et al., 2007). If most teacher interaction with students is as part of a group, many children will feel lost or invisible. When the teacher interacts with children as individuals, they know that they have the teacher's attention. Communicating on an individual basis also makes it easier for the teacher to interact appropriately with children of various cultures. Mrs. Jensen makes sure to notice and comment to each child about his or her activity during free-choice time and lets children know she is tuned in to them at other times. Her comments and questions help each child feel important and valued. Her students don't need to engage in inappropriate attention-getting behaviors to get her to notice them. Because each child has her undivided attention at some time, they more easily share her attention during group times or when she is working with another child.

Conferences between teacher and child both provide for individual attention and focus on individual progress. Mrs. Jensen usually manages to meet with each of her students once a week for 5 or 10 minutes. She is convinced that the weekly one-on-one time is much more valuable than meeting with all children daily in a group. Interacting with children individually in this way also assists in building the relationships with them that are crucial to the teaching-learning process.

∞ Mrs. Jensen found time to meet with Nick after making the rounds of the room during quiet reading time. Everyone seemed engrossed in a book, so she hoped that she and Nick wouldn't be interrupted too much. During their conference, Nick told Mrs. Jensen about the books he had read recently and showed her how long his list of books completed had become. Then he read a particularly funny part from a book about King Bidgood in the bathtub. He also showed his teacher the letter he was writing to his pen pal in the third grade. They discussed whether or not Nick's letter clearly explained the way the classroom snake shed its skin. A copy of the final polished version of the letter would go into Nick's writing portfolio. Mrs. Jensen suggested some books about snakes that Nick might be interested in. Nick went back to his work with confidence and a renewed sense of purpose. During the conference, Mrs. Jensen made brief notes about Nick's progress and what skills he was ready for next. ∞

Conferences like the one between Mrs. Jensen and Nick are increasingly being used as a formative assessment of student knowledge (Hatherly, 2006). These types of assessment offer teachers immediate, authentic feedback of student's progress toward learning standards. Traditional, competitive ways of assessing children's progress make only the best students feel proud and accomplished. All except the top few feel just the opposite. Too many minority youngsters are evaluated without regard for cultural influences (Volante, 2008). Evaluation systems that compare children to one another have a much different effect than systems that compare children's current work with their own work a few months earlier.

When a child competes with a past personal record instead of with classmates, each child can feel a sense of accomplishment. Each can feel motivated to keep trying. For instance, children who look at a folder containing their writing and drawing for the year can see for themselves how much progress they have made. New approaches to evaluation help youngsters to set personal goals for themselves and take pride in their progress toward those goals (Szente, 2007). The ways in which you assess children's educational progress can help each child feel individually important and can help each feel successful.

Success   Children experience feelings of success or failure during many different kinds of activities in school, during playground games, as well as through teacher assignments. Zan and Hildebrant (2003) urge us to look at the kinds of games we encourage, pointing out that games that require cooperation better promote children's use of higher-level negotiation skills than do competitive games.

Competitive situations are a setup for failure, since not everyone can win. Therefore, the others become losers. In addition, competition is incompatible with the goal of building a caring community. If you pit children against one another, you undermine the development of kindness and cooperation. In order to foster a caring community and help everyone feel successful, you will want to arrange for cooperative games, contests, and projects. Situations where children work as a team for a common goal are productive. If you can't do without competition, have children try to beat their "personal best" rather than one another.

When all children are expected to complete the same assignment in the same way, comparisons are inevitable, with results similar to those of competition. Open-ended activities allow for individual differences and discourage comparison by allowing children to use their creativity in how they complete a task. Open-ended activities are those with no one right outcome, and therefore no possibility of failure. Success is ensured because children can choose to work at their own appropriate level of challenge. Some children will easily succeed at almost any task the teacher comes up with, but they may not be sufficiently challenged to feel good about succeeding. Other youngsters are more vulnerable to failure. In both cases, open-ended activities can help all children feel challenged and experience success.

Open-ended activities do not have set limits and they allow for extension beyond the expected levels, creating an additional challenge where needed. In this case, youngsters can make a project as challenging as they wish. Open-ended activities are also an important aspect of inclusion. Often, children with special needs require open-ended activities in order to participate with classmates. Feelings of success do not result from easy schoolwork; they result from the appropriate match between the challenge and the child's ability.

∾ The writing center in Dennis's preschool class provides for many levels of abilities and adapts to a variety of interests. It has a selection of paper in many sizes and colors, both with and without lines. There are also pencils and markers, staplers, and hole punches. Children are free to use these materials as needed for their work and play. Naomi's "pretend" writing, Joshua's scribbles, and Shakir's drawing are all acceptable. Each of the children uses writing for different purposes. Naomi uses writing for social purposes, putting a combination of pictures and symbols on a scrap of paper and giving it to a friend to establish contact. Joshua is interested in how different types of crayons and markers make different kinds of marks. Shakir shows an impressive literary background in the picture stories he creates and makes into books. Children frequently choose to spend time at the writing center, and they are making progress in their understanding of how print works. ∾

Contrast Dennis's open-ended options with Joanne's closed-ended activity described next. Joanne thinks the only important thing about writing is learning the correct way to make letters; she decided it was time the children learned the right way to write.

∾ Joanne got out the lined paper and some charts showing proper letter formation. She told the children they could make any letters they wanted, as long as they made them look like those on the charts. Sarah wanted to make "her" S and tried hard to make it look like the chart. Somehow it kept coming out more like a backwards C; sometimes it was a C with a tail. However, it looked fine to

Sarah until Joanne told her it was wrong. Sarah resisted Joanne's efforts to show her the right way and left the writing center in tears. ∞

Certainly, there is also a need for activities with just one correct response; but these need to be implemented with care for individual differences. You need to provide a balance of open and closed activities in your classroom to meet the needs of all youngsters. Sometimes Kelsey seeks the challenge of closed tasks in preschool, such as putting a puzzle together or learning how to weave paper mats at the arts and crafts table. As she challenges herself with the specific task and succeeds, she builds her feelings of competence. At other times she seeks the freedom to test what she can build with various manipulatives or to explore freely with art materials.

Choice   How can you, as a teacher, possibly provide just the right activity and material for each child all the time? You can't. What you can do is allow children a freedom of choice among a wide variety of interesting educational materials and activities. You can count on each child almost always choosing the appropriate level of challenge and the right type of activity for the moment. Here is another value of child choice: Not only does it enhance the development of autonomy, but it also is invaluable for matching the curriculum to the child (Brumbraugh, 2008). Obviously, providing choice for your students is an important teaching strategy (e.g., Brumbraugh, 2008; Feeney, Christensen, & Moravcik, 2006).

Offering children choices of a range of activities aimed at a particular educational goal teaches decision-making skills, ownership of learning, and student engagement. Just at there are different types of learners, there should be different types of learning materials and activities. In a prekindergarten classroom, choice may be provided by supplying children with various materials in the art area, or various levels and types of books (e.g., board books, wordless, picture books, nonfiction books, etc.) in the library area. In the primary classroom, teachers can provide a choice in the ways in which children represent their learning. For example, when learning about the life cycle, some children might conduct an experiment with caterpillar eggs and document how they change over time. Another group may use the Internet to research how native plants in their region grow and create a PowerPoint presentation of their learning. A third group may plant a vegetable garden and document how varying environmental conditions influence the life cycle of the vegetables they planted. All of theses activities would lead to a deeper understanding of the life cycle, yet students have the opportunity to learn the content in a variety of ways. See Figure 4–2 for strategies that encourage student autonomy.

Ability Grouping   Self-selection of an academic challenge also provides an alternative to ability grouping, which is a less effective effort to match the task to the child's ability (Conrad, 2008). Research has demonstrated the negative effect

---

- Decision making
- Multiple ways to represent learning
- Personal responsibility for learning
- Acceptance of diverse ways of knowing and learning

FIGURE 4–2   Instead of Controlling You Could Be Teaching

of ability grouping on self-esteem and classroom dynamics (Tomlinson, 2003). It doesn't take much time in a classroom to notice that children in the "low" group are most likely to act out or quit trying academically.

If you follow youngsters onto the playground, you also see that children in the low group are frequently rejected as playmates by children from the other groups. This rejection creates a segregation effect among youngsters of different academic achievement levels. It is especially disconcerting in light of the fact that a disproportionate number of minority children tend to be placed in the low group (Tomlinson, 2003). Teachers need to take special care that being a child from a certain ethnic group doesn't result in an academic disadvantage. Teachers also need to take care that children are not socially disadvantaged because of academic labels.

The purpose of ability grouping is for supposed efficiency when the teacher is giving information. Ability grouping, with its many negative side effects, is part of a teacher-centered classroom where the teacher makes most of the decisions about what happens. In contrast, child choice is basic to what is known as a child-centered classroom. The teacher provides an array of interesting activities, moves among the youngsters as they work at their choice of activities with their choice of friends, and makes comments to encourage thinking. There is no place for ability grouping here. Instead, children choose learning activities based on their learning styles and interests, and children of various ability levels work together to contribute in their own ways. This approach builds community.

The teacher is responsible for the external order and rhythm of the classroom, but giving children the freedom to make choices within that structure helps children find learning experiences that are individually appropriate (Tomlinson, 2003). We don't recommend allowing children to make all the choices, but children cannot grow emotionally in an overly rigid setting. Both chaos and rigidity damage children's ability to grow emotionally (Koplow, 2002).

Positive Teacher Expectations

The teacher's attitude can create an environment that encourages either positive or negative behavior (DeVries & Zan, 1994). Naturally, no teacher would deliberately encourage negative behavior, yet it is possible to send messages unconsciously that are better not sent. Nonverbal communication is especially likely to reveal your inner feelings. Body language, tone of voice, and intensity often speak louder than words.

If you are convinced that children want to work and play constructively, your whole manner of relating to them communicates that expectation. However, you may be convinced that children want to get away with whatever they can and have no interest in learning. This expectation, too, will be communicated by your tone of voice as you speak to children and by the amount of freedom you give them. You can pretty well count on children to behave according to your expectations.

∾ Mrs. Jensen's first-grade class has just come in from recess, and the youngsters are moving purposefully around the room as they prepare for their next activity. They have the freedom to choose among the classroom centers and to decide individually whether to eat a snack now or later. The classroom is alive with the sounds of decision making as children refocus their energies. Some go first to wash up before a snack and find a comfortable spot to relax and eat. Beau and Dylan are hungry but want to finish the block structure they were working on before recess. Food isn't allowed in the block area, so they postpone their snack. Yaisa and Shayla take their snack into the playhouse, where eating is allowed, and happily incorporate snack time into their dramatic play. Now that the youngsters have learned the routines and the classroom rules, Mrs. Jensen sometimes feels she really isn't needed. She is able to use this time for observing and recording children's progress.

Mrs. Jensen has trusted her children to self-direct their free-choice time, and they have lived up to her expectations. This makes school more pleasant for her and for her students. Contrast Mrs. Jensen's room with Miss Wheeler's.

Next door, Miss Wheeler has no time for observing. She is busy directing and controlling everyone's behavior. In her first-grade class, all the children must eat their snack as soon as they come in from recess, whether they are hungry or not. This schedule makes a long wait in line for hand washing, with lots of pushing and shoving during the wait. It isn't easy, but Miss Wheeler makes the children all sit still until everyone is finished eating before they are excused for the next activity. Then she assigns them by table to specific centers, where they must stay until she flashes the lights signaling rotation to the next center. Jose is a constant problem, always trying to sneak out of his assigned center to the math area. Emily cries a lot, saying she doesn't want to play with those "mean kids" from her table. Miss Wheeler is in constant demand to settle disputes and make children stay where they are supposed to be. She sees this situation as clear evidence that these young children aren't capable of self-direction. Actually, she is getting in the way of their self-direction. ∞

Unfortunately, many teachers run their classrooms like Miss Wheeler does, and they create discipline problems for themselves. Their lack of trust in children to make good choices makes them overcontrolling, which means individual children don't get their needs met.

Clear Guidelines

It is essential that children understand exactly what behaviors are acceptable in school and which ones are not. Your positive outlook is not enough if children are confused about what they are to do. Young children often do not have the experience to know what is and what is not acceptable. Social norms are not self-evident.

∞ Mrs. Jensen started the school year by reading a book called *Little Monster Goes to School*. Little Monster does a lot of bad things, like sticking his arm out of the bus, tripping other kids, and getting into their lunches. Mrs. Jensen's first graders were properly horrified at this behavior. The story provided a good start for a discussion about how to act at school. Then the class was invited to brainstorm behavior limits. Mrs. Jensen helped them to combine their ideas into a few main ideas and to phrase them in positive instead of negative terms. "Don't run" became "Be careful." "Don't hit, don't shove, and don't spit" became "Be kind and talk things over." Mrs. Jensen wrote these as the children watched.

Children are more likely to follow guidelines they have created.

They were displayed on a bulletin board that the children decorated with monster pictures they created at the paint easel. Most of the children learned to read the guidelines and referred to them when a classmate didn't follow one. ∞

Children will more likely follow guidelines they themselves have helped to determine. They may also actively remind other children to do the same. However, young children's ability to describe appropriate and inappropriate behavior greatly exceeds their ability to act accordingly (Koplow, 2002). Therefore, the teacher's role goes beyond including children in the development of classroom rules; regular class meetings must be held for the purpose of problem solving when children do not live up to the guidelines.

Class Meetings   Class meetings help the group function as a community and include discussing ways in which people have been kind and helpful as well as discussing problems. Sharing feelings, working together to solve conflicts, and supporting one another as children strive toward common goals create a unified group (Styles, 2001). Class meetings allow children, and the teacher, to bring problems and concerns to the group for discussion. The goal of these discussions is to find a solution for the next time the issue arises, not to place blame or give out punishment (Rightmyer, 2003). Such meetings allow thoughts and feelings to be expressed without fear of embarrassment or punishment. This feeling of safety has a positive effect on the school day and improves children's ability to concentrate on learning (Vance & Weaver, 2002).

Children come to understand the ideas behind class guidelines as a result of ongoing discussions that apply the guidelines to problems shared in class meetings. Have you noticed that we aren't talking about making rules, but instead use the terms *guidelines* and *limits*? Reynolds (2000) points out the differences between limits and rules: Limits and guidelines are flexible, taking circumstances into consideration; rules are rigid and tend to apply regardless of circumstances. Limits or guidelines encourage thinking and decision making; rules allow neither. Therefore, limits and guidelines foster moral autonomy, and rules foster heteronomy. Consider the difference between "Be careful" and "Don't run." The rule "Don't run" or even "Always walk" encourages children to test it and see what happens. Obviously there are times when kids can run, and even times when they should. The limit of being careful encourages children to reflect on what it means to be careful; "Being careful" becomes a topic of discussion to encourage children to self-evaluate their behavior according to that standard.

∞ Nick was driving a toy car on the block road he and Kyle had built. The car zoomed faster and faster as Nick began a fantasy about a jet car. Kyle was absorbed in building a bridge over his part of the road and wasn't paying attention to the jet car. He had finally gotten the right combination of blocks and the right balance to make his bridge stay up when Nick's jet car crashed into it. Dennis heard the heated exchange of words between the boys and managed to get to them before the disagreement escalated to blows. "He knocked down my bridge!" complained Kyle. "I didn't mean to!" exclaimed Nick. What a perfect opportunity for important teaching. Dennis could use this situation to help Nick and Kyle to think about the effects of their actions. His question, "Were you being careful of Kyle's bridge when you drove your car so fast?" is designed to encourage thought. So is the question, "How could you make your car go fast and still be careful of what other children are doing?" Notice, Dennis isn't giving answers—he is helping the kids think. ∞

Young children have much to learn, but you might assume that they should at least know better than to sit up on their knees during class meetings and story time. Surely they realize that sitting that way blocks the view of the person behind them, and that means they are not following the guideline "Be kind." But remember that young children think about their own needs and have trouble considering someone else's position. There are ways to help them understand another person's view during group time.

∞ Mrs. Jensen doesn't constantly remind children to sit down in the front rows; instead of nagging, she structures a learning experience to help them begin to understand consideration for others. She assigns each table of children to a specific row during the first group meeting of each day. During other group sessions, they are allowed to choose their own places, but for this one group time they take turns experiencing how it feels to be in the back rows with other children in their way. Mrs. Jensen encourages the children who can't see to remind the others politely when they are thoughtlessly blocking the view. This experience provides an important lesson in seeing things from another person's perspective and in communicating a problem. The children soon take responsibility for reminding one another to be considerate, and eventually remember most of the time not to kneel in front of someone. ∞

CONCLUSION

Teachers who understand how the environment influences children's initiative, perspective taking, sense of belonging, and need for security have smoother days. Adults who expect the best from children and communicate their expectations clearly find that children behave more positively. Adults who respect individual children, their families, and their cultures create caring classroom communities. Adults who provide choices and otherwise share power with children find them more eager and helpful. Teachers who help youngsters find friendship, success, and recognition help them to learn more effectively. Teachers who make an effort to build relationships with individual children and their families create the necessary foundation for learning social and academic skills. When you meet children's needs in the physical and emotional classroom environment, many common discipline problems never arise.

∽ *FOR FURTHER THOUGHT*

1. What are the behavior guidelines in an early childhood education program where you have spent time? How were these guidelines determined? Why do you think the youngsters either do or do not follow the guidelines?

2. In what ways have you seen teachers demonstrate respect for young children? In what ways have you seen teachers show lack of respect for youngsters? Which examples most closely match your own interactions with children?

3. How are friendships encouraged or discouraged in an early childhood program with which you are familiar? Would you recommend any changes to help children develop meaningful friendships?

4. Analyze an early childhood program for open-ended and closed activities. Is there a balance, or does one type dominate? How do children's responses to the two types differ?

5. Observe teacher–child interaction, watching for the amount of individual attention provided. How do youngsters respond differently to individual interaction with the teacher than they do to interacting as part of a group?

6. Analyze the physical setting of a classroom. In what ways does the room arrangement prevent or create opportunities for building friendships, teaching organization, fostering initiative, and meeting privacy and other learning needs?

∽ *RECOMMENDED READINGS*

Copple, C., & Bredekamp, S. (Eds.) (2009). Developmentally appropriate practice in early childhood programs serving children from birth through age 8 (3rd ed.). Washington, DC: National Association for the Education of Young Children.

Conrad, D. J. (2008). An early start: Skill grouping and unequal reading gains in the elementary years. *Sociological Quarterly, 49*(2), 363–394.

Derman-Sparks, L., & Ramsey, P. G. (2005). What if all the children in my class are white? Anti-bias/multicultural education with white children. *YC Young Children, 60*(6), 20-4, 26-7.

Greenman, J. (2005). *Caring spaces, learning places, children's environments that work.* Redmond, WA: Exchange Press, Inc.

Kirmani, M. H. (2007). Empowering culturally and linguistically diverse children and families. *Young Children, 62*(6), 94–98.

Koplow, L. (2002). *Schools that heal: Real-life solutions.* New York: Teachers College Press.

Seefeldt, C. (2002). *Creating rooms of wonder: Valuing and displaying children's work to enhance the learning process.* Beltsville, MD: Gryphon House, Inc.

Wasik, B. (2008). When fewer is more: Small groups in early childhood classrooms. *Early Childhood Education Journal, 35*(6), 515–521.

WEBSITES

Child Development Project. Developmental Studies Center. http://www.devstu.org/cdp/#

∞ Chapter **5** ∞
Planning Programs That Prevent Discipline Problems

NAEYC Standards Addressed in This Chapter

Standard 2c: Involving families in their children's development and learning.

Standard 4b: Using use a wide array of effective approaches, strategies, and tools to positively influence young children's development and learning.

Standard 4d: Using your own knowledge and other resources to design, implement, and evaluate meaningful, challenging curriculum that promotes comprehensive developmental and learning outcomes for all young children.

GUIDING QUESTIONS

- How do teachers design an active, engaging curriculum that will support children's social development?
- How does a curriculum that does not meet children's needs affect their social development?
- How do the daily schedule and transition routines support children's engagement in learning and their behavior?
- What makes a successful group time?

*W*hen children are interested and involved in learning, they don't have time for troublesome behavior. Which do you think would keep young learners involved better? Tracing and copying a different letter each day, or exploring print in books and signs that have an interesting message? Counting the number of dots on a worksheet, or figuring out how to divide the raisins equally for snack time? Educational objectives or standards and the instructional practices used to meet the objectives make up a school's *curriculum* (National Association of Early Childhood Specialists in State Departments of Education [NAEYC/NAECS/SDE], 2003). Decisions about curriculum for young children are influenced by many factors, such as community values, policy mandates, and individual children's needs (NAEYC/NAECS/SDE, 2003).

Young children are better able to cooperate in school when curricular goals and educational approaches match their developmental stages. Therefore, teacher expectations and instructional methodologies must be geared to the maturation level of the students. When practices and materials created for older students are used for younger ones, many problems arise (Zaslow & Martinex-Beck, 2006). Developmentally inappropriate curricular content and teaching results in inappropriate behavior from children. This occurs because forcing children to achieve unattainable expectations or learn through ineffective teaching strategies leads children to believe they are simply not good at learning (Jalongo, 2007).

Research shows that children in programs that are not developmentally appropriate exhibit more stress (Marcon, 2002; Ruckman, Burts, & Pierce, 1999). Obviously, stress has negative effects on learning and on behavior. Therefore, it is no surprise that developmentally appropriate classrooms are also more emotionally positive environments (Jenson, 2006; Marcon, 2002). As a result, children in programs that are developmentally appropriate demonstrate higher levels of social skills than those in other kinds of programs (Marcon, 2002). This chapter describes approaches to the design of developmentally appropriate curriculum and instruction that will serve to eliminate the causes of many behavior problems.

MAKING LEARNING MEANINGFUL

How do children act when they are bored or disinterested? Most likely, you remember from your own childhood how you acted under those circumstances. Most youngsters will create some action when the teacher doesn't offer any. Often, however, these creative efforts do not conform to acceptable group behavior, and teachers call them discipline problems.

The National Association for the Education of Young Children and the National Association of Early Childhood Specialists in State Departments of Education (NAEYC/NAECS/SDE, 2003) provide curriculum guidelines for preschool and primary-grade youngsters. The Association of Childhood Education International (ACEI; Jalongo, 2007) provides guidelines on the role of motivation in children's learning and effective teaching practices that promote motivation and interest in learning (see links to both documents at the end of this chapter). Taken together, these guidelines emphasize the characteristics of thoughtfully planned, meaningful curriculum for young children and approaches to teaching young children that build on children's interests and motivation to learn. Figure 5–1 shows the major components of the recommendations from these organizations and the alignment between the two. The following discussion explains how adhering to these guidelines will eliminate many potential discipline problems you might otherwise face as a teacher or caregiver.

Relevance and Interest

Interest has a strong effect on children's attitudes toward learning (Jalongo, 2007). According to Jalongo (2007), interest in learning can be personal, which is unique to individual children and stems from their prior knowledge and experiences. Interest can also be situational. Situational interest stems from being exposed to a new or novel experience. Situational interest is usually short lived, unless learners find the experience to be relevant or valuable to their lives. A relevant and interesting curriculum allows children to investigate things that affect their lives, things they care about. Cutting out snowflakes in Miami just because it is January would not be relevant. A unit on farming

NAEYC/NAECS/SDE Indicators of an Effective Curriculum	ACEI Policy Statement on Motivation and Interest in Children's Academic Achievement
Children are active and engaged.	Capture the learner's attention. Motivation is key to achievement.
Goals are clear and shared by all.	Set, monitor, and attain goals.
Curriculum is evidenced-based.	Establish a rationale for learning.
Valued content is learned through investigation, play, and focused intentional teaching.	Interest is essential to children's learning. Learning is social and cultural.
Curriculum builds on prior learning.	Learning something new depends on prior learning.
Curriculum is comprehensive.	Attaining higher standards demands attention to the affective domain.
Professional standards validate the curriculum's subject matter content.	Understand the role of choice in children's learning.
The curriculum is likely to benefit children.	Expectations for learning need to be respectful of children. Learning is unevenly paced.

Modified from NAEYC/NAECS/SDE (2003) and Jalongo (2007).

FIGURE 5–1   Overview of NAEYC/NAECS/SDE and ACEI Policy Statements on Curriculum

would not be relevant to youngsters in Nome. How the weather affects children's activities is relevant in both locations, as is how people get their food in each place. But kids themselves might be more concerned about the problem of the mudhole beneath the tire swing. That, too, offers an opportunity for meaningful study. Relevant learning helps keep youngsters motivated to learn (Jalongo, 2007), which in turn keeps them on task—a classroom management challenge.

The NAEYC/NAECS/SDE (2003) guidelines recommend planning curriculum that is challenging and engaging. Don't we all get more involved in things we are interested in? Mrs. Jensen is alert to questions and comments from youngsters that indicate their current interests. She knows that children have some well-developed interests by first grade; she encourages children to pursue these ideas and incorporates many child-generated topics into class activities. She is prepared for many of the ideas with collections of books and activity ideas for topics that frequently catch children's interest in her classes. Mrs. Jensen knows from experience that kids are generally interested in dinosaurs, space, animals, and insects.

Ideas from individual youngsters often become a major curriculum focus in Mrs. Jensen's first grade. She understands that it doesn't really matter whether children are studying the life cycle or how to create a class newspaper (Shan & Reichel, 2008); children can practice the basic skills, broaden their knowledge base, expand their interests, and increase their feelings of competence with almost any topic. She uses children's various interests to provide a purpose for learning. For instance, reporting about the daily events in the classroom orally and through writing and illustrating stories is a good way for children to practice valuable literacy skills. Activities such as this provide children with the motivation to stay engaged in learning and increase opportunities for social interaction and community building (Shan & Reichel, 2008).

Mrs. Jensen also knows how to help children become interested in subjects included in state standards. For instance, the topic of nutrition may sound boring or beyond the reach of young children. It probably was when you had to memorize the food groups, but it isn't when you take a trip to the supermarket to buy items from each food group and use them for class cooking projects. Interest is sustained in the subject when a play store is set up next to the playhouse. Much thought and energy goes into writing grocery lists that reflect nutritious meal planning. These children are going far beyond mere memorized social knowledge; they are constructing logico-mathematical understanding about food and nutrition. When you channel children's energy constructively, they don't have so much excess to burn off inappropriately.

Dennis uses the same curriculum guidelines when planning instruction for his preschool students. The instructional principles are the same, although the expectations for children differ according to their grade level. He, too, ensures that the curriculum makes sense to kids. Instead of rote learning about letters, his students have frequent opportunities to see their names and the names of their friends used for labeling artwork and for keeping their place on a waiting list. Many children can recognize their own names and those of their closest friends. Some discuss how confusing it is when names start with the same letter, like the names Anton and Anna or Kelsey and Katlyn. Lessons such as these are a precursor to young children's alphabet knowledge (Justice, Pence, Bowles, & Wiggins, 2006). Most important, the thinking that goes on during these discussions results in true construction of knowledge, genuine involvement in learning about letters, and social connectedness.

Sometimes the most relevant curriculum deals with unresolved developmental issues, such as making friends, separating from parents, dealing with disappointments, or facing fears (Hyson, 2004; Koplow, 2002). If we ignore these emotion-laden issues and try to focus only on teaching academics, children will be unable to learn and may suffer socially and emotionally as well as academically (Wilson, Pianta, & Stuhlman, 2007). Policymakers, educators, and community members agree that all academic programming should emphasize curricular goals for children's social emotional development and their approaches toward learning (Boyd, Barnett, Bodrova, Leong, & Gomby, 2005; Cohen, Onunaku, Clothier, & Poppe, 2005; Vespo, Capece, & Behforooz, 2006).

Recent reviews of early learning standards for prekindergarten children urge early childhood educators to place as much, if not more, emphasis on social and emotional skills and approaches to learning as they do to teaching academic content (Kagan & Scott-Little, 2004). The Center for Social Emotional Education (*http://www.csee.net/climate/aboutcsee/*) has waged a similar campaign for students in K–12 classrooms. These movements to include social and emotional learning in the curriculum stem from the knowledge that children's understanding of curricula content, and hence their achievement, is directly related to their social and emotional development.

Integrated Curriculum

It is widely accepted that children learn more from integrated units of study or projects than they do from curriculum that is focused on a single subject area (Loughran, 2005). An *integrated curriculum* gives a context for learning and therefore makes learning more meaningful, as is recommended by the curricular guidelines published by leaders in the field of early childhood education (Jalongo, 2007; NAEYC/NAECS/SDE, 2003). Curricular integration is also related to children's engagement and motivation to learn, and thus is an effective tool for preventing discipline problems related to lack of interest, off-task behaviors, or under- or over-challenging expectations.

PEARSON
myeducationlab

To see an example of how teachers integrate the curriculum, go to MyEducationLab and select the topic "Math and Science" and watch the video "Mathematics."

Themes and project work are approaches to integrating the curriculum. They offer teachers an alternative to organizing a curriculum focused on disconnected pieces of information and isolated drills in basic skills. Both themes and topics are *conceptual organizers* used to link multiple components of the curriculum in the exploration of one topic of study. A teacher-selected theme, such as a study of birds, offers possibilities for a variety of teacher-selected activities related to the topic of birds. However, the theme approach may not be as compelling a reason to learn about birds as a project, such as caring for the classroom finches who just laid eggs. Projects are guided by children's interest in real-world phenomena that they are trying to understand. For this reason, projects tend to have more immediate applicability to children's lives (Katz & Chard, 1989/2000).

Children learn social skills and academic content when working collaboratively on projects that interest them.

An integrated curriculum allows children to practice reading, writing, and math skills as they explore topics of interest. The topic itself usually involves social studies or science information. Mathematics, art, music, and drama are incorporated as children investigate the topic of study. Children can learn in most subject areas using almost any topic. Dennis knows that actually using arithmetic to explore a subject is more useful than merely practicing arithmetic skills, so he helps children find the mathematics potential in the topics they are interested in.

∞ When the resident preschool expert on dinosaurs reported that a certain type of dinosaur had 200 teeth, Dennis challenged the child and others who were interested to discover just how many 200 is. They got out Unifix cubes and worked together as a group to identify 200; then they arranged them like top and bottom teeth to visualize the dinosaur's mouth. Ahmed commented, "I'll bet dinosaurs can eat faster than we can!"

That remark led Dennis to suggest the idea of getting a partner and counting each other's teeth. Megan decided that they should count out the number of teeth in their mouths and make a display of them using the smallest Cuisenaire rods. Counting dinosaur teeth and their own teeth turned into quite a project, attracting different children over a period of several days. It led to further reading and further science information as a result.

Olivia was motivated to make pictures representing herself with her teeth and the dinosaur with its teeth. Several other children followed her example. Thus, artistic representation was added to mathematics, science, and reading as the curriculum was integrated around a dinosaur-teeth theme. ∞

The play store in Mrs. Jensen's classroom is another example of a theme for an integrated curriculum. Children thought about foods for good nutrition while playing store. They practiced writing when they made their grocery lists, and they practiced reading both the lists and the labels on the food packages. They extended their mathematical thinking about counting and money as they made price tags and tried to figure out proper payment for each item. The class book in which each child contributed a drawing and a dictated message about the trip to the supermarket also helped children learn to read and write. The children learned more about their community during their field trip to the supermarket. Thus, the trip was part of the subject of social studies.

There was also lots of social studies involved in resolving the inevitable disputes during these activities. Important negotiation skills were practiced while making group decisions. When children encounter others' points of view while studying the same topic, it compels them to take on the perspective of others. As children challenge one another's ideas, they learn to negotiate. Through their attempts at negotiation, children learn to express and defend their ideas, and sometimes they learn that their ideas need modification. Project work also offers students opportunities to strengthen their skills without external pressure or rewards. If children are genuinely interested in knowing how many teeth are in a dinosaur's mouth, or how much money they have to spend at the store, they will be motivated to use *and improve* their math skills.

Ideas for projects also come from outside the classroom. Second graders in Mr. Davis's classroom discovered a project during recess; they ended up using math and literacy in a study of science focused on environmental conservation.

∞ Fall rainstorms were eroding the steep hillside at the end of the playground. During recess, the playground aide told everyone to stay off it so it wouldn't get worse. But the hill was almost everyone's favorite place to play, and she had trouble enforcing the rule. She blew her whistle again and again, sending children inside who wouldn't obey her.

Mr. Davis heard his students complaining about the loss and their doubts that it was really necessary to close the area. The conversation became a topic for a class meeting, and Mr. Davis asked the class if they would like to go back outside and study the problem some more. Always eager for any reason to go outside, the children threw their coats back on and grabbed the notepads Mr. Davis handed out.

Active debate ensued as they checked out the hillside, riddled by rivulets of water, with sloughing topsoil and gravel slides. Gradually, the observations became more critical. Mr. Davis encouraged them to write down what they saw and what they wondered about. He helped them focus on what might happen there and what they might be able to do to help the situation. Healthy disagreements arose, and Mr. Davis kept on saying, "I wonder what others think about your plan!"

Regrouping in the classroom, the second graders shared what they'd seen and what they thought might help. Ideas included using rip-rap rock, staking burlap over the hill, putting in drainage, and even letting it slough away to a more stable slope. Some children cited their observations of city projects to stabilize slopes and a couple said one of their parents knew all about how to fix things like that.

They decided they wanted to take on a "save the hill" project, but first they needed more information. Mr. Davis warned them that this project would take some serious planning, work, record keeping, and evaluating. The children were excited and wanted to get right to work. They planned walking field trips to observe some other sites, the children with expert parents said they would invite them as guest speakers, and Mr. Davis worked with the librarian to obtain relevant research materials. ∞

Counting dinosaur teeth, playing store, and saving the hill are authentically integrated activities because children think critically about a topic and use their skills as a means of investigation. These children probably never ask the question, "Why do I need to know this?" Not everything labeled "integrated curriculum" fits this criteria for projects. Too often teachers superficially use themes as a means to cover required subject-area content. Poor Miss Wheeler does just that and wonders why her students don't act interested.

∞ Miss Wheeler has a different theme each week. This week it is rocks. She brought many different rocks to school for the children. (She thought it would take too much time for them to go outside and collect their own.) For writing time, each child is to write a letter to his or her rock. For art time, children are allowed to paint their rocks. For snack, they get a little piece of rock candy along with something more nutritious. ∞

These activities may involve rocks, but they don't help children learn anything about rocks. This is a *correlated* rather than an *integrated* curriculum (Fields, Groth, & Spangler, 2004).

Real Experiences and Real Materials

Both Dennis and Mrs. Jensen know that children will benefit more, and the school day will be smoother, if teaching is compatible with how children learn naturally. Integrating the curriculum is one way to match your teaching with children's learning and your curricular goals. Children certainly don't separate the world into the categories *science, math,* and *social studies.* They just want to make sense of their world, with all its interrelationships, as they experience it. Therefore, school also needs to reflect the real world and children's own experiences in order for youngsters to perceive school as important. Teachers need to remember that learning is social and cultural. One way to do this is to build children's background knowledge and experiences into the curriculum (Jalongo, 2007; NAEYC/NAECS/SDE, 2003). Another way to get children to think deeply about a project is to use real materials as a source of inspiration (Tishman, 2008).

∞ Nathan brought a bird's nest for sharing time, and other children began talking about birds' nests they had seen. Mrs. Jensen encouraged the discussion by asking what they knew about birds and birds' nests. Most of the children in this suburban area had some sort of experience to share. Tony told a story about when his mom had cut his hair outside on the patio; he had seen birds come and take the hair for their nests. Other children told about being careful of nests with eggs in them. The teacher decided to follow up on the children's experiences and build on the knowledge they already had.

Mrs. Jensen got out her own collection of birds' nests from past years for the children to examine. She had protected the nests by keeping them in clear plastic bags, which kept the nests from falling apart. A discussion about the kinds of things birds use to make nests was preparation for a field trip around the schoolyard to collect materials for making birds' nests. Each child had

Children use real materials to show their knowledge about a variety of topics.

the opportunity to make a bird's nest model with the materials collected. Mrs. Jensen provided the "mud" to hold the material together; she had previously discovered that glue mixed with dirt and water allows for a successful nest-building experience. ∾

Children's way of learning starts with real experiences and real objects from which to make sense. Mrs. Jensen's students would not have made much sense out of a lesson on birds' nests without both their personal experience and the concrete materials the teacher provided. The students made observations, posed questions, and developed explanations about how birds make nests. These are the ingredients for thinking that transcend subject-area boundaries (Tishman, 2008). Students engaged in this type of lesson, with real objects, apply their knowledge to other investigations (Epstein, 2008). Some teachers don't understand this; they waste precious time lecturing children about topics totally outside their realm of experience. Of course, this approach leads to discipline problems because children don't pay much attention to a discussion they cannot understand.

Some teachers cover the same topics year after year without responding to the enthusiasms and questions of the children in *this* class *this* year. Then they follow up the meaningless lessons with developmentally inappropriate worksheets. Many youngsters will dutifully go along with the teacher and complete these purposeless tasks, but many others will cause classroom problems by trying to find something interesting to do.

Mrs. Jensen not only started with a topic of personal importance to her students when they studied birds, but she also provided opportunities for children to investigate at the concrete level. Examining real nests, collecting real material to make nests, and going through the process of creating their own models are the kinds of concrete experiences that match the way young children learn. They have the opportunity to construct their own understanding of birds' nests from the experience of creating replicas. The children engaged in these educational experiences are involved in the business of learning and therefore aren't likely to disrupt anyone else's work. They are also building the base for thinking further about birds. This will help children to make sense of reading material on that subject.

PEARSON
myeducationlab

To see an example of how teachers incorporate real materials into social studies lessons, go to MyEducationLab and select the topic "Social Studies" and watch the video "Social Studies."

Too often, teachers forget young children's need to focus on the real world of the here and now. Well-meaning teachers frequently lead youngsters into the totally unintelligible world of long ago or far away. Thanksgiving time is particularly likely to motivate teachers to explain the history of the original feast. However, young children have notoriously inaccurate ideas about time and space. They may not understand the difference between something happening 300 years ago and something happening last week. Ask a young child who has heard the story of the first Thanksgiving to tell you about it, and you will hear truly amazing misconceptions. Wasting children's time with a presentation of incomprehensible historical facts may result in children acquiring misconceptions

To view an example of how a teacher prepares engaging activities for young children, go to MyEducationLab and select the topic "Guiding Children." Under Activities and Applications, watch the video Making Orange.

about the people and events from the past. For example, after studying Thanksgiving, many children believe that all Native Americans paint their faces, wear feathers in their hair, and live in teepees.

Active Learning

Children's direct involvement in learning is related to how they approach learning and how they come to view themselves as learners. If children are in a classroom where the teacher tells children everything they need to know, children will not develop an inquiring disposition. If teachers are the only people in the classroom that get to touch and manipulate objects, children will come to believe that learning is a passive endeavor. Mrs. Thomas had a recent reminder of how important it is to plan learning experiences with students' active involvement in mind.

∞ The salmon were running in a nearby stream when school started, and many children had been fishing with their parents. Interest in fish was high, and Mrs. Thomas decided to capitalize on it. She planned a trip to the local fish hatchery so that her students could see the salmon fighting their way up the fish ladder. They also got to see the eggs being taken, fertilized, and put in tanks to grow. The field trip was just right for young children: lots of action and the talking limited to answering some questions.

The follow-up portion of the plan went differently. The hatchery donated a few salmon for the children's closer study. One of the children's parents is a fish biologist who has offered to donate her time to help with this study. Back in the classroom, children crowd around a small table to watch the biologist cut open the fish and see what is inside. But first, the fish expert wants to tell the youngsters some things: how fish move through the water, the name and purpose of each fin, how fish breathe, how the gills function, and how fish are marked for study.

Mrs. Thomas personally finds the lecture fascinating, though the Latin names for the various parts go over her head. She realizes, however, that a lecture appropriate for her is not appropriate for her students. Some children have started to talk among themselves, others are jockeying for position to see the fish better. One has wandered over to a table where other fish are displayed; he is engrossed in stroking their scales. A few youngsters are still interested in the biologist, but they want to tell her what they know about fish. The biologist sees that the children are restless and decides to get on with the dissecting. Unfortunately, most children have lost interest. Mrs. Thomas realizes she should have planned more specifically with the guest to ensure that the presentation would allow the children's active involvement rather than require only passive listening. ∞

Active learning promotes reasoning as well as academic and social problem-solving abilities. In the previous vignette, children were not asked to reason or think about salmon or how they behave during spawning season, and the children's behavior reflected this. Leaving the group, talking out of turn, and

Negotiating rules for play helps children to understand how to interact with others in a variety of situations.

interrupting are the ways in which children show adults that the lesson is not meeting their needs. Even the best-developed lesson plans can go awry if they do not offer children opportunities to be actively involved in learning.

The Role of Play

Young children learn through play; it enhances their intellectual curiosity and helps them to construct knowledge on a variety of topics (Riggings-Newby, 2005). Play promotes exploration, thinking, and inquiring, all of which are essential ingredients for learning (NAEYC/NAECS/SDE, 2003). Learning through play opens the emotional brain, which in turn opens up the intellectual brain (Jenson, 2006).

PEARSON
myeducationlab

To see an example of how children learn through play, go to MyEducationLab and select the topic "Play." Under Activities and Applications, watch the video "Making a Discovery: The Water Table."

Feelings play a significant role in motivation, interest, and academic achievement (Jalongo, 2007). Feelings are also related to and how much and what type of material we remember (Nelson, 2007). It is no wonder, then, that children show higher rates of social competence and academic achievement when they are in classrooms that support their play.

The play store project in Mrs. Jensen's classroom is not only an example of integrated curriculum (Jalongo & Isenberg, 2004) but also has many other benefits. There are lots of important decisions to be made and problems to solve during play, whether it is pretend play, such as the play store, or games such as checkers or cards: Who gets to run the cash register? How do we resolve it when everyone wants to do it now? Which rules for Crazy Eights should we use today? Can Nathan change the rules if he is losing?

Vygotsky (1978) points out that play necessarily involves learning about rules and abiding by them. He contends, "Whenever there is an imaginary situation, there are rules" (p. 95). Rules are necessary for guiding behavior in an imaginary situation because children have to agree on the "script" and the cast of characters (Bodrova & Leong, 2007). As children construct the rules necessary to keep their pretend play situation going (e.g., how to go shopping, or cook a meal, etc.), they develop logical reasoning skills and also both creative thinking and critical thinking abilities (Bodrova & Leong, 2007). Teachers can enhance children's cognitive and social development by encouraging pretend play and engaging children in discussion of the rule-bond situations they create (Weber, 2002).

It is interesting to note that as children get older, their play increasingly emphasizes rules. Vygotsky described this development as moving from play that is obviously imaginary and subtly rule-bound (playing house) to play that focuses on rules but has subtle imaginary contexts (board games). Weber (2002) concludes that the rules involved in play help children understand expectations for desirable behavior and encourage children to act accordingly. This is another one of many reasons to include play in your curriculum.

The Teacher's Role in Play   Teachers take on various roles during children's play, such as being a stage manager, co-player, or play leader (Christie, Enz, & Vukelich, 2006). Each of these roles can serve to promote children's social competence. The stage manager sets up children's play activities, assists in beginning interactions, and then quietly slips out of the play situation so that children can work on their own. This role is particularly good for children who don't know how to enter play. The co-player asks to enter children's play and takes on an assigned role. This is the least intrusive teacher role and is used to promote the skills of children with well-established play behaviors or to support a child who may need some assistance. The play leader is the most teacher-directed role; it is used to support groups of children who don't make any attempts to enter play on their own. The play leader begins the play interaction, assigns children various roles (e.g., "I'll be the mother and you be the father."), and directs the play. The play leader stays with the group until the play ends.

Using Time Wisely

Perhaps the most critical curriculum guideline has to do with making sure that what children are asked to learn is worth knowing. Respect for children should guide us away from the trivial and cute school activities that are all too common. As stated by Dark (2007), cute has to count! Instead of wasting children's time by having them all make identical red flowers for the bulletin board, let's think about what is truly important in their lives. Feeney and colleagues put things into perspective by reminding us that one of the most important things any of us can learn might be "how to find a friend when you're sad" (Feeney, Christensen, & Moravcik, 2006). Feeney et al. make this statement in the context of a broad view of what is worth knowing; it includes understanding the physical and social environment and yourself in order to better respect and care for the world and its people. For example, evaluate the importance of colors and shapes in comparison to goals of becoming more humane and helping our world survive. Respecting children involves respecting their time and using it wisely. Mrs. Jensen was surprised at how well the birds' nest activity met this goal.

∽ When the children finished making their birds' nests, Mrs. Jensen called them together for a group discussion. "What did you learn when you made the birds' nests?" she asked. Expecting answers about the way the mud felt and what ingredients worked best, the teacher was astounded to hear a whole different level of response: "Birds' nests are really hard to make!" "I'll never knock one down out of a tree," and "I won't ever shoot a bird" were the type of ideas generated. Making birds' nest models encouraged these youngsters to think about the birds' viewpoint, and it helped them develop an appreciation for birds and their struggle for survival. Certainly, these children will be better able to respect and care for the world they live in. ∽

You also need to ask yourself whether what you are teaching is worth the effort at this time in children's lives. Many teachers have discovered the hard way that trying to teach kindergarten-age children to tell time is not worth the effort. Others have decided that trying to teach everyone how to make change in first grade is wasted energy. Trying to teach these symbols too soon is about as productive as trying to teach a 5-month-old baby to walk. Some topics are a waste of time because they are too easy and can be learned without specifically spending school time on them. For instance, directed instruction on colors is not necessary for most children. Colors are a part of life and are generally picked up at a very young age as children decide which color crayon to use, which shirt to wear, or the color of their favorite ice cream. Talking with children about color as they engage in other activities is all the instruction most of them need.

However, some ideas are well worth the time and effort. We hope for greater emphasis on helping children learn to respect and protect the environment and to live peaceably together with respect for individual differences. Some call these areas of study science and social studies; we call them basics.

Three Kinds of Knowledge

Other curriculum guidelines can be derived from an understanding of the learning process. Any learner is more engaged and on-task when teaching approaches match the ways in which people learn. Planning curriculum without attention to the ways in which people learn different types of knowledge will not benefit children. Teachers who understand the differences between how children learn and *physical knowledge, social knowledge,* and *logico-mathematical knowledge* are able to plan learning activities that will benefit learners (Kamii, 2000; NAEYC/NAECS/SDE, 2003).

According to Piaget, physical or empirical knowledge is derived from our engagement with objects in the world (Piaget, 1970). Physical knowledge is learned through the senses. When children discover that a ball placed on a ramp rolls downward, or that when pushed forward a swing will only go so far before returning, they are acquiring physical knowledge. Physical knowledge also involves the observation of changes caused by the way one object acts on another (e.g., an ice cube melts if left in the sun). This type of knowledge can only be acquired through the direct action on objects (i.e., active learning) and is the reason why most national curriculum guidelines promote children's active engagement in inquiry using discipline-related materials (e.g., Michaels, Shouse, & Schweingruber, 2008; National Council of Teachers of Mathematics, 2000; National Research Council, 2005).

Social knowledge is the knowledge shared among members of a group and differs based on the group's language, norms, and customs. It is passed from one person to another. How to greet your elders is social knowledge. So are the names we've assigned to the days of the week and months of the year. Social knowledge complements other types of knowledge. For example, the names assigned to numerals are social knowledge, but acquiring an understanding of numbers and how they work (number sense) is logico-mathematical knowledge.

Logico-mathematical knowledge deals with our ability to reason about the relationship between objects and actions and the rules or theories we generate about both. Now, there is nothing in the object itself or, for that matter, how the object is transformed, that will reveal the relationship; this is something children must conjure up in their own minds. For example, Piaget tells a story of how a young boy came to understand the commutative property (i.e., changing the order of numbers or objects does not change the results or sum of the objects). The young boy had 10 pebbles and he laid them all in a row. He counted the pebbles from one end and got 10. He counted them from the other end and got 10, which surprised him. He then placed the pebbles in a circle, counted, and got 10 again. He soon came to realize that the order in which the pebbles were placed did not affect the quantity. The boy didn't learn this from the pebbles or from rearranging the pebbles; rather, he learned this from reflecting on what happened, or in this case, didn't happen, to the pebbles each time he moved them.

Logico-mathematical thinking provides the framework for classifying, and therefore making sense of any information. Physical knowledge and social knowledge are used in the construction of logico-mathematical knowledge, and logico-mathematical knowledge is necessary for the construction of physical and social knowledge (DeVries, 2001). Therefore, in order to truly engage children's minds and help them be successful learners, teachers must ensure opportunities for experimentation and reflection with content related to all types of knowledge. Too many classrooms trivialize education and children's capabilities by limiting teaching to transmitting social knowledge—asking children to remember lists of facts without understanding the underlying mechanisms that make the facts believable. For example, we can teach children to memorize the steps of scientific inquiry, but until they experience each step of the process during an authentic investigation, they probably won't understand the importance of asking questions, collecting data, or analyzing and sharing results.

Another example of this results from the recent emphasis on test scores and teachers feeling forced to "teach to the test" rather than teaching children. Teachers who know this is poor education see the negative effects on children's learning and on behavior, but are unsure how to plan learning experiences that take into consideration the three kinds of knowledge, children's interest and motivation to learn, the benefits of active learning and play, and state standards. All of the strategies discussed thus far will help you to accomplish this task. The information in the next section of this chapter will help you to organize active, engaging learning experiences to assure that they are meeting children's social and academic needs.

ORGANIZATIONAL STRATEGIES

Teachers with knowledge of how children learn, how emotions affect learning, how to organize the classroom environment, adult–child and peer interactions, and curriculum also know when behavior problems are most likely to occur. Children often experience behavioral difficulties when they are unsure of the routines and expectations in the classroom, and during transitions from one activity to another. To avoid these types of problems, teachers use a combination of strategies, routines, and rituals to avoid turmoil during transitions, waiting periods, and group times.

Routines

We all like routines. Think how you feel when you wake up late and can't enjoy your morning routine. Chances are you feel disorganized and disheveled and are worried about what the rest of the day will hold for you. Children experience similar feelings when put into situations where they don't know what will happen next. Stable routines help children know what to expect and therefore can assist them in being cooperative members of the group. Routines also provide emotional security through predictability (Hyson, 2004), which is especially important for children who live in chaotic environments.

Because the children know the routine, it doesn't take any time at all for Mrs. Jensen's first graders to assemble for group time. They have a system for moving smoothly from their seats to the group area, and each child knows just what to do. Routines save the teacher from constantly having to tell the children what to do next; they know what comes next and what they are to do.

However, having a routine does not mean being ruled by the clock, stopping whatever else is going on at exactly 11:15 each day to have story time. But it is important that children have an idea of the sequence of events and what their role should be. Dennis helps the children in his prekindergarten classroom learn the routine by posting photographs of children engaged in each of the day's events in sequence on the daily routine board (see Figure 5–2). Children in Dennis's preschool class know that they will get to work and play at their choice of activity when they first arrive at school and that there will be a time to gather together about mid-morning. They know where they can fix and eat their snack when they are ready for it. They know where to put their coats and belongings when they arrive, and they know where to find the materials they might need for a project. If they forget the next activity in the sequence, Dennis takes them to the routine board and discusses what will happen next. This is particularly important when children are worried about when their parents will return or when they are anticipating an exciting event such as having a visitor in the classroom.

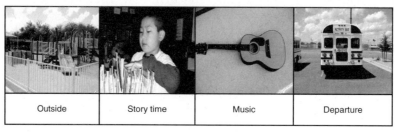

FIGURE 5–2 Picture Routine Board

Dennis purposefully plans his routines around children's needs; he alternates periods of active exploration with more quiet times and plans for daily outdoor play. He does this to prevent behavior problems that arise when children are expected to be quiet for long periods of time or when they are overexcited and need some downtime. Although Dennis follows the same routine each day, the exact timing of transitions between activities is based on his observations of the children in his preschool program. Using these observations, he can determine how the change in activities will affect the work students have in progress. One of Dennis' goals is to be sensitive to children's needs for extended periods of uninterrupted concentration. He is aware that it takes young children time to set up quality play and exploration and wants to make sure they have time to finish what they have started. Dennis also knows that children have long attention spans when they are doing something important to them, and he has made a conscious decision to build on this strength by not reducing the children's ability to concentrate by making them constantly change activities.

When it appears that most of the youngsters may be winding down on their choice-time activities and reaching closure, Dennis moves around the room, telling each child that it will be group time in 5 minutes. This advance warning allows children to finish what they are doing and mentally prepare to move on. Occasionally a child will be too engrossed to quit and will ask to be excused from group or to join in a few minutes. Dennis's respect for children and their work comes through as he honors these requests. When Dennis can't honor a child's request for more time, he takes the time to explain his reasoning and helps the child plan for alternative arrangements, such as saving the work in a protected area of the room until the child has a chance to complete it. See Figure 5–3 for a sample prekindergarten schedule.

It is equally important to honor the social needs of primary-age children. They too benefit from a consistent daily routine that offers them the flexibility to spend a bit more time on activities in which they are deeply engaged. Teachers in

Pre-K Daily Schedule		
8:00–8:20	Arrival and Morning Meeting	Children check in on attendance board, select lunch preference (i.e., buy or pack), share news, and discuss the day's events.
8:20–9:20	Center Activities	Children share plans and work on self-selected activities in a variety of centers (e.g., art, math, literacy, dramatic play, blocks, science, etc.). Teachers work with children, extending content knowledge and documenting student work.
9:20–9:40	Snack Time	
9:40–10:10	Small-Group Activities	Children work with teacher on small-group projects.
10:10–10:40	Outdoor Recess	
10:40–11:00	Shared Reading and Departure	Whole-group reading/children share reading responsibilities with teacher. Children also share work in progress, discuss the day's events, prepare the classroom for the next day, and organize belongings for departure.

FIGURE 5–3 Sample Prekindergarten Schedule

primary-grade classrooms not only have to consider children's needs when planning their schedules, but they must also consider organizational needs. For example, principals plan the schedules for lunch times, recess, and specialists (e.g., physical education, music, art) by taking the needs of all children and staff into account. While this reality may make planning the primary-grade schedule a bit more difficult, it is just as important to provide older children with a consistent daily routine that offers a balance of activities and options for flexibility during transitions between activities or classrooms. See Figure 5–4 for a sample primary-grade schedule.

Making Transitions

Many discipline problems occur during transition times, when children are moving from one activity or one place to another. Some children's temperaments can't handle the noise and movement associated with transitions in a child-centered classroom (Hyson, 2004). These youngsters need help figuring out how to cope. Most transition-time behavior problems happen because teachers unrealistically expect children to wait patiently for too long while other children get ready to join them. Adults who respect children do not waste their time with prolonged periods of waiting. If they do, you can almost guarantee that children will be clever enough to find some way to alleviate their boredom. Unfortunately, this activity usually takes the form of poking or pushing the person in front of them. Few teachers appreciate these creative outlets.

PEARSON
myeducationlab

To view an example of how teachers transition students from one activity to another, go to MyEducationLab and select the topic "Guiding Children." Under Activities and Applications, watch the video Transitioning: "Stand Up . . .".

Primary-Grade Daily Schedule		
8:00–8:30	Arrival and Morning Meeting	Children check in on attendance board, select lunch preference (i.e., buy or pack), share news, and discuss the day's events.
8:30–10:00	Literacy Workshop	Reading centers, guided reading, independent reading, writer's workshop.
10–10:30	Snack and Morning Recess	
10:30–11:30	Math Workshop	Children work on the problem of the day, math centers, and teacher-directed math groups.
11:30–12:15	Lunch and Recess	
12:15–12:45	Shared Reading	Whole-group reading/children share reading responsibilities with teacher.
12:45–1:45	Project Work Integrating Science and Social Studies	Children work on long-term projects emphasizing science and social studies content. They apply previously learned reading and mathematics skills during their investigations and presentations.
1:45–2:15	Specials	Physical education, art, and music on rotating days.
2:15–2:45	Community Meeting	Children share work in progress, discuss the day's events, prepare the classroom for the next day, and organize belongings for departure.
2:45	Dismissal	

FIGURE 5–4   Sample Primary-Grade Schedule

∞ Mrs. Jensen dislikes having to line up her students and make them walk all together in a row. She knows that waiting in line is terribly boring for them and invites behavior problems. When her students go out for recess, she lets them leave individually or in small groups as they get ready. At the beginning of the school year, she spent time with her class discussing and practicing good manners when walking through the elementary school hallways. Her children generally remember to walk instead of run and to keep their voices down. When they forget, their classmates remind them. Not having lines is less trouble for Mrs. Jensen and her students and causes fewer discipline problems.

The librarian, Mrs. Hill, insists on lines, so Mrs. Jensen's class gets practice in lining up when they go to the library. Instead of making the students who get ready quickly wait around and be bored while she gives her attention to the procrastinators, Mrs. Jensen creates some action of her own in the line. She leads the group in their favorite songs and finger plays to head off inappropriate kinds of activity. This approach also hurries the stragglers faster than nagging does; they are eager to join in the fun.

Mrs. Jensen uses a similar approach when she is gathering children together for group time. If it takes a while for everyone to arrive, she engages

Transition times are difficult for young children. Provide activities to help them pass the time.

in a discussion with those who are there. She often uses this time to help children evaluate their activities, with questions such as, "What book did you read today?" At other times, she asks children to share their writing or progress on project work with the group. ∾

Getting to and from the mid-morning gathering are the only significant transitions children must make in the morning preschool component of the Midway Children's Center day. An extra, time-consuming transition is avoided by having outdoor play just before children go home at noon. That way, they are already in their coats when it is time to leave. Dennis's use of advance warning helps most children get prepared for a change of activity. When they are not interrupted in the middle of a project, they are much more agreeable. Keeping transitions to a minimum also keeps disruptions to a minimum. For most of the morning, youngsters are free to change learning activities as they are individually ready to do so.

When group time is over, Dennis avoids a stampede to the snack table by making a game out of sending a few children at a time. Sometimes he says, "Everyone wearing stripes today may go to the snack table." Next it might be those with plaid or print designs on their clothing. On other days, Dennis focuses on hair or eye color. Sometimes he holds up name cards to excuse the children one at a time; the youngsters practice reading their own and their friends' names to determine whose turn it is. These games keep children involved and learning during their short wait. Those who arrive at the snack table first must also have something to do besides waiting. They either need to be allowed to begin eating immediately, or else another adult must be there to engage them in a song or activity.

Those children who remain at the center for the full-day program are faced with a number of transitions: lunch time, nap time, getting up from nap, going outside again, and parent arrival time. Each of these changes requires that children change gears and move from one mode of activity to another. Most also involve movement of groups from one place to another. Both aspects of transition are frequently upsetting to youngsters (Hemmeter, Ostrosky, Artman, & Kinder, 2008). Young children need the support of teachers they know and are comfortable with as they move through these activities. Teachers may not consider transition times to be central to their educational goals, but the ways in which children are moved from place to place, or activity to activity, affects how children will approach the new task or environment and how much they will learn.

Tuning in to children as individuals will help remind you not to herd them into the next activity. One key to making smooth transitions lies in not unduly rushing children. As soon as you start to hurry kids, they immediately start to rebel. Respecting individual differences in youngsters is another important guideline for smooth transitions (Hemmeter et al., 2008). Joshua is always hungry at lunchtime and eagerly gets going on his meal. Anna makes slower transitions and has trouble tearing herself away from the dramatic play she is usually involved in. These two children require different treatment. Forcing Anna into Joshua's schedule won't work for her.

Mrs. Jensen used increased flexibility to allow for differences and solve a problem at the end of daily choice time.

> Children in Mrs. Jensen's classroom were not being cooperative about cleaning up after choice time and getting ready to go out to recess. She wasn't interested in Miss Wheeler's approach of giving out candy as a reward to get children to clean up. Instead, she carefully watched to see what was happening instead of clean-up.
>
> What she noticed was that many children were just not ready to stop what they were doing because they hadn't had enough time. Many were bouncing around for about 10 minutes before they settled in to what they wanted to do with their choice time, and then didn't really have enough time to complete anything before they were told to clean up. She decided to try something radical for a public school: a choice of staying in or going outside to play. Since the primary playground was just outside her back door, she could allow children to go out during recess if and when they were ready.
>
> This plan worked very well, with clean-up coming after recess instead of before, and going much more smoothly. On nice days, some of the indoor activity flowed outdoors and children didn't have to choose between their choice-time project and being outdoors. >

Planning for transition times prevents behavior problems from occurring while children wait for the next activity. As noted, some teachers use songs or movement activities to ease transition times. Others see transitions as an additional opportunity for learning. In these classrooms you'll see children saying tongue twisters (practicing phonological awareness), counting the number of cracks in the sidewalk on the way to recess (mathematics), or solving riddles posed by the teacher (problem solving). Large-motor activities also make waiting more pleasurable; marching in place, standing on your tiptoes, or tapping different body parts are activities that all children enjoy. Planning transition activities reduces behavior problems by helping children to learn how to pass time constructively

Waiting in Line	Activity-to-Activity Transitions	Arrival and Departure Transitions
Sing a song.	Describe children by hair color, eye color, letter in first name, clothing, family members (e.g., if you have a sister . . .), birthdays, etc.	Sign in on a large piece of paper. Pre-writers can draw a picture.
Do a fingerplay.	Release by the first letter in their names (e.g., If your name begins with . . .).	Move name tag from "not-here" to "here" on an attendance chart.
Solve mental math problems.	Give a 5-minute warning (e.g., In 5 minutes, we will clean up).	Walk with a buddy.
Play Simon says.	Turn on music to signal a change of activities.	Make a train.
Rhythmic	Randomly select names from a basket.	Walk like an animal, fly like a plane, clapping, tip-toe like a ballerina, etc.

FIGURE 5–5   Transition Activities

and it offers additional opportunities for playful learning. Figure 5–5 lists additional suggestions for transitions activities for prekindergarten and primary-age children.

Group Time

Group time serves many different purposes and has many different names. We bring children together in groups for stories, songs, lessons, planning, and problem solving. Whether it is called *story time, circle time, class meeting,* or something else, gathering together as a group is essential for building a sense of community in a classroom. This feeling of belonging and caring for one another is necessary for developing a social conscience. When youngsters meet together regularly, sharing rituals such as favorite songs and stories, they come to see themselves as a group. As a group, they can discuss mutual problems and create solutions that transcend the wishes of the individual (DeVries & Zan, 1994). This process promotes moral reasoning and de-centering from an egocentric viewpoint. Children in classrooms with a sense of community tend to be more cooperative, supportive of one another, and empathetic (Bartel, 2005; Noddings, 2005).

To get the most out of group time, teachers need to truly encourage student input and get children thinking. Some group times don't really engage children's minds, but instead drag them through a series of repetitive rote exercises. How engaged are children in merely reciting the responses to questions such as, "What day of the week is this?" "What is today's date?" and "How many days have we been in school?" We see lots of bored youngsters and frustrated teachers during this kind of group time (Beneke, Ostrosky, & Katz, 2008). We also see children getting into trouble because they can't sit still and give the desired responses. Group time is much more productive when it is spent helping children work on intellectual or moral issues they care about.

As important as group time can be, bringing young children together often creates trouble. Teachers complain about feeling like police officers as they continually remind children to sit down or pay attention at group time. Young children talk when they aren't supposed to; they wriggle and squirm and poke one another, and they even just walk away. Teachers with child development knowledge realize that these behaviors are related to children's maturational stage. They understand that young children are not good at sitting still or being quiet, that they have trouble dealing with large groups, and that they aren't good at pretending to be interested in things they don't understand (Beneke et al., 2008). Many of these teachers seriously question the appropriateness of a group time at the preschool level; some question it in kindergarten as well. Yet, these same teachers usually wish to have at least a brief period of togetherness.

Successful group times cannot be passive listening experiences for youngsters. They must truly involve all children in the group activities and discussions (Beneke et al., 2008). Some teachers find that a circle seating arrangement works best with this goal. A circle allows children to see one another during discussions and read body language as well as hear words. The group circle is consistent with a child-centered approach and with the purposes of group interaction; the teacher at the front of a group suggests a different purpose.

Another approach allows choice about participation in some group activities. Dennis is able to allow choice with his preschool group because there are other adults available to supervise children who do not choose to join. Dennis tries to make his circle time so attractive that youngsters will want to join in and stay involved. If he doesn't get much enthusiasm, he treats that response as useful feedback regarding the appropriateness or relevance of what he is offering at group time. For instance, if several children leave during the story he is reading, he might think twice about sharing that story again.

Dennis allows for a partly involved presence at group time as another way of meeting individual needs. Some youngsters can't seem to sit and listen without having something to occupy their hands. Therefore, children in his program are allowed to look at books or work on puzzles at the back of the group area. Only activities that are quiet and do not disturb the group discussion are allowed. Allowing quiet activities lets children who might not otherwise be able to cope with the enforced passivity benefit from the discussions and stories. Through this flexibility, Dennis provides a transition into group time for children who need it.

In other programs, teachers feel strongly about full participation but try hard to make group time more compatible with the needs of young children. They keep the time short and respond to signals from youngsters that they have reached their limit. Frequent opportunities to move and actively participate extend the amount of time children can cope with group times. Songs and rhymes that involve full-body movement provide useful breaks. Nevertheless, 15 minutes may be long enough for most preschoolers to be involved in group time. This time period will gradually increase as children get older, but teachers need to take their cues from the children.

Many will argue that youngsters need to learn the social skills involved in a traditional group gathering because the next teacher will expect it. Others reject that argument on the grounds that children will more easily gain those skills

Watch children's body language during large group activities to determine if they have reached their limit.

when they are a little older. They believe there is no point in putting everyone through the misery of pushing the skills before youngsters are ready. This argument is similar to the prevailing view of toilet training: Wait until the child is ready, and it will happen quickly and painlessly.

Waiting a Turn

We have already talked about problems caused by waiting in line and waiting for groups to start. They are invitations to discipline problems as well as a serious waste of children's time. However, there is another kind of waiting that causes just as many problems: when children must wait their turn.

Waiting for a turn is incredibly hard on young children for several reasons. One reason is that they don't have a sense of time. Because time is an abstraction, telling a child to wait 5 minutes for a turn with the tricycle is meaningless. Another problem is that young children don't understand why they must wait. They can't see things from another person's viewpoint, so they don't relate to another child's claim. Colin wants the tricycle. That desire is the only reality for him. The fact that Alex also wants it is irrelevant to Colin. With help from adults, youngsters gradually learn about the needs and feelings of others. With experience and maturation, they also learn to approximate time spans. While youngsters are in the process of learning, understanding teachers can help them cope.

∞ Kenji ran into the large-muscle room. He was eager to get onto the climbing tower, his favorite place to play. Suddenly, a teacher came to tell him that he must get off and wait his turn. There were already four other children on the climbing tower. Four is the limit; that's the rule.

Kenji looked confused and sad but climbed down. He gazed longingly at the children climbing and shouting. He kept asking Sheri, the adult in charge, when it would be his turn. Gradually, tears welled up in his eyes. Sheri realized that Kenji was in distress. She tried to explain to him that the other children were in the room first. Seeing that her explanations were getting nowhere, Sheri thought about other alternatives. Center rules allow youngsters to use equipment until they decide they are finished, so she couldn't even promise Kenji a certain time for his turn. She tried to distract him with suggestions about the block-building or woodworking centers. But Kenji was determined to be there to stake his claim as soon as someone got off the climbing tower.

Then Sheri remembered the sign-up sheet that helped children wait their turn to hold the new pet rabbit last week. She asked Kenji if he would like to start a sign-up sheet to use the climbing tower. He agreed to this plan and helped Sheri locate paper, tape, and a marker. Kenji wrote his name, 4-year-old style, on the page and taped it to the wall near the climber. He seemed to feel better now that his claim to a turn was officially in writing. He said he would wait in the block center nearby. Sheri assured him she would call as soon as someone got off the climber. Without someone hovering nearby waiting for a turn, the pressure to stay on the climber eased. Soon there was a vacancy, and Sheri notified Kenji. He had been helped to cope with a hard situation. His feelings were respected even though he didn't immediately get his way. The experience helped him build understanding and trust in the waiting process. ∞

Many teachers use sign-up sheets to ease turn taking and waiting. This approach fosters literacy development as well as social development. Of course, it works better if there aren't so many children in the group that it takes days for everyone to get a turn. When children are limited to a set amount of time for a turn, the sign-up sheet can be combined with an egg timer. Watching the timer ticking away or seeing the salt pour from one side to the other can help youngsters to experience the passage of time, making it a little less abstract. Of course, these timed waits must be short in order to be humane.

Much of children's waiting involves waiting for help from an adult. Children have to wait less if there are more adults available to them. Public school classrooms generally not only have larger groups than recommended, but also have too few adults for the number of children. The maximum group size in kindergarten and the primary grades should be no more than 15 to 18 children with one teacher. If the group size is up to 24, there should be two adults. For preschool-age groups, it is necessary to have two adults responsible for no more than 20 youngsters (NAEYC, 2006). See Figure 5–6 to see how to prevent discipline problems.

Working with Families

Parent volunteers can make a major contribution to planning and implementing an engaging curriculum and a smoothly running classroom. Families can contribute real materials for children's investigations, and they can serve as "experts"

| • Enough adults to engage children
• Interesting activities
• Appropriate spaces
• Predictable routines
• Intellectual challenges | Prevents → | • Loss of instructional time
• Lack of engagement
• Overcrowding
• Confusion
• Off-task behaviors |

FIGURE 5–6 Preventing Discipline Problems

on topics children are studying. They can also improve the ratio of adults to children during project work, cutting down on the length of time children wait for adult assistance and providing support when problems arise.

When families are involved in children's learning, it sends a clear message that all of the adults who care for them think school is important; therefore, the child also believes school is important. Additionally, when parents spend time helping, they tend to gain a better understanding of the school's curriculum and the classroom routines. Their increased understanding of the teacher's goals and methods makes parents better able to support their children's learning at home. The messages parents send to their children about school last a lifetime, so it is a priority to help them feel welcomed at school.

There are a variety of approaches to family involvement. Kindergarten and primary-grade teachers generally ask for parent volunteers at the beginning of the school year. Many find that posting a list of specific jobs and asking parents to sign up is a good strategy. Parents whose work doesn't allow them to spend time at school may volunteer for something that can be done at home in the evening. Some preschools follow the same pattern, but cooperative preschools exhibit the ultimate in parent involvement. Cooperative preschools are run by parents who determine school goals and procedures, administer the budget, collect tuition, and hire the teacher. Parents take turns as teacher assistants to create appropriate adult–child ratios for their programs. Child-care programs generally exist because parents are not available during the day. However, with encouragement, parents may find it rewarding to visit during their lunch time and even to take occasional time off to be part of their youngster's child-care day.

CONCLUSION

Prevention of discipline problems is based on caring relationships with children and families. Prevention of behavior problems also has much to do with respecting children. Respecting children involves making it easier for them to meet school expectations, including their parents in their education, accepting their emotional needs as valid, planning curriculum carefully to fit their level of development, helping them learn to think about others, and using their time and energy wisely. When you do these things, you will find that most children are more cooperative, hardworking, and committed to learning.

∽ *FOR FURTHER THOUGHT*

1. Observe a planning session at a preschool or local elementary school. How do the teachers plan to keep children active and engaged in learning? How do they use their knowledge of individual children to plan instruction? How do the curriculum goals of the program influence the teachers' instructional planning?
2. Observe a large group-time activity in a prekindergarten or primary classroom. Note any behavior problems that occur. Using information from the chapter, explain what the teacher might have done to prevent the behavior problem(s). If you do not witness any behavior problems during your observation, describe the strategies used by the teacher to prevent them from occurring.
3. Interview a group of young children about their interests or what they would like to learn. Describe how you might use the children's interests to plan an integrated activity.
4. Plan a daily schedule for a group of young children in a full-day prekindergarten program. Justify the rationale for your schedule using information from the chapter.
5. Try some techniques described in this chapter to help youngsters wait for a turn or transition from one place to another. Analyze the successes and the failures to learn from them.
6. A problem to solve: The kindergartners were lining up to go to the library. Tony got into line and immediately began pushing Tim, who was in front of him. Next, Tony grabbed Tim's arm and then began playing with his hair.
   a. What is the probable cause of this problem?
   b. How can you best deal with it now?
   c. How can you prevent similar situations in the future?

∽ *RECOMMENDED READINGS*

Bredekamp, S., & Rosegrant, T. (Eds). (1995). *Transforming early childhood curriculum and assessment* (Vol. 2). Washington, DC: National Association for the Education of Young Children.

Chaille, C., & Britain, L. (2003). *The young child as scientist: A Constructivist approach to early childhood science education.* New York: Longman.

Davidson, J. (1980). Wasted time: The ignored dilemma. *Young Children, 35*(1), 13–21.

Developmental Studies Center. (1998). *Ways we want our class to be: Class meetings that build commitment to kindness and learning.* Oakland, CA: Author.

Hyson, M. (2004). *The emotional development of young children: Building an emotion-centered curriculum.* New York: Teachers College Press.

Jalongo, M. R. (2007). Beyond benchmarks and scores: Reasserting the role of motivation and interest in children's academic achievement. An ACEI position paper. *Childhood Education*, International Focus Issue, Association of Children's Education International.

Jones, E., & Reynolds, G. (1992). *The play's the thing: Teachers' roles in children's play.* New York: Teachers College Press.

Kamii, C. (2000). *Young children reinvent arithmetic: Implications of Piaget's theory.* New York: Teachers College Press.

Katz, L. G., & Chard, S. C. (2000). *Engaging children's minds: The project approach.* Norwood, NJ: Ablex.

Koplow, L. (2002). *Creating schools that heal: Real-life solutions.* New York: Teachers College Press.

National Association for the Education of Young Children/National Association Early Childhood Specialists in State Departments of Education. (2003). *Early childhood curriculum, assessment, and program evaluation: Building an effective accountability system in programs birth through age 8.* Washington, DC: Author.

Vance, E., & Weaver, P. (2002). *Class meetings: Young children solving problems together.* Washington, DC: National Association for the Education of Young Children.

∞ *Chapter* **6** ∞
Teaching Desirable Behavior Through Example

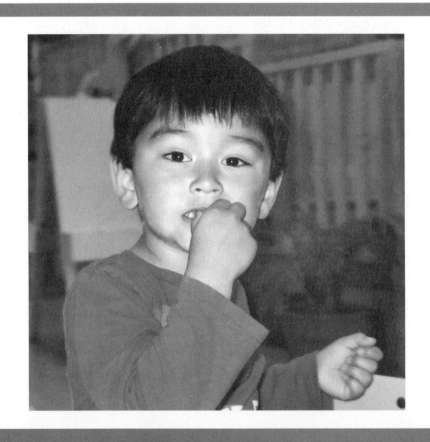

GUIDING QUESTIONS

- How do observation and imitation influence behavior?
- How do role models influence behavior?
- How can adults use literacy to model behavior?
- How does the media influence behavior?

Discipline is a teaching activity, and teaching by example is a powerfully effective method. Children use the examples of admired adults as they construct their own ideas of appropriate behavior (De Schipper, Riksen-Walraven, Geurts, & Derksen, 2008). Therefore, teacher and parent examples are productive methods of guidance and discipline. The more that teachers take the time to model appropriate expressions of emotions and action, the less time they will spend on discipline issues as the year progresses (Brady, Forton, Porter, & Wood, 2003). This chapter will give examples of how models of desirable behavior help children learn to behave in socially acceptable ways (Bandura, 1986).

Sometimes the cause of inappropriate behavior is that children have learned from inappropriate role models. If you doubt that children pick up the example of adults, watch them during pretend play (Nielson & Christie, 2007). Parents and teachers are often embarrassed as they see children mimic parts of adult behavior they'd rather not have repeated. Children also imitate the behavior they see on television and movies, with some extremely antisocial results (Wilson, 2008). Positive adult models are crucial to counteracting such pervasive and violent influences (Wilson, 2008).

When adults provide examples and children imitate them, we say that adults are *modeling* behavior. Let's look at how children learn desirable and useful ways of behaving through modeling.

MODELING

Bandura developed the *social cognitive theory of human functioning* in the late 1980s (Bandura, 1986). He believes that people are active agents in the construction of knowledge. He says that learning is a process of reciprocal determination—children and adults use observation and imitation to learn new information. In essence, the basic tenant of social cognitive theory is that people are products and producers of their environments. While Bandura agrees that modeling plays a role in learning, his research shows that people adapt and reconstruct the actions they observe to meet their own goals, capabilities, and circumstances. It is Bandura's focus on cognition that differentiates his social cognitive theory from behaviorist learning theories.

Bandura believes we are products of our environment because we learn, in part, through vicarious experiences. When we witness something in our environment, we store it in our memory through symbolization—the creation of visual images and verbal codes that correspond to what we witness in the environment. If an event we observe is extremely important to us, we produce an image of the event and a verbal script, or a set of rules, to accompany our mental image. When placed in a situation where we might need such information, we will call upon the mental rules we have created about the event and modify them to fit the circumstances of our situation. Thus, children do not merely imitate the actions of others, but utilize models of behavior that they have created through the cognitive process of symbolization.

When faced with an experience that requires us to call upon our mental rules, we also use forethought. Forethought is a cognitive function that involves planning a course of action, anticipating likely consequences, and setting goals to guide and regulate our activities. It is during the planning phase of problem solving that we are most likely to sift through all of the experiences we have stored in our memories to find one or more that applies to our current situation. Once we find an experience in our memories that relates to our current situation, we *reflect* upon the visual and verbal scripts we have assigned to the model to determine how, or if, we might apply it to our current circumstances.

During reflection, we think about our ability to re-create and organize the actions stored in our memories to meet our immediate needs. Bandura calls this self-efficacy—our belief in our ability to re-create a series of specific actions in order to solve a problem or manage a situation. Motivation corresponds to our level of self-efficacy. If we perceive ourselves to be capable of combining and carrying out a series of actions to solve a problem or meet a goal, we are more motivated to do so. Once we have selected a model, thought about our ability to use the model effectively, and feel motivated to do so, we reproduce or re-create the actions in an attempt to meet our goal(s).

After we reproduce the actions, we use self-regulation to judge the outcomes of our behavior. If our actions were successful, we will most likely try them again. If our action was not successful, we either modify it for future use or decide to abandon the action altogether. According to Bandura, it is our use of the cognitive functions of *symbolization, forethought, reflection, recreation,* and *self-regulation* that make us producers of knowledge rather than passive recipients who merely imitate the actions and thoughts of others. Now let's look at how you can use your knowledge of these processes to teach children desirable behaviors.

INTERACTION STYLE

Teachers with a positive disposition tend to show more respect for children's autonomy, and provide higher-quality instruction than teachers with an unhappy disposition (De Schipper et al., 2008). In turn, children in these classrooms display higher self-concepts and autonomous behavior (De Schipper et al., 2008). A teacher who speaks in a kind, respectful tone to students tends to have a classroom where children speak more kindly and respectfully to one another. However, a teacher who uses sarcasm and put-downs to keep kids under control will certainly generate more of that type of interaction among students.

To view an example of how teacher and child rules come into conflict, go to MyEducationLab and select the topic "Guiding Children." Under Activities and Applications, watch the video "How Many Fingers Did You Use?".

Some classrooms and centers have a warm and friendly feeling as you walk into them, and others exude tension. The teacher usually sets the tone for the classroom, with children taking on the interaction style of the adult (DeVries & Zan, 1994). Likewise, teachers who are sensitive, responsive, and involved with their children have youngsters who behave in ways that make them more popular with their peers (Rimm-Kaufmann, Fan, Chiu, & You, 2007). Children notice when adults respectfully consider children's ideas and feelings. From this example, they gain both attitudes and skills for getting along with other children and peacefully negotiating solutions to disagreements. Teachers who exhibit very controlling behaviors are setting an example of demanding their own way without regard for others. If that attitude is the adult example, then youngsters will learn to behave in the same way.

EXPRESSING FEELINGS

How do you deal with your emotions? Do you hold them in and try to hide the fact that you are upset? Or do you find yourself "flying off the handle," and yelling when things go wrong? The holding-in approach might sound like a more desirable model for kids, but we believe it is actually worse for them—and you—in the long run. You may know from your own experience, or from others who are close to you, that suppressed emotions will eventually surface in some form or other and can cause debilitating emotional and physical problems. As discussed later in this chapter, a person's culture often determines how emotions are expressed. Cultural norms affect how both teachers and students express their emotions, and their expectations of one another. Some people with loving, responsive families are taught to completely suppress their negative emotions. Teachers who had this experience in their childhoods may need to overcome some of their discomfort with expressions of anger or sadness. Looking at our own life experiences is an important step in our ability to model healthy expressions of our emotions.

While we don't advocate that teachers "stuff" their emotions, throwing a tantrum to express your feelings isn't productive either. Adults who have learned to accept and work with their emotions achieve a socially acceptable medium between the extremes of too little emotional outlet and too much. Many find that it is important to let off steam as it arises instead of allowing it to accumulate into a blowup. Teachers with this kind of self-knowledge can provide a beneficial model for youngsters. Figure 6–1 provides a summary of the ways in which teachers can model behavior.

Letting It Show

You teach a lot when you share your feelings with children and allow them to see how you express your frustration, excitement, sorrow, or joy. Beginning in infancy, children acquire what is called a "like-me" developmental framework (Meltzoff, 2007). First children learn about the consequences of their actions by observing the actions of others. As children test the actions they've witnessed,

Behavior	Example
Let it show	I'm frustrated because I can't get the Smart Board to work properly.
Apologize	I'm sorry, Julie. I see that you did put your paper in your cubbie. I was looking at Carrie's cubbie and not yours. That's why I couldn't find your paper.
Accept feelings	I can tell that you're disappointed that you are not the line-leader today. Let's look at the calendar and see when it is going to be your turn.
Teach about diversity	Yes, my skin is a different color than your skin. My skin is a mahogany color and yours is light peach.
Show kindness	You spilled your juice on your shirt. I can help you clean it up.
Engage in risk taking	Pronouncing that name is difficult for me, but I will learn to say it correctly if I keep practicing.
Help with responsibilities	Wow, we have a lot to clean up today. Why don't you hand me all of the triangle blocks and I'll put them on the shelf.
Keep your promises	I am working with Tommy right now. I will put your name on our appointment list so I don't forget to meet with you as soon as I'm finished helping Tommy.
Show, don't tell	Walk with the scissors pointing to the floor. Keep your desk or work area free of clutter. Pretend to put on your life jacket before getting into the rocking boat with children.
Follow the rules	Sit where you want children to sit. If you want them on the floor, don't sit on the table.
Share similarities	I have a brother too. His name is Jim and he is bigger than I am. I like cinnamon toast too!
Be likable	Smile, show your sense of humor, and join activities that children initiate.

FIGURE 6–1 Model Expected Behavior

they come to understand not only the consequences of their own actions, but the intentions of others who perform similar actions (Meltzoff, 2007). As a result of these early imitative experiences, children come to see a "like-me," "like-them" relationship—which is the foundation for emotive expression, perspective taking, and empathy.

Children learn the most when adults talk about how they feel, also letting it show in their face, body language, and tone of voice. By listening and observing, children begin to understand what feelings are, what situations are likely to create which feelings, and how to express feelings (Hyson, 2004). The daily life of the school offers ample opportunity for modeling the expression of emotions. But, as Hyson (2004) says, "Early childhood educators should not be content to leave this process entirely to chance. Competent, thoughtful professionals consciously decide what emotions and emotion-related behavior to model" (p. 130).

∞ Mrs. Jensen was pushed past her limit one day by the several children in her classroom with behavioral disorders. Her friends always told her that the "reward" for being a great teacher is that you get more of the needier children. But that thought was of no comfort when she was being kicked and hit on a daily basis. Then there was the additional problem of trying to keep the other children safe from those who were out of control.

Mrs. Jensen's voice was loud, yet controlled as she told the students, "Kids, I need your help. I am getting too frustrated right now to help anyone. I am going to take 2 minutes to sit and breathe in a calming place. I will talk with those of you who need me when I have calmed myself down." While the kids stared with curiosity, Mrs. Jensen walked to the window and took some deep breaths with her eyes closed. She reminded herself what her goals were for this class, and that the weekend was almost here. Slowly she opened her eyes and returned her attention to the classroom. She spoke more quietly than before as she told the class, "I feel more calm now and I will try to stay that way while I talk to those of you who need my help." As the children took their turns talking with Mrs. Jensen, her calming mood seemed to be contagious and the frenzy began to mellow. ∞

After all her years of teaching, Mrs. Jensen has learned when she has had enough. This time she could tell she had reached the limits of her patience. She knew it would be good for her, and a good model for the children, to take a break. She really did feel better after stepping away from the chaos and taking some deep breaths.

A personal time-out is often the best answer when you are overwhelmed. Obviously this is more easily accomplished when there are several adults in charge of a group of children. Unfortunately, the option of leaving the scene is seldom available for public school teachers. Even if you are the only adult with a group of children, you can still stop and take a deep breath when things begin to feel overwhelming. You do not need to respond instantly to the problem. However you do it, your model of how to calm yourself will teach your students best if you explain to them what you are doing. Children benefit in two ways when teachers briefly remove themselves, either physically or emotionally, when they become overstressed: The cooling-off period helps the teacher to deal more rationally with child behavior, and the example set by the teacher shows children a useful way of handling their own stress.

This is just one of the many possible social skills that can be taught by adult example. It is helpful to think about the individual needs and developmental stages of children in a class when determining what emotions and behaviors to model. Your priorities and personality will also determine how and what emotions you choose to deliberately express to your class. You can make a point to express some of your emotions during your daily routine tasks or make a special time for dealing with some more complex emotions or issues. Dennis tells the kids around him when he is feeling frustrated with the stapler that won't work. He also uses puppets during circle time to discuss feeling both sad and excited about the vacation time ahead. As mentioned in Chapter 2, there are packaged curriculum programs addressing many of the important lessons about feelings, but Bandura contends that observing an adult who is actually coping with an emotional situation is much more likely to help children learn.

Apologizing

Sometimes even wonderful teachers get overwrought and lose control before they have a chance to take a break. This offers a teaching opportunity also, as in the following example.

∽ Dennis usually didn't mind the children's inevitable messes, but the director's reminder to "spruce up" for open house that night had him on edge. It seemed like everywhere he looked was a disaster area. He snapped at Anna when she ripped the border edging on his bulletin board while she was trying to reach the shelf next to it. He complained to Jackson that he was spilling sand from the sand table. Then Dennis saw the easel careen forward, with violet, green, and red paint spewed all over the adjacent block area. He let out a "Hey!" so loud it silenced most of the class. Maddie, who had tripped on the easel, cowered and looked fearful of punishment.

Dennis took a few deep breaths, recovered his composure, and smiled to reassure the frightened girl. Then he told the class, "Wow, I'm really getting nervous about all the people coming to see our classroom at the open house tonight. When I saw that paint spill, I got upset. I'm sorry I yelled. I've been pretty irritable about messes all day because I want our room to look nice when your families come to visit tonight. I'll bet you want it to look nice, too. What can we do to fix this problem?" The children were eager to help and immediately got busy cleaning up the paint. ∽

Dennis apologized for frightening the children and explained his feelings to them. Then they worked together on a solution. Because there is so much inappropriate expression of feelings in the world, and in some children's homes, it is essential that schools model better ways. For instance, how we express our anger makes the difference between a violent situation and a nonviolent one, and between a destructive use of anger and a productive one (McKay & Maybelle, 2004; Sanders et al., 2004).

ACCEPTING FEELINGS

As teachers acknowledge and appropriately express their emotions, they demonstrate to children that emotions are not wrong, though there are good ways and bad ways of expressing them. Teachers also have the opportunity to model acceptable ways of expressing all emotions. This is particularly important for negative emotions, such as anger, sadness, or even shame. Some children have rarely seen appropriate expressions of these difficult emotions. These emotions may be expressed in violent ways in their household or may be denied altogether in their experience.

Sometimes adults try to deny children's negative feelings because they so desperately want them to be happy, or they don't want to deal with the potential tantrums that could result from children not getting their way. Therefore, some adults try to make bad feelings go away by distracting children with treats or activities. A common response to children's unhappiness is often, "Don't cry; do you want a cookie?" Some adults punish or belittle children when they feel strong emotions. For example, "You do not hate your friend; you will go to time-out if I hear that again." Although well intentioned, these responses don't help children learn to deal with their feelings effectively. Instead, they may learn that their feelings are wrong and end up feeling guilty (Plattner, 2003). This guilt, added to repressed feelings, is likely to result in negative behavior.

Instead of trying to make children's bad feelings disappear, you are already helping children learn to accept and express their feelings when you accept and express your own feelings. Beyond modeling, identifying and acknowledging children's emotions are a critical part of teaching them how to deal with their emotions in a healthy way.

Permit children to experience and express a range of emotions.

Use Your Words

When Amelia says, "I hate you!" she is expressing anger. The anger may or may not be justified from your perspective, but she does have that feeling and it needs to come out. Young children usually lack the language skills to express their feelings adequately. Your role as the teacher can be to help the child clarify feelings by modeling more appropriate words. In this case, your response might be "It sounds like you are angry with me."

If you can find out what made Amelia angry, you can help her find the words to say specifically what she is upset about. Perhaps she wanted to be the line leader, and you chose someone else. You can accept her feelings while helping her express them more suitably. This approach involves demonstrating expressive language for her, perhaps by saying, "I can tell you are very *disappointed* that you weren't chosen." Then you can let Amelia know that it is more productive to tell you that she wanted to be the line leader than to say she hates you. Teaching effective communication will be discussed further in Chapter 7.

By allowing children to experience a range of emotions and helping children to name their feelings, you are teaching them valuable, lifelong skills. Important learning can result from facing negative feelings. For instance, a child who has never faced the loneliness of being left out is less able to feel compassion for someone who is being excluded from a group. Children who experience empathy for their feelings will be able to treat others with empathy as well (Pfeifer, Iacoboni, Mazziotta, & Dapretto, 2008).

Acknowledging and Listening

Sometimes just acknowledging bad feelings and lending a listening ear can help a child get over them. Children who perceive social support from teachers display an increase in motivation toward academic and prosocial goals (Rimm-Kaufmann et al., 2007). Listening is one of the most powerful sources of social support we can offer children. Listening while children talk about their feelings, without telling them what to do, shows your acceptance of the child and his or her feelings. This is often all that children need. Children then free their energy to begin their own process of problem solving.

We can see the power of acceptance and acknowledgment in the following example. Jealousy of a new sibling is a common problem that most adults don't want to accept; however, Maureen provides Anzhelika with a safe place to feel her jealousy and begin to move beyond it.

∞ Anzhelika was glued to the goodbye window at preschool. She was trying to get her mother's attention for a wave, but her mother's back was to the window as she adjusted the baby's carseat. Maureen noticed the look on Anzhelika's face and asked if she'd like to step outside to catch her mom. Anzhelika spat back, "She's too busy with that baby!" and turned away, her face scrunched in anger and sorrow.

Maureen appreciated Anzhelika's irritation since she had been the only child in her family, too, until her brother came along and burst her bubble. She remembered what adults usually said to her when she was feeling sad about having to share her parents' attention, "You love your baby brother, don't you? He loves you. You are so lucky to be a big sister!" Maureen knew that Anzhelika wasn't feeling lucky. She said gently, "It's not always fun being the big sister is it?" Then she gave Anzhelika some time to respond. Anzhelika looked sad but didn't have anything to say.

Maureen sat down and asked if Anzhelika would like to sit on her lap. Anzhelika quickly accepted and settled into Maureen's lap. Maureen held her for a while and then told her, "I am a big sister too, and I remember feeling pretty angry at my mom when she was always holding my baby brother. I felt sad sometimes too." Anzhelika looked surprised and asked, "Do you like your brother?" Maureen thought for a moment and then said, "I didn't like him much when I was little because he was always taking my mom away from me." Anzhelika seemed relieved; she agreed and began to smile. Maureen was tempted to tell Anzhelika that she would like her sister one day, but she refrained. She knew that Anzhelika was hearing enough of that. Anzhelika then volunteered that her mom was going to pick her up and take her to the park, alone! Maureen cheered for Anzhelika and the two walked to the art table, where Anzhelika decided to make a picture for her mom. ∞

Anzhelika needed someone who could understand her and make her feel safe expressing her feelings. This may have been harder if Maureen didn't share a similar experience. Regardless, Maureen could still take the time to identify Anzhelika's feelings and give her some time to feel them without trying to talk her out of her feelings.

Gender and Emotions

Similarities can be particularly helpful in modeling, as we discuss later in this chapter. Male role models are especially important for little boys. However, actual brain function as well as social pressure tend to make it harder for males to deal with emotions. The old idea that big boys don't cry hasn't disappeared from society. Many men not only feel uncomfortable expressing sadness or fear, but they also have trouble expressing positive feelings of affection and caring. For some men, anger is the only emotion they can easily express. Therefore, it may be difficult for teachers to tell when some boys feel sadness, loneliness, or jealousy. Brain research demonstrates that processing emotions is more difficult for males than it is for females. Boys are more likely to become aggressive or withdrawn when confronted with an emotionally difficult situation. Experts propose that boys are slower to process their emotions and may first need a physical outlet to help access their emotions. Due to some boys' inherent difficulties dealing with emotions, helping them identify their feelings and put them into words is particularly important (Gurian, 2001).

Providing children with opportunities to learn about emotions from both male and female role models is important to children's development. When male teachers are not available, bringing in male volunteers from the community or older boys from upper grades can provide male mentors. This is especially important for boys without father figures at home (Gurian, 2001).

Dennis does his part to wipe out the macho stereotypes and gives boys and girls plenty of time and opportunities to express all of their feelings. He freely expresses affection for his young students with hugs, smiles, and verbal feedback, such as "I like being with you." He demonstrates his joy in small things: a sunny day, a delicious snack, or a child's artistic creation. He also shows feelings of sadness when the guinea pig dies. Although Dennis doesn't cover up his feelings of frustration when something goes wrong, he is careful to show negative feelings in ways he wants children to imitate. He knows the children are likely to follow his example, whether it is positive or negative.

Cultural Differences

As always, your cultural background, and that of the children you work with, is an important consideration as you deal with emotions in your classroom. Some children get very different messages at home about how to express emotions than what they get at school. Some children come from a culture that allows aggressive expressions of anger. Others come from a culture that does not allow for any expression of emotion (Hyson, 2004). Cultures also differ in the ways children are taught to show respect for others, beliefs about whom they should trust, and polite ways of speaking (Barrera & Corso, 2003). Whether to speak loudly or softly and whether to look at the person spoken to are examples of cultural variations on politeness. The many possible differences between home and school expectations emphasize the importance of getting to know parents and coming to a mutual agreement with them on behalf of their children. Asking families about their cultural norms helps to clear up any confusion or misunderstandings that occur due to differing expectations.

Perhaps your own cultural background makes you disagree with this text about the best ways of dealing with feelings. This book explains one viewpoint; your professional judgment will have to guide you in how to use this information in ways that work best for you and for your students.

CARING FOR OTHERS

You may have noticed that some youngsters have sharp tongues and say cruel things to other children, and others show concern for anyone having a hard time. Much of that behavior is learned through example. We now know that the brain is wired to mirror actions and emotions, and that the mirror neuron system in the brain plays an important role in social cognition (Pfeifer et al., 2008). We also know that children use adults as mirrors; they learn from watching others (Hyson & Molinaro, 2001). Because adults are powerful role models for young children, your example has a great impact. When adults model caring behaviors coupled with reminders about people's feelings, children learn to think about the impact of their words. In a classroom where students are being unkind to one another, the teacher needs to examine what type of role models children are experiencing.

Children's cultural backgrounds are important considerations in dealing with emotions at school.

Modeling Acceptance

There is an increasing amount of evidence that children emulate adults' implicit and explicit displays of prejudice (Sinclair, Dunn, & Lowery, 2005). Because of this, more and more early childhood teachers have come to recognize that teaching tolerance outright in the curriculum is as fundamental and as far-reaching as teaching children how to read (Teaching Tolerance, 1997). The tolerance referred to here is actually about appreciating that there are differences and learning to respect the opinions and ways of people who are different from you. This is a lesson clearly not learned in most of the world: wars between people of different religions, skin colors, and cultures throughout the world testify to the lack of tolerance.

How can you, as a teacher, work to counteract ethnic and racial stereotyping that creates divisiveness in the classroom and in the world? In the past, teachers have considered it enough to treat all children the same and ignore differences, with the intent to give the message that everyone is equally acceptable. However, those approaches have not been effective in the face of outside influences. It is now clear that schools must take a proactive stance in combating intolerance. For instance, instead of hushing it up if a child repeats a racial slur, use it as a "teachable moment" for a class discussion. Instead of pretending there are no differences in skin color, offer activities that celebrate those differences. Whole boxes of crayons devoted to various skin colors can contribute to such celebrations. *Starting Small* (Teaching Tolerance, 1997) is one source of activities designed to increase children's appreciation of diversity.

Sometimes you will have students who have personal difficulties that make them the target of cruelty from other children. Maybe a youngster with a bed-wetting problem comes to school smelling of urine, and another wears ragged and ill-fitting clothes. Sometimes the child is like Aiden, who has such damaged self-esteem that he actually seems to invite abuse from other youngsters. These children have many needs, but one of them is the teacher's example to encourage their class-mates' kindness toward them. These children are often hard to like and unap-pealing to be around; however, they are the ones who most need your acceptance and caring.

Starting with their families and friends, children can begin to understand and accept differences and similarities. Later they will be able to expand this awareness to the greater world. Learning to care about others and to get along together in our diverse world are central issues in the curriculum area called *social studies*. Some teacher guides seem to suggest that social studies only covers the food and music of other lands, so some youngsters are never exposed to lessons aimed at develop-ing attitudes and understandings that might promote the welfare of humanity—civics. If educators recognize that compassion and learning how to establish caring relationships are among the most important things anyone can learn, they will spend time in the classroom assisting the development of such social skills.

Modeling Kindness

Children first need to learn these ideas at the concrete level—in their own envi-ronment and through their own experience. People and problems far away are too abstract for young children's thinking. Concepts such as compassion become un-derstandable to children when they witness the principles in their own homes, classrooms, and communities (Landy, 2002).

Children learn these lessons best through situations that constantly arise during the course of the day, as 25 people attempt to live and work harmoniously together in a classroom. Because Mrs. Jensen considers that learning to live harmoniously is an important issue, she doesn't hesitate to spend school time helping children learn to settle a group problem. She calls it her social studies curriculum and considers it time well spent. By making time for interpersonal re-lations skills, she shows that she considers such skills important.

She and other educators are concerned about the prevalence of bullying in school (Kochenderfer-Ladd & Pelletier, 2008). Bullying in schools is a worldwide problem that affects children's ability to feel safe in school and to learn (Kochenderfer-Ladd & Pelletier, 2008). The bullies and their victims both feel the negative effects: The bully, left unchecked, learns a pattern of abuse that may carry over into violent relationships in the future, and the victim suffers from low self-esteem, anxiety, and insecurity (Berger, 2007). Too often teachers do nothing about bullying, either because they are unaware of it or because they want to discourage tattling (Kochenderfer-Ladd & Pelletier, 2008). Teachers do not ignore bullying if they realize how serious the effects are.

Mrs. Jensen lets it be known that she will not tolerate such behavior. The guide-lines in her class emphasize being kind to one another, and any deviation from that is a matter of grave concern for the whole class. Any child who does not feel safe in class, on the playground, in the lunchroom, or even on the school bus is encouraged to let the teacher know. If a child has a pattern of bullying, Mrs. Jensen closely observes the child, and works with the parents and others to get help for the child.

Mrs. Jensen also takes a proactive approach to bullying: She combats bullying and other unkindness when she creates a classroom climate that fosters cooperation instead of competition, when she helps children learn ways of calming themselves, and when she involves children in discussions about the kind of class they want to have. Whenever you work at meeting children's needs and at creating a caring classroom, you are combating bullying.

Vivian Paley's stories of classrooms (1999) show us that young children are capable of caring and concern for others. Paley encourages understanding of others through the stories she shares with children: stories of helpfulness and compassion to give children the ideas and the models needed.

TAKING RISKS

Teachers can also be role models for risk taking (Hyson, 2008). Why would a teacher want to encourage risk taking? Rest assured, we don't mean dangerous physical risks, but rather intellectual risks. Intellectual risks involve following up on an idea or hypothesis to see if it works. When people talk about intellectual risk in the field of science, they refer to it as generating and testing hypotheses. When they talk about the arts, they refer to intellectual risk as creativity.

Why Bother?

Risk taking is an essential part of the learning process and therefore a highly desirable behavior. Unless people are willing to think about concepts and test out new ideas, they are only able to memorize what other people say is true. Such rote learning is a very limited and limiting aspect of education. People who only learn this way will never add to the knowledge of the world. Throughout history, the great scientists, mathematicians, composers, artists, and others who have made major contributions to civilization have been those who risked questioning the status quo.

Some people might argue that children who don't think for themselves are easier to manage. They might even suggest that encouraging risk taking will increase discipline problems. After all, a child who debates the fairness of adult-imposed rules and consequences can be a real pain. But you can also consider such debates a challenge with valuable teaching potential. How you feel about this idea relates back to Chapter 1 and decisions about your goals for children. Because we, the authors of this book, are committed to the goals of intellectual and moral autonomy, we definitely want to encourage children to take intellectual risks—think for themselves.

We believe you will find that teaching for autonomy, rather than conformity, makes guidance and discipline easier, not harder. As you help children learn to make their own responsible decisions, you are released from having to make and enforce all the rules. Additionally, children who are challenged intellectually to think for themselves tend to get excited about learning (Hyson, 2008). As they explore their hypotheses, children become self-directed and self-motivated learners, which makes the job of classroom management easier. The teacher is released from the job of police officer and freed for the role of educational guide and facilitator of learning.

How to Do It?

How does the teacher demonstrate risk taking? The first step is to work on fear of failure or mistakes. This fear is a serious block to trying new ideas of any type (Dweck, 2007). Mrs. Jensen starts by calling attention to all the mistakes she makes herself. She freely shares her failures, such as a fall on her new mountain bike. She doesn't belittle herself for natural human failings, but rather demonstrates acceptance of them. If she misplaces a book or some needed supplies, she might say, "I got so interested in Frencesca's block creation that I didn't pay attention to where I put the book for story time today. Can you help me look for it?" Then she might use the situation to encourage children to disclose times when they, too, forgot where they put something. Her acceptance of their forgetfulness, as well as her own, provides an example for them to learn similar acceptance. It is also important for teachers to model taking risks as part of their own learning experience.

∞ Russian visitors were coming to Lincoln Elementary School. One of the school aides spoke some Russian, so Mrs. Jensen invited him to her classroom to teach some basic greetings. Never having heard the language before, Mrs. Jensen was right with the children at a beginner's level. First, the aide told them how to say, "My name is. . . ." "Menya zavoot," he said. Mrs. Jensen tried, "Menizoot." He repeated, "Menya zavoot." She struggled, smiling, "Menyesavoot?" The children giggled with her as she tried again. She admitted, "This is a little hard for me," and she invited the children to try with her: "Can you help?" Their keen young ears quickly picked up the nuances of sound, and within a few minutes everyone was saying, "Menya zavoot Abby. Menya zavoot Jacob." Eventually, even Mrs. Jensen mastered it! ∞

Relation to Academics

Mrs. Jensen believes that risk taking is especially related to children's progress in writing. Emergent literacy research indicates that children learn about letters and their sounds best when they work on their own hypotheses about writing and spelling (Kamii, Long, & Manning, 2001). Therefore, Mrs. Jensen encourages children to try out their ideas through "kid writing" or invented spelling. This approach involves risk taking. Some children charge into kid writing with gusto, but others hesitate, afraid of making a letter wrong or spelling a word wrong. Some are risk takers and some are not.

The fearless ones produce pages and pages of scribbles; they also include some words they have memorized, such as their own name and *Mom, Dad,* and *I love you.* They proudly tell everyone about what they have written. Soon these youngsters are making good progress on their sound-symbol hypotheses, trying out different ideas about which letter makes which sound (Fields, Groth, & Spangler, 2008). Those children who are afraid of failure may be hampered in their learning (Dweck, 2007).

∞ Isabel just joined Mrs. Jensen's class and obviously has not done any writing except copying. She is so terrified of making a mistake that she does nothing for most of journal time. As Mrs. Jensen tries to encourage her that "kid writing" is just fine, Isabel blurts out, "What if I mess up?" Mrs. Jensen tries to reassure her, but knows it will take awhile before Isabel gets the courage to try to express herself in writing. ∞

Ideas about perfection in one area, such as writing, can carry over to other topics and get in the way of other learning, too. Some children feel incapable of artistic creativity, always wanting someone to show them the "right" way to approach an open-ended project. Others will read the same book over and over, not just because they enjoy the book, but because they know all the words and it is safe. These children desperately need the teacher to model acceptance of imperfection and the courage to venture into the unknown. They need help becoming more comfortable with learning through their mistakes (Dweck, 2007). They need such help in order to become effective learners and self-directed students.

TAKING RESPONSIBILITY

Adults tend to lecture a lot about being responsible. Picking up after yourself, taking care of materials, finishing what you start, and doing work on time are common themes. A good way to teach children these important ideas is by modeling them yourself.

Helping with Clean-up

Clean-up time is a good place to start. You read about Dennis's power struggle over this issue, and you may know that cleaning up frequently causes conflict. It is often a problem at home as well as at school. Many young children are simply overwhelmed by the mess; they don't know where to start and think it is impossible to clean up. Adults who tell kids to clean up are assuming that the children know how to do it. That is not a logical assumption. Young children need to be taught how to pick up a mess; the best way for them to learn is for you to show them what you mean by cleaning up. In other words, you work with them. Seeing you help with clean-up also gives children a clear message that the teacher thinks cleaning up is worth doing. You are an effective model. Contrast the following scene with one where the teachers merely tell youngsters to hurry up with the clean-up.

∞ The block area was strewn with a jumble of blocks and littered with the small toy cars and trucks that had been driving on the block roads. Nancy, one of Dennis's assistant teachers, saw Sadie and Luke standing in the midst of this mess looking hopeless. Nancy went over to the children and offered to help. She started picking up blocks, handing the long, rectangular ones to Sadie to put on the shelf and giving the small, square ones to Luke to put away. Nancy made sure the youngsters were able to match the blocks with the outlines painted on the shelves showing what kind of block goes where. She called their attention to the different sizes and shapes as they worked together.

Soon Nancy positioned herself by the shelf and asked the youngsters to hand her all the triangle-shaped blocks. Next, the children got to choose which shape to work on, and before long the job was complete. Sadie and Luke felt good about their hard work, and they gained skill in organizing the clean-up of the block area. Eventually, they will be able to do it themselves with only a few verbal clues. Having Nancy work with them helped them to value the work they were doing.

Meanwhile, Dennis was working with children washing out paint brushes. As they worked, he talked about the importance of using cold water so as not to loosen the glue holding the brush in the handle. He also encouraged his fellow brush cleaners to experiment with ways that most quickly get the paint out.

While Dennis and Nancy helped with blocks and paint clean-up, Sheri, another assistant, circulated among other clean-up tasks. She stopped to help get the doll babies comfortable in their bed instead of on the floor in the playhouse. Then she complimented Rawan and Anna on how orderly the kitchen cupboard looked before moving on to help Megan and Joshua at the manipulatives table. ∞

Keeping Your Promises

Trustworthiness is associated with children's adjustment in school, their formation of friendships, and their academic competence (Betts & Rottenberg, 2007). Thus, it is important for children to have good examples of trustworthy adults. One of the easiest ways for teachers to promote trusting relationships with their students is to keep their promises.

Following through with a plan or a promise is important to building trust and responsibility. Mrs. Jensen teaches promise keeping effectively through modeling. She starts each day with a discussion of the day's schedule, writing it on the board while the children watch and learn about writing as well as planning. They get practice in reading as they refer back to the schedule during the day. Mrs. Jensen treats the daily plan like a contract, or promise, of what the day will bring.

If weather causes the cancellation of a nature walk that the children are looking forward to, she discusses the change and plans with them to do it another day soon. She makes sure to follow through with this plan, never deciding that the children will soon forget. She models consistent follow-through, and she talks to the children about her commitment to keeping her word. She wants to be sure they realize what she is modeling for them. Some children have no experience with consistency and follow-through in their homes. These children may need help recognizing it when they see it.

Children in Mrs. Jensen's class can count on this same follow-through on an individual level as well. If their teacher is too busy when they want to talk to her, they know she will soon get back to them.

∞ Mrs. Jensen was deep in discussion with Ling Ling about the story she was reading when Trey came up and tapped his teacher on the shoulder. A tap on the shoulder is an approved signal for a child to communicate the need for teacher attention when she is in conference with another student. Mrs. Jensen smiled at Trey and made a signal with her fingers indicating she would be with him in a short while. To make sure that she didn't forget, Mrs. Jensen wrote Trey's name on a note to herself. Trey went back to his seat, secure in the knowledge that his teacher would soon be with him. As soon as she was finished with Ling Ling, Mrs. Jensen went over to see what Trey wanted. Trey and his classmates have begun writing reminder notes to themselves in imitation of their teacher. ∞

Sometimes Mrs. Jensen's list of requests for attention gets too long, and she knows she can't reach so many children in a timely manner. Rather than keeping them waiting, she makes appointments with them for later on. They can still count on her, even if not immediately. Of course, if children have an urgent need, they communicate it. Mrs. Jensen then helps them find whatever assistance is required. As part of encouraging their autonomy, Mrs. Jensen has shown her students how to use a variety of resources, including other children, to solve problems or get their needs met. Therefore, these children are quite capable of helping each other when their teacher is working with an individual child.

Caring for Property

The children in Mrs. Jensen's class are able to work alone and together without constant attention because she dedicated a significant amount of time teaching her children how to use the classroom materials in a responsible way. Her students have learned these lessons well because their teacher doesn't just lecture about their proper use. You guessed it: She shows them how instead.

∞ Mrs. Jensen spends time working with children in each learning center as a way of helping them learn the independent use of materials. Independent use is much different than prescribed single use. It is not a way to limit how children use things, but rather to provide guidelines for their creative expression. Mrs. Jensen finds that her students soon take over the modeling job and begin to show one another important points. Dylan learned that a tile is needed under the plastic clay to protect table tops. He then took the responsibility of reminding Nathan when Nathan forgot. Mrs. Jensen also follows the class guidelines when she uses any material. She knows that to do otherwise would undermine her efforts. ∞

Following the Guidelines

Beth's first day of student teaching taught her a lot about the importance of adult role models. At least some children pay a lot of attention to whether adults follow the rules.

∞ When the teacher called everyone together for the morning meeting and everyone began to gather, Beth took a seat on the couch in the gathering area. Riley loudly informed her that, "It isn't your day for the couch." Beth asked him how he knew whose day it was, and he pointed to a list. Beth went and examined it and said, "You're right, it's not my day for the couch." Beth joined the children on the floor.

After the meeting, children were dismissed to the designated learning centers. Beth was busy helping a group of children when she noticed that Riley had climbed up onto the table. She looked at him questioningly. He looked back. Beth said, "Are you supposed to be sitting on the table?" He just looked at her, and in that instant she realized that she was sitting on the corner of the table. She immediately acknowledged, "But I'm sitting on the table, aren't I?" Riley nodded yes. Beth replied, "Well, I'll have to get off then, won't I?" Riley waited until Beth stood up, then he jumped back down onto the floor. Later, when Beth forgot and sat down on the table again, Riley started to scramble back up again. Beth quickly got up and Riley got down. ∞

Effective teachers model all types of guidelines. According to Weber (2002), we live by three types of guidelines: "social convention, moral issues and issues of personal prerogative" (p. 107). Sitting on the table is a social convention guideline, which helps to keep the classroom orderly. Guidelines dealing with moral issues are more difficult for young children to understand; they deal with issues of harm and fairness (e.g., "Be kind" or "Include everyone"). Guidelines dealing with personal prerogatives focus on protecting our personal rights (e.g., right to privacy, right to learn, right to free choice, etc.).

Guidelines focused on personal rights often come into conflict with social conventional and moral rules. For example, when a child has a need for privacy and walks away from the group, he is most likely breaking the social conventional guideline "sit down and listen to your teacher during circle time." Guideline conflicts generally occur because children do not always put their personal needs in relationship to the needs of others. Teachers can model how to deal with this type of conflict by using reflective self-talk (e.g., I wish I could have one of Julie's cupcakes right now, but I'll wait because she hasn't offered them to me).

KEEPING SAFE

"Do as I say and not as I do" won't work in teaching safety behavior, either. All the teachers at Midway Children's Center remind each other to carry scissors with points down to keep their example consistent with their words to children. They are also careful not to walk too close to a child on a swing, and they model safe street crossing when taking walks with children. When using a car or van for a field trip, teachers, as well as children, wear their buckles.

∞ Mrs. Jensen makes sure she always pushes in her desk chair when she's not using it. Pushing in chairs is an important safety rule in her school. This rule is primarily to keep passageways clear for fire drills, but it also saves a lot of tripping over chairs on a daily basis. Mrs. Jensen helps her students internalize this safety rule by her example. ∞

Maureen became convinced of the impact of adult models while watching preschoolers in dramatic play one day.

∞ Several youngsters were engrossed in a make-believe trip on the boat in the play yard. Megan ran to get some life jackets that had been donated as props. She offered them to Jack and Tory, who scorned them, saying, "We're the dads! We don't wear those." These children had obviously noticed during family boat outings that the children had to wear life jackets but that their fathers did not wear them. ∞

CHILDREN'S LITERATURE

Children's literature is sometimes helpful for providing examples of behavior for discussion and analysis (Hansen & Zambo, 2007). For instance, *The Grouchy Ladybug* (Carle, 1977) or *Mufaro's Beautiful Daughter* (Steptoe, 1987) might spark discussion about how to treat others. Children's books may also help you discuss bullying and teasing with your students: We suggest you try *Chrysanthemum* (Henkes, 1991), *Oliver Button Is a Sissy* (de Paola, 1979), *The Meanest Thing to Say* (Cosby, 1997), and *The Crow Boy* (Yashima, 1976). *Alexander and the Terrible, Horrible, No Good, Very Bad Day* (Viorst, 1972) and *Spinky Sulks* (Steig, 1988) provide examples of how not to have children express their feelings, but offer children the opportunity to be wiser than the book character and offer suggestions for improvement. Figure 6–2 provides additional examples of children's literature that will assist you in teaching children a range of healthy behaviors.

EFFECTIVE ROLE MODELS

The act of social mirroring leads us to match our behavior with that of other people (Byrne, 2005). Of course we don't match all of the behaviors we see, only those of significant others (Byrne, 2005). Role models are most effective when they are people whom children look up to: important, powerful, nurturant people (Hyson, 2004). Primary-age children, both boys and girls, look up to people they perceive to be helpful, gentle, warm, energetic, hardworking, brave, confident, happy, and nice (Shayla-Holub, Tisak, & Mullins, 2008). This belief puts a large responsibility on you as an adult who works with young children. Seize the opportunity! As children get older, they look less to adults for their models and turn more to peers they admire.

Someone Similar

The ability to identify with role models is important to all ages. Erikson believes that role models serve as a mechanism for children to understand their culture and society (1963). As discussed previously, children are more likely to copy people who are similar to them in some way. Teachers can emphasize similarities with their students by commenting on similarities of interest and feelings. For instance, Anna's favorite color is purple. Nancy makes a special point to tell Anna that she likes purple the best, too. Sadie and Luke both have pet beagles that they talk about. Nancy makes sure to ask about their dogs.

Feelings	• *Alexander and the Terrible, Horrible, No Good, Very Bad Day* (Viorst, 1972) • *Spinky Sulks* (Steig, 1988) • *The Feelings Book* (Parr, 2005) • *When Sophie Gets Angry . . . Really, Really Angry* (Bang, 1999) • *Today I Feel Silly: And Other Moods That Make My Day* (Curtis, 1998) • *Move Over Rover* (Beaumont, 2006)
Kindness	• *Hands Are Not for Hitting* (Verdick, 2000) • *Teeth Are Not for Biting* (Verdick, 2003) • *Sometimes I'm a Bombaloo* (Vail, 2002) • *Hooway for Woodney Wat* (Lester, 1999)
Acceptance	• *Lizzie Logan Wears Purple Sunglasses* (Spinelli, 1998) • *Nobody Asked Me if I Wanted a Baby Sister* (Alexander, 2005) • *Will There Be a Lap for Me?* (Cory, 1992) • *Two Eyes a Nose and a Mouth* (Intrater, 2000)
Responsibility	• *Max Cleans Up* (Wells, 2002) • *Once upon a Banana* (Armstrong & Small, 2006) • *Good Work, Amelia Bedelia* (Parish, 2003) • *Do I Have To? A Book for Children Who Find Themselves Frustrated by Everyday Rules* (Leventhal-Belfer, 2008) • *Lilly's Purple Plastic Purse* (Henkes, 1996)
Friendship	• *How to Be a Friend* (Krasney-Brown, 2001) • *Rainbow Fish* (Pfister, 1992) • *Best Friends Together Again* (Aliki, 2000) • *Who Will Be My Friends?* (Hoff, 1985) • *Horace and Morris but Mostly Delores* (Howe, 2003)
Empathy	• *It's Okay to Be Different* (Parr, 2001) • *Louie* (Keats, 2004) • *Jamaica's Find* (Havill, 1987) • *Princess Pooh* (Muldoon, 1989)
Risk Taking	• *Not a Box* (Portis, 2006) • *Olivia* (Falconer, 2000) • *I Ain't Gonna Paint No More!* (Beaumont, 2005) • *Hi Fly Guy* (Arnold, 2006) • *Sheila Ray, the Brave* (Henkes, 1987)

FIGURE 6–2 Use Children's Literature to Teach Social Skills

Older children often look to others of the same age for models, and models of the same gender and culture are important because of their similarities, too. Children whose first language differs from their teacher's or whose skin is a different color may benefit less from the model of their teacher (Brazelton & Greenspan, 2000). When this occurs it is important for teachers to help children recognize other ways in which the teacher and the child are similar. Providing all children with role models that are similar to them is one reason why it is important to recruit more teachers and aides from a variety of cultural groups.

Someone to Be Like

You are more likely to be an effective role model if children want to be like you (Hyson, 2004). This means that youngsters need to see you as being fun and pleasant. It also means having a positive relationship with youngsters. They want to be like you because they like you.

Children often want to be like sports stars, television characters, and superheroes. The companies who use these stars to market their products count on this and use it to their advantage. Advertising can be very powerful and, unfortunately, is increasingly aimed at children (Linn, 2004). At Kidscreen's fifth annual conference on Advertising and Promoting to Kids, some of its stated missions were to teach attendees how to "own kids" and create "lifelong consumers" (*The Lancet*, 2002, p. 959). The philosophy now in advertising to kids is to "teach kids to influence their parents' purchases" (Shore, 2004). Children are inundated with these persuasive role models in games, clothes, foods, and especially toys.

There are other problems with media's strong influence on children. Children pick up whole behavior patterns by emulating the models they see in the media (Wilson, 2008). In some television programs, sarcastic put-downs are presented as humorous and entertaining, teaching impressionable young people that this is a desirable way to interact (Wilson, 2008). The greatest concern with the influence of superheroes and some cartoon characters is the likelihood that children will copy the violent behavior they have observed.

MODELS OF VIOLENCE

The American Medical Association, the American Academy of Pediatrics, the American Psychological Association, and the American Academy of Child and Adolescent Psychiatry made a joint statement about media violence. These health professionals concluded that violence in television, music, video games, and movies can make children more aggressive, fearful, disrespectful, and insensitive to the effects of violence (TRUCE, 2008, in Appendix A). The National Association for the Education of Young Children (NAEYC) has also published a position statement cautioning about the media and violence. Media is clearly a significant influence when we consider the amount of time some children spend watching television or playing video games. Violence affects children of all ages. Children are never too young to have their trust development or desire to explore their world threatened by exposure to violence (Osofsky, 1997).

Teachers can guide children's thinking about super heroes seen in media.

Organizations such as TRUCE (Teachers Resisting Unhealthy Children's Entertainment) actively work to eliminate violence in children's television and toys. Other coalitions, including CCFC (Campaign for a Commercial Free Childhood), specifically work against marketing aimed at children. A quick search on the Internet will bring up many more groups with similar missions.

When children see violence they will often bring it into their play. This is their way of processing what they have witnessed and trying to make sense of it all. Creating class guidelines about violence and safety in the classroom is essential. However, when violent play arises, teachers have a great opportunity to help children learn from what they have seen. When children imitate their favorite superheroes, we can use these opportunities to discuss fantasy versus reality, the impact of violence, and support positive images of being helpful and feeling powerful (Levin, 2004). Instead of imitating superhero plots seen on the screen, you can encourage children to develop their own plots for superhero play. This may be a great opportunity to discuss true heroism and how our actions affect others. Some children develop real fears from violence they have actually experienced or observed. In some cases, your openness to discuss violence may allow you to help a child who is tormented by fear or who is in real danger.

Working with Families to Combat Media Violence

Fortunately, when parents supervise children's media activities, they can help them make sense of the violence they see. Educational programming is known to have a positive affect on children's social emotional development (Wilson, 2008).

Therefore, teachers are urged to encourage parents and guardians to talk to their children about the content of advertising and media and to provide families with educational alternatives. Children need to know that, contrary to what they may be seeing on TV, most people really do not carry weapons—they avoid violence and talk about their disagreements instead of forcing their opinions on others. Educational programming provides children with these positive examples. It is the responsibility of adults to help children think about and analyze the positive and negative social interactions they are sure to encounter in real life and on television. Youngsters will learn negative behavior patterns from models as easily as they learn positive ones. Teachers and families must work together to ensure that the negative doesn't overwhelm the positive.

Resources are available to help children and families use discretion in choosing positive media images and to facilitate discussion about the effects of media. Workshops and newsletters for parents are great ways to communicate these messages. In Appendix A at the end of this book, you will find some useful handouts to send home; they include some startling statistics about the impact of media on children. These handouts also offer suggestions for facilitating family discussions about potentially negative media images. We can also encourage the use of open-ended toys that allow children to use their imaginations instead of toys that represent specific characters connected with violent media (Levin, 2004). We can all work together to decrease the amount of violence exposure in children's lives.

Fortunately, all media is not harmful. Some books that may be helpful for fostering critical thinking about the media are: *The Bionic Bunny Show* (Brown, 1999); *Mouse TV* (Novak, 1994); and *Box-Head Boy* (Winn & Walsh, 1996). These books may aid a discussion about the harm and good that can come from media and inspire children to consider alternatives to watching television (Hesse & Lane, 2003).

CURRICULUM PROGRAMS THAT PROVIDE EXAMPLES

The principles described in this chapter are accepted pieces of violence prevention and are included in published violence prevention programs. Lesson plans to promote productive expression of feelings, caring for others, and being responsible for yourself can be found in programs such as the *Resolving Conflict Creatively Program* (Lantieri, 2003), *Tribes* (Gibbs, 2001), *Second Step: A Violence-Prevention Curriculum* (Committee for Children, 2003), and *Educating the Heart* (Siccone & Lopez, 2000).

Creating a caring classroom reduces violence by addressing the major causes of violent behavior: unmet emotional needs, values of exclusion rather than inclusion, and lack of skills for peaceful conflict resolution. If a program does not work toward these goals, then we question its worth. A worthwhile program also includes intensive training for teachers as well as for the school administration and staff. The most effective programs have lessons for children integrated throughout the day—lessons that are relevant to their real lives. For best success, schools must commit to a program for a significant span of time (Wheeler, 2004).

Even if your school doesn't adopt a formal program schoolwide, you may find that some of the materials from these programs offer helpful ideas for class discussions and activities to promote kindness, caring, and cooperation. Mrs. Jensen uses many of the esteem-boosting and appreciation expression activities from the *Tribes* curriculum as part of building her classroom community (Gibbs, 2001). We encourage you to critically review published programs and decide the worth of the lessons for yourself. We find that some focus on paper-and-pencil or cut-and-paste activities rather than on actual interpersonal experiences. We prefer activities that involve children with one another, using the skill or disposition to be learned. These include exercises such as practice in giving compliments, expressing and interpreting feelings through pantomime, and partner interviews.

CONCLUSION

Your positive examples will result in more positive child behaviors. If you have a caring relationship with your students, your models of respect and fairness toward children will be emulated in how children treat one another. How you deal with your own feelings and those of others will affect how children handle their feelings. Your demonstrations of caring and kindness will make lasting impressions on young people. Your willingness to take risks in learning new skills and trying out new ideas will help youngsters more bravely try out their emerging skills and ideas. When you set an example of being responsible and of following good safety habits, children are more apt to pay attention than when you lecture about those issues. As an adult, you have a powerful influence on young children. You are teaching by everything you do.

ᕯ FOR FURTHER THOUGHT

1. Observe young children and the adults with whom they spend their days. Note the ways in which the children imitate the examples set by adults.
2. Analyze your own expression of feelings in your personal life. Are you able to express fear or loneliness to trusted friends or family? Do you have a tendency to cover up other negative feelings with expressions of anger? How do you express your anger? Do you need to work on your own ability to express your feelings

effectively in order to set an example for children?
3. Notice how adults respond when children get hurt or are upset. Do they deny children's negative feelings or accept them? Do they try to distract children from physical or emotional pain? What is your own common response? Do you need to work at learning new ways to respond to a child's pain?
4. Observe ways in which teachers encourage or discourage children in

thinking for themselves. Do you see any relationship between a teacher's own intellectual autonomy and that teacher's encouragement of children's intellectual autonomy? How would you rate yourself for intellectual autonomy?

5. Observe the difference in classrooms where teachers merely tell children to clean up and those where teachers work with youngsters, showing them useful clean-up approaches.

∞ RECOMMENDED READINGS

Froschl, M., & Sprung, B. (1999). On purpose: Addressing teasing and bullying in early childhood. *Young Children, 54*(3), 70–72.

Hesse, P., & Lane, F. (2003). Media literacy starts young: An integrated curriculum approach. *Young Children, 58*(6), 20–26.

Hyson, M. C. (2004). *The emotional development of young children: Building an emotion-centered curriculum.* New York: Teachers College Press.

Jackson, C. (2007, January). The ABCs of bullying. *Teaching Tolerance, Classroom Activities.*

Levin, D. E. (2004). Beyond banning war and superhero play: Meeting children's needs in violent times. In D. Koralek (Ed.), *Spotlight on young children and play.* Washington, DC: National Association for the Education of Young Children.

Plattner, I. E. (2003). Granting children their emotions. *Child Care Information Exchange, 152,* 34–36.

Stassen-Berger, K. (2007). Update on bullying at school: Science forgotten? *Developmental Review,* 27(1), 90–126.

Teaching Tolerance. (1997). *Starting small: Teaching tolerance in preschool and the early grades.* Montgomery, AL: The Southern Poverty Law Center.

∞ Chapter 7 ∞
Effective Discipline Through Effective Communication

NAEYC Standards Addressed in This Chapter

Standard 4a: Teaching and Learning, Connecting with Children and Families: Candidates know, understand, and use positive relationships and supportive interactions as the foundation for their work with young children.

Standard 4b: Teaching and Learning, Using Developmentally Effective Approaches: Candidates know, understand, and use a wide array of effective approaches, strategies, and tools to positively influence young children's development and learning.

Standard 4c: Teaching and Learning, Understanding Content Knowledge in Early Education: Candidates understand the importance of each content area in young childrens' learning. They know the essential concepts, inquiry tools, and structure of content areas including academic subjects and can identify resources to deepen their understanding.

GUIDING QUESTIONS

- How can teachers communicate with children so they will listen?
- What makes a good listener?
- How can teachers guide children through social problem-solving situations?

> "Get to work, young man."
> "Stop acting like a baby."
> "You're such a good little girl."
> "No recess unless that paper is finished."
> "You are being rude."
> "Everything will be fine; just wait and see."
> "Your picture is beautiful."
> "You're okay. There's no reason to cry."
> "You need to improve your attitude."

*D*o any of these statements sound familiar? Perhaps you heard them from your parents and teachers as you grew up. Perhaps you have said them to children yourself. You may be surprised to hear that these statements have a negative effect on behavior (Gordon, 1989). This chapter will look at how such comments build barriers to communication in addition to teaching children that their feelings aren't okay. In his discipline classic *Parent Effectiveness Training,* Thomas Gordon (1970) calls them "roadblocks to communication."

Many parents and teachers grew up with these counterproductive ways of communicating, which have become second nature to them. These adults automatically resort to the ways of talking to children that they have heard in the past. Knowledge about effective communication can drastically alter relationships between people of all ages. Some people use the information to improve marriages, friendships, or working relationships (Gordon, 1989). Parents and teachers can apply the information to effective communication and better relationships with children. Effective communication is an essential part of effective discipline, as are good relationships.

This chapter helps you build better relationships as you communicate more positively with children. Being a role model of effective communication, plus your explicit teaching, will help children learn to use these forms of communication so that they can get along better with others. Your classroom will be a more peaceful place when you and your students talk, listen, and negotiate differences according to the guidelines shared in this chapter.

WHY CHILDREN DON'T LISTEN

Adults frequently complain that children don't listen to them, and they often have no idea why. Few adults ever consider that it might be their own fault. Think about the following situations:

1. You have just warned Kenji to be careful of that puddle, and now he's splashing right into the middle of it.
2. You have given the directions for the math activity three times, and still individual children are coming up to you and asking how to do it.
3. You hear yourself saying, "How many times have I told you not to do that?!"

These incidents may be symptoms of ineffective ways of talking to children. Of course, we can't guarantee that Kenji will stay out of the puddle no matter what you say, but you can improve your success rate. How you talk to kids makes a big difference in whether they listen to you. How you talk to children and other people also makes a big difference in whether they care what you have to say.

Criticizing and Lecturing

It isn't too surprising that people don't listen to what is unpleasant to hear. It seems like a natural self-protective device to tune out what is unpleasant. Yet, many teachers and parents express dismay when children don't listen to their persistent nagging. The adults consider frequent reminders and corrections as forms of teaching. Certainly, teaching is the intent, but the teaching approach obviously is not effective if the teaching is ignored.

No matter what their age, people rarely like to hear someone tell them how badly they have behaved. Similarly, no one wants to be called derogatory names such as *selfish* or *tattletale*. Most people also get irritated at being told how they should be acting. Well-intentioned comments analyzing possible causes of your behavior are perhaps the most infuriating of all. Remember, kids are people, too, and if you want them to listen to you, avoid talking to them in ways that turn off listening. Think about how you would feel in the following situation.

∞ You were late for work and feeling awful about it. It was a terrible morning: Everything that could go wrong did go wrong. Your alarm didn't go off, the clothes you had washed and put into the dryer last night to wear today didn't get dry, and the bus pulled away just as you got to the bus stop.

You finally arrived at work, frustrated, hungry, and disheveled. Your supervisor pointed out that you were late once last month, too, and said that you have been inconsiderate. She went on to tell you how disappointed she was in your thoughtlessness and suggested that you might have a problem dealing with authority and rules. She finished by lecturing you on the importance of being on time. ∞

Would this supervisor's approach make you open to her instruction? Would you pay close attention to what she says and want to learn more from her? How would it affect your feelings about her in general? How would your attitude about work that day be affected? Most people would get very angry, tune out the supervisor, and have an even worse day as a result. Yet, many teachers regularly talk to students in this way and expect improved behavior to result. Gordon (1970) calls this behavior "sending put-down messages." It is fortunate that kids often tune such messages out because they are so harmful to self-esteem.

Giving Orders

It is fairly easy to recognize the unpleasantness of hearing about your errors. However, you may not have thought about why kids (and adults) also dislike constantly being told what to do and how to do it. These instructions communicate disrespect for the other person's ideas and abilities. When you tell people everything they need to do in a situation, you also tell them that you don't think they are capable of figuring it out for themselves. Gordon (1970) calls this communication approach "solution messages." When you communicate this kind of disrespect, you don't get much cooperation in return. You are more likely to generate resistance to your directions instead. Of greater concern are the long-term effects on the child. Such disrespect not only damages self-esteem, but it also short-circuits growth toward autonomy. When you solve problems for them, children learn not to trust their own solutions. You are creating an unhealthy dependency.

∞ Ariel couldn't get the glue to come out. She turned the dispenser's end, chewed on it, and squeezed as hard as she could. Finally, she just took off the lid and tried to pour glue onto her collage. When it didn't immediately come out, she shook the container. Glop! As Ariel considered the best way to approach the puddle of glue, Miss Wheeler stepped in and ordered, "Get a sponge!" Ariel frowned. She would have scooped up most of the glue with a scrap of mat board first. Then she would have gotten a sponge to finish the job. Why didn't Miss Wheeler ever let her decide how to do things?, Ariel wondered. ∞

Haim Ginott also wrote a child-guidance classic, *Between Parent and Child* (1965). Thomas Gordon and Ginott both discuss how differently adults talk to children than to other adults. They point out that few teachers or parents would talk to a friend or acquaintance in the bossy, rude ways that many speak

Children listen to adults who speak to them with respect.

to children. It tends to sound ridiculous if you think of talking to an adult in the disrespectful terms often used toward youngsters. If Ariel had been an adult, would the teacher have spoken to her that way? More likely, Miss Wheeler would have said, "You may use my table sponge if you'd like."

Inauthentic Communication

Speaking to children with respect, as you would expect to do with adults, can be a helpful guide. But many people don't know the best ways to express themselves to people of any age. You may be one of those people who don't say anything when someone offends or upsets you because you don't want to be rude or unpleasant. Or, you may be bold about speaking up to defend yourself. Too often, it is hard to defend yourself without expressions of anger, which generate anger in response.

If you say nothing when someone hurts or frustrates you, your resentment builds. Your nonverbal communication will be negative, indicating your true feelings. The relationship will be damaged by the unexpressed feelings and the unresolved conflicts. This is not an honest way of relating. Children with parents and teachers who provide this model of behavior do not have productive examples to follow.

If you find yourself speaking in anger frequently, you may also be covering up your true feelings. Anger is often a secondary emotion. It results from a primary emotion such as fear, hurt, or embarrassment. Expressions of anger focus on what the other person did, without acknowledging your own feelings. Some teachers and parents feel that revealing their own fear or hurt is not compatible with their authority role. They may think that the expression of true feelings demonstrates weakness and that their job is to demonstrate power. Like holding in unpleasant feelings, expressing them as anger also damages relationships. It is dishonest and, therefore, a poor role model as well.

The idea that an adult cannot demonstrate fear, sadness, or other feelings associated with vulnerability is linked to the power-based authoritarian discipline style, with its repercussions of negative behaviors and negative self-esteem. The invincible adult role is counterproductive to long-term discipline goals in other ways as well. We have already discussed in Chapter 6 how children's ability to express their emotions in a healthy way is affected by their adult role models. Additionally, the invulnerable adult model gets in the way of authentic relationships with children because the adults cannot reveal their true selves. Authentic relationships between adults and children, like those between peers, encourage cooperation and empathy. These traits are clearly linked to more desirable behavior.

TALKING TO CHILDREN RESPECTFULLY

It is important to communicate your personal needs and limits. Doing so effectively means you state your feelings without labeling the child as bad and without ordering the child to change. In this way you balance the expression of self-respect with that of respect for others. Gordon (1970) was the first to call this simple statement of your own feelings an "I message."

I messages are appropriate when the problem is yours: what is happening is upsetting to you personally. Children need to learn to give I messages when someone does something that bothers them. Sometimes adults seem to get confused and assume that all problems are the adults' problem; that view gets in the way of teaching children to express their own feelings with I messages.

In contrast with "you messages," I messages do not blame or condemn another person, and they do not contain put-downs. I messages also don't tell someone else what to do, thus avoiding a "solution message." They focus on your needs instead of on the other person's actions. Therefore, people are more willing to listen to this type of communication; it generates little argument or defensiveness.

A complete I message has three components, according to Gordon's book *P.E.T. in Action* (Gordon & Sands, 1976):

1. It is specific about what the unacceptable behavior is.
2. It states your feeling.
3. It explains why it makes you feel that way.

We add another component:

4. It stops after saying those three things.

Too many people start out with a good I message and then ruin it by telling the child what he or she should be doing differently. Some social skills curriculum programs also make this mistake in teaching I messages: they actually say to tell the other person how to change his or her behavior. That sends a solution message—another roadblock to communication. If you don't stop after stating the problem and its cause, your listener hears the instructions for improvement and tends to react negatively.

Situation	I Message	Result
While Mrs. Jensen was reading a story to the group, Abby was talking to her friend quite loudly.	Mrs. Jensen looked at Abby and said, "I can't read with so much noise in the room. It gives me a sore throat to try to talk loudly enough for people to hear me."	Abby had a reason for keeping her voice down and willingly complied.
Dennis was bending over to help Anna with her boots when Sam came up behind, threw his arms tightly around Dennis's neck, and hung on his teacher's back. Dennis nearly fell over backward, but understood that Sam was expressing affection and meant no harm.	Dennis told the affectionate child, "I'm afraid I'm going to fall over with you on my back, Sam, and I can't help Anna with her boots this way."	Sam hopped off, and Dennis gave him some attention as soon as Anna had her boots on.
Karina was spilling paint on the carpet as she exuberantly worked on the class mural.	Mrs. Jensen walked over to where Karina was working and told her, "I am worried that this paint won't come out of our rug, especially after it dries."	Karina got a sponge for clean-up and then put down papers to catch the drips.

FIGURE 7–1 Effective "I Messages"

It is more effective and respectful to communicate the nature of your problem and then back off, allowing the child to make things right. Figure 7–1 shows examples of effective I messages.

Relationships

I messages assume that the person you are speaking to actually cares about how you feel. If you don't have a caring relationship with Alexis, you can't expect her to be concerned when you tell her you are having a problem. Once again, we are reminded of the central role played by relationships. Piaget (1965) identified mutually respectful relationships as the basis of moral development. In order to be effective with guidance and discipline, you must cultivate relationships with the children in your care.

The children in the previous examples (see Figure 7–1) were free to think about their teachers' concerns instead of defending themselves against accusations of wrongdoing. The children were also free to think about how they could make things right again. Did you notice that Mrs. Jensen didn't tell Karina what she needed to do about the problem, but instead respected the child to come up with a solution? This approach helped Karina feel good about herself and increased the likelihood of future desirable behavior. If Mrs. Jensen had tacked on a solution message, it would have taken away from the effectiveness of the communication. Instead, Mrs. Jensen indicated belief in the child's ability and desire to figure out a solution.

Misconceptions

Sometimes people get confused about what an I message is. They think that it is any statement that starts with "I feel. . . ." Remember, an I message is the expression of your own perspective; it is an I message because it doesn't aim the blame at someone else. Be careful, or you might actually send a "you message," fooling yourself into believing that it is an I message (Gordon, 1970). For example, Mrs. Jensen might have told Mica, "I feel irritated when you are being such a messy painter." Her "I feel irritated" would then have only been a preface for an insult.

The real key to I messages has little to do with using the word *I*. Instead of saying, "I feel hurt when you kick me," it would be much more natural to say, "Ouch, that hurts!" The message is the same: It isn't calling the youngster bad for kicking; it is just expressing your feelings about being kicked. The statement, "I am proud of you" may, at first, sound more like an I message than saying, "thank you." Analysis of the two statements, however, reveals just the opposite. "Thank you" actually tells your feelings and means "I feel appreciative of what you have done." The statement "I'm proud of you" really is a judgment of the other person.

Effectiveness

According to Curwin and Mendler (1990), I messages are effective for the following four reasons:

1. They say how you feel about what a child is or isn't doing.
2. They give a reason why the behavior is a problem.
3. They never criticize or blame the child.
4. They allow the child to solve the problem.

It takes practice to get good at I messages, but eventually you can retrain yourself so that it comes more naturally to express your own perspective instead of judging someone else's behavior. You will find that the results are worth the effort. People of all ages will respond much more positively to what you say. The situations in Figure 7–2 contain "you messages." Read each statement and change it into a positive I message.

Teaching Children to Use I Messages

Your model will go a long way toward encouraging your students to express themselves with I messages, but coaching them in how to use them will help, too. Remember, the person who has the problem is the one who gives the I message. So, when Sarah is upset because someone took something she was using, it is an appropriate time to help her use an I message. Often, the other child involved will have a different perspective on the problem and can be helped to give his or her own I message in response. I messages are an important first step in conflict resolution. You may recall that Chapter 3 recommended I messages for helping children gain perspective-taking ability, too.

Situation	I Message
You are taking a group of children on a walking field trip that involves crossing a few streets. Sam runs ahead of the group instead of staying with you as instructed. Frantic, you yell to Sam, "You have to stay with us! Come back here right now!"	
A co-teacher is clearing a counter for a project and doesn't notice that five children behind her have their hands raised. You are overwhelmed by trying to meet their demands for attention alone and say to the co-teacher, "You should be more attentive to the children!"	
A parent brings in a child late, as is her habit, which disrupts your morning reading time. Beside, this boy really needs help with his reading fluency. You wish she would bring him to school on time. You say to the mother, "You really need to make sure Max gets to school on time."	

FIGURE 7–2   Create Effective I Messages

BEING A GOOD LISTENER

Maybe one of the reasons why children don't listen to adults is that adults often don't really listen to children. Too often teachers and parents respond to children's problems by brushing them off. Sometimes adults believe that children's concerns are trivial, or they worry too much about children getting upset. Sometimes an adult is unable to deal with real feelings. It is also possible to be so busy that you don't realize you are not truly listening. You may even think you are paying attention to a child and still respond in ways that prove otherwise.

Not Listening

Many common, well-intentioned ways of responding to what a child says amount to quick brush-offs. Trying to distract a youngster from feeling sad is one way of not really listening. Diversions may be something like the old "let's have a cookie" routine or other words that say, "Let's think about something nice instead." Quick reassurances that everything will be fine also communicate that you are not interested in hearing the child's concerns. Therefore, these are roadblocks to communication. Even trying to solve the child's stated problem with advice is a way of not really listening. Think about how you feel when someone does those things to you.

∞ Maureen has a friend, Jane, who is quick to give out advice. Maureen really hates it when she is upset about something, then confides in Jane, and gets an instant solution. The advice is always shallow and nonproductive anyway, because Jane hasn't had time to think through the problem. Naturally, Maureen has thought of all those obvious and easy solutions and already come to the conclusion that they won't work; otherwise, she wouldn't still have the problem.

Because Jane doesn't know all the complexities of the situation, her thoughts are mostly irrelevant. What Maureen really wants is someone who hears and understands how upset she is. Instead, Jane's response shows that she isn't hearing the seriousness of the problem; her offer of an easy answer clearly says to Maureen, "Your problem isn't any big deal. If I were in your place, I could solve it in a minute. You aren't handling things very well." ∽

No wonder Gordon lists giving advice as one of the roadblocks to communication.

Talking Instead of Listening

Sometimes adults are so busy telling kids what they think that they don't hear what a child is saying. When children bring up a problem, many teachers and parents think it is their job to tell youngsters what to do. Some talk to kids about what they "should" do from a moral standpoint, while others tend to dish out facts, trying to influence young people with logic. Still others just give orders and expect compliance. None of these approaches results in listening to the child or respecting the child's ability to figure out answers to problems. You can surely remember how you felt when you got these kinds of lectures yourself. They didn't make you feel like listening!

Passing judgment on a person confiding in you is another sure way to stop further communication. You have heard responses like "It's your own fault" or "You're not making any sense." You may have even heard worse. One of the worst things anyone can say to a young child striving hard to be grown-up is "You're being a baby." Such name-calling is just one way of shaming children and making them feel worthless. Some teachers unfortunately use ridicule and other forms of humiliation to keep youngsters from challenging authority.

On the opposite end of the spectrum, have you ever noticed that praise is another way of passing judgment? In this case, you have judged that things are good, but the implication is clear that you will continue to judge and next time may come up with negative findings. We further discuss problems with praise, and offer alternatives, in Chapter 9. Messages of praise are also counterproductive to the communication process. Gordon (1970) includes praise, along with reassuring, diverting, and probing, in his list of roadblocks to communication. These methods are attempts to help the child feel better; but like the rest of Gordon's 12 roadblocks to communication, they are nonlistening responses.

Adults can teach good listening by being good listeners. Adults can also learn a lot by listening to kids and finding out what they are thinking. In addition, you can build productive relationships with children by showing that you care enough about them to genuinely listen. When you have a good relationship with children, they try harder to cooperate with you. Good listening can reap many rewards.

Passive Listening

One way to show you are listening is to stop talking yourself. Some people just can't seem to be quiet long enough to hear what anyone else is saying. Quiet attention to a child's words with only minimal comments, such as "Is that so?" or

"How interesting," can be very effective. Even a sympathetic "hmmmm" is better than a roadblock (Faber & Mazlish, 1996; Porter, 2000). Sometimes more is required, such as asking "What do you think about that?" or "Would you like to talk about it?" These responses indicate acceptance and respect for the child's opinion. They are basically passive listening approaches.

Reflective Listening

Reflective listening, coined by Carl Rogers in 1951, is a specific way to sequence interactions with the intention of focusing on the speaker on understanding how he or she is making sense of the issue at hand. Rogers, a psychologist, argues that reflective listening is the core of client-centered practice. Similarly, many educators believe that reflective listening is key to effective teacher–child interactions in both social and academic situations (Arcavi & Isoda, 2007). Gordon (1970) was the first to operationalize reflective listening. Building on Rogers's theory, Gordon designed Parent Effectiveness Training, a parent education program designed to improve parent–child relationships. Subsequently, he designed Teacher Effectiveness Training to improve teacher–child interactions.

Reflective listening is central to Gordon's training programs. Gordon uses the term *active listening* in his books; however, we prefer the term *reflective listening* and thus will use this term in our discussion. Reflective listening includes restating and validating the concerns and/or feelings of another person. Reflective listening can be used to ensure the accuracy of communication by reflecting back to the speaker what the listener has heard. Figure 7–3 outlines the steps of reflective listening.

When you practice reflective listening, you will discover how often misunderstandings occur. When you say what it is you think the other person meant, you allow the speaker to confirm or correct your interpretation. The different experiences and perspectives of the people involved can give totally different meanings to the same set of words. Reflective listening involves the speaker and the listener in a mutual effort to ensure accurate communication. When you give this kind of effort to understanding a child, you show the child you care. You are also more likely to find out what's really going on.

∞ Maddie was often upset when her mother dropped her off at preschool. However, today her reaction was more extreme than usual. As was sometimes the case, Dennis had to gently restrain Maddie from following her mother out the door. Today, Maddie did not stop crying 30 seconds after her mother's departure as she usually did.

Dennis knew that Maddie and her family had been out of town for the last 2 weeks, and this was probably the reason for her increased difficulty with

---

- Stop talking—listen to the problem from the children's perspective.
- Wait, don't rush to pass judgment—find out what children are thinking.
- Restate what you hear in your own words—allow children to confirm that you understand the situation.
- Validate children's concerns and feelings—show that you care.

FIGURE 7–3   Steps to Reflective Listening

separation. He settled himself into a seat where he could be eye level with Maddie and said to her softly, "It looks like you really didn't want to come to school today."

Maddie sniffled, "I want to go home."

Dennis reflected, "You went on a trip with your mom and the rest of your family didn't you?" Maddie nodded as Dennis continued, "Sometimes it is hard to come back to school after you've been gone for a while. Everything seems new again."

Maddie just nodded her head, leaning on Dennis' shoulder, and continued sniffling.

Dennis wondered if Madeline was feeling tired too, after her big trip. He told her, "When I go on a long trip, sometimes I feel extra tired when I get back."

Maddie sat up, and said, "I was tired when I got a fever at Aunt Debby's house."

Dennis asked, "Were you sick on your trip?" As Maddie nodded, all the pieces seemed to fall into place. Maddie's difficulty with separation was exacerbated by her time away from school, and she was recovering from the exhaustion of traveling and being sick. It was easier for Dennis to have empathy for Maddie when he knew why she was feeling so needy. Dennis summed it all up, "It is really hard to play at school when you miss your mom and you're tired."

Maddie offered, "I don't want to play right now." Dennis understood her need and sat with Maddie as she continued to lean on him and look around for a few more minutes. Maddie eventually stopped crying. When her friend Sarah stopped to ask if she wanted to "be Clifford," Maddie accepted and went off barking across the room. ∞

There are many important benefits to reflective listening. In this example, acknowledging and reflecting Maddie's concerns without forcing solutions or attempting to distract her reduced her need to be oppositional and created a connection between Dennis and Maddie (Koplow, 2002). By encouraging children to talk about a problem or concern, you also encourage them to think about it and give them time to deal with their needs. Children are then free to figure out their own solutions. Chances are good that their solutions are similar to yours, but they are more likely to implement them because they are their own. Chances are also good that their solutions are more in tune with the child's perspective.

Cautions About Reflective Listening

When you practice reflective listening, be sure to watch for some common pitfalls. Most people find it very hard to avoid trying to give advice. Sometimes the tendency to take over the problem is shown by inappropriate probing questions, such as "Why do you think that happened?" or "When do you feel this way?"

Reflective listening is appropriate when the problem belongs to the child; remember to use I messages for your own problems. When the problem belongs to the child, the best solution is the child's own. If you decide how the problem should be solved, then you communicate a lack of respect for the child's problem-solving ability. You get in the way of children's learning when you try to figure out and solve their problems for them. The experience of personally resolving a problem teaches children how to do it and empowers them in the future. Besides, kids generally don't use adult solutions. If they do use an adult's solution, it only creates dependency.

Feeling Awkward or Phony   You may initially feel awkward when trying to find the right words for reflective listening. This type of listening involves telling the speaker what you heard him or her say, but it should be your own interpretation rather than mere parroting of the same words. When you provide your interpretation, you are asking for confirmation that you did understand the speaker's intent. The process of clarifying the message encourages the speaker to continue and to delve more deeply into the subject. By clarifying the idea for the listener, the speaker tends to clarify his or her own thinking.

The reflective-listening process may sound contrived to you at first, and you may feel like a phony paraphrasing back to someone what he or she just said to you. If you are honestly trying to understand what the other person is saying, however, your sincerity will come through. Keep focused on the other person's feelings and on accurate communication; then you will not only feel more comfortable with reflective listening, but you will also be a more effective listener. Your model will help children learn to be better listeners for one another, but few preschool or even primary-grade children are capable of this sophisticated type of communication.

Children's Communication   Very young preschoolers not only can't do reflective listening, but they can't easily use words to tell us what is bothering them. Their vocabulary generally doesn't have precise words for feelings. In addition, they often lack a clear idea of what is bothering them. Reflective listening with very young children requires you to tune in to the children carefully and pay close attention to their nonverbal communication, as we saw in the Dennis and Maddie example. With children you know, you can usually get clues from their behavior about what is bothering them. You can follow up these clues by checking out your impressions with the child.

The process of reflecting these nonverbal messages is the same as reflecting back what you hear being said with words. Just as with oral communication, you may not receive the message accurately. Instead of immediately solving the problem you assume is at hand, you verbalize your hypotheses until you identify the actual concerns of the children involved.

∽ Jake grabbed the handlebar of Sam's tricycle, yanking him sideways. Sam tried to shove him away and screamed for the teacher. When Nancy arrived, Jake was saying, "Off! Off!" The teacher assumed he wanted to use a tricycle. There were other free trikes she could help him get, and she almost offered. But she thought she'd better check to see if that was really his problem. "You want to ride a trike?" she asked. Jake had planted himself firmly in front of the trike. "No, I want Sam off!" he replied, still clinging to Sam's handlebar.

Nancy thought again, looking around for other clues. Then she saw the chalk dust smeared all over Jake's hands and clothes. Nancy looked ahead on the sidewalk and saw a big colored section. "It looks like you are worried Sam will drive over your picture," she guessed. Jake nodded, "Yeah." Nancy then modeled some words Jake could use to ask Sam to please go around his drawing. They communicated to the best of their ability, and the conflict was resolved. Both boys returned to their play. ∞

Cultural differences can present another barrier to reflective listening. For instance, some families discourage children from speaking their minds to adults, or teach children not to look at people who are talking (Trawick-Smith, 2006). So, if you are trying to use reflective listening with a child and you become frustrated that the child isn't looking at you, be sure to consider whether this is a cross-cultural misunderstanding.

HELPING CHILDREN RESOLVE CONFLICTS

Both reflective listening and I messages come in handy when conflicts arise. When your needs and the needs of a child conflict, sophisticated communication skills can help you to negotiate a solution. You can protect your own personal limits and still respect the needs of children. When youngsters experience conflict among themselves, you can coach them in using effective communication to resolve their differences. Your classroom can become a laboratory for learning the fine art of conflict resolution. This skill may be one of the most important subjects you can teach.

It is important for adults to take time to teach children the steps of conflict resolution.

Many people think that conflict is bad and should be avoided; however, avoiding conflict usually means repressing feelings. Rarely can people live and work together in total harmony with no one's needs impinging on those of another. Conflict in the classroom and on the playground can be viewed as a learning opportunity. It is a chance for children to learn about the needs and wants of others, and it is also a chance for them to learn lifelong skills for mutual problem solving. In the process of practicing conflict resolution, children have the opportunity to learn more about perspective taking, empathy, self-control, and collaboration (Landy, 2002; Wheeler, 2004).

Consistency in Schools

Schools have traditionally used a power model rather than a negotiation model (Gordon, 1989). Because children have so often seen adults use threats and intimidation as ways of resolving differences, it may take some effort to teach children a peaceful, respectful alternative. However, you will find it is worth the effort both to enhance the social skills of your students and to increase peace in your classroom.

Many of the social skills curriculum programs adopted by school districts include conflict resolution instruction based on the same principles of negotiation and consensus that Thomas Gordon described (e.g., Siccone & Lopez, 2000). The success of these programs may require that schools let go of authoritarian approaches to discipline. It is difficult to teach students a cooperative approach to resolving their problems if you model a different style when adult-to-child interactions are involved. If adults use a "power-on" model, instead of learning negotiation and cooperation, children learn that "might makes right." Children must feel trust, knowing that they are emotionally and physically safe, in order for conflict resolution to be successful (Levin, 2003).

Everyone Wins

Negotiating mutually acceptable solutions allows both sides to have power and respect. No one says, "You do it my way or else." No group says, "We have more votes. You lose." No one ends up angry and resentful. Therefore, general attitudes and relationships are more pleasant. Because everyone is involved in selecting the solutions, each person is more likely to follow through on them.

In addition, the solutions tend to be of higher quality, reflecting the needs and ideas of all involved. The process helps children to consider the views of other people. Consideration of others and the thinking process involved in problem solving both contribute to the long-term goals of intellectual and moral autonomy. It takes a lot more work to get consensus than just to vote, but that's what makes negotiation such a great learning opportunity.

Mutual problem solving not only assists children toward long-term goals, but it also makes life more pleasant in the here and now. It relieves youngsters from the anger and the fear of punishment that accompany teacher-power approaches. It relieves the teacher from constantly having to nag, enforce, and police instead of teach. Mutual problem solving makes school a much more enjoyable and productive place for teachers and children.

Conflict Resolution Programs

The violence prevention programs listed in the end of Chapter 6 include conflict resolution in their comprehensive approach. Some other programs for teaching conflict resolution are *Peacemaking Skills for Little Kids* (Schmidt & Freidman, 1992), *Teaching Conflict Resolution Through Children's Literature* (Kreidler, 1999), and *Conscious Discipline* (Bailey, 2002). Gordon (1970, 1989) presents the basic model for peaceful negotiation and problem solving; many other authors present variations of these steps. Diane Levin's book *Teaching Young Children in Violent Times: Building a Peaceable Classroom* (2003) is another helpful source on conflict resolution.

These programs are most successful when they are implemented schoolwide, so that not only the teachers, but also the playground and lunchroom aides, the principal, the librarian, and all adults in the school, treat children respectfully and know how to encourage peaceful conflict resolution. When parents are brought onto the team, the benefits are much greater. Even if your school doesn't adopt such a program, you will find that the materials offer helpful ideas for class discussions and activities to promote kindness, caring, and cooperation. Some programs, such as *Peacemaking Skills for Little Kids* (Schmidt & Friedman, 1992), suggest children's literature to help teach ideals of the caring community; others, like *Teaching Conflict Resolution Through Children's Literature* (Kreidler, 1999), use children's stories as the main focus. Whether your school uses a formal program or not, you can informally help your students learn conflict resolution. When conflicts arise, you can support children in using the problem-solving approach to conflict resolution. Seizing the teachable moment is often more effective than any formal program.

Figure 7–4 shows the steps for several well-designed programs. We will use Gordon's model to discuss the basic steps.

STEPS FOR NEGOTIATING SOLUTIONS TO PROBLEMS		
Thomas Gordon's Steps	**Peaceworks Steps**	**William Kreidler's Steps**
Identify the problem.	Keep both hands on the peace table while you are talking and listening.	Ask: What's the problem?
Generate solutions.		Brainstorm solutions.
Evaluate solutions.	Tell the truth.	Choose the best.
Make a decision.	Listen without interrupting.	Do it!
Implement the plan.	No name-calling or blaming.	
Evaluate the plan.	List ideas to solve the problem.	
	Choose the best solution.	

FIGURE 7–4 Negotiating Solutions to Problems

Identifying the Problem

How does the problem-solving process work? You may begin the process in a class meeting or on the spot during a conflict. When children are very upset or angry, the process will be unsuccessful unless they have some time to calm themselves before beginning (Landy, 2002). In some programs, calming techniques such as breathing are taught with the process. In others, children leave the scene of the conflict and go to a peace table (Schmidt & Freidman, 1992). Whatever the setting, the steps are the same. The first step in conflict resolution is identifying the problem. This step is where I messages come in to help each side express how its needs or expectations are not being met. Reflective listening is useful for hearing the other side, and often it's necessary for discovering the actual cause of the problem. If you see your role as the storyteller, you can remain objective and let the kids do their own work. Being a storyteller means describing both sides of a situation to all the children involved. You may also point out any feelings that the children are expressing.

In the following example, the teacher helps the children use conflict resolution and effective communication to solve their conflict.

∞ During the after-school child-care program, Ann, the program director, noticed some tension on the basketball court. "Hey guys," Ann said as she approached. "Looks like you've got a problem."

"They won't let us have the ball!" complained the younger children.

"They won't, huh?" she reflected. The kids responded by telling her more about the situation. "They never throw the ball to us," said some of the younger children. "They always lose the ball when they dribble down the court," retorted some of the older children. Ann summed up their comments without blaming either side and defined the problem as a shared one (Levin, 2003), "You both have a problem here, don't you? Everyone wants a chance with the ball, and the way you were playing doesn't give you both time with the ball. It's no fun for you younger kids to be left out and it's frustrating for you older kids to keep losing the ball to the other team." The kids were obviously glad that Ann understood and confirmed her thoughts about what they were feeling. ∞

Brainstorming Solutions

Once the problem is identified, everyone involved needs to help think of possible solutions. Many conflict resolution programs include setting limits about blaming or criticizing any specific children during this step (Rightmyer, 2003). No idea is too wild, and no ideas are rejected at this point. In fact, no ideas should even be evaluated yet. Be sure to continue getting ideas until everyone has run out of possibilities. Sometimes, writing down all the ideas where everyone can see them is helpful, even if the children are too young to read yet. You can refer to the list as you review, and they will recognize their ideas.

Ann asked all of the children, "Can you think of what you could do so that everyone can play and have some time with the ball?" The group proposed many ideas, and Ann wrote them on a big piece of paper so all could see.

∞ "Big kids play and then little kids have a turn," suggested Stephen, a competitive and competent player.

"Little kids play an easier game," offered Abby, trying to be helpful.

"Don't take the ball when we dribble," Eli said assertively.

That seemed to spark an idea for Blake: "I know!" he said excitedly. "Let's make a rule that the little kids can either dribble the ball or they can hold it and run down the court."

"OK," chimed in Riley. "And when they dribble, no big kids can try to get it; but if they carry it, we can try to get it away."

The brainstorming seemed over at this point and it was time for the next step in problem solving. ∞

Evaluating Solutions and Making a Choice

The next step is to evaluate the suggestions. Which ones are just impossible or totally unacceptable to someone? Cross those out immediately. Now what is left? Do any of them stand out as great ideas? Continue the discussion until everyone agrees to try one or a combination of solutions. Make sure the children understand that choosing a solution means a commitment to carrying it out. Voting is not a part of the process. This is a consensus model: Everyone agrees to try a solution, and no one is forced into it by a "someone loses" or "minorities lose" method, such as a vote.

∞ Choosing among the suggestions for the basketball conflict didn't take long. Will held out a bit for his idea of the big kids playing without the little kids, but the little kids nixed that one. There was lots of support for the idea of new rules that created some equality between older players and younger ones. Consensus soon emerged around that plan, and the new basketball rules were clarified. ∞

Implementing the Plan

There's more to the process than simply determining a solution. A plan isn't worth much unless you figure out how to implement it. Who will do what? When and how often? Where and how? To what standards? Who checks? When children make these kinds of decisions and plan to implement them, they tend to follow through with little teacher direction.

∞ Blake and Riley felt ownership of the new plan. They took leadership roles in setting up teams of fairly equal ability and getting the game going again. All the children reminded one another of the new rules as they played. ∞

Evaluating the Plan

What if the solution doesn't work? There are many reasons why it might not. Perhaps it was too difficult to implement or perhaps there were conditions you and the children neglected to consider. Evaluating the solution after you have tried it for a while is an essential final step. If you find that things aren't working, that situation isn't a signal for you to take over. It just means that the group needs to try again to generate workable solutions.

∞ Ann watched with pleasure as the game went on for a full 45 minutes without a single problem. What a relief! Complaints and arguments had been the main event on the basketball court for days. In addition, she noticed that these new rules encouraged the younger children to practice dribbling the ball. The older children were now working in partnership with the younger ones on their team, giving them the ball and urging them to dribble it, since that protected it from being stolen. Everyone seemed to be having a good time.

Ann checked with the group the next day after school, asking them how their new "big kid—little kid" rules worked out. There seemed to be unanimous agreement that they worked great. ∞

Saving Time

Does conflict resolution sound like it takes a lot of time? This is a common concern. Sometimes problem solving can be accomplished in just a few minutes; at other times, it does take quite a lot of time. However, if you have a recurring problem, that takes a lot of time, too. Teachers and parents who use this problem-solving approach report that it saves a lot of time in the long run. Instead of ineffectively dealing with the same problem over and over, time is set aside to deal effectively with the problem until it is resolved. The time spent on this problem-solving session was certainly time well spent for Ann; the problem had been disrupting play and dividing the group for quite some time.

Independent Problem Solvers

You can save yourself time and trouble by teaching youngsters to negotiate solutions to their own problems. The model you provide in group problem solving is an important part of this teaching, but you will need to talk children

Taking the time to teach conflict resolution skills helps children learn how to solve their own problems independently.

through the process individually while they are learning. Teaching conflict resolution during class meetings is a great way to work toward fostering independent problem solvers. You can begin teaching the process slowly, starting with the first two steps. Later you can work with the kids on evaluating the solutions and choosing the best one. Eventually the kids will be able to do these steps in one sitting. Gradually you can add in the implementation and evaluation of plans.

You can teach these steps as you work on real class issues. Some teachers have a sign-up sheet available for children to record their name or an issue that will be solved through conflict resolution during class meeting (Adams & Wittmer, 2001). The use of puppets and children's literature is also a great way to bring up conflicts to discuss with groups of young children. There are many sources for finding meaningful children's books and tips on how to use them, such as *Teaching Conflict Resolution Through Children's Literature* (Kreidler, 1999) and *Class Meetings: Young Children Solving Problems Together* (Vance & Weaver, 2002). When using children's stories, you can ask questions that help children apply the lessons to their own lives.

If you continually practice the same steps for conflict resolution with individual children and in your class meetings, it will come naturally to the children. It takes practice for teachers, too, to ask meaningful questions that allow children to solve their own problems during this process (Koplow, 2002). Kreidler's (1999) simplified *ABCD* version of negotiation is probably easiest for children to remember: A. Ask: What's the problem? B. Brainstorm solutions. C. Choose the best. D. Do it! Let's see how Jacob and Blake work out their problem at the sand table.

∞ Jacob and Blake were trying to play together at the sand table again, but as always, they had very different game plans. Jacob was trying to make carefully groomed patterns in the sand. Blake was chugging around with a bulldozer, trying to get all of the sand up against the edges, exposing the bottom.

Jacob complained as the bulldozer kept undermining his space, making the patterns sluff away. Mrs. Jensen observed the conflict and got things rolling by helping them define the problem. "It looks like you two are getting in each other's way here," she commented. Then she suggested that the boys try to brainstorm a way to play together at the sand table.

Jacob frowned, wishing the teacher would just tell Blake to stop ruining his work. Then Mrs. Jensen reminded him, "You guys have been solving problems so well during our class meetings. I bet you could come up with a way to fix this one!" Jacob brightened up.

Mrs. Jensen then asked, "Do you remember how to brainstorm solutions?" Blake had liked that part; anything you thought of was okay, so you could be silly or serious. Blake was silly: "Measure every grain of sand and divide it exactly!" Jacob got into it and offered, "We could take turns at the sand table." "I know! We could build the Great Wall of China, and neither one could cross it!" Blake said excitedly, remembering a picture he had seen of the wall. Jacob thought again and came up with one last idea: "Blake could play with the funnels instead of the bulldozer."

Mrs. Jensen reminded the boys that choosing the best solution meant they had to both agree on a solution to try. Measuring sounded like a challenge and both boys thought it would be too hard. Taking turns was rejected because neither wanted to be second, and Blake wasn't interested in playing with the funnels. But the "Great Wall" idea intrigued both of the boys. They asked if they could use some blocks in the sand table to make a barrier wall.

Mrs. Jensen thought to herself that the idea might not work but told them to go ahead anyway. They were eager to try out their solution. It didn't perfectly hold back sand, but it was completely effective at resolving the conflict between the boys. Whenever it collapsed, they ignored their patterns and bulldozing to rebuild their barrier cooperatively, the new major focus! ∽

If you teach children how to negotiate their own solutions, soon they will be teaching each other and won't constantly be coming to you with their arguments or to tattle-tale (Rightmyer, 2003). Even preschool-age children are capable of problem solving. In the past, adults generally just separated children who were in conflict, or else the teacher decided who was in the right and would "win." Teaching children to arrive at a mutually satisfying solution to their disagreements is a more productive use of your time (Watson, 1999). In the process of learning to problem-solve, your young students will learn about peaceful negotiation of differences. Perhaps they will even put this skill to work as adults, possibly helping the people of the world to resolve their differences peacefully.

FAMILY AND COMMUNITY

Imagine what a different world it would be if children grew up feeling so cared for that they could never imagine doing harm to themselves or anyone else! What if families, schools, and communities worked together to protect children and teach them, by example, about cooperation and caring for others? Would the United States still spend more on the prison system than on education? Is it conceivable that schools could be a model for families and communities? When children know they are valued, worthy of time and attention, heard, and treated with kindness and respect, they will pass this treatment along to others they encounter throughout their lives.

Comprehensive violence prevention programs, such as the Resolving Conflict Creatively Program (RCCP), teach effective communication and peaceful conflict resolution to teachers, children, parents, and school administration and staff. Using this program in a school for only 1 year showed some encouraging results: "92% of children felt better about themselves; and more than 90% of parents reported an increase in their own communication and problem-solving skills" (Lantieri, 2003, p. 84).

We believe that any approach that enables schools to model and teach respectful and peaceful communication to children and parents will have a positive impact that echoes throughout our communities. If children internalize these skills when they are young and continue experiencing and using them throughout their growing years, the implications for their adult years are staggering. Maybe they would become world leaders able to peacefully resolve international disputes, without war. Maybe child abuse and domestic violence would only be a bad memory of our past. These are lofty goals, we realize. However, starting with one classroom in one school, building positive relationships with children and their families, is well within your realm of possibility. Through your example, class meetings, and other integrated classroom activities, children can learn how to treat others with kindness. Through workshops, newsletters, community events, and your own interactions with families, they can also learn more effective and peaceful communication skills. If more teachers and schools used this approach, the impact would be well worth the effort.

CONCLUSION

When we communicate with children respectfully, we can prevent many discipline problems and solve many others. When we state our own needs respectfully, children are more apt to behave considerately in the first place and are generally more willing to change their behavior if it has become inappropriate. By reflectively listening to children, we can help them resolve their own problems, either before their behavior is adversely affected or in time to remedy the situation. When we teach problem-solving skills, children learn to avoid disputes as well as to resolve them. Communicating with kindness and respect, and teaching children to do the same, has far-reaching implications. Our dedication in the beginning of this book reflects the aim of our interactions with children. This book was written "For the cause of worldwide peace and harmony. May it begin in the hearts of children and spread. And may teachers be the sowers of the seeds of peace and harmony."

∞ FOR FURTHER THOUGHT

1. Listen to adults talking to children. Think about those same words used with another adult. Do they sound ridiculous or reasonable? Analyze your own ways of talking to children. Do you show less respect to children than to your adult acquaintances?

2. Practice using I messages when someone upsets you. What were the results? Were you careful not to send a disguised "you message"? Were you able to stop yourself from also telling the other person what to do or not to do? Keep on trying. It takes time to break old habits.

3. Practice reflective listening with friends who confide in you about a problem. Be careful not to give advice or reassurance, but only to clarify your understanding of the other person's feelings. How does this attitude affect the communication? Is it difficult to do?

4. A problem to solve: Angie comes to you complaining because another child is using the swing and she wants to swing.
   a. Describe a common ineffective response.
   b. Describe a reflective-listening response.

5. A problem to solve: Matt and Jason are experimenting with magnets at preschool. Jason goes off to play elsewhere, and Matt starts crying.
   a. What might a teacher say who is skilled in reflective listening?
   b. What might a teacher say who doesn't understand about roadblocks to communication?

6. Try out the steps to negotiating conflicts as described in this chapter. Analyze the results to learn how to be more effective in the future.

∞ RECOMMENDED READINGS

Adams, S. K., & Wittmer, D. S. (2001). I had it first: Teaching young children to solve problems peacefully. *Childhood Education, 78*(1), 10–17.

Faber, A., & Mazlish, E. (1996). *How to talk so kids can learn at home and in school.* New York: Fireside/Simon & Schuster.

Ginott, H. (1965). *Between parent and child: New solutions to old problems.* New York: Macmillan.

Gordon, T. (1970). *Parent effectiveness training.* New York: Wyden.

Gordon, T. (1974). *T.E.T.: Teacher effectiveness training.* New York: Wyden.

Gordon, T. (1989). *Teaching children self-discipline: At home and at school.* New York: Random House.

Kreidler, W. J. (1999). *Teaching conflict resolution through children's literature.* New York: Scholastic.

Levin, D. E. (2003). *Teaching young children in violent times: Building a peaceable classroom* (2nd ed.). Washington, DC: National Association for the Education of Young Children.

Schmidt, F., & Friedman, A. (1992). *Peacemaking skills for little kids.* Fresno, CA: Peace Works Inc.

Siccone, F., & Lopez, L. (2000). *Educating the heart: Lessons to build respect and responsibility.* Boston: Allyn & Bacon.

Vance, E., & Weaver, P. (2002). *Class meetings: Young children solving problems together.* Washington, DC: National Association for the Education of Young Children.

❦ *Chapter* **8** ❦
Helping Children Understand and Accept Limits

NAEYC Standards Addressed in This Chapter

Standard 4a: Teaching and Learning, Connecting with Children and Families: Candidates know, understand, and use positive relationships and supportive interactions as the foundation for their work with young children.

Standard 4b: Teaching and Learning, Using Developmentally Effective Approaches: Candidates know, understand, and use a wide array of effective approaches, strategies, and tools to positively influence young children's development and learning.

GUIDING QUESTIONS

- How do you handle immediate behavioral concerns?
- What types of consequences might best guide children toward moral autonomy?
- What is the difference between consequences and punishment?
- How do adults select consequences?

*W*hat do you do if prevention, modeling, listening, and problem solving don't work? What if you need to change a behavior immediately? What do you do when it's too late to prevent a problem because it is already happening? Do you then turn to punishment?

In *The Moral Judgment of the Child* (1965), Piaget identifies two types of sanctions that serve to guide children toward higher levels of moral autonomy. The first is an expiatory or punitive sanction—a punishment. This type of sanction is delivered with coercion and is designed to make the child suffer. Piaget points out the arbitrary nature of punishment and its negative affect on autonomy as a reason for not using punishment to guide children's behavior. The second type of sanction Piaget suggests is a reciprocal sanction. DeVries calls Piaget's sanctions *consequences*, and we adopt that term here (DeVries & Zan, 1994).

Reciprocal sanctions further social functioning because they are based on relationships. In this sense, Piaget argues that the consequence should help the child understand how the misdeed affects others. As was the case in modeling good behaviors, reciprocal consequences depend on the child's relationships with adults and peers. The child learns that misbehavior has a negative affect on relationships, so he or she is motivated to behave to keep the relationship intact. The consequences in this case are designed to guide children toward self-regulation.

Piaget describes five types of sanctions or consequences that are alternatives to punishment. These sanctions or consequences may be imposed by adults or peers, or they may occur as a natural outcome of the child's actions.

1. *Natural consequences:* The child experiences the direct results of his or her own behavior. Piaget uses the example of a child who has a cold room as a result of breaking his or her own bedroom window.

2. *Exclusion:* A child who hits another child is asked to find something else to do until the he or she feels ready to behave appropriately.

3. *Deprivation:* The child may not have access to materials that have been abused or misused until the child feels ready to behave appropriately.

4. *Restitution:* The child pays for, or replaces, that which has been damaged or lost; the child assists a person injured through that child's fault.

5. *Doing to the child what the child has done:* What the child has done to another is done back to the child. Piaget is very clear that this response does not mean an adult doing evil for evil, such as biting a child who has bitten another. He says that action is not only a poor model but also "absurd" (Piaget, 1965, p. 208). Instead, he refers to a response such as not doing a favor for a child who has not helped with assigned chores. Thus, if the child doesn't help you, you don't help the child.

Dreikurs's concept of natural and logical consequences is basically the same as Piaget's concept of reciprocal consequences. In his book *Children: The Challenge* (1964), and subsequent writing (Dreikurs, Greenwald, & Pepper, 1998), Dreikurs identifies two types of consequences. Like Piaget, he identifies *natural consequences* as those that automatically result from the child's behavior with no intervention from an adult. Dreikurs identifies *logical consequences* as those imposed by an adult but linked to the child's actions. The important distinction between punishment, Dreikur's logical consequences, and Piaget's reciprocal consequences is that the consequences of children's actions, whether naturally occurring or imposed by a peer or adult, are directly related to the action. With punishments, this is generally not the case. Children only come to understand the logical relationship between their actions and the consequences if they are related.

To emphasize the necessity of consequences being related to the behavior, we use the term *related consequences* to describe imposed consequences that help a child learn. It is important to remember that related consequences are designed to help children think: think about why certain behaviors are unacceptable and others are desirable. They are designed to help children view themselves as capable and willing problem solvers.

NATURAL CONSEQUENCES

As noted, both Piaget and Dreikurs recommend the use of natural consequences as one method for addressing misbehavior. Adults do not impose natural consequences. This type of consequence happens naturally as a result of children's actions. Children learn from natural consequences because the consequence is immediate and directly related to the action. Natural consequences also release teachers from the need to deliver reminders or reprimands or constantly nag about what might happen if they engage in a specific behavior.

Natural consequences are mostly a matter of getting out of the way and allowing children to learn from their experiences. Too often adults deprive children of the chance to experience the consequences of their actions because they care about the children and don't want them to have unpleasant or disappointing experiences. Unfortunately, the result is that the children don't become responsible for their own actions (Kamii, 1982). The following example is a type that most teachers see frequently.

∞ Travis is tipping his chair backwards again. Mrs. Jensen has reminded him numerous times that he might get hurt if the chair tips over and he falls backwards. His action indicates that the nagging hasn't helped the situation. Before Mrs. Jensen has a chance to remind Travis again, the chair tips over. Travis catches himself and breaks the fall, but he is clearly shocked by the jolt. Mrs. Jensen helps Travis up from the ground and asks if he is hurt. He indicates that he is fine, but it is clear from the look on his face that he is embarrassed by the commotion he has caused. Mrs. Jensen does not tell Travis, "I told you so"; instead she lets the consequence speak for itself. ∞

The Inevitable Does Happen

Although teachers and parents are often uncomfortable with allowing natural consequences, children still manage to experience them often. They will build an unstable block tower and experience its collapse. From this natural consequence they can begin to learn about balance, physical limits, and maybe the way hard blocks feel when they land in their lap. That is, they will learn if adults don't stop them by controlling their constructions. Social behavior and friendships are also

Sometimes children's behavior leads to natural consequences such as peer rejection.

molded a great deal by natural consequences (Riley et al., 2008). A child who repeatedly hurts others physically or hurts their feelings may reap the consequence of peer rejection, as in the following example.

∞ On the playground at Lincoln Elementary School, the ratio is 2 aides to 250 children. Here, free from the ever-watching eyes and ears of the classroom teacher, the children learn how to get along on their own. Alli had been particularly bossy to her table mates in class one morning. She told Rosa to get out of the book corner and ordered Ling Ling to clean up her mess. When Alli came out for recess, they all avoided her, leaving her out of their games. She complained, "Why can't I play?" Rosa answered directly, "Cause you always have to be the boss!" Alli was experiencing a delayed natural consequence for her earlier behavior. ∞

The teacher can help Alli by helping her to think through this experience, not by saving her from it. Although showing sympathy for her hurt feelings is appropriate, fixing the problem Alli created will not help her learn. Some adults would insist that no child should be left out; this would ruin Alli's lesson. A much kinder teacher response is to encourage Alli to think about how she might act differently in the future in order to be accepted on the playground.

Avoiding Overprotection

Mrs. Jensen does try hard not to protect children from learning through their mistakes. She reminds herself not to take over their responsibilities when they forget. She doesn't nag, coax, and remind children to do the things they are supposed to remember on their own. Mrs. Jensen thinks that youngsters learning to take responsibility for themselves is more important than making sure everyone remembers to take home the book order list or even the class newsletter. She teaches effectively by helping them to figure out the cause-and-effect relationship between their actions and the results. They soon find out that they don't get to buy a book if they don't take the book order form home, get permission and money to place an order, and then return the form with the money to school. She knows that children learn through their experiences and that learning takes time.

The real world offers much more opportunity for natural consequences than school does. By its nature, school is an artificial environment that doesn't allow much opportunity for natural responses. At home, Mrs. Jensen can allow her own children to learn much more freely from their mistakes than she can at school with her students. If her own children don't put away their things at home, they naturally get lost. At school, the custodian picks things up and gets cross when they are lying around. When her own children go running outside without a coat on a cool day, she lets them find out for themselves that they need to come back for a coat. At school, she worries that parents will think she is shirking her responsibility if she lets her students go out to recess without coats. Besides, school rules don't allow youngsters to run back inside for coats in the middle of recess. Mrs. Jensen has trouble allowing for natural consequences at school.

RELATED CONSEQUENCES

When natural consequences are not feasible, teachers can use related consequences to help children learn about the results of their actions. Related consequences are consequences that are directly tied to a behavior. They communicate
through actions that certain behaviors will not be tolerated. At the same time, related consequences help children learn why that behavior is undesirable, giving
them personal reasons to change. Instead of merely forcing children to do what
adults know is best, related consequences help youngsters reflect on how their
actions affect others. Related consequences use children's own experiences as
the basis for teaching desirable behavior. This form of discipline helps develop the
personal responsibility necessary for self-discipline and moral autonomy. At the
same time, this kind of discipline respects the child's right and ability to choose
an action that is more appropriate.

Natural consequences are not always acceptable in school situations. Adults
do have the responsibility of keeping children safe from harm. Obviously, no one
allows a child to experience the natural consequences of playing in the street. Instead, adults watch carefully and plan related consequences to help youngsters
learn to stay away from traffic.

There is general agreement that children cannot be allowed to take risks that
could result in serious injury. Therefore, adult-imposed consequences are often
the only learning experiences available. Following are examples of four types of
related consequences. Note that the purpose in each case is to help children relate their behavior to its results.

Doing to the Child What the Child Has Done

From a Piagetian perspective, doing to the child what the child has done is appropriate for teaching children how a behavior can break trust or the relationship
bond. This type of consequence is not revenge. Piaget's example of this type of
consequence is sending a child who pretends to be sick to bed for the day, or not
helping a child who has not helped you when asked. To walk the fine line between
punishment and imposed consequences, it is essential to keep anger and recrimination out of your response.

At school, it is more often the children who "do unto others." For instance,
Nicole may not help Karina with her project because Karina got mad and
messed up Nicole's project last time they worked together. Mrs. Jensen helps
Karina to learn from this experience but doesn't insist that Nicole help her.
What if Sam hits Zach? Do you allow Zach to hit him back? Occasionally, Dennis
decides that this response is the learning experience one of his preschoolers
needs. Perhaps the child hasn't had enough social interaction to realize that
hitting gets a negative response from peers. In that case, Dennis pretends not
to notice what is happening; of course he cannot appear to condone hitting. In
the rare times he might allow it, Dennis definitely keeps an eye out to be sure
no one really gets hurt.

Exclusion

Usually, however, Dennis doesn't allow hitting and uses related consequences instead. In the following example we see how Dennis uses the consequence Piaget (1965) called exclusion.

∞ Sam wanted to play with Zach after nap time. Unfortunately, Zach was waking up slowly and just wanted to be left alone. Frustrated, Sam got increasingly aggressive and eventually resorted to physical contact to get Zach's attention. Action escalated from nudges to pushing, and then to hitting. Zach wailed and Dennis intervened. Sensing that Zach was in no condition to verbalize his need for privacy at the moment, Dennis chose to impose the consequence of telling Sam he had to find somewhere else to play, explaining that he could not let him hit Zach. "Hitting hurts," Dennis said as he calmly helped Sam find something to do in another area of the room. He told the child, "You may go back and play with Zach when you are ready to use your words instead of hitting. Zach is hurt and he needs to feel safe." ∞

Notice that Dennis did not tell Sam how long he had to stay away from Zach. Instead of using his adult power to make all the decisions here, Dennis allowed the child to be in charge of how much time he needed. He allowed Sam to reflect on his own actions and to decide when his feelings were under control. Also notice that Dennis didn't confine Sam to a specific place. He excluded Sam from contact with Zach, not contact with everyone and everything. Sam offended Zach so the exclusion should only apply to Sam's contact with Zach. This approach helps Sam recognize the results of his actions on Zach—he can no longer play with him. It also helps to teach Sam that he is responsible for making the choice between playing with Zach in a peaceful manner and playing alone.

Although exclusion may seem related to time-out, there is a difference. Time-out banishes the child from all activities and all of the children in the group. Exclusion permits the child to remain a member of the group, but removes him or her from the person the child offended. The intent is to teach the child that his or her actions broke the relationship bond. In our example, Sam wanted to play with Zach and the consequence was designed to capitalize on Sam's desire to have a relationship with Zach. If Sam wants to repair his relationship with Zach and be permitted to play with him, he will be motivated to show Zach respect by honoring his wishes. Ideally, a teacher or aide can stay with the excluded child to support the thinking process and encourage rejoining the offended person as soon as possible so that the relationship can be repaired.

Deprivation

Chapter 1 mentioned the problem of Kenji knocking over other children's block constructions. In addition to helping Kenji learn a better way of showing that he wants to play, the teacher might also explain to Kenji that he cannot play with the blocks until he is ready to play without damaging the blocks or anyone else's constructions. This is an example of the consequence involving deprivation: not being allowed to use materials that were misused. Telling Kenji he may not play in the block area until he decides he can play without knocking over blocks is very different from making him sit in time-out. Asking him to decide when he is ready to return gives him the message that you have faith in his ability to make the necessary adjustments in his behavior. Making him sit in time-out teaches him that the teacher needs to control his behavior.

Restitution

The example from Chapter 1 in which Anton wipes up the water he spilled is also a related consequence. Cleaning up the mess you make is a way of making restitution, a method that Piaget (1965) recommends. Restitution is our favorite type of related consequence, one that isn't likely to get mixed up with punishment. An example of making restitution that we particularly like involves children who hurt each other through carelessness. If Dylan is throwing rocks and one accidentally hits Jessie, Dylan learns much more about the dangers of rock throwing by holding a cold cloth to Jessie's head than by being banished to the principal's office. Kenji and the block destruction could also be handled with restitution. If it seemed appropriate to the circumstances, the teacher might ask him to help rebuild what he knocked down. Making restitution helps youngsters see themselves as helpful people rather than bad ones. All of these examples describe ways of motivating children to build rules of conduct for themselves from within.

Combining Teaching and Consequences

In a situation like the one with Sam hitting Zach, be sure you don't ignore the child's feelings that lead up to an incident, although this doesn't mean you should interrogate the children to determine who started it. An interrogation would put the adult back in charge of the kids' behavior. Instead, think about how you can help the children deal with their feelings or learn needed skills.

Imposing consequences to stop the hitting doesn't preclude the use of other guidance techniques. For instance, after Sam and Zach have calmed down from the incident, you could work with them on the communications skills discussed in Chapter 7. Each boy could be helped to tune in to his feelings and put them into words. Hitting is often a primitive form of communication; learning higher-level communication skills can help a child give up hitting.

WHEN CONSEQUENCES BECOME PUNISHMENT

Many people use the term "consequence" when they really mean "punishment." "He has to face the consequences" often means a spanking or loss of privilege. In this book we are trying to make a distinction between punishment and consequences. Consequences respond to a behavior problem in a way designed to solve the problem rather than to punish the child. As they were originally described (Dreikurs, 1964), consequences were not intended to be punitive. Yet many people began using that "nicer" term when they really meant punishment, and as a result the terms became confused. Figure 8–1 compares discipline terms.

Natural Consequences	Related Consequences	Punishment
Natural consequences happen without an imposed intervention.	Related consequences are imposed without anger or intent to harm. They are logical and respectful: logical because they are directly tied to a behavior, and respectful because they are intended to teach rather than harm.	Punishment is intended to cause pain, either physical or emotional distress.

FIGURE 8–1 Comparing Discipline Terms

Watch Your Attitude

Even an excellent related consequence can be turned into punishment. For instance, if the adult expresses anger about the garbage, then not fixing dinner will come through as a retaliation rather than a consequence. Instead, the parent might use an I message and say, "I don't want to fix dinner until the garbage is out. The garbage makes the kitchen smell too bad for me to be in there cooking." It is important to be calm and matter-of-fact about imposing consequences. In fact, it is important not to be angry, or your anger will be all that is heard. Effective consequences involve adult intervention without anger or recrimination (Brady, Forton, Porter, & Wood, 2003).

If you use the impending consequences as a threat, that treatment also turns them into punishment (Dreikurs et al., 1998). "Take that garbage out before I come home from work, or no dinner tonight" is not in the spirit of related consequences. There are times when you want to inform children in advance of consequences, but it needs to be done in a nonthreatening and calm manner.

Variations of the "I told you so" theme are another way to ruin the educational value of related consequences (Dreikurs, 1964). Perhaps, in addition to not fixing dinner, the parent might be tempted to say, "Maybe that will teach you a lesson." These words take the focus away from the actual problem and invite an angry power struggle. Often it is better to say nothing. Let the consequences speak for themselves.

The bottom line is respecting children. If you take away a child's dignity as you deal with his or her behavior, you damage that child. Sarcasm and humiliation have no role in teaching better behavior. Instead of trying to avenge a wrong, the helpful approach is to work on a solution to the problem. A constructive guidance approach using consequences looks for ways to make things right again. Helping a child make restitution to someone he or she has harmed is probably the most useful consequence of all.

Use Consequences with Caution

The big difference between punishment and consequences is in how they make children feel about themselves. Punishment convinces a child that he or she is "bad" and damages self-esteem. Consequences aim to empower children in their

Consequences are not the same thing as punishment. Consequences teach understanding; they do not hurt or humiliate.

efforts at self-control and to help them see themselves as good people (Brady et al., 2003). Nevertheless, related consequences can easily turn into punishment if the adult is not careful (Charney, 2002). Because the adult administers them, they demonstrate adult power over children. For this reason, other, less-intrusive methods of discipline should be tried first. Prevention of problems is the least intrusive approach to discipline. Teaching by example, coaching, I messages, and conflict negotiation all teach discipline without the use of adult power.

However, if none of those approaches works on the cause of the misbehavior, then another approach is needed. If a lack of understanding is the behavior cause, then consequences can be used to help the child understand. Also, there are times when judicious, respectful, and limited use of adult power is required in order to keep children safe. If safety guidelines are being tested, it may be time to plan a related consequence. These are the two reasons to rely on consequences as discipline: (1) to teach understanding or (2) to enforce necessary limits while you work on the cause of a behavior problem.

Plan Ahead

Sometimes it's hard to remember the judicious and respectful aspects of related consequences. Imposed consequences can quickly lead to a power struggle for the unwary adult. Remember Dennis's problem with the "no lunch until you clean up your mess" ultimatum in Chapter 4? Dennis had a practical rationale for that ruling: He wanted to clear the room for lunch. However, it was really Dennis, and not the situation, that was depriving Amy of her lunch. Amy's dress-up clothes weren't on the lunch table, and she couldn't see any reason why they had to be put away before she could eat. Dennis had only his power as an adult to enforce his hasty ultimatum, and that power led to the confrontation. Effective consequences strive for adult withdrawal from power rather than an application of power. Fortunately, Dennis's ego allowed him to back down, listen reflectively, and negotiate a solution with the child.

Related consequences take planning and forethought. They require the teacher to step away from adult needs and to look at the behavior from the perspective of the child. When imposing a related consequence, the connection between the child's behavior and the results must be clear to the child. Dreikurs (1964) reminds us that if the consequence isn't related to the action, children will not learn how their behavior affects others. Instead, they come to see adults as unjust and often seek retaliation to the injustice by engaging in power struggles.

SELECTING REASONABLE CONSEQUENCES

Selecting a consequence related to the action takes thought and understanding. Many people don't understand how to apply consequences. They impose totally unrelated outcomes on children's behavior and call them consequences. They don't realize that without the relationship between the action and the result, there is no learning involved; the result is merely punishment (DeVries & Zan, 1994; Thornberg, 2008).

Public school discipline guides often list a variety of punishments they call consequences: losing a recess for chewing gum, staying after school for talking back to a teacher, or doing push-ups for hitting someone. Totally unrelated to children's behavior, these punishments teach resentment, calculation of the risk of getting caught, and consideration of whether the benefits are worth the costs (Dreikurs, Cassel, & Dreikurs-Ferguson, 2004). Gum chewing might have a reasonable consequence if there is a need to scrape gum off floors and desks. Discipline for talking back to a teacher or hitting someone should depend on the causes for those behaviors. No pat solution could address all the various sources of those behaviors. Discipline solutions are of questionable value if they are not based on the cause of the behavior as determined by information about the nature of the individual child, the particular situation, and the relationship between those involved (Goodman, 2006).

Careful Thought

Related consequences are supposed to help children judge the pros and cons of a certain behavior as they experience the ramifications. Therefore, consequences must be selected carefully. Besides picking something related to the behavior, you need to think of a consequence that matters to kids. Telling them they have to hurry up or they'll be late may carry no clout if being late isn't important to the

Teaching social responsibility through related consequences requires as much careful planning as teaching academics.

child (Thornberg, 2008). The consequence also needs to be something that you can live with and are actually willing to follow through with, unlike Joanne's threat in the following scenario.

∞ The children kept running across the plot that had been rototilled for a garden at Midway Children's Center. They delighted by how the fluffy soil felt! The parent who had promised to build a fence to protect it kept putting off the job. Joanne tried steering the children away, telling them that the ground would get packed down too hard to plant in, but they had no concept of the problem. As yet another group raced through the garden area, she gave up. Crossly, she told them, "That does it! We just won't have a garden if you step in there again!" Intimidated by her anger, the children avoided the tempting dirt for most of the afternoon.

Then Kenji blew it. Right before pickup time, he got carried away with a game of tag and tromped through the forbidden zone. A few minutes later, the parent volunteer arrived with an armful of tools to work on the fence. Olivia piped up, "We don't need a fence anymore. We can't have a garden 'cause Kenji stepped in it!" Embarrassed, Joanne looked at the confused parent. She wondered how she could get out of this one. She really wanted to have a school garden. ∞

Clear Teaching Goals

Living and working harmoniously in a group requires great mutual consideration and cooperation (DeVries & Zan, 1994). Related consequences can be very useful in helping children develop and remember these attitudes. Mrs. Jensen plans this part of her curriculum as carefully as the academic aspects. As she plans, she keeps in mind her goal of assisting the children's growth toward autonomy. She wants to give them freedom while helping them understand that freedom implies responsibility.

This responsibility includes not impinging on the freedom of others, such as the rights of other classrooms not to be disturbed. Mrs. Jensen's plans are also built around the principle of respect for each child, which she demonstrates through her belief in the child's ability and desire to behave responsibly. She firmly believes that all people, including children, have an equal claim to dignity and respect. She likes the way Dr. Seuss puts it in *Horton Hears a Who* (Geisel, 1954): "A person's a person, no matter how small."

Mrs. Jensen employs a variety of strategies to help her students determine the value of mutual consideration and cooperation. In addition to imposing related consequences, she also demonstrates desirable attitudes and behaviors through personal example. She makes sure that the class environment encourages harmonious social interaction, too. The best approach to guidance and discipline is to use a combination of preventative strategies, consequences, and opportunities for reflection.

Combining Strategies

Dennis wants to do more than merely stop the misbehavior; he wants to get at the cause as well. If the cause is simply that the child does not understand why an action is inappropriate, then consequences and reflection are sufficient. If the behavior is signaling an unmet need, as it may have when Sam hit Zach, that need must also be considered.

∞ When Sam was harassing and eventually hurting his friend Zach, Dennis stopped the escalating behavior by removing Sam—an exclusion consequence. If he thought that Sam's behavior was a symptom of an unmet need for attention, Dennis could have helped Sam get that need met. If Sam had complained that Zach wasn't his friend anymore, Dennis could have listened reflectively to find out more. Maybe Sam just wanted a playmate, so Dennis could have coached him in ways to play cooperatively. ∞

PEARSON
myeducationlab

To view an example of how teacher and child rules come into conflict, go to MyEducationLab and select the topic "Guiding Children." Under Activities and Applications, watch the video "How Many Fingers Did You Use?"

The key to successfully combining strategies is to evaluate the situation and all of the possible causes of children's behavior. First you must decide if you need to change behavior immediately to keep children safe, or if it is appropriate to let the child experience a natural consequence. Next, you need to determine the cause of the behavior. Is the behavior a result of the environmental arrangement? Is it a result of curricular demands? Is the behavior typical for the child's developmental level, or does he have a need that is not being met? Finally, you need to consider what you or other adults have and haven't taught the child. Have adults in the child's life modeled examples of good behavior? Has the child been coached in effective communication skills?

Evaluating Expectations

As a result of trying to think up reasonable consequences, Mrs. Jensen sometimes finds that there really is no good reason why some actions displayed by children aren't acceptable. She knows that children will more easily accept limits when they can see their value (Thornberg, 2008). She believes children deserve an explanation of reasons why certain behaviors are unacceptable. If she can't think of such an explanation, she is inclined to change the expectation or to allow the behavior. Sometimes her decision means not conforming to school traditions, such as walking in lines.

∞ Walking through school hallways in regimented lines under the stern gaze of the teacher is a time-honored tradition. Yet Mrs. Jensen can't convince herself that lines are necessary or helpful.

Why shouldn't youngsters be allowed to walk in quiet groups like adults? Won't they learn more about respecting others if they are in charge of their own behavior than if the teacher is standing guard? Won't many behavior problems be solved if kids aren't walking so close together and don't all have to go at the same time? Mrs. Jensen sees many children poking the child in front of them just from the sheer frustration of waiting until everyone is ready.

She has been working to teach her students about walking through the halls without disturbing other classes or blocking the hallway for people coming in the opposite direction. She finds this approach a much more productive use of her energy than enforcing the lines.

It is much easier for Mrs. Jensen to explain to her students the importance of not bothering others than to explain why they have to stay in a line. She feels good about the time spent helping children learn to be independent in the halls. She leads class discussions about what hall behaviors would bother other classrooms. During these discussions, Mrs. Jensen sees careful thinking; the children are definitely making progress in understanding the views of others. She sees children feeling important and proud as they practice being responsible for their own behavior in the hallway. Children who continually forget about thoughtful behavior can be helped to remember by experiencing a consequence. Mrs. Jensen simply asks forgetful children to walk with her until they think they can manage on their own. ∞

You probably have seen a child being punished for hallway misbehavior by having to walk with the teacher, and you may be wondering why we are calling this a consequence and not a punishment. Walking with the teacher is a deprivation consequence—the child is being deprived of walking alone because he or she is breaking the bond of respecting others' rights to a quiet workplace. Notice that the child only walks with the teacher until the child decides he or she can manage alone. Giving the child this power is important. Also remember that the adult attitude toward the child is a key factor in the difference between punishment and consequences. A helpful attitude is much different from an angry one and makes a child feel much differently about walking with the teacher. Of course, the way the child feels about the teacher in general also plays a part. Your relationship with each child is the foundation for any guidance or discipline approach.

Teachers using natural or related consequences must be careful not to ruin the learning experience by adding sermons or scolding.

USING CONSEQUENCES

Because of the thought and planning required, you usually will not implement consequences the first time a certain behavior occurs. Typically, a teacher analyzes an ongoing problem, trying out various hypotheses about the cause. When it becomes clear that the cause is not unrealistic adult expectations, missing skills, or unmet needs, the adult may decide that the cause is the child's lack of understanding. At that point, the teacher must first decide whether natural consequences will suffice or whether related consequences are required. If related consequences are needed, the adult's challenge is to figure out something that will demonstrate the link between the behavior and the outcome. Figure 8–2 compares how natural and related consequences might be used in a variety of situations.

Helping Children Make Connections

Preschoolers may be somewhat less adept at linking cause and effect, but they are able to learn from related consequences. Dennis and Maureen know that they can use related consequences to help their students learn. Adults can assist

Natural Consequences	Exclusion	Deprivation	Restitution
Stephen is playing with three other children in the sand box. He gets angry and throws the truck. *The wheel breaks and he can no longer drive it.*	Stephen is playing with three other children in the sand box. He gets angry and throws his truck. *The teacher asks Stephen to leave the sandbox until he feels ready to play there safely and not throw anything.*	Stephen is playing with three other children in the sand box. He gets angry and throws his truck. *Mrs. Jensen calmly tells him he'll have to find something else to play with. She puts the truck in the storage shed.*	Stephen is playing with three other children in the sand box. He gets angry and throws his truck. *Mrs. Jensen discusses the consequences of throwing the truck and helps him fix it.*
Allie pokes Meghan during shared reading. *Meghan cries out, "Ouch! And pokes Allie back."*	Allie pokes Meghan during shared reading. *The teacher has Allie go back to her seat for the rest of shared reading time.*	Allie pokes Meghan during shared reading. *Mrs. Jensen says, "If you can't keep your hands to yourself, you'll have to go to the library and read by yourself."*	Allie pokes Meghan during shared reading. *Mrs. Jensen asks, "Meghan, do you need some ice for your poke?" Meghan says "yes." Mrs. Jensen asks Allie to get the ice pack and give it to Meghan.*
Emma blurts out answers during whole-group math instruction. *Mrs. Jensen ignores her.*	Emma blurts out answers during whole-group math instruction. *Mrs. Jenson gives Emma the math problems on a piece of paper and asks her to go work on them in the math center.*	Emma blurts out answers during whole-group math instruction. *Mrs. Jenson writes the math problem on a small white board and shows it to children one at a time. Emma is last.*	Emma blurts out answers during whole-group math instruction. *Mrs. Jensen says, "Emma, your friends like to do their own thinking. What can we do to give them time to think before you tell the answer?"*

FIGURE 8–2 Comparing Types of Consequences

children in thinking about cause and effect as well as about how their actions affect others. Therefore, experiences with related consequences are a valuable part of their preschool curriculum. As the following example shows, the teacher is careful not to ruin the learning experiences with sermons or scoldings.

∞ Celest and Kyle were being too rough with Pinky the guinea pig. As the frightened creature squealed and tried to pull away, Celest grabbed its fur. Tufts of fur came out in her hand. Kyle thought the tufts were neat and tugged off another bunch of fur. The teacher heard Pinky's cries and came to his rescue. As he examined his patchy coat, he decided he deserved a respite to recover. He moved his cage up out of the children's reach, explaining as he did so, "Pinky's hair has been pulled out, and I want him to have a chance to grow it back. He needs to be in a safe place for a while. After he gets better, and when you feel you can play gently with him, he can come back down." ∞

Depriving the children of Pinky's company matches one of Piaget's recommended responses—deprivation. Dennis finds that his young students respond to the inherent justice of such a consequence. They do not usually resent or rebel against a truly related outcome. Noting this fact, Dennis is challenged to think of the best possible consequences. Still, he keeps in mind that the behavior may be a symptom of another problem that needs attention.

CONCLUSION

Natural and related consequences are ways of helping children construct moral rules and values by reflecting on their experience. Like teaching through example, teaching through experience is an extremely effective method (Goodman, 2006; Thornberg, 2008). Of course, just the experiences themselves are not sufficient for learning. Teachers must provide opportunities for children to reflect on the experiences and try to make sense out of them. It is this process of thinking about the experiences that results in learning. Children construct their own sense of right and wrong in this way. Moral rules that children construct from within are compelling to them, unlike rules that have been imposed by others (Goodman, 2006). Children are best guided by their own understanding. Similarly, the values they construct for themselves are more likely to guide their actions in future situations.

Thus, consequences teach self-discipline. They not only help children take responsibility for their behavior at the time, but they also assist with the development of lifelong autonomous behavior. When you help children move toward autonomy, you work toward the ideals of a democratic society. Instead of being imposed by authority, order is maintained by each person for the benefit of all. When schools employ democratic principles and treat students according to those principles, students will rebel less and learn more (Goodman, 2006).

∞ FOR FURTHER THOUGHT

1. Observe an early childhood education program, watching for how often children experience the results of their actions through natural consequences and how often an adult protects them from those results. Describe the situations and determine if adults are getting in the way of children's learning, or if they are merely protecting them as necessary.

2. As you observe children's interactions with one another, watch for situations

in which making restitution would be the most educational consequence for inappropriate behavior. Describe the situations you witness and discuss how you might help children make restitution for their actions.

3. List three to four misbehaviors that you have witnessed while observing children play together. Describe how you might use natural or related consequences (i.e., deprivation, exclusion, doing to the child what he or she has done, or restitution) to help the children make connections between their actions and the result of their actions. Provide a rationale for the consequences you select for each situation.

4. A problem to solve (use this chapter and the previous ones to help you): Chelsea and Katie are playing in the block area with four other children. Chelsea backs up and accidentally knocks over Katie's block construction. Katie is yelling at Chelsea and threatening to knock down what Chelsea has built.
   a. Describe how this problem might have been prevented.
   b. Describe the types of guidance approaches that might help the girls solve their own problem.
   c. Describe how you might use natural or related consequences to guide the children toward a respectful resolution to their problem.

∽ *RECOMMENDED READINGS*

Dreikurs, R., Cassel, P., & Dreikurs-Ferguson, E. (2004). *Discipline without tears: How to reduce conflict and establish cooperation in the classroom.*

Goodman, J. F., & Lesnick, H. (2004). *Moral education: A teacher-centered approach.* Boston: Pearson.

Kamii, C. (1982). Autonomy as the aim of education: Implications of Piaget's theory. In C. Kamii (Ed.), *Number in preschool and kindergarten* (pp. 73–87). Washington, DC: National Association for the Education of Young Children.

Piaget, J. (1965). *The moral judgment of the child.* New York: Free Press. (Originally published in 1932.)

⮾ Chapter **9** ⮾
Controlling Behavior Externally

NAEYC Standards Addressed in This Chapter

Standard 1b: Promoting Child Development and Learning: Knowing and understanding the multiple influences on development and learning.

Standard 5d: Becoming a Professional: Integrating knowledgeable, reflective, and critical perspectives on early education.

Standard 5b: Becoming a Professional: Knowing about and upholding ethical standards and other professional guidelines.

GUIDING QUESTIONS

- What are the major tenets of behavior modification?
- What are the issues related to behavior modification?
- How do constructivist and behaviorist principles of guidance differ from one another?
- What things should teachers consider before implementing a behavior modification program?
- How do teachers' views about the aims of education influence their selection of guidance programs?

*I*n this chapter we discuss *behavior modification*, a discipline practice aimed at controlling children's behavior externally. First we provide an overview of the basic principles of behavior modification and describe popular behavior modification systems used in classrooms and schools. Because there are many concerns with the use of behaviorist techniques in schools and the impact they have on children's behavior and learning (Kohn, 2005; Landrum & Kauffman, 2006; Reeves, 2006), we also discuss the concerns with behavior modification.

Behaviorists are concerned with behaviors that can be observed. They believe that learning is shaped by environmental influences—control the environment and you can control the individual. They discount the fact that learners construct knowledge internally, a fact that is central to constructivist theory. As discussed in Chapter 1, our approach to guidance and discipline is based on constructivism. We believe that children learn from their experiences and from reflecting on those experiences. We also believe that process of becoming morally autonomous takes time. As such we end this chapter by revisiting the long-term goal of moral autonomy—nurturing children toward self-governance—and how we believe this goal is compromised by those who use behavior modification to control children's behavior.

BEHAVIOR MODIFICATION

Behavior modification is based on B. F. Skinner's (1948) work with operant conditioning. Skinner believed that behavior could be "conditioned" through a system of positive or negative reinforcers and punishments. He tested his theory by conducting experiments with both animals and people. Through his experiments Skinner discovered that a change in environmental conditions does indeed cause a change in behavior. The basic premise of Skinner's theory of behavior modification is that behavior that gets pleasant results is likely to be repeated. Behavior that gets unpleasant results probably won't be repeated.

Reinforcement

According to behaviorist thinking, behavior is changed through positive reinforcement, negative reinforcement, and punishment. It is important to know that in behaviorist terminology, *positive* means to add and *negative* means to subtract or remove. The goal of both positive and negative reinforcement is to *increase* good behavior. *Positive reinforcement* increases good behavior by adding something the child finds good or pleasurable each time he or she shows a desired behavior. *Negative reinforcement* increases good behavior by removing something the child finds bad or unpleasant. In negative reinforcement, the child is offered relief from an unpleasant condition as a means of getting the child to complete a desired task.

Positive reinforcement
→ *add* something pleasant → increase desired behavior

Negative reinforcement
→ *remove* something unpleasant → increase desired behavior

Positive Reinforcement Positive reinforcement involves giving children rewards for good behavior. Rewards are divided into three categories: tangible rewards, praise, and privileges. Tangible rewards include stickers, stars, points, and food. Praise can be verbal, such as saying "good job," or nonverbal, such as a smile. Privileges include things like having a party, taking a trip, watching a movie, or playing a game. Children must think the rewards are interesting or pleasurable if they are to work as expected. For example, flower stickers may not motivate preschool-age boys to behave as expected, but girls may find them enticing. Because older children are better at delaying gratification, privileges usually work well for them.

From a behaviorist perspective, how often teachers give a reward is also important. When children are first learning an expected behavior, adults give praise or a tangible reward after each instance of good behavior. As children come to behave as expected, they receive fewer rewards and/or praise. If you have ever seen a parent toilet training a toddler, you have witnessed how adults provide a great deal of reinforcement during the beginning of the process and then gradually withdraw the rewards over time.

Negative Reinforcement Negative reinforcement is one of the most difficult concepts in behaviorist theory. It involves removing something unpleasant to motivate children to complete a task or behave in a certain way. An example of negative reinforcement is telling students that you will not assign homework (removal of something unpleasant) if they behave when a visitor is in the classroom.

Publicly scolding children results in humiliation.

Punishment   In behavior modification programs, *punishment* is also divided into two categories: punishment through aversives and response-cost punishment. *Punishment through aversives* is the addition of an unpleasant experience to decrease the child's use of an undesirable behavior. *Response-cost punishment* is the removal of something the child enjoys in the hopes of increasing positive behavior. Again, the goal is to increase good behavior.

Punishment through aversives
→ *add* something unpleasant → increase desired behavior

Response-cost punishment
→ *remove* something pleasant → increase desired behavior

Punishment by delivery of aversives includes physical or emotional punishment such as spanking or scolding. These methods are intended to cause discomfort. Behaviorists believe that physical and emotional pain remind children to act appropriately. You have probably witnessed this type of punishment in action. When a parent smacks a child's hand and says, "don't touch," the parent is using an aversive to remind the child about appropriate behavior. Although behaviorists believe that aversive punishments should only be used as a last resort for children who have no control over their behavior, punishment is still practiced within many homes and educational settings. Consider the fact that corporal punishment is still permissible in 21 states (Human Rights Watch, 2008). We are also sure that you can remember instances when you've heard a teacher publicly scold a child, which results in humiliation and is very punishing.

In response-cost punishment systems, positive reinforces (stickers, candy, privileges, etc.) are removed as a means of controlling behavior. When praise is used as the positive reinforcement, ignoring the negative behavior is the response-cost punishment. In both situations it is thought that the negative feelings associated with removal of the reward or praise will motivate children to act appropriately. The thinking here is that children prefer pleasurable experiences so they will repeat behaviors that get pleasant results. Conversely, they will avoid behaviors that get unpleasant results.

BEHAVIOR MODIFICATION SYSTEMS

Teachers frequently use the behaviorist principles discussed thus far to create their own behavior modification systems. However, several packaged behavior modification programs are available through educational publishers. Regardless of who creates the system, most behavior modification programs combine positive reinforcement and cost-response punishment. Although some teachers rely solely on punishment by aversives as their guidance approach, behaviorists discourage this strategy. We discuss the negative effects of punishment further in Chapter 10.

While we don't advocate the use of behavior modification, we do realize that you will see this approach to guidance in schools. We are also aware of the fact that the administrator in your school may require you to follow such a system. To assist your decision-making process in these situations, we use this section of the chapter to provide an overview of the most common types of behavior modification systems you may encounter in your practice.

The following section of this chapter describes token economy systems, praise as a positive reinforcement, packaged behavior modification systems, group contingency systems, and the use of punishment to control behavior. Following the descriptions of these systems we discuss how behavior modification negatively affects children's social and academic development.

Token Economies

Positive reinforcement is a tradition in the public schools. You have experienced it as a student, and you will see it as a teacher. You are probably most familiar with positive reinforcement through tangible rewards, such as stickers and stars. The use of tangible rewards to control behavior is part of a behavior modification system called a token economy. In a token economy children are given rewards for good behavior. In some token economy systems, children can exchange rewards earned during the week for a better prize or privilege. For example, if a child earns 10 stars during the week, she can exchange them for a candy bar on Friday. In other token economy systems this is not the case. The stars or stickers are the only rewards children receive.

When children misbehave under a token economy system, teachers impose a cost-response punishment—a fine. The fine is the removal of the reward. The logic behind this type of punishment is that if children desire the reward, they won't act in ways that get the rewards revoked. If stars are the reward, the child pays the fine by returning stars.

Token economies are difficult to establish and manage (Carr, Fraizer, & Roland, 2005). Therefore, teachers do not always implement them in ways described by proponents of behaviorism. Many teachers begin a token economy system without attention to which behaviors will receive awards and which will receive punishments. They also neglect to think about how often rewards will be distributed and how they will determine that they no longer need to reward the behavior. Another issue that teachers don't consider is how they will account for differences in children's interests and developmental abilities when distributing rewards and punishments. All of these things will affect how well the system works to increase desired behaviors (Carr et al., 2005).

Before implementing a token economy system the teacher must determine which behaviors will receive rewards and which warrant a punishment. This is difficult to do. How many stickers should children receive for coming to school on time? Is pushing your chair under the table before leaving the classroom worthy of one sticker or five stickers? How about cleaning up your own mess? Do students earn more rewards if they clean up a mess created by someone else? What is the cost-response punishment for not completing these behaviors? If you earn one sticker for pushing in your chair each time you get up, do you lose one every time you forget to push in your chair? What about if you clean your mess 20 days in a row, but on the 21st day you're not feeling well and can't face a cleaning task? Should you lose all of your stickers for slacking off during cleanup time, or should you only lose one sticker? Should students earn more rewards for being kind and generous, or should they receive the most compensation for listening during teacher-directed activities?

Regardless of how rewards are distributed, it is important to make sure that the rewards and punishment are just and fair. This is extremely important given the fact that even young children can tell if a system is fair or not (Thronberg, 2008). Think about the times during your childhood when you thought teachers or other adults weren't being fair in the distribution of rewards or punishments. Remember how it made you feel about these people.

The next step in designing a token economy system is deciding on the type of reward that children will receive for good behavior. This is also tricky. Some students may do just about anything to get a happy face sticker, and for others getting a sticker will provide no motivation to change their behavior. You should also remember that novelty items lose their allure over time. While working to complete an assignment so you can receive a star may be motivating in August, it is usually not quite as enticing in February.

The cost associated with reward systems must also be taken into consideration so that you can budget for the expense. While stickers are inexpensive, having a pizza party for 20 to 25 children every Friday can be quite costly. Using food as a reward is also risky. Allergies and other health conditions may prohibit you from giving children food as a reward, not to mention the risk you run with teaching children inappropriate eating patterns.

Once a teacher makes a decision about which behaviors to reward and what type of rewards to use, she must explain the system to her students. Remember, the more complicated the system, the less likely children will be able to follow it. It is also important to remember that young children have a limited memory capacity, so they will be prone to forgetting long lists of good and bad behaviors.

A final consideration in establishing a token economy system is time. Teachers often underestimate the time and effort it takes to reward 20 to 25 children following each good behavior. They also forget that taking time to distribute rewards for good behavior takes away from instruction. Most teachers find it difficult to cover all of the content they want to get to during the course of any given day. Taking time to reward a child each time he or she does something good further limits the amount of time teachers and children have for other activities.

Praise as Positive Reinforcement

Praise is another common form of behavior modification. It is often recommended as a tool for guidance and discipline, and most people mistakenly think it is positive and helpful. Teachers and parents are often told to praise children for desirable behavior. It is common to hear teachers make these kinds of statements: "Good job" or "I like how you are sitting so straight and quiet." Although there is considerable research to the contrary (Kohn 2005), most people still think that praise in response to children's good behavior or performance on schoolwork gives children a reason to repeat the behavior.

As was the case with the token economy system, the delivery of praise as a positive reinforcement must be fair and just for all. Think about the times that a teacher praised one of your classmates for a job well done but neglected to praise you when you did the same assignment with the same degree of success. Chances are that you noticed the situation and probably wondered why you didn't receive a compliment. Again, children are aware when one child gets praise for something but another doesn't. If you don't praise all children who do a good job, they are likely to think that they are being punished or that they have failed at the task (Henderlong & Lepper, 2002).

Packaged Programs

While there are many prepackaged behavior modification programs used in schools, *assertive discipline* (Canter, 1976) is one of the most popular. It uses many of the principles of a token economy system but departs from true behaviorist principles because it gives precedence to addressing misbehavior, rather than rewarding good behavior. Teachers trained in assertive discipline learn to address misbehavior in a swift, consistent manner using canned guidance techniques.

To get started with assertive discipline, teachers create four or five classroom rules. They then teach the rules to their students. When students break the rules they are given a reminder. Reminders can be verbal or nonverbal. The most common nonverbal technique used by teachers implementing this program is proximity. When a teacher sees a student breaking a rule, the teacher moves near the student. The teacher doesn't say anything, but may tap the student's shoulder to get his or her attention. The most important goal of proximity is to let the student know that you are watching the misbehavior. Teachers trained in this technique believe that children won't misbehave if an adult is nearby. However, this is not always true.

If nonverbal reminders don't work, the teacher is to use a verbal reminder. To stay true to the assertive discipline techniques teachers must follow specific guidelines when giving verbal reminders. The first reminder consists of a description of the rule the child is breaking, followed by a description of what the child should be doing. Saying, "You can't lie down at circle time; you have to sit crisscross applesauce" is an example of this technique. If the student opposes or doesn't respond to the request teachers use the "broken record" technique. This technique is designed to help the teacher avoid power struggles with the student. To apply the broken record technique, the teacher calmly acknowledges the student's opposition and then repeats the request again. In our situation a teacher might say, "I understand that you want to lie down, but you need to sit crisscross applesauce at circle time." The goal is to reinforce the rule by repeating it over again. If a student doesn't respond to the second request he or she is given a choice: "You can sit crisscross applesauce or be punished." If the student doesn't immediately follow the rule after being given a final choice, a punishment is delivered.

∞ Miss Wheeler has just completed a summer training course in assertive discipline. She had watched the course videos and filled out the worksheets. Now she was excited to try it out. The authors, Lee and Marlene Canter, promised a well-behaved classroom if she followed the rules. She was all prepared to write names on the board and put marbles in a jar.

On the first day of school, Miss Wheeler clearly told the children her list of firm rules. They were to sit in their seats until they had permission to get up. They were to follow directions the first time they were given. They were to raise their hands and wait to be called on before they spoke. Each time they did those things she would put a marble in a jar. At the end of the day if they had earned enough marbles, they could have a popcorn party.

Next, she told them what would happen when anyone disregarded the rules. For a first infraction, the students would receive a reminder. The second time a student misbehaved, his or her name would be put on the board. For a third failure, the name would get a checkmark by it, and the child would stay in for the first 5 minutes of recess. A second checkmark meant the student would lose the whole recess. Anyone who received more than two checkmarks would have his or her parents called. (She didn't tell the children that the course had recommended that she make a point of calling the parents at work to be sure to embarrass them.)

Kayla was worried. She said, "But I'm allergic to popcorn." Miss Wheeler decided to use the girl as an example, saying, "You talked without raising your hand, Kayla. Raise your hand." Kayla replied, "I'll get sick if I eat popcorn." "Kayla, you did not raise your hand, so I will put your name on the board to help you remember to do that," Miss. Wheeler responded. Pleased with herself for swiftly addressing the misbehavior, Miss Wheeler went on with her classroom orientation. But Kayla wasn't listening to the detailed descriptions of how to use classroom centers properly—only one book from the shelves at a time, and so on. Kayla just kept staring at her name on the board, flushed with embarrassment.

Delighted when her table was dismissed to the reading center, Kayla eagerly skipped over, taking three attractive books off the shelves and nestling into the beanbag chair to decide which one to read first. She had settled on *Frog and*

Toad Together, one of her favorites from home, when she saw Miss Wheeler's feet next to where she had put down the other two books. Miss Wheeler looked down at the girl and reprimanded her: "Kayla, because you didn't follow the instruction of one book at a time, you have chosen to have a checkmark by your name. You will lose part of recess now. You can use the time to think about the rules of our classroom."

Miss Wheeler caught the group's attention as she checked Kayla's name, saying, "I'm sorry, but we all need to work on remembering the rules. Maybe you can help Kayla learn so we can start getting marbles in the jar." Several children frowned at Kayla and she squirmed. She hated Miss Wheeler and her dumb rules. She hated school! ∽

Group Contingency Systems

One of the positive reinforcement systems recommended in the assertive discipline approach is a group contingency program. In a group contingency program all children have to behave for a specified time to get the reward (Massetti & Fabiano, 2005). During the day, the group is expected to collect a specific number of tokens (marbles, etc.) for good behavior. If the class acquires the required amount of tokens, they get a prize at the end of the day. This type of positive reinforcement is designed around the premise of peer pressure. Teachers who choose this type of guidance technique hope that children will help them maintain good behavior. For example, if everyone follows the directions and does as they are told, the group gets one marble. If one child forgets the rules, the group doesn't get any marbles. This jeopardizes the group's chance for receiving the prize at the end of the day. It also jeopardizes children's relationships with their peers.

THE USE OF PUNISHMENTS AS REINFORCEMENT

Many teachers use punishment as their sole guidance technique. This is a misapplication of behaviorist theory. In fact, Skinner was opposed to punishment except in the most extreme cases (Landrum & Kauffman, 2006). Nonetheless, you'll see several forms of punishment in preschool and primary grades. Time-outs, taking away recess privileges, and being sent to the office are common forms of punishment used in early care and education centers and grade schools. If you've ever seen the same children "on the wall" during recess time, or the same child in the time-out chair each day, you've seen how ineffective punishment can be.

Time-Out

Time-out is a pervasive school tradition. It is considered a punishment by behaviorists because it is a time-out from positive reinforcement (Martin & Tobin, 2005). The procedure was initially designed for use with children with disabilities in self-contained classrooms (Martin & Tobin, 2005), though you are sure to see it used with all children. Teachers send children to time-out when they misbehave. Short time-outs of 2 to 3 minutes seem to work best (Simpson & Sasso, 2005). Children in time-out are usually placed where they are unable to see other children or the activity in the classroom (removal of pleasure). As children get older, they may be sent to the hallway or office to take their time-out.

Teachers who use time-out believe that problem behavior will be reduced if positive reinforcement is withheld. However, time-outs are ineffective if the classroom isn't rich with activities that the student finds pleasurable and the teacher doesn't give the student positive reinforcement for engaging in those activities (Martin & Tobin, 2005). Unfortunately, this is how time-outs are most often used. In most cases teachers provide little positive reinforcement for good behavior and overly rely on time-out to reduce behavioral issues. When this occurs, children are likely to do things to be sent to time-out because they consider it a pleasurable way to escape an uninteresting classroom.

∞ Joanne prides herself on her discipline during circle time at Midway Children's Center. When all the children are on their designated rug scraps in their circle spots, she begins singing, "I like the way that Christie sits; she's got her legs crossed, and her hands are in her lap. I like the way that Ling Ling sits; she's got her legs crossed, and her hands are in her lap. I like the way that Ashley sits; she's got . . ." until all the children are dutifully in position. Then she begins the "educational" presentation part of her circle program. If children get out of position, she says, "I need your whole body's attention, and you can't do it that way. Please sit up crisscross-applesauce style!" Some children continue to resist the rigid posture.

Joanne's firm rule is that the second time they get out of position, youngsters are sent to a time-out chair for the remainder of circle time. Sheri, the aide, usually has her hands full supervising the time-out chairs by the end of Joanne's circle time. She wonders if this approach is really working. The same kids are in those chairs almost every day. It sure doesn't seem to be teaching them anything. ∞

THE LIMITATIONS OF BEHAVIOR MODIFICATION

There are many issues associated with behavior modification systems (Landrum & Kauffman, 2006). We mentioned some of them already. It is difficult for teachers to design a behavior modification system that is fair to all children and easy to implement. Young children recognize when behavior systems are unjust, and this influences how they view the teacher and learning. Keeping a consistent schedule of positive reinforcement takes a great deal of time and effort on the part of teacher. The demands associated with implementing behavior modification often limit instructional time. Less instructional time equals less learning.

It is important for you to consider the problems teachers have when designing and implementing behavior modification programs if your administrator requires you to use this type of guidance system. However, you need to know about other, more serious issues with behavior modification before you decide if this type of guidance system is right for you. Many people express concern about how behavior modification programs affect children's development (Landrum & Kauffman, 2006).

Concerns About Motivation and Engagement in Learning

Motivation is our reason for engaging in specific behaviors. We may engage in a behavior to get our needs met, to meet a personal goal, or because we believe a specific behavior is right or just. This is called intrinsic motivation. *Intrinsic motivation* means doing something for its own sake, without an external incentive. Stopping to help a stranger change a flat tire, hobbies, reading a good book, or volunteering for an extra assignment at work are examples of behaviors that are intrinsically motivated. In each of these activities you made a choice to act or not to act without thinking about an extrinsic reward. We help people without reward because we believe it is the right thing to do. We read, paint, sew, or golf because these activities bring us joy or provide some challenge. The value lies in the behavior itself, and the reward is in how you feel about it: The reward is internal to you. Self-disciplined, autonomous people don't behave appropriately only when a reward is offered. They have come to appreciate the natural benefits of positive interactions and making good choices.

Extrinsic motivation is the opposite; it means doing something for a reward or out of fear of punishment. The value lies not in the behavior, but in what may happen as a result of the behavior. You often hear teachers say, "If you do your reading quickly, I'll give you 5 minutes of extra recess. This teaches that reading for enjoyment isn't as important as reading to get recess.

It is a little-known fact that people who perform only for rewards perform at lower levels (Reeve, 2006). External controls cause students to become passive and to withdraw their interest and investment in learning (Dweck, 2007). External controls turn activities students find enjoyable into work, which reduces student interest and engagement (Henderlong & Lepper, 2002; Reeve, 2006). They also shift student focus from engagement on the task to the reward (Reeve, 2006). In addition, there is compelling evidence that rewards aren't really effective in changing behavior; they may actually be counterproductive (Henderlong & Lepper, 2002; Kohn, 2005; Landy, 2002; Reeve, 2006).

Many studies have compared two groups of people doing the same task, rewarding one group and not the other. Results are clear that those who are rewarded for their performance did less well than those who were not (Kohn, 2005; Reeves, 2006). This is important when we consider the pressure on teachers to have all children reading on grade level by third grade. For instance, programs that give children rewards for reading actually reduce children's inner motivation and enjoyment for reading (Reeves, 2006). Rewards also teach children to choose quick, easy tasks rather than striving to accomplish something more challenging (Reeves, 2006). Surprised? You probably are, which goes to show how much society has unquestioningly bought into a false premise.

It is possible to destroy intrinsic motivation by rewarding behavior that a person was doing for personal satisfaction (DeVries, Hildebrandt, & Zan, 2000; Kohn, 2005; Nucci, 2006; Reeves, 2006). Such a counterproductive result is an unfortunate aspect of extrinsic motivation.

   ∞ Mandy was in third grade but loved to go to her old first-grade classroom and help. She would frequently offer to stay after school and help clean chalkboards or tidy up the shelves. Helping made her feel good, and it also made her

Behavior modification results in poor teacher–child relationships.

feel grown-up. Miss Wheeler decided she should reward Mandy's helpfulness and began giving the girl a prize each time she came in to help. Somehow helping wasn't as much fun anymore, and Mandy went to Miss Wheeler's room less and less often. Neither the teacher nor the girl understood the relationship between the rewards and Mandy's lessened enthusiasm. ∞

In this case, Mandy's reaction to rewards caused her to discontinue her volunteer work. Another risk associated with behavior modification is that it affects teacher–child relationships.

Concerns About Relationships

Many people believe that behavior modification gets results, so why do so many researchers advise against it (e.g., Charney, 2002; DeVries et al., 2000; Gartrell, 2004; Kohn, 2005; Noddings, 2005)? And why do so many teachers and parents refuse to use it as their discipline approach? Many adults are personally uncomfortable with using their power to coerce someone with less power. To do so violates their value system and ethical principles (Weiss & Knoster, 2008). They prefer to address behavioral issues through a person-centered rather than a problem-centered approach (Weiss & Knoster, 2008). Adults who reject reward and punishment to control children's behavior do so primarily out of concern for the child's long-term welfare.

As we have said before, caring, mutually respectful relationships are an essential component of teaching desirable behavior (DeVries et al., 2000; Kamii, 1982; Piaget, 1965; Pianta, 2006). Rewards and punishment both damage relationships (Brady, Forton, Porter, & Wood, 2003; Kohn, 1996; Reynolds, 2000). You probably already knew that punishment damages relationships; after all, who wants to be around someone who hurts you? But, isn't getting rewards just the opposite? The answer is no.

Getting rewards means you are dependent on someone else to judge you worthy of getting something you want. This causes you to try to impress or flatter the person who gives rewards; this is not an honest relationship. Such an unauthentic relationship cannot foster the trust and genuine caring that inspire students to do their best. In addition, the process of judging and rewarding is not respectful; it emphasizes the power and status differences between the person giving the reward and the person hoping to get one. Besides, if the authority figure withholds the reward, in essence the subordinates are punished by not getting it.

Relationships are damaged by the strict, rule-bound discipline typical of behaviorist theory (Pianta, 2006). Behavior modification programs lay out the rules and also the punishment for breaking a rule (Canter & Canter, 1992). This focus on the rules does not take into consideration the reason a rule was broken; therefore, the relationships and contexts for the behavior are ignored (Noddings, 2005). This model does not teach children sensitivity to the needs and concerns of others, since their own needs and concerns are not considered.

Mutual trust is essential to caring relationships, but the impersonal nature of a reward and punishment system damages children's trust in adults. Rather than caring and compassionate protectors, adults become feared authority figures. The lack of trust goes both ways, as a teacher's use of such a management system implies adult mistrust of children as well. Teachers who believe that children want to be kind and cooperative will not feel the need for constantly monitoring and coercing children to do their bidding. Behavior modification is based on the belief that people will not do the right thing on their own.

Perhaps most damaging is that some behavior modification programs use public humiliation as a component of punishment, which seriously damages self-esteem. "The pain is forever!" wrote one college student who became upset while reading about assertive discipline and remembering how it felt to have her name on the board as a child. Twenty years after experiencing it, she couldn't discuss the system without crying.

Concern About Addressing Learning Goals

As discussed in Chapter 5, most states have academic standards related to children's social and emotional development. All have standards related to children's communication skills. Therefore, all discipline approaches should target "children's ability to communicate their emotions in appropriate ways, regulate their emotions, solve common problems, build positive relationships with peers and adults, and engage in and persist in challenging tasks" (Hemmeter, Ostrosky, & Fox, 2006, p. 585). Schools and teachers who use behavior modification to get children to comply with behavior but ignore the research literature that says you cannot change children's misbehavior without taking the time to teach appropriate social-emotional and communication skills are missing the point (Feinberg, Lewis, & Williams, 2005).

These teachers are willing to give children the gift of time when guiding them toward reading independently, but they are less willing to be patient when guiding children toward behaving independently. When children can't decode text, or don't have vocabulary skills, teachers teach the missing skills; when children can't take the perspective of another person, or don't know how to express their emotions, they are punished.

Many who embrace behavior modification forget that no guidance system works without consideration of each child's unique needs (Feinberg et al., 2005). Discipline approaches need to be individualized (Hemmeter et al., 2006). For example, teachers need to be able to distinguish the difference between inappropriate behaviors related to misunderstandings associated with second language learning. They also need to understand the relationship between children's social and emotional development, cognitive development, communication skills, and problem behavior. Children who feel comfortable in their environment, have learned to solve problems, and have been given time to learn social and communication skills are less likely to engage in problem behaviors (Hemmeter et al., 2006).

Behavior modification programs do not focus on teaching children why certain behaviors are more desirable than others or which behaviors to use in specific situations. Instead, they use rewards and punishment as a means of quickly stopping children's misbehavior (Reeve, 2006). As long as the cause of a behavior problem continues, any efforts to change the behavior can only be superficial. Like the weed whose roots live underground, the problem will pop back up again soon. Long-lasting approaches to change have to search for the cause of problem behavior and work on that cause (Hemmeter et al., 2006).

Think about behavior modification and causes of behavior problems. If Kayla behaves inappropriately because of missing social skills, does it help to put her name on the board? If unmet power needs cause Noah to act out, does it help to send him to time-out? If a lack of communication skills leads Tenzin astray, does it help to punish the entire class? Teachers need to consider a range of strategies to address children's behavioral issues because each has a different cause. One size does not fit all. Therefore, it is extremely important that teachers shift their thinking from monitoring and controlling children's behavior to teaching social skills (Algozzine & Algozzine, 2007).

If a teacher has to use rewards to keep kids on task with the learning activities provided, the obvious question is, "Why?" Why aren't students interested or involved? Perhaps it is because the schoolwork isn't interesting or challenging enough. That means that teachers need to stop asking, "How can I get my students to behave?" And need to start asking, "How can I create a curriculum that motivates students enough to remain on task?" Watch any teacher who has a collaborative, independent group of students and you're sure to see an interesting and engaging curriculum.

Concern for Children's Self-Esteem

Many behavior modification programs rely heavily on praise as a positive reinforcement. However, it is important to note "that every approach that does not rely on aversive or restrictive procedures is not by default a positive approach" (Weiss & Knoster, 2008, p. 72). And they don't always have positive outcomes for children (Dweck, 2007).

Both praise and punishment have a negative influence on children's self-esteem.

Believe it or not, praise is evaluative (Dweck, 2007; Kohn, 2005). "You're so smart" is evaluative praise. So is "You're so pretty." These types of comments judge children's intelligence or their worth as a person. Evaluative praise has the same side effects as other forms of behavior modification (Kohn, 2005). Certainly, it has the same effects on performance, self-esteem, moral autonomy, self-discipline, and intrinsic motivation as any other reward system. This is probably hard for you to believe, as most people have bought into the idea that we are supposed to praise children. However, there is compelling evidence that praise not only is counterproductive in increasing desired behaviors (Reeve, 2006), but actually has a negative influence, even on self-esteem (Dweck, 2007; Nucci, 2006).

How can it make people feel less good about themselves to have someone tell them they are smart or pretty or capable? Think about the importance of unconditional love for self-esteem and then think about praise: Praise doesn't say "you are important and lovable because you are you." Instead it says, "I approve of you because you are smart or pretty or capable." Also think about the flip side of the praise coin: If a person judges you wonderful today, that same person can make a different judgment tomorrow. Instead of making kids feel confident, praise makes them insecure and fearful of rejection (Dweck, 2007; Kohn, 2005).

Few seem to have considered that evaluative praise is an external judgment about another person (Katz & McClellan, 1997; Reeve, 2006). When you praise someone, you are setting yourself up as an authority who knows what is best. This attitude implies that you are able to evaluate others' performance better than they are. These messages can make children dependent on others to tell them whether they are doing well or not. It keeps them from judging for themselves and developing autonomy (Reeves, 2006). Praise is also condescending because it implies a power imbalance; rarely does a lower-status person praise a higher-status person (Brady et al., 2003). Would you tell your boss you are proud of her?

Encouragement

So, what *can* you say to kids? Should you never say another nice thing? You can learn to give positive verbal feedback that is not judgmental by substituting comments that help children learn to self-evaluate and self-congratulate. Instead of telling them what you think about their accomplishments, you can help children identify their own feelings of pride or success. We want to convey interest, appreciation, and respect, but not impose our judgment on children.

Responding to children by describing their actions and asking questions is often called *encouragement* rather than *praise* (Hitz & Driscoll, 1988). Encouragement describes children's behavior, asks important questions about their work, or offers genuine thanks for their participation in the life of the classroom. Examples of encouragement include: "Jose told me that you helped him to understand his math. He was grateful for your help." "Can you tell me how you solved that problem?" "I really appreciate that you helped me clean the guinea pig cage. Working together made the job more fun!" Encouragement doesn't evaluate: it shows genuine interest in and appreciation for children's behavior. It also teaches children that what they do and think is important.

Simply describing what the child did is one good alternative to praise (Kohn, 2005). For example, instead of giving your opinion by saying something like "You did a nice job" or "I'm proud of you," you could put more energy into the process and describe what it is you saw the child do. You could say, "I saw you share the doll buggy with Devon. That made her happy." You don't need to tell the child that she is generous or kind; it is better for her to draw that conclusion for herself. Describing instead of praising might involve such changes as saying, "You got all the blocks put away in their right place!" rather than "What a good worker you are." These examples take the focus away from praising the person and emphasize the behavior. In addition, they are specific about what the child did and therefore provide more useful information. Describing what a child did requires you to pay more attention to the child than is required for a judgment such as "Good job!" Children recognize and appreciate the difference.

Asking questions is another valuable alternative to praise. When a child shows you a drawing or other project, resist the temptation to judge. It is quick and easy to say something like "That's great!" or "How beautiful." But such responses actually *take away* children's confidence, interest, and pleasure in their work, causing them to do less well in the future (Kohn, 2005). Instead of judging the work, it is far more respectful and supportive to ask questions about the child's process.

∞ Luis has been at the paint easel for quite a while. Dennis stops by to see how he is doing and Luis asks, "Do you like my picture, teacher?" Dennis is working at using encouragement instead of praise, and so he doesn't fall into the trap. Instead of a direct answer, he says, "Wow, look at all the colors in your painting! How did you decide which ones to use?" Luis responds that he used his favorite colors, so Dennis has a short discussion with Luis about why he likes those colors.

Nearby, Dennis sees Nick and Tory, who have made an intricate block structure they want to show off. Dennis kneels down to examine it more carefully and asks, "What was the hardest part of building this?" When they mention the bridge, Dennis asks, "How did you figure out how to make this bridge stay up?" The boys explain their trial-and-error process in detail and Dennis listens attentively. ∞

As shown in the examples, it doesn't require praise to show your enthusiasm for a child's efforts. Comments that focus children's attention on their own judgment of accomplishments and behavior help them feel good about what they have done without damaging their autonomy.

Teachers who model honest communication are more likely to get it from their students. *Honesty* is the key word here. Honest expressions of appreciation or admiration are quite different from praise given to manipulate someone's behavior. As you work to reduce your use of praise, focus first on stopping evaluative praise, especially that which puts kids into competition with one another. A private statement to the child, rather than a public statement to the class about one child's performance, is less likely to be manipulative.

Encouragement as Effective Communication

It might be helpful to think about praise and encouragement in relationship to the communication skills described in Chapter 7. Praise is another of the "roadblocks to communication" described by Gordon (1970, 1989). In contrast, encouragement can be a form of reflective listening. This type of encouragement responds to the message sent by what a child says or does. If Blake calls you over to look at his block tower, you can tell by his expression that he is pleased with himself. Reflective listening and encouragement respond to that message about his own feelings. "It looks like you feel big for making such a big tower" tunes in to the child's feelings rather than judging what he has done.

Positive "I messages" are a form of encouragement also. For instance, when a child does something helpful for you, a sincere "thank you" gives a more respectful message than praise. If you decide you do want to give a value judgment, think about what you say to children in comparison to what you would say to an adult acquaintance. Then you might decide that "Congratulations," or "WOW!" is more respectful than "I'm proud of you." Figure 9–1 provides you with more examples of how to change praise into encouragement.

Do you recognize the difference between praise and encouragement? Is it clear to you how examples of external adult judgment are different from helping children think about and evaluate their own behavior? Do you think the change is

Praise	Encouragement
I'm proud of you.	I noticed that you helped Zeth with his coat.
	You got all the books in your backpack by yourself.
	You hit that ball hard! It almost made it to the fence.
Good work!	The end of your story made me laugh.
	Will you show Becka how you solved that problem?
	Yes, that letter C makes the /k/ sound.
I like how Emily is cleaning up.	Thank you for your help.
I like your new shirt.	You have a green shirt like Sophia.
	Did you go shopping?

FIGURE 9–1   Praise versus Encouragement

worth the effort? If not, read Kohn's article, *Five Reasons to Stop Saying "Good Job!"* listed in the Recommended Readings at the end of this chapter.

QUESTIONS TO ASK ABOUT GUIDANCE APPROACHES

Some teachers use behavior modification techniques without question simply because that is what they experienced during their K–12 education. Many teachers revert to the use of behavior modification because that is what they witnessed during their internships or student teaching experiences. Neither of these groups of teachers is acting in an intellectually autonomous way.

Teachers have an ethical imperative to read the research evidence, reflect on that evidence, and teach using evidence-based practices. Before choosing any guidance system, it is important to ask yourself several questions (Weiss & Knoster, 2008). Is the approach learner-centered? What will the approach teach children about self-control, altruism, empathy, justice, and fairness? Will the approach improve the quality of life for individual children, the classroom as a whole? Will it improve the climate in the classroom? Will children learn to build positive relationships with one another? Will they learn trust and initiative and eventually become industrious in their work? Does the approach address the cause and purpose of the behavior? Is it sensitive to children's developmental, physical, and emotional needs? Will it help them grow as individuals and as members of a community? The most important question for you to ask yourself is whether you would use this approach with your own children.

The answers to these questions lie in your beliefs about children, teaching, and learning and the importance of the relationships you wish to have with your students. Ultimately, the way you answer these questions depends on what you consider to be the aim of education.

THE AIMS OF EDUCATION

> *Education, for most people, means trying to lead the child to resemble the typical adult of his society . . . But for me, education means making creators . . . You have to make inventors, innovators, not conformists.*
> —(Piaget, 1980, p. 182)

Autonomy versus Heteronomy

Piaget believed that autonomy is the aim of education (Kamii, 1982). If people are morally and intellectually autonomous, they behave and think in ways that are free of coercion. When people discuss an "outside the box" thinker, they are describing an intellectually autonomous person. Albert Einstein, Bill Gates, the founder of Microsoft, and Larry Page, the founder of Google, are considered intellectually autonomous people. None of these individuals limited their thinking to what they had learned was the right or true way to solve a problem. They each created new solutions to solve the issues with which they were faced.

Moral autonomy means that a person will make decisions based on internally constructed convictions about right and wrong (DeVries, 1999; Nucci, 2006). A morally autonomous person will be respectful of others whether or not someone in authority is watching. Morally autonomous people consider the pros and cons of a situation and act based on their own reasoning. They think, decide, and act independently in ways that are just and fair. Both moral and intellectual autonomy require that a person be skilled in thinking about issues and coming to personal conclusions (Kamii, 1982). These skills require practice. They are learned progressively through experience.

By taking responsibility for the child's behavior, the adult denies the child the opportunity to learn by experience and by reflection on those experiences (Piaget, 1965). If you are constantly in charge of children's behavior, the message to the children is that they are not capable of making good decisions for themselves. Their confidence in themselves as thinkers and decision makers is damaged (DeVries, 1999).

It is ironic that schools advocate teaching critical thinking and problem-solving skills in academic subjects, but do just the opposite for social and emotional development (Goodman, 2006). This mix of incompatible approaches not only harms moral autonomy, it also counteracts the intellectual autonomy necessary for critical thinking. You cannot teach children to think for themselves about certain issues while simultaneously disempowering them in other areas (DeVries et al., 2000).

CONCLUSION

Behavior modification happens if you plan it or not. Recognizing that many common discipline systems are forms of behavior modification can help you make informed decisions about your own guidance plan. Thinking about the negative effects of behavior modification can help you decide whether to implement it purposefully or not.

This chapter has explained why behavior modification ultimately tends to be counterproductive. It has also discussed why rewards and praise are not compatible with a relationship of mutual respect. Such respect is crucial to the type of human relationships that nurture the development of caring, morally autonomous people. If autonomy and self-discipline are your long-term goals, you do not want to use behavior modification approaches to discipline.

∽ FOR FURTHER THOUGHT

1. Describe the discipline approaches used by two of your primary-grade teachers. Discuss which you felt was most effective and why.
2. Spend a day observing in an early childhood setting. Identify the type of guidance approach used by the teachers in the setting. Discuss the effectiveness of the approach in terms of the questions to ask about guidance approaches discussed in this chapter.
3. Observe in a classroom, watching for the focus of the teacher's attention. Is inappropriate behavior or desirable behavior more apt to get attention? What are the consequences for child behavior?
4. Talk to children about the stars and stickers they get for school performance. Do the children focus on the learning or on the prizes? How do you think getting rewards affects a child's education and attitude about learning?
5. A problem to solve: Courtney finally wrote something in her journal today instead of just drawing in it: a major breakthrough!
   a. If you were praising her, what might you say?
   b. If you were using encouragement, what might you say?
   c. How are the two approaches and their goals different?

∽ RECOMMENDED READINGS

Bilmes, J. (2004). *Beyond behavior management: The six life skills children need to thrive in today's world.* St. Paul, MN: Redleaf.

Flicker, E. S., & Hoffman, J. A. (2006). *Guiding children's behavior: Developmental discipline in the classroom.* New York: Teacher's College Press.

Gartrell, D. (2001). Replacing time-out: Part one—Using guidance to build an encouraging classroom. *Young Children, 56*(6), 8–16.

Gartrell, D. (2002). Replacing time-out: Part two—Using guidance to maintain an encouraging classroom. *Young Children, 57*(2), 36–43.

Kohn, A. (2001). Five reasons to stop saying "good job!" *Young Children, 56*(5), 24–28.

Loomis, C., & Wagner, J. (2005). A different look at challenging behavior. *Young Children, 60*(2), 94–99.

Watson, M. (2003). Attachment theory and challenging behaviors: Reconstructing the nature of relationships. *Young Children, 58*(4), 12–20.

∞ *Chapter* **10** ∞
Punishment Versus Discipline

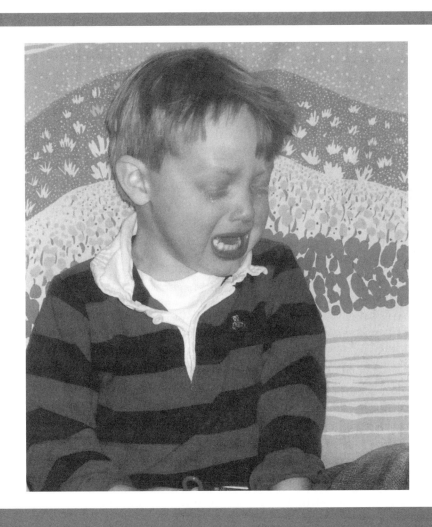

NAEYC Standards Addressed in This Chapter

Standard 1b: Promoting Child Development and Learning: Knowing and understanding the multiple influences on development and learning.

Standard 5d: Becoming a Professional: Integrating knowledgeable, reflective, and critical perspectives on early education.

Standard 5e: Becoming a Professional: Engaging in informed advocacy for children and the profession.

GUIDING QUESTIONS

- What is the difference between punishment and discipline?
- How does punishment affect child development?
- How does punishment affect moral autonomy?

*S*ociety is gradually coming to recognize the negative effects of punishing children physically (Donnelly, 2005; McCord, 2005). For example, spanking or slapping children is outlawed in most states. However, there are 13 states that still allow physical punishment in schools (CEASE, 2004). In addition, many other types of punishment are still commonly used to control and direct students. Although this chapter examines various forms of punishment and their negative effects on children, this book is primarily about alternatives to punishment. Chapters 4 through 8 explained how and why other approaches work far better. In those chapters, we explained which causes indicate the approaches described there. However, we do not accept punishment as an appropriate treatment for any cause of misbehavior.

Punishment is intended to hurt or humiliate a person in response to undesirable behavior; its goal is to make a person pay for misconduct (DeVries, Hildebrandt, & Zan, 2000; Piaget, 1965/1932). Emotional pain is often more intense and lasting than bodily harm. You may have personal memories of intense embarrassment about being banished to the hallway for an offense. You might still be able to feel your childhood despair and frustration at being denied an eagerly awaited outing after an infraction of the rules. Or perhaps your worst memory of school is the shame and anger you felt from a teacher's sarcastic put-down. These are all punishments.

RESULTS OF PUNISHMENT

Most people who use punishment believe it will improve behavior (McCord, 2005). In fact, it can appear to stop the undesirable behavior because punishment may force negative behaviors "underground" (e.g., Butchart & McEwan, 1998; McCord, 2005).

This quick result convinces many people that punishment is effective. However, extensive research proves that punishment is not an effective way of correcting behavior (e.g., Bredekamp & Copple, 1997; Dodge, Bates, & Pettit, 1990; Sabatino, 1991). It is clear that punishment does not improve behavior (McCord, 2005; Scheff, 2005). Even if the action being punished does stop for the moment, worse behavior is almost sure to follow. Punishment creates seriously counterproductive feelings that are demonstrated in numerous ways (McCord, 2005).

Anger and Aggression

Anger is a common reaction to punishment. Children who are punished have a need to get even, to assert their own power after having been the victim of someone else's power (Turner, 2005). Because anger tends to be expressed as aggression, children often vent their anger by hitting and hurting others (Rich, 2005). The negative feelings inside these angry children inevitably surface. Having experienced punishment, they have learned from a powerful role model how to give punishment (McCord, 2005). Children who have been hit when they have displeased a big person are very likely to hit a smaller person who displeases them. This is very clear in the following example, where Kyle seems to be echoing an adult as he tries to justify hitting Joshua.

> ∽ Five-year-old Kyle and 3-year-old Joshua are working side-by-side with some magnets. Kyle decides he wants the magnet that Joshua has and tries to take it. Joshua resists by running away from the bigger boy, clutching the precious magnet. Kyle chases after Joshua, catches him, and hits him to get him to relinquish the magnet. As Sheri comforts the sobbing Joshua, Kyle keeps saying over and over, "He didn't pay attention. He didn't pay attention." ∽

Children who experience other forms of punishment tend to be physically aggressive, too (Vissing, Straus, Gelles, & Harrop, 1991), and they will have learned other methods of getting even. These kids might call other children names, ruin their work, or take their possessions. Such unacceptable behavior is then likely to be punished, creating further misbehavior. This negative cycle is behind the behavior of many "bad kids." Unfortunately, many parents use punishment as discipline at home (McCord, 2005; Springen, 2000). The teacher then has to deal with the results at school.

> ∽ Mrs. Jensen chose her words carefully as she shared her concerns about Tony with his parents at their conference. "When Tony doesn't like what someone else is doing, he often hurts them." Looking concerned, his mother said, "Oh, dear. What does he do?" Referring to her observation notes, Mrs. Jensen described an incident. "When he didn't like a classmate's singing, he told her to quit it. She did for a while but started up again. Tony hit her and said, 'I told you not to do that!' He usually says that right after he hurts someone." A flash of recognition came across the mother's face. She knew where he got that line! And the hitting, too! She glanced accusingly at her husband. He retorted, "That sounds like a normal kid thing."
>
> The father questioned Mrs. Jensen, "What do you do to him when he hits?" The teacher explained how she generally handled the situations, with attention

to the hurt child and modeling alternative ways for Tony to get what he needs. Tony's dad leaned back in his chair and said knowingly, "Yeah, well, that soft-touch stuff just doesn't work with this kid. You have to tell him not to do something and then just don't let him do it! Giving him a quick wallop works at home." The mother stared intently at the pattern on the carpet, trying to avoid both the teacher's and her husband's eyes.

Mrs. Jensen could tell she had touched on a sensitive area with this couple. Still, she was glad she had brought it up. She promised to keep them updated on Tony's progress. In the meantime, she had some new insight about why Tony was exhibiting such physically aggressive responses; it seemed he was following his father's model. ∞

Damaged Relationships

Punishment also creates feelings of hostility and resentment toward the person administering it (e.g., McCord, 2005; Thompson, 1998). This result is particularly serious when it damages relationships between children and their parents. Whether the negative feelings are aimed at parents, teachers, or other authority figures, those emotions get in the way of positive discipline teaching (McCord, 2005). People don't want to be around someone who hurts them or makes them feel bad. Certainly, no one is eager to listen to, or learn from, that person. Some children merely withdraw from contact, and others try to get even. Getting even takes many forms, depending on the experiences and the personality of the child. One child may be openly defiant and rude, and another may retaliate through helplessness and refusal to try anything. Still another may become a bully, using smaller children as substitute targets.

All of these responses to punishment are self-defeating, and all are only made worse by further punishment. It isn't only relationships with punishers that are damaged; children who are punished tend to have trouble with peer relationships also (e.g., Hart, Olsen, Robinson, & Mandleco, 1997; Turner, 2005). Because these youngsters use aggression to get their way, other children don't want to play with them. Being rejected for hitting or shoving truly confuses the child who has been punished; the experience of being punished teaches children that hurting others is an appropriate response when they don't get their way. They erroneously believe that their aggressive behaviors will have positive social outcomes. All too often these youngsters end up as social outcasts, exhibiting escalating antisocial behaviors in retaliation.

Damage to Self-Esteem

Punishment also damages self-esteem because children get their opinion of their worth from how others treat them (Garbarino, 2005; Miller, 2004). Being punished can convince youngsters that they are inferior (DeVries, 1999) and that they are bad (McCord, 2005). Feeling like a worthless or bad person is likely to become a self-fulfilling prophecy, resulting in further undesirable behavior. Many children routinely experience verbal abuse at home, internalizing the labels such

Being punished can make children feel like "bad people" and damage their self-esteem.

as "stupid" or "damn brat" and acting accordingly. A child who is verbally or physically punished does not feel respected or valued. Any kind of punishment attacks personal dignity by putting the child at the mercy of a more powerful person. Additionally, many punishments are humiliating, as shown in the following example.

∞ "Beep! Beep! Beep! Beep!" sounded the intercom, as the library light kept flashing. The secretary had two people on hold on the telephone and new parents at the counter needing forms. She switched on the speaker, "Yes, this is the office." The librarian sounded distraught. "Ian bit Serge and then ran out of the room. He's somewhere in the halls, and I can't leave the group to go find him." The secretary responded, "Sorry, but I'm the only person in the office, so I can't go look for him right now." Leaning by the message board, the custodian overheard the exchange. He volunteered, "I'll go get him." Relieved, she called the library back and said, "George is going to go look for Ian. I'll let you know when we find him."

The custodian strode down the hall on his mission to bring in the wayward child. Not finding him on the first floor, he went upstairs. Still failing to see the boy, he checked the playground. Darn it, he needed to go set up the lunchroom soon. Where was that kid? Then he thought of the bathroom. Sure enough, there were two feet standing in the back corner of a stall. "Come on out!" ordered George. The boy froze, wondering if the custodian could see him. "Come out now!" he repeated. The other boys in the bathroom giggled as George crouched to look under the door and demanded, "Move it!" Ian slowly opened the stall door, his eyes darting around like those of a trapped animal. His mind raced as his playmates, Alex and Tory, teased him about being caught.

Once outside the bathroom, George scooped Ian up like a bag of potatoes. He hauled the boy past the library while the child flailed and demanded to be put down. His classmates crowded to the door to glimpse the spectacle. Humiliated, Ian's temper flared. He pounded on the back of George's leg, but the custodian just held him more tightly and headed for the office, proud to have successfully completed his mission. Dumping Ian in the detention room, George announced, "Here's your biter!" Ian felt about 1 foot tall as the custodian described the bathroom scene to the secretary. And Ian noted that the woman listening at the counter was his friend Kenji's mom. Ian wished he were invisible! ∞

Unfortunately, this disrespectful treatment of children is not uncommon. The damage to a child's self-respect is immeasurable. The idea of mutual respect between adult and child is the absolute opposite of this scenario.

For some kids, fear of punishment becomes the only reason to behave in socially acceptable ways.

Fear

Punishment controls through fear (Brady, Forton, Porter, & Wood, 2003). This fear keeps some children from positive activities as well as negative ones. When they are punished without warning for something they didn't know was unacceptable, many children will tend to avoid any new activity. Their strategy is to use caution about anything that might possibly get them into trouble. Exploration and initiative are sacrificed to the need for safety and security. Therefore, fear of punishment can hamper academic learning. Remember Kayla from the assertive discipline example in Chapter 9? Scared of checkmarks on the board by her name and of classmates who blamed her for not getting marbles in the jar, Kayla rarely initiated conversation or joined activities. The following example of Beau and the broken bracelet shows the results of a different approach.

∞ Beau's face showed surprise as he held the two pieces of what had been Shayla's bracelet, and Mrs. Jensen could see that he had not purposely broken it. Mrs. Jensen acknowledged Shayla's concern and accepted Beau's protests of an "accident." She encouraged each child to hear the other's side of the story.

That evening, Mrs. Jensen called Beau's parents and explained what had happened. She made it very clear that Beau had not been "naughty," just clumsy in examining the bracelet. She discussed the concept of making restitution and asked if they thought they could help Beau figure out a way to make it up to Shayla for her loss.

A few weeks later, Beau arrived at school and handed a delighted Shayla a package with a small assortment of child-size bracelets. It had taken Beau those weeks to earn the money, buy the bracelets, and wrap them up to give to Shayla. Mrs. Jensen knew that Beau's heartfelt "You're welcome!" to Shayla's "Thank you!" could never have been the result of punishment. Beau understood the significance of his carelessness, but he felt good about himself for making things right. He saw himself as a good boy, not a bad one. ∞

Sadly, many adults who were themselves punished, and suffered from the results, nevertheless use punishment to control children in their care. They may realize that it harmed them, but that model has been strongly imprinted on them (Garbaino, 2005; McEwan, 1998).

Missed Opportunity for Learning

Punishment actually undermines children's learning about appropriate and inappropriate behavior. Instead of youngsters thinking about the behavior that caused the problem, they end up thinking resentfully about the punishment. Punishment also focuses attention on what *not* to do rather than teaching what *to* do. Young children need information about acceptable ways of behaving, and they need help in understanding why certain actions are better than others (Roffey, 2005). In other words, they need teaching instead of punishment.

∞ Caroline, the children's center director, was concerned about the row of sad faces in the back of the room during afternoon choice time. It was Joanne's policy to remove kids from play if they weren't able to get along with others. Caroline decided to discuss this policy with Joanne.

Caroline met with Joanne and shared her concern that the children who most needed practice with social skills were not getting that practice. When they were removed from play, they were no longer in the learning situation. She asked Joanne to problem-solve with her about ways to help these youngsters learn to get along instead of just expelling them from play.

As they discussed the kinds of learning experiences these problem children needed, Joanne began to think of ways to teach instead of punish. But she realized that the changes required more than one adult in the large playroom. "I'll have to ask Sheri or Maureen to work the blue room with me during choice time," she planned. That change, however, meant having fewer options available for children. The teachers would have to alternate between opening the woodworking center and the painting area. Joanne decided that the sacrifice was worth it. With two adults to intervene, teachers could help children individually resolve disputes.

Caroline was pleased with the outcome of the discussion. She and Joanne reviewed the kinds of role modeling and problem-solving assistance that would be most helpful in teaching social skills. Joanne arranged a meeting with her assistants to go over this new plan. ∽

Lack of Critical Thinking

Punishment doesn't just limit learning about acceptable behavior: it limits learning in general. Brain research shows that events that create fear, anxiety, or humiliation have negative effects on mental growth (Jenson, 2006). Even strict environments that require superficial, automatic responses can inhibit the growth of mental capacity. The gruff and threatening order to "Do as you're told!" and the expectation of instant obedience are examples of this type of environment. Children raised with this type of discipline usually have low motivation to think beyond parroting memorized answers. They tend to be submissive to the ideas of others and accept what others say uncritically instead of learning to think for themselves (DeVries, 1999). Such submissiveness may sound good to some parents, unless they realize that it will mean submitting to peer pressure when the child is a teenager.

In contrast, events that encourage reflection and other thinking promote mental growth and intellectual power. An example of an event that encourages thinking is Beau and the broken bracelet. Through his experience, he comes to realize the connection between his action and the broken bracelet, and then the connection between his work to earn money and making up for the damage. This type of discipline encourages children to think for themselves and strive to understand the world (DeVries, 1999). A brain that is exercised becomes stronger and more capable.

Lack of Inner Controls

For some kids, fear of punishment becomes the only reason to behave in socially acceptable ways. These youngsters are only likely to act appropriately when someone is there to catch them. Even then, the seriousness of the punishment is often weighed against the potential pleasure of the inappropriate action (McCord, 2005). Often youngsters will choose to go ahead with the action and "face the music" later. Accepting the punishment can even become a sort of challenge to their courage. Not getting caught can become another type of challenge. Kohlberg's (1984) extensive studies of moral development concluded that punishment is ineffective in promoting moral development, whereas the opposite approach, a de-emphasized use of adult power, assists the development of a child's internalized conscience (e.g., DeVries, 1999; Kochanska, 1991).

Deceitfulness

Many people whose only restraint comes from fear of punishment become incredibly sneaky (Kamii, 1982; McCord, 2005). They become skillful at lying and other forms of deceit. You have probably known people who have adopted this dishonest approach to life. They get what they want behind people's backs. Although they can act innocent, others soon catch on to them and learn to distrust them. Certainly, this behavior is not a desirable outcome of discipline.

Recent headlines tell us that juvenile crime is increasing alarmingly. The public response is to "get tough" and punish harder, while punishing the kids' parents, too. Suggestions such as publishing the names of juvenile offenders are evidence of how little most people understand about how to improve behavior (Polakow, 2007). How can publicly labeling a young person as a criminal possibly help that child behave better? When suggestions focus on prevention of juvenile delinquency instead of punishment, the plans aim at older kids who are already in trouble. Kindergarten teachers can tell you which of their 5-year-old students are likely to end up in jail unless they get help; the problems begin early, and therefore need to be addressed early (Papatheodorou, 2005).

Those who would address the problems through punitive measures need to read the research showing that children who are punished are most likely to turn to crime (McCord, 2005). In 2001, nearly three of every hundred American adults had served time in prison, according to the U.S. Justice Department. Almost a third of those who had served time were still under correctional supervision, including parole, probation, and in local jails (U.S. Department of Justice, 2004). Punishment clearly isn't working, since building more and more prisons and incarcerating more and more people have not significantly reduced crime. Figure 10–1 summarizes the results of punishment.

WHY PUNISHMENT IS USED

Obviously, the results of punishment are totally incompatible with the goals of self-discipline and autonomy. Punishment undermines the development of personal responsibility. Adults who rely on punishment are looking for the quick fix referred to in Chapter 1, but they may not get that result because some children are not submissive enough to give in.

- Anger and aggression
- Damaged relationships
- Damage to self-esteem
- Fear
- Missed opportunities for learning
- Lack of critical thinking
- Loss of self-control
- Deceitfulness

FIGURE 10–1 Results of Punishment

Children's defiance leads to escalation of punishment and even greater defiance. When punishment clearly doesn't stop the behavior, many parents and teachers still persist in using it because they don't know any other methods. In the rest of this chapter we discuss this lack of skills and other reasons why some adults may use punishment. Figure 10–2 provides suggestions to eliminate corporal punishment from the schools.

ADULT STRESS

Even adults who really don't believe in punishment and know better than to use it sometimes resort to it (Broderick, 2005). A survey of American parents found that 70% believed that yelling and swearing at children cause psychological problems (Daro, Abrahams, & Robson, 1988). Yet, that same study, as well as others, revealed that most parents had insulted or sworn at their children during the past year (Vissing et al., 1991). There are times when the stresses of life push people beyond their limits, when an adult's behavior doesn't live up to his or her personal expectations. If this is a frequent occurrence, counseling is needed. If it is a rare occurrence, it is best to forgive yourself and try to redeem the situation.

∞ Mrs. Jensen had such an experience several years ago when she was driving across the state on a very hot summer day with her four children in a van with no air-conditioning. The children were uncomfortable and fussy from the heat and from being confined in the van. Andrew was screaming that he wanted out of his car seat, and Joe was teasing John by snatching his hat. There was no place to pull over and deal with the problem sensibly, so Mrs. Jensen reached back and grabbed Joe's arm, yanking him into his place with a barking order: "Sit!" She just didn't know what else to do. Besides, it actually made her feel better at the time. But later she felt bad and apologized to Joe, explaining her frustration. When everyone was calm and cooled off, the family was able to problem-solve about the situation. ∞

Such instances are less likely in the controlled environment of Mrs. Jensen's classroom. Sometimes, however, a child does push her beyond her limits. In her professional role, Mrs. Jensen maintains her professional ethics. She would

Classroom Alternatives	Schoolwide Prevention Strategies
Set age-appropriate limits.	Provide parents with information on child development.
Teach conflict resolution and mediation skills.	Provide new parents with information and classes on temperament and responsive parenting.
Reason and talk with children about behavior.	Offer parenting classes on behavior management.
Model patience, empathy, kindness, and cooperation.	Provide teachers and other staff with professional development opportunities focused on supporting positive behavior and student engagement.
Provide opportunities for children to practice problem solving.	Establish partnerships with community-based counseling and mental health programs.
Encourage appropriate behavior.	Promote collaboration with other community agencies that service children and families.
Include children in establishing community guidelines.	Provide a unified system of advocacy on behalf of children.
Provide structure, continuity, and predictability.	Provide parents with information and activities to teach children about school guidelines.

FIGURE 10–2 Strategies to Eliminate Corporal Punishment

never hit a child or even grab a youngster in anger. She knows the importance of being in control of herself to effectively deal with discipline problems.

∞ Robert began making screeching noises again during the Spanish lesson. Señora Lupita was trying to keep the group interested in the Spanish language songs and stories she was sharing with the class, but the group was clearly becoming distracted by Robert's antics. Mrs. Jensen tried to make eye contact with him to communicate with him, but he avoided looking at her. Finally, she went and sat beside him to calm him, but his disruptions only escalated.

Out of respect for Señora Lupita, Mrs. Jensen felt she had to remove Robert from the group. However, Robert was not receptive to the idea and was not cooperative when Mrs. Jensen tried to escort him away. He yelled louder and flailed around, kicking her in the process. It was an unpleasant scene, and Mrs. Jensen was very upset.

She knew she shouldn't try to deal with Robert at that moment. Instead, she privately told him, "I'm feeling too angry to talk to you about this right now. When I'm feeling calmer, we'll talk about the problem." ∞

Any time you feel angry, you run the risk of punishing behavior rather than teaching self-discipline (Powell, Cooper, Hoffman, & Marvin, 2007). Chapter 8 described how anger can change related consequences into punishment, just by the inevitably negative tone of voice and body language. Similarly, anger destroys the technique of holding a child to calm him or her. Restraining a child when you are infuriated is different from the reassuring embrace needed by an out-of-control youngster. It is important to know when you are not emotionally able to provide helpful guidance to youngsters and to call in someone with a fresh perspective. In order to help children control their emotions you need to understand your own emotional state in relation to the needs of the child (Powell et al., 2007). Understanding your emotional state when a child is misbehaving is called "reflective functioning" (Powell et al., 2007, p. 178). When adults display high levels of reflective functioning, they have more secure, cooperative children.

Misconceptions

Some adults say they don't believe in punishment and yet routinely rely on it. Apparently, they don't perceive their actions as punishment. Some teachers humiliate children in front of classmates and call it peer pressure. Others pride themselves on their "humor" when they cut down a child with a sarcastic response. Still others call it a "consequence" when they take away privileges totally unrelated to a behavior problem (Landrum & Kauffman, 2006). All of these responses inflict hurt, create anger, and fail to teach. They are all punishment because the intent is to inflict emotional pain (Landrum & Kauffman, 2006).

∞ Ahmed was notoriously slow at cleaning up before circle time. The truth was that he didn't like going to circle time, so he dragged his feet. It distracted Joanne to have a child otherwise occupied during her circle. One day she decided to break Ahmed of his habit. She announced in a voice that carried across the room, "We're waiting for Ahmed to join our group so that we can begin our circle."

Embarrassed because all of the kids were staring at him, Ahmed hurried. Trying to carry both the basket of trucks and the box of animals at once, he dropped everything with a clatter. With his classmates laughing, he got even more flustered and put some trucks in the animal box. Joanne noted his error and asked, "Can anyone tell Ahmed which container the trucks go into?" "The orange basket!" taunted several children, enjoying what seemed to be the teacher's approval to pick on Ahmed. By now, Ahmed was nearly in tears, but Joanne couldn't see his face. She made another effort at using what she called peer pressure to bring his behavior into line. "Ahmed, we'll wait for 3 more minutes; then we'll have to start our circle. It's just not fair to keep your friends waiting." Thoroughly upset, he fumbled at putting away the rest of the toys. Finally, the teacher pronounced, "Time's up! Sorry, but you have used up too much of our time being a slowpoke." Steaming, Ahmed thought, "You're not sorry at all! I hate you!" ∞

Lack of Discipline Skills

Many people fear that children will go wild without fear of punishment; it is the only discipline approach these adults understand (Feld, 2005; Reynolds, 2000). They are not informed about how other approaches to discipline set limits and communicate expectations about desirable behavior. Not understanding these other approaches, they think their choice is either punishment or a total lack of discipline, as we discussed in Chapter 1. To many people, discipline means punishment. That was clearly the case with a father who told Mrs. Jensen, "I just don't know what to do with him anymore. Hitting him doesn't make any difference."

Any concern about a lack of guidance and discipline is justified (Feld, 2005). Overly permissive child rearing can be as damaging as a punitive approach. Freedom without limits or responsibility is chaotic and dangerous. There are times when adults must step in to keep youngsters safe as well as to help them learn. Children must be helped to learn socially acceptable behavior and respect for the rights of others. These understandings are good for the child who learns them, as well as for those around that child. Young people who don't learn socially acceptable behaviors are not pleasant to be around. They damage property and are rude and inconsiderate. Naturally, no one wants to spend time with them, which leads to feelings of rejection and damages their self-esteem. Understanding the rights and needs of others is also essential to the development of self-discipline. Self-discipline doesn't result from forced behavior, but neither does it occur by itself. It is a product of careful teaching through constructivist approaches to discipline.

Family and Societal Norms

Many truly loving and caring families are firmly convinced that punishment will have long-term, positive results (Feld, 2005; Springen, 2000). They mean well but their beliefs are based on tradition rather than evidence (Feld, 2005). They are merely doing what their parents did with them, unaware of the negative effects punishment had on their own development (Powell et al., 2007). Education must be used as a tool to help parents and teachers learn the other, more useful approaches explained in this book. Most books on guidance and discipline are research-based and firmly reject punishment as an option. Unfortunately, a few are written by people without a background in child development or knowledge of relevant research; parents may not know the difference and can be led astray (Feld, 2005). Your suggestions of constructive discipline books or parenting classes may be a helpful way to introduce parents to discipline approaches that are less punitive. In the Recommended Readings section at the end of this chapter and Chapter 7, we suggest some of our favorite parenting books.

Some people justify punishment for broken rules based on the model of our legal system. However, our legal system is merely designed to control behavior, not to teach acceptable behavior or to socialize citizens (Paintal, 2007). In contrast to our legal system, parents and other educators could be the antidotes to punitive measures. "It does not make sense for educators to use the criminal-justice model as the first resort, before employing what they were professionally prepared to use—educational and mentoring approaches" (Gathercoal, 1998).

The violent traditions of society make it difficult for many people to give up punitive approaches to discipline. Movies and television promote violence as a legitimate way for the "good guys" to win. Many sporting events involve violence that is eagerly applauded, and world leaders still rely on force to settle differences. The use of force is continually glorified.

Yet, society also recognizes values that should counteract the use of force to discipline children. Respect for the rights of all people is increasingly evidenced in laws and attitudes. Minority groups are speaking up and insisting on respectful treatment. Perhaps the least represented group is the one with the smallest voice: the children. The U.S. Constitution guarantees equality, rights, and the protection of all. Perhaps children, too, will soon be included in this guarantee. Teachers can be effective advocates for the rights of young children. Professional organizations representing early childhood teachers, such as the National Association for the Education of Young Children (NAEYC) and the Association for Childhood Education International (ACEI), have been vocal about the subject of punishment (NAEYC, 1996; Paintal, 2007).

CONCLUSION

We have hope that punishment will cease to be considered a reasonable means of discipline. We believe that when parents and teachers understand the dangers of punishment and learn more effective approaches to child guidance, the world will become a better place. There will be fewer angry people who need to get even with society through violence. There will be fewer people who have come to believe they are worthless. There will be less dishonesty and less energy spent to avoid being caught. Personal inner controls and concern for others will become the norm among morally autonomous people.

∞ FOR FURTHER THOUGHT

1. Corporal punishment is legal in nearly half of the states in the United States. Discuss how corporal punishment might affect our national goal to "leave no child behind."

2. Were you given constructive discipline as a child? How has it affected your life, your attitudes, and your self-esteem?

3. Observe a group of young children on the playground. Determine which seem to be socially competent and which seem "aggressive"; listen carefully to their interactions. Describe how adult models might have contributed to the competence level of both groups.

4. How would you explain to someone the fundamental differences between punishment and discipline? Can you relate those differences to the differences between moral autonomy and heteronomy?

∞ RECOMMENDED READINGS

Butchart, R. E., & McEwan, B. (1998). *Classroom discipline in American schools: Problems and possibilities for democratic education.* Albany: State University of New York Press.

Gordon, T. (2000). *Parent effectiveness training.* New York: Three Rivers Press.

Gottman, J. (2004). *What am I feeling?* Seattle, WA: Parenting Press.

Kamii, C. (1984). Obedience is not enough. *Young Children, 39*(4), 11–14.

Nelson, J., Erwin, C., & Duffy, R. A. (2007). *Positive discipline for preschoolers: Raising children who are responsible, respectful and resourceful.* New York: Three Rivers Press.

PART 3
Matching Discipline Causes to Discipline Approaches

Part 2 explained the different approaches to discipline. Although this information is essential, its organization is not in the format most useful in real life. In the real world, we are first confronted with the behavior, not the discipline approach. Part 3 looks at discipline from the real-world perspective: we discuss behaviors and then move backward to discover the cause, select the related approach, and then implement that approach.

Because discipline is effective only if it addresses the cause of the problem, we begin Chapter 11 with a discussion of observation techniques that will assist you in matching behaviors to probable causes. Observing behaviors is the only way to get at the root cause of the problem. Observation is designed to assist you in planning an appropriate course of action to enhance children's social and emotional development. If you don't know what is causing children's behavior, you have no means by which to analyze the multiple developmental and contextual variables that may cause children to behave in a given manner. The remainder of Chapter 11 discusses typical childhood behaviors and strategies for addressing those behaviors. In this section of the chapter we will focus on matching discipline approaches to the causes of behavior, not to the behavior itself.

In Chapters 12 through 14, we discuss other causes of children's behaviors and provide you with examples of how you might match discipline approaches to each. We believe that ability to match discipline approaches to the cause of problem behavior is essential to maintaining nurturing relationships with children and assisting them in learning to manage their own behavior.

∞ *Chapter* **11** ∞
Immaturity

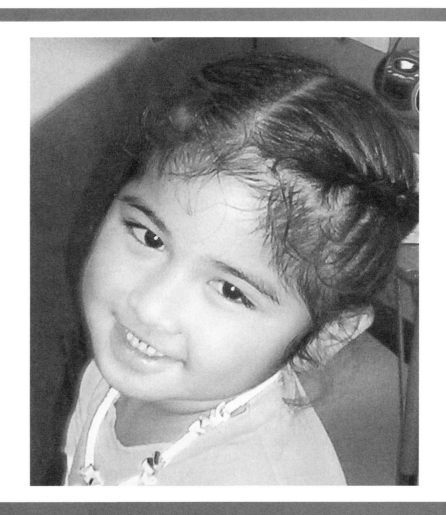

NAEYC Standards Addressed in This Chapter

Standard 1a: Promoting Child Development and Learning: Knowing and understanding young children's characteristics and needs.

Standard 1b: Promoting Child Development and Learning: Knowing and understanding the multiple influences on development and learning.

Standard 1c: Promoting Child Development and Learning: Using developmental knowledge to create healthy, respectful, supportive, and challenging learning environments.

Standard 3a: Observing, Documenting, and Assessing to Support Young Children and Families: Understanding the goals, benefits, and uses of assessment.

Standard 4b: Teaching and Learning, Using Developmentally Effective Approaches: Candidates know, understand, and use a wide array of effective approaches, strategies, and tools to positively influence young children's development and learning.

GUIDING QUESTIONS

- How can teachers use observation to determine the cause of children's behavior?
- How do children's normal developmental trajectories affect their behavior?
- How can knowledge of child development assist teachers in guiding children toward self-governance?

It's playtime in preschool and the teachers are busy: Kyle just hit Sophie, Ellie has grabbed Olivia's toy, Meadow wet her pants, and Jack is sobbing hysterically over something. This is a glimpse into a normal day with young children; these are examples of typical behaviors for little people with a lot to learn. Such immaturity is the cause of many behavior problems among children. This chapter examines the types of behaviors caused by immaturity. It also demonstrates some appropriate responses to specific examples of immaturity. In doing so, we revisit the information presented in previous chapters about child development and appropriate child guidance.

The word *immature* means not fully grown; therefore, being young means being immature. Although teenagers may use the term in a derogatory way to one another, even teenagers have a right to be immature. Just being young is often the cause of problems; the younger the child, the more this is so. Early childhood teachers face this issue daily as their students demonstrate a lack of skills needed for success in daily living. Experienced teachers of young children know that each day will bring spilling, falling, spitting, biting, hitting, crying, and screaming. These behavior problems can be directly traced to immature coordination, undeveloped communication ability, childish social skills, and other perfectly normal aspects of early childhood. Knowledgeable adults are able to distinguish between misbehavior and childlike behavior. This distinction is essential for helpful guidance.

Recognizing that immaturity naturally causes many problems gives you a more productive way to deal with those problems. Your challenge is to determine the exact cause of the problem so that you can provide the appropriate teaching for the child or make the needed change in the program. Because the exact same behavior can have different causes, you need to work at discovering the cause. This involves observing for patterns in individual children's behavior, listening and observing to determine a child's understanding of a situation, and communicating with families so you have information about each child's experiences outside of school.

OBSERVING AND RECORDING BEHAVIOR TO DETERMINE THE CAUSE

Collecting data on children's behavior patterns is essential to meeting their developmental needs. All effective teachers use data to inform their instructional plans. Preparing to meet long-term goals for children's social and emotional development is no different. Teachers use a variety of techniques to observe children's behavior, including written records, videotapes, audiotapes, and photographs. The most common forms of observation for the purposes of discovering the causes of children's behaviors are written records; anecdotal note taking, event sampling, and time sampling.

Without information about the children involved, it is not possible to diagnose a problem accurately. Without an accurate diagnosis, discipline approaches are likely to go astray.

One useful observation technique is anecdotal note taking. Anecdotal notes are short recordings of children's actions and words during a particular situation. Most anecdotal notes contain the date of the observation, the place the observation took place (e.g., science center, circle time, arrival, etc.), and a brief, objective description of the situation. An objective description of an event includes specific words and actions used by the child in the situation. It does not contain your feelings about the event or your interpretation of children's behavior. Following are examples of objective and subjective anecdotal notes.

> **Objective:** S cried when the bus driver dropped her off at the classroom door. Sat in a chair in the library area and did not respond to any interactions for 10 minutes. Came to morning meeting and asked, "Will you read *Silly Sally* today?"
>
> **Subjective:** S was sad when she came to school today. She ignored everyone but finally settled into the routine.

As you will note, the objective observation contains descriptions of the child's actions as well as her language. The subjective observation contains inferences about the child's mood and an unsubstantiated interpretation of the child's actions. First, we cannot conclude that crying implies sadness. Children may cry to display of a range of feelings, such as frustration, anger, or joy. Second, we cannot conclude that a child sitting in a chair and not responding to conversational overtures is ignoring people. She may in fact be doing just the opposite—testing the emotional climate of the setting before she chooses to interact. Finally, just because a child follows the routine and initiates a conversation, we cannot assume that he or she is "settled in." Figure 11–1 shows a sample anecdotal record form.

If we wish to uncover patterns in children's behavior, we must collect objective records over time. This practice limits our tendency to think about behavior in terms of adult feelings or inferences, and instead keeps us focused on the feelings and needs of the child. With a series of observations the patterns of children's behaviors become obvious, thus limiting the need for subjective interpretation.

Event sampling is another observation method that is useful when you see a pattern in children's behavior, but still can't pinpoint the cause. For example, if you notice that Allison hits others on the playground, but not in the classroom, you plan your observations around the events on the playground. To conduct an event sample you must remain focused on Allison during the situation in which the behavior occurs. As soon as you witness the behavior, you must document the events that immediately preceded the behavior and those that followed. Figure 11–2 shows an example of an event sampling form.

Name of Child:	Date:	Time:

Description of place: *Playground*

A is watching B, C, and D play catch with the red ball. She is smiling. The ball rolls near her—she watches but does not touch it. C gets the ball and runs back to the group. A moves closer to the group. D misses the ball and it rolls near A. A picks up the ball. D says "That's our ball." A hits him and runs away with the ball.

FIGURE 11–1 Anecdotal Note

Name of Child:	Date:	Place:
Trigger	**Behavior**	**Intent**
A is watching B, C, and D play ball. She is smiling.	D's ball rolls near A. She picks it up. D says, "That's my ball." A hits D.	A runs away with the ball. D follows and tries to pull the ball from A's hands. A hits him again and says, "I want this ball."

FIGURE 11–2   Event Sampling

Documenting the sequence of events will help you uncover the cause of the behavior as well as the result or goal of the behavior. What happens before the behavior is the "trigger" for the emotional response. More often than not, triggers go unnoticed by adults. What happens after the behavior is related to the goal of the act, but is not necessarily the cause of the behavior. For example, if Allison is watching a group of children tossing a ball to one another and she hits someone to get the ball, we might infer that the behavior was directed at getting the ball. However, we don't know that for sure. What we need to ask ourselves at this point is what was she doing before she hit the person and took the ball. Was she watching the group? Did she ask for a ball? Were there other balls in sight? Did she attempt to get into the play? Did the ball accidentally hit her while the other children were tossing it about? Did the other children tell her to move away from their play? Did they invite her to play? The trigger often reveals the cause of children's behavior and it helps us to make informed decisions about the intent.

As was the case in using anecdotal records, you must collect several event samples to reveal the patterns of children's behavior. If after observing on the playground for several days you begin to see a pattern of hitting each time Allison watches another group of children playing, you might conclude that she has not yet mastered entering play on the playground. Remember that children's development is uneven, so we can't expect that they will use all of the skills they possess in every situation. Some children will do just fine entering play in the classroom where interactions are calm, but will have difficulty breaking into a high-intensity activity such as tag or kickball. It may be the case that Allison has not had an opportunity to engage in group games in outdoor settings and is unsure how to enter the play.

Time sampling is another type of observation technique that can help you determine the cause of children's behavior. This method is useful in determining how often and in what situation a behavior occurs. In many cases, adults generalize children's bad behavior, saying Max is shy or Jonathan is aggressive. However, it is likely that Max is not shy in every situation and the same is true of Jonathan's aggressiveness. To determine in which situations the behavior does or doesn't occur, we use time sampling.

In time sampling, each instance of the problem behavior is recorded according to a predetermined timeframe. The interval for time sampling corresponds to the information needed about the behavior. At first, the interval should be broad (e.g., arrival, math, reading, lunch, recess, etc.). Observation using a broad time interval will assist you in determining the time of day that the behavior most frequently occurs and when it is less likely to occur. Once you've identified the situations in which the behavior does or does not occur, you can begin to focus on

Name of Child:	Max	Date:			
Behavior	Circle	Center	Snack	Playground	Story
Crying	x				x
Thumb sucking	x		x		x
Sitting alone				x	
Painting alone		x			

FIGURE 11–3   Time Sampling

the cause of the behavior. This is best accomplished through the use of event sampling or anecdotal records. We want to caution you not to ignore the situation in which the behavior doesn't occur because it often holds the key to determining how to modify the environment in which the behavior does occur. Figure 11–3 shows an example of a time-sampling form.

Strategies for Collecting Observations   You can collect observations at any time during the day. The easiest times to collect observations are when children are working independently or in small groups. Watching behaviors on the playground, in the lunchroom, or during arrival and departure times will help you to determine how children interact when adults are not nearby. You can also jot short notes about students while you are engaged in small-group activities. If children ask what you are writing about, tell them the truth—"I'm writing a story about what you're doing during reading time."

Collecting observations over time will not only reveal the cause of behavioral issues, it will provide you with valuable information to use when making decisions about instructional or environmental modifications that will facilitate children's learning. Observation can help you analyze children's developmental trajectories (e.g., what skills the child has mastered) and how the environment and your teaching methods are meeting children's needs. As we begin our discussion of possible causes of children's behavior, we encourage you to revisit Figure 1–3 in Chapter 1 to guide your thinking about possible causes of children's behaviors.

PHYSICAL IMMATURITY

Let's start by looking at problems typically related to physical immaturity. We will also examine emotional, social, and intellectual development as causes of undesirable behaviors. Figure 11–4 provides an overview of these behaviors.

Inability to Sit Still

Children often get into trouble for moving around when they aren't supposed to. The inability to sit still for very long is another example of the physical limitations of being young (Bredekamp, 1997). Forcing young children to sit still or control their bodies for long periods of time can cause problems. Unable to satisfy this unreasonable expectation, the young child will move around regardless of what the teacher wants. Chapter 2 described this aspect of early childhood

Lack of:	Causes:
• Large motor control	• Bumping
• Attention	• Disrupting group times
• Fine motor coordination	• Spilling
• Bladder control	• Wetting
• Expressive language skills	• Hitting, kicking, biting
• Emotion regulation	• Tantrums, tears
• Social skills	• Grabbing, hitting, kicking, biting
• Perspective taking	• Lying, being selfish, fighting
• Understanding ownership	• Taking without asking
• Following rules	• Cheating

FIGURE 11–4 Normal Childhood Behaviors Interpreted as Misbehavior

PEARSON
myeducationlab

To read about how teachers meet children's needs to be active, go to MyEducationLab and select the topic "Guiding Children." Under Activities and Applications, read the strategy Attention Span.

development, and Chapter 4 explained the importance of allowing children to move around as a way to prevent discipline problems. Let's look more closely at ways to meet that need.

First the teacher must let go of plans that require children to sit still and be quiet for very long. The teacher's understanding and acceptance of young children's needs will go a long way toward solving some behavior problems. You certainly don't want to be the cause of the problem. However, if you find that you have been, changing yourself is much easier than changing someone else.

Then you need to analyze your classroom and your program for levels of physical activity. Children need a lot of large motor activity (Stork & Sanders, 2008). Be sure to include activities that involve the arms, shoulders, and trunk muscles since these normally get used less than lower body muscles. A woodworking area is usually a big draw if it is well supplied with usable tools. Large, hollow blocks are also great for upper body development. If your program doesn't include them, large, hollow blocks would be an excellent investment. Then make sure there is plenty of time and space for using them. Varying the types of props to use with them will enhance children's interest. Pretend play can encourage physical activity too.

Dennis set up a fitness center for children's play (King & Gartrell, 2003). Many of his students have parents who go to a gym to exercise before or after work, so the children are familiar with this type of activity and are excited about having their own workout area. Dennis included typical preschool materials such as the balance beam and climbing structure, and he created others.

One of the parents volunteered to transform an old school tricycle into a stationary bike exercise center. Maureen and Sheri filled plastic bottles with sand to use as weights. Plastic floor mats were included for calisthenics and lively music for aerobics. Stable child step stools allowed for step aerobics.

The teachers had fun playing with the children and demonstrating some of the less familiar activities. Both boys and girls were attracted to the area and it became a permanent part of the classroom throughout the winter when outdoor active play was less available.

Allowing children to move freely about the classroom and to find comfortable body positions lets children meet their need to move. Teachers who are aware of children's physical development provide meaningful reasons for them to move around. These teachers are also sensitive to the group's energy level. They recognize squirming and children's frequent requests to move—to go get a drink, to go to the bathroom, to go!—as symptoms of their need for movement. These teachers know that sometimes the only reasonable thing to do is to have everyone push the tables back and play an energetic game or sing an action song!

PEARSON
myeducationlab

To view an example of how teachers use movement to teach content, go to MyEducationLab and select the topic "Guiding Children." Under Activities and Applications, watch the video Using Songs, Actions, and Chants to "Teach English Language Learners."

Movement can be incorporated into many areas of the curriculum (Stork & Sanders, 2008). Children can use large muscles when they do art projects that require large pieces of paper and large tools. For instance, children can be encouraged to paint with feather dusters on large cardboard boxes. Math activities can offer movement as children use large manipulatives or practice one-to-one correspondence by moving themselves around. The following example shows how even a normally sedentary activity like reading can accommodate the movement needs of young children.

∞ Mrs. Jensen asked Andrea, her student teacher, to take a group to the library corner to read *The Three Little Pigs* together. Most of the children settled right in and found their place in their individual books. But Isabel, Jason, and Tomas couldn't get settled. They pushed and jostled for seats. They juggled their books into every conceivable position, flipping pages and occasionally dropping the books. Andrea was having a hard time keeping them still and focused on reading. How could she get them through the story with all of this activity and fighting? Deciding to ask for help, she excused herself from the group for a minute and described her difficulty to Mrs. Jensen.

Aware of the high energy level that morning, Mrs. Jensen suggested they try acting out the story. Andrea checked with the children to see if they'd like to do a play. Affirmative! She assigned the roles of three little pigs to—you guessed it—Isabel, Jason, and Tomas. They went to the adjacent block area to build their houses. She sent Brianna, a strong reader, along with them in the narrator/cueing role. Brianna brought the book to each construction site as the part came up in the story. Andrea read the part of the wolf to help pull the play together. The piglets frantically built while the narrator read. They read their pig parts with intensity. Then they squealed in delight and scrambled to the next house as Andrea huffed and puffed. There was no more pushing or dropping books; everyone was fully involved. ∞

Andrea could have wasted a lot of energy trying to squelch the children's surface behaviors. Fortunately, Mrs. Jensen accurately recognized their off-task behaviors as symptoms of an undeniable need for movement. Her recommended discipline approach dealt directly with the cause of the problem.

Mrs. Jensen knows her students well and is in a position to know the cause of behaviors such as why Isabel, Jason, and Tomas had a problem sitting still. But the same behavior could have had a different cause. It is possible that the "troublemakers" might have been uncooperative due to their inability to read the

Be sure to provide enough time for children to complete tasks that require the use of fine motor skills.

material. Or the problem could have been just the opposite: The material may have lacked challenge for them. Similar disruption could have been caused by one child's attention-getting tactics. Often there are multiple causes, which create an even greater challenge for helpful adult intervention.

Without information about the children involved, it is not possible to diagnose the problem accurately. Without an accurate diagnosis, discipline approaches are likely to go astray. Knowing students well enough to guess fairly accurately about the cause of problems involves establishing authentic relationships with the child and the parents.

Immature Coordination

Spilled juice at snack time is an everyday occurrence in preschool. Usually it is a result of the immature coordination that is normal for young children. Providing child-sized pitchers and furniture increases children's successful independence, but it doesn't eliminate all spills. Adults with realistic expectations prepare for this inevitable outcome by having paper towels handy for clean-up. Piaget (1965) calls it "making restitution" when children clean up their mistakes. We call it helping children take responsibility for themselves without making them feel bad. This approach to accidents is an example of using related consequences, as described in Chapter 8. Teachers also prevent spills from becoming a problem by locating snack tables on a washable floor surface. These preparations help teachers remain calm and allow for productive responses to mistakes. This attitude is a description of the approach to discipline we call *creating environments that prevent discipline problems* (see Chapter 4).

Unfortunately, not all adults realize that spilling is a natural part of learning to pour. Some act as if they think that yelling insults at a child will improve his or her pouring ability. Common adult responses to a spill are "Not again!" or "That's the third time today! Can't you be careful?" Other adults simply eliminate spills by denying children the chance to practice. Both responses are counterproductive to the child's skill development. Both approaches also damage the child's self-esteem and hinder the development of autonomy. Being yelled at makes youngsters feel ashamed and afraid to try, and having things done for them makes kids feel inept and unable to succeed. Both responses create helplessness. In contrast, related consequences help children feel capable and proud (Curwin & Mendler, 1999).

Young children frequently experience negative feedback for the clumsiness natural to their age. As a teacher, you may see a lack of sensitivity not only from other adults but also from the children's own peers. The following example demonstrates how an opportunity for making restitution can make everyone involved feel better about an accident. It is another example of a related consequence.

∞ Sophie and Anna were at the inventions table, busily cutting out pictures from catalogs and picking bits of ribbon, shells, and Styrofoam to glue onto larger pieces of paper. Anna accidentally spilled some of the gooey white glue on Sophie's paper. Sophie started yelling in frustration and anger about her spoiled project. Anna kept saying over and over how sorry she was, but Sophie kept on screaming.

Maureen quickly came to the rescue. Anna looked frightened and fearful of punishment as the teacher came near. Maureen reassured her that accidents do happen and then turned her attention to the screaming Sophie. "I know you are angry about your paper, but such loud screaming hurts everyone's ears. Let's see what we can do to fix your paper. Anna feels bad about spilling on it, and I'm sure she will help you clean it up. What would be a good thing to wipe up glue with?"

Anna did indeed want to help. She suggested that Kleenex might work to wipe up the glue and ran to get some. Together, the girls carefully wiped away the excess glue, leaving Sophie's paper almost as good as new. Then they were able to continue working cooperatively together. ∞

Such accidents don't stop when children reach grade school; they are still a normal part of the children's development.

∞ Several second graders in Mr. Davis's class were busy painting for a class project. They were working on a countertop in the uncarpeted part of the room designated for messy projects. This was fortunate since it wasn't long before the blue paint had spilled on the countertop and was dripping down the lower cabinets onto the floor. The children happily and obliviously continued to paint, while making blue shoe tracks all over the tiled floor.

Mr. Davis saw the mess and said, "I see that paint drips a lot. It's going to be a lot of work cleaning it up when you're finished; what do think will be the best way to do it?" He also asked for their ideas about how they could keep from tracking the paint from their shoes onto the carpet. He helped them find the sponges and paper towels they decided they needed, but let them take charge. He was pleased to discover that his students figured out for themselves how to wipe their shoes off, as well as how to get all the paint cleaned up. In fact, the cleanup project turned out to be even more interesting than the painting, attracting help from many who hadn't even been painting. It didn't take long before there wasn't a trace of blue paint left. ∞

Other Physical Limitations

"Someone wet on the floor!" Physical immaturity sometimes means a youngster doesn't make it to the toilet on time. The accident can be a serious blow to a child's pride and must be handled with care to preserve his or her self-esteem (Fleisher, 2004). Mrs. Jensen remembers how her kindergarten teacher publicly humiliated children who had accidents. They had to wash out their underpants, and then the teacher would hang them up to dry in the classroom for all to see. Mrs. Jensen is sure she can improve on that technique. She doesn't consider the incident to be a discipline issue; her only approach in the following example is to treat Meadow with compassionate respect. Mrs. Jensen knows this is not a discipline problem, but rather a maturation issue.

∞ Meadow was working on a puzzle during choice time when she suddenly realized she had to go to the bathroom. She was very uncomfortable, but it wasn't time for the bathroom break yet. She knew she could ask permission to go any time she wanted, but it was just too embarrassing. Everyone would know where she was going. She decided to wait until the scheduled time. Oh, oh! She couldn't hold it any longer. Meadow was mortified but hopeful that no one would notice the puddle on the floor around the chair. She quickly got up and moved away from the evidence. Her skirt didn't seem too wet and maybe no one would see that her underpants were soaked. Meadow just didn't think she could stand it if anyone knew what she had done.

"Mrs. Jensen! Someone wet on the floor!" shouted Jimmie indignantly. The teacher replied calmly, "I guess it will have to be wiped up. Just don't walk there for now." Mrs. Jensen noticed Meadow's damp skirt and furtive looks. She quickly put the pieces together and realized how distressed the shy girl must be. The teacher's challenge was to get the floor cleaned, help Meadow get dry, and still preserve the child's privacy and dignity. Mrs. Jensen noticed that recess was in 10 minutes, and decided to wait until then for the custodian to come and clean up. It would make much less fuss that way. Recess would also be a good time to get Meadow aside and quietly give her some dry undies as well as a plastic bag for her wet ones. ∞

If wetting incidents became frequent, Mrs. Jensen would contact the child's parents and look further for a cause. However, this isolated incident appeared to be simply a case of waiting too long.

UNDEVELOPED COMMUNICATION ABILITY

Consider the activities of hitting, kicking, biting, and spitting. Although these behaviors are unacceptable, they generally only indicate a need to learn more productive approaches for expressing needs and feelings. One common cause of this

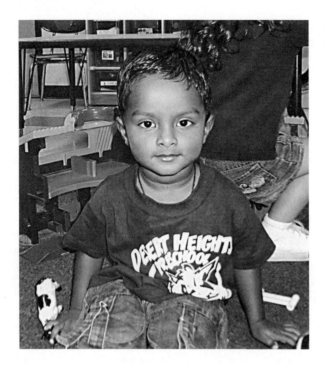

Lack of language skills can cause behavior problems.

type of behavior among many preschoolers is their lack of communication ability (Horowitz, Westlund, Karolina, & Tomas, 2007). Young children are still beginners with language (Vygotsky, 1962). They haven't yet had sufficient practice to find the exact words they need, and in times of stress what they do know may fall apart. A child who is angry, frustrated, or otherwise upset often has trouble expressing those feelings in words. Instead, the child hits, kicks, bites, or spits to communicate.

Productive discipline does more than simply stop the behavior; it doesn't just let kids know what not to do, it teaches them what to do. Therefore, when a lack of communication skills appears to be the cause of the behavior, adults need to help children express themselves with language. Teachers of young children can frequently be heard reminding them, "Please use your words," as in this situation with the rocking boat.

∽ Three children were in the rocking boat happily rocking and pretending to fish. Three-year-old Celeste went over to them and stood by the boat. The children kept on rocking. Celeste started whining and screaming at them, but used no words. The other children looked at her but did not stop what they were doing. Celeste kept on whining and screaming.

Dennis came to the rescue. He bent down to Celeste and said, "You seem very upset." The child acknowledged her teacher's reflective listening with a nod and told him she wanted to play on the boat. Dennis asked her if she had used her words to tell the other children what she wanted. Celeste shook her head "No." So Dennis asked her to think of what words she could use. Celeste smiled at him and said to the children in the boat, "I want to ride."

Thank heavens it worked! The children in the boat stopped and let her in, then the four of them proceeded to rock and fish. Dennis hoped that this successful experience would help Celeste remember to talk instead of scream in the future. ∞

When a lack of language skills causes behavior problems, the proper discipline approach is to teach the missing skills. Possibly the most valuable communication skill is how to use an "I message," as described in Chapter 7. Notice how Mrs. Jensen helps Abby find a better way of expressing herself in the following scenario.

∞ Abby was reading by herself in a secluded spot in the room. She had had a hard day at school and needed to be alone. Suddenly Cole plopped down beside her and began reading his book aloud, laughing at how funny it was. Abby was in no mood for such nonsense, so she kicked him. Cole yelped and indignantly complained to the teacher, "I didn't do nothing to her!" As she comforted Cole, Mrs. Jensen thought about what might have brought this on.

She was aware of the conflicts Abby had experienced during the day and knew that Abby hadn't come out well in them. Mrs. Jensen had been pleased to see that Abby was making good use of the soft private area of the room to comfort herself. She hadn't noticed Cole go over there, however. Maybe she could use this situation as a teaching opportunity.

Mrs. Jensen went over with Cole to where Abby was pouting, her arms crossed and a big scowl on her face. Mrs. Jensen used some reflective listening to acknowledge what she thought Abby's feelings were. "It looks like you wanted to be alone over here," she said. Abby nodded, still scowling but perhaps more able to be reasonable.

So Mrs. Jensen decided to work on "I messages." She encouraged Cole to tell Abby how he felt about being kicked. "You hurt me and made me feel bad," Cole said. Then she tried to get Abby to use an "I message" to express her feelings: "Is there a better way for you to let Cole know what you wanted?" Abby was able to say, "I want to be by myself." And she spontaneously added, "I'm sorry I got mad and kicked you." ∞

Another discipline approach might have been appropriate for this behavior if there had been a different cause. You may recall that we recommended in Chapter 8 that a child who hurts another child should help the injured youngster. Do you know why that wouldn't be the best learning experience in this case? Remember, you select your discipline approach based on what you believe the child needs to learn. Mrs. Jensen saw the need for communication skills here, apparently having reason to believe that Abby already knew that kicking hurts. Additionally, a child who desperately needs time alone is not in the best condition to offer nurturing help right then. The choice of discipline approach was based on the teacher's perception of the child's current intellectual and emotional needs.

UNDEVELOPED EMOTION REGULATION

Hitting, kicking, biting, and spitting, as well as screaming, crying, and other out-of-control behaviors, can also be caused by an inability to regulate emotions. As explained in Chapters 2 and 6, learning to express emotions productively is not automatic, and some children require more assistance than others. Adults can support and coach children in the difficult process of learning to deal with emotions and express them productively.

Coaching Emotion Regulation

Being aware of a child's emotions and recognizing emotional moments as teachable moments are the critical first steps. Accepting children's feelings is also an essential part of helping them cope; you don't need to accept the screaming or hitting that may accompany them, but you do need to acknowledge the validity of the feeling. The reflective listening process described in Chapter 7 is an excellent way to show empathy and to validate a child's feelings. It also allows you to help the child verbally label emotions and provides an opportunity to support the child in thinking about more useful ways of expressing feelings. Remember, we aren't trying to stop them from expressing how they feel, but rather to express their feelings in a reasonable way. Notice how Mrs. Jensen works on this process with Robert:

∞ Robert was involved in a math game when Mrs. Jensen gave the 5-minute warning for cleanup and lunch time. Robert immediately flung his cards and playing board into the air and wailed, "I didn't get to finish my game!" Then he got up and ran out of the classroom. Mrs. Jensen found him standing in the hall beside the door with his fists clenched, eyes shut, and face red. She could see that he was working on getting control of himself, but that trying to reason with him right then wouldn't work. She kept an eye on the students in the room, seeing that they were cleaning up. A couple of them were even cleaning up Robert's mess. Soon the others were on their way down the hall to lunch. "Have a good lunch," Mrs. Jensen said as they left.

Then she had time to help Robert. He no longer had clenched fists, his eyes were open, and his face wasn't quite as red. He did have a few tears, though. "You really wanted to play that game, didn't you?" Mrs. Jensen said sympathetically. "Yeeeeeeeeeees, I never got to play that one before. I want to play it!" replied Robert angrily.

Mrs. Jensen asked Robert to come back to the room and look at the classroom calendar with her. She showed him that they would have math game time every day this week and the next and the next. Robert began to relax, and acknowledged that he could play the game tomorrow. "Can I go to lunch now?" he asked, obviously feeling much better.

As she walked down the hall with him, Mrs. Jensen asked Robert if throwing the game had made him feel better. "Yes, but I'm not supposed to do that, am I?" he answered. "What do you think?" smiled Mrs. Jensen. "No." Then Mrs. Jensen asked him why he thought he wasn't supposed to. "I don't want to hurt the game," he replied. It wasn't a perfect answer, she thought, but Robert had come a long way in these first 3 weeks of school. Last week he was spitting when he was upset.

Mrs. Jensen thought that in addition to needing help with emotion regulation, maybe he would benefit from more time to make transitions. Perhaps the pressure of a tight school schedule was making it harder for him to control his feelings. The next day Mrs. Jensen approached Robert a little before the 5-minute warning and asked him to be in charge of flicking the lights as the warning signal. This put Robert in charge and gave him a feeling of power over the situation that had been upsetting him. ∞

Notice that Mrs. Jensen used a combination of guidance approaches, based on her assessment of the cause of Robert's outburst. She used reflective listening to acknowledge his feelings, she allowed him to express his feelings in words, and she helped him put the problem into perspective. All of these responses helped him with his emotion regulation. Notice, too, that she didn't try to do emotion regulation coaching until she had gotten the other children off to lunch. It is unwise to engage in such work when you are rushed or when you have an audience (Riley, San Juan, Klinkner, & Ramminger, 2008).

In addition to working on emotion regulation with Robert, Mrs. Jensen used her observations of his behavior to determine that transitions were hard for him and that he might be helped by feeling more control over his day. So often there are interactive causes for a behavior problem; it is necessary to deal with all the causes.

Emotion Regulation Curriculum

Most children need help with emotion regulation; therefore, many teachers include that topic in their curriculum as a preventive measure (Riley et al., 2008). Coaching and scaffolding children's emotion regulation during emotional moments is extremely useful, but some discussion during calmer moments can help too. Role-play with puppets can be a fun way for children to practice better ways of expressing their feelings. Hyson (2004) suggests games to help children think about and talk about emotions.

Reading books about emotions with children can lead to important discussions of feelings and how to cope with them (Hansen & Zambo, 2007). What children's books do you know that deal with the expression of feelings? Some children learn from the old favorite *Alexander and the Terrible, Horrible, No Good, Very Bad Day* (Viorst, 1972). Have you read *Spinky Sulks* (Steig, 1988) with children? Both provide examples of how not to express feelings, but offer children the opportunity to be wiser than the book character and offer suggestions for improvement. See the Recommended Readings list at the end of this chapter for some useful children's literature titles.

Class meetings often include discussions about feelings, offering the observant teacher valuable insights into individual children's thinking. Some teachers have pictures of faces showing various emotions and encourage children to pick the one that matches their feelings. Art projects offer a way to express feelings, and journaling can be used by older children. Pretend play offers outlets for children to express and explore emotions; observing children's pretend play can give adults valuable information about children's feelings.

It is rewarding if children can plan ahead for ways to calm themselves when their feelings get too intense. Someplace they can retreat to while getting their feelings under control is essential. The soft and secluded classroom area we recommended in Chapter 4 provides for this need. Children can be encouraged to bring comfort items from home: for some children it is a special blanket, for others it might be a stuffed animal or doll. Taking a teddy bear and retreating to a beanbag chair away from other children can provide an age-appropriate, self-soothing process.

Children who don't know how to find playmates often hit, shove, or grab things from the child they want to play with. These children need adult help to learn more effective approaches.

Helping children with emotion regulation requires a knowledgeable teacher; professional development specific to this topic is recommended for best results (Paintal, 2007).

UNDEVELOPED SOCIAL SKILLS

Learning the complexities of human interaction takes at least a lifetime. No wonder small humans with very little experience often have problems. To make matters worse, society groups these inexperienced beings into crowds, where they have to compete for limited space and resources. Some children don't face this test until kindergarten, but many are in preschool or group care at much younger ages. They are expected to "get along" by "sharing" the attractive toys and being "nice" about letting others infringe on their play territory. When children are unable to rise to these challenges, adults generally consider it a discipline problem. Those who understand discipline as teaching respond in one way, but those who view discipline as controlling behavior respond in another way (DeVries & Kohlberg, 1987). You can observe this contrast in these next two examples.

PEARSON
myeducationlab

To view an example of how teacher's help children to share ownership, go to MyEducationLab and select the topic "Guiding Children."
Under Activities and Applications, watch the video "Guiding Children Through Property Disputes."

∞ "Teacher! Kyle is messing up my cakes!" yelled Colette. Colette had been making cakes out of playdough and Kyle was making them into something else.
   Joanne immediately came to the rescue. "Kyle, you can't take the playdough Colette is using."

"But I want to help her!" exclaimed Kyle. Joanne ignored his explanation; she gave Kyle another ball of playdough and set him up at another table. Kyle gave up on playing with Colette when teacher Joanne told him, "If you bother Colette again, you will go to time-out." Dejectedly, Kyle pounded on the playdough a bit and then wandered off.

Sheri, the aide, watched this incident with interest. Because her hours at the center were from mid-morning to mid-afternoon, she noted the contrasting teaching styles of the morning and afternoon head teachers. Sheri had to admit that Joanne's style got the incident over with quickly, but children definitely got along better in the morning under Dennis's management system. The next morning, Sheri closely observed as Dennis handled a similar situation.

Sarah was working with the large, interlocking tubes, trying to build a tower. Suddenly Dennis heard her crying and screaming at Jack, "No! No! Bad!" Dennis saw that Jack was pulling apart the pieces that Sarah had been putting together, ignoring Sarah's cries.

"Whoa. Wait a minute here," Dennis said, putting his arm around Jack and stopping the action. "What's going on?" he asked. Sarah was sobbing that Jack was wrecking her tower. Jack looked confused and said he wanted to help Sarah build.

"Does Sarah like what you are doing?" asked Dennis. Jack shrugged. "Look at her face," the teacher told Jack. "Listen to what she is saying."

Dennis got Sarah to stop screaming and crying and instead to use an "I message" to tell Jack how she felt. Then he got Jack to tell Sarah that he wanted to help her build. Things had calmed down enough now so that some negotiation could go on. Dennis scaffolded the process as Jack proposed how he could help and while Sarah made it clear that helping did not involve taking apart what she had put together. Before long, the two children were working happily together and Dennis was off helping other children. ∞

Notice that Dennis not only scaffolded communication of feelings in this example, but also helped Sarah control her emotional outburst, and then assisted both children in interpreting one another's feelings. These are important social skills directly linked to peer acceptance (Riley et al., 2008).

∞ Sheri could see that Jack was feeling more cooperative at the end of this exchange than Kyle had after his unsuccessful attempt to play with Colette and the playdough. Yet Dennis had to spend several minutes working with the youngsters on the problem. Sheri found a chance to ask Dennis, "Why didn't you just tell Jack to stop bothering Sarah instead of spending so much time with that problem?"

Dennis was glad to discuss his approach with Sheri; she seemed to have a good rapport with the children, and he hoped she would stay in this job for a while. He explained that children don't learn how to make friends if the teacher sends them away for mistaken approaches. He communicated his goals of teaching youngsters how to get along and helping them learn to consider the feelings of others. He told Sheri that he considered this knowledge one of the most essential outcomes of early childhood education; therefore, he was happy to spend his time working on it.

Dennis commented further on the time element, mentioning that he seemed to spend less and less time on arguments between youngsters as the school year progressed. Sheri was inclined to agree; Dennis spent more time on individual problems, but Joanne had many more continuing problems to deal with. ∞

Sometimes a problem between children initially looks like it is about sharing toys or materials, but actually has another source. As shown in the previous examples, many young children don't know how to initiate play with another child (Riley et al., 2008). It is common for these youngsters to grab a possession away from someone they really want as a playmate. Sometimes they will punch or shove to get attention from someone they want as a friend. This behavior is a primitive way of saying, "I like you." Adults who don't understand young children's social development will simply try to stop the behavior. Adults who realize the cause of the problem will help children learn more productive ways of making friends. It is difficult to stop unacceptable behavior unless you help children find another behavior to take its place. In the following example, Eric learns something about using one of the play entry approaches described in Chapter 3.

∞ Eric, a very quiet 4-year-old, was watching three girls who were engrossed in playing "puppy dog." One girl was the dog and the other two were leading her around, each one with a leash on the same puppy. Eric went up to them and tried to take hold of one of the leashes. "No, go away!" the girls told him.

Dennis had been documenting Eric's play entry techniques and realized that Eric needed assistance entering play. Dennis saw Eric's ineffective attempt at joining the puppy dog play and went to see if he could help. "You want to play with them, don't you?" he asked Eric. When Eric affirmed that he did, Dennis suggested a play entry strategy: "They have two leashes but only one dog; maybe they will let you be a dog too if you ask them."

Eric went over to the girls but hesitated to speak to them, so Dennis supported the shy little boy by saying, "Eric wants to ask you if he can be a dog too, since you have two leashes." Then Eric was able to add, "I be dog?" The girls answered, "OK," and unhooked one leash from the girl being a puppy and hooked it into Eric's belt loop. Dennis was happy to see that the children played cooperatively until it was time for snack. This was a big breakthrough for Eric. ∞

Children don't automatically figure out how to successfully enter play as they get older; many primary-grade children still use inappropriate methods for gaining a playmate. It is not unusual for first graders to shove or grab something from a person they want to play with. These children still need lots of help figuring out how to accomplish their social goals. As they learn, there will continue to be conflicts. When you accurately diagnose the cause as missing play entry skills, you can begin reducing conflict by teaching the missing skills.

EGOCENTRISM

Young children want their own way, and they want it now. Adults would actually like the same thing, but they have learned not to insist on it. Adults have learned that other people's wishes don't necessarily match their own. They have also learned that give-and-take is part of getting along with others. Young children need help in learning these things. In the meantime, their behavior often appears selfish and inconsiderate (DeVries & Zan, 1994) and is difficult to deal with. They wander off during group time and start a distracting activity, they take what they want regardless of who is using it, and they generally disregard others. That's because they are so concerned with their own wishes, they cannot think about anyone else's.

Many adults believe that such behavior should be punished, but those who understand child development know otherwise. Punishing selfish behavior doesn't make children more thoughtful; it only makes them more careful about being caught and resentful about sharing (Kamii, 1982; McCord, 2005). Youngsters will become more considerate and less selfish only when they are able to understand that other people have important needs and feelings, too. This understanding takes time to develop and requires experience in order to be learned. Constructive discipline gives children both time and experience.

∞ Luis was thrilled to see the new toy car that he could really ride in; he could hardly wait to get in it. As he drove around and around in it, he wore a huge grin on his face. But after about 15 minutes, other children began asking when they could have a turn. Zach finally decided to take things into his own hands; he climbed onto the back of the car and tried to force his way in.

Nancy, the assistant preschool teacher, saw serious trouble brewing and hurried to head off any injuries. "One at a time," she cautioned as she gently removed Zach from the car. She assured Zach and the others who wanted a turn that she understood their desire to drive the car. At the same time, she tried to defend Luis's feelings. "How would you feel if someone got on the car when you were driving it?" she asked. However, it is hard for young children to understand another person's feelings. All Zach knew was that he wanted a turn. All Luis knew was that he didn't want to stop.

To assure others that they would get a turn, Nancy helped them make a sign-up sheet for showing whose turn was next. The preschoolers had used this system for other situations and understood the significance of writing their names on the chart. But Katya still complained, "Luis is taking too long a turn!" Nancy agreed that something needed to be done with so many children wanting to use the attractive new toy.

She asked the youngsters what they thought would be the right amount of time. Should it be the length of a song on a CD, or should they use an egg timer, or did they have another idea? Nancy knew that clocks were meaningless to these children and she didn't want to be the time-keeper: the "ogre" who makes people give up their turns. With Nancy's help, the children began learning ways of resolving such conflicts. By the end of the school year, they independently made sign-up sheets and turned on the CD player as a timer. ∞

What if Nancy had taken a different approach? What if she had just solved the immediate problem either by forcing Luis to give up the car to Zach or by removing Zach to time-out for his behavior? Or what if she had just tried to distract Zach with another activity instead? Many people would consider those to be good solutions, yet they would not help the children learn anything useful. Notice the errors made by the adult in this next situation.

∞ Several preschoolers were lined up waiting to foot paint. Tory finally just couldn't wait any longer. He plunged past the others waiting in line and started shoving his way into the paint pan. The other children hollered at him indignantly. Teacher Joanne reacted quickly and firmly. She pulled Tory away and told him that he would have to go to the back of the line. Tory began wailing loudly.

Needing to get back to supervising the messy activity, Joanne asked her assistant, Maureen, to quiet Tory. While Maureen was desperately trying to think of what to do, her eye fell on the gerbil cage next to Tory. "I think you are scaring Pinky," Maureen told the crying boy. Tory's attention was successfully diverted to the gerbil, and the problem was over for the moment. ∞

Is this what we want to teach children about dealing with their own feelings? What about the feelings of the other children when Tory crowded them? Neither teacher tried to help him understand the viewpoint of those who were waiting in line. Tory needs help learning to deal with his own feelings and those of others. They are important realities that prepare a child to function effectively in society, whereas feigned concern about the gerbil's feelings is only a manipulative tactic.

A more productive approach to handling Tory's problem involves only a subtle shift in the teacher's response. The teacher could have used the guidelines (provided in Chapter 8) for implementing a related consequence. Instead of just pulling Tory away, Joanne could have told him to leave until he decided to get back into line and wait his turn. This method gives him some power over his own situation and focuses his attention more clearly on the problem. Instead of just thinking about how mean the teacher is, he is free to think about how he can change his behavior to get a turn (Riley et al., 2008). A related consequence addresses the immediate problem but needs to be supplemented with other approaches. Tory also obviously needs help with perspective taking—understanding the feelings of other children.

Emotion regulation helps children manage their own feelings; perspective taking helps children tune-in to other people's feelings. Both skills are essential to socially acceptable behavior.

Therefore, it would be useful for him to listen to how they feel about his crowding. Tory also would benefit from the security of knowing that he would get a turn eventually. The sign-up sheet and the egg timer used with the trampoline line would address the children's needs in this situation. A combination of causes calls for a combination of approaches.

By the time they get into the primary grades, children usually have gained a little awareness of the needs of others. However, they still need help thinking about what others want when it conflicts with what they want. At this stage, they can make better progress with exchanging viewpoints through "I messages." Primary-grade children can be helped to use I messages effectively as a starting place for negotiating resolution to conflicts, as these second-grade boys did.

∞ Henry, Anders, and Jeremy were playing a game they had made up that involved kicking a ball within the confines of a large box. Will was watching them kick the ball back and forth, asking if he could play but being refused. Will saw Mr. Davis on the playground and told him, "They won't let me play." The other boys defended themselves by saying, "You play too rough and you always kick the ball out." Will retorted that he didn't kick the ball out any more than Henry did. Henry then replied, "You wouldn't let us play with you and your friends last recess so you can't play with us now." Jeremy and Anders nodded in agreement.

Mr. Davis asked Will how he felt about not being allowed to play. Will said he felt bad. Then Mr. Davis asked the other boys how they felt when Will didn't let them play. They said they, too, felt bad; Henry especially seemed to feel that a payback was necessary. Mr. Davis acknowledged everyone's feelings, saying "It's not fun to feel bad." He could see by Will's face that he suddenly realized how his earlier rejection made his friends feel.

Mr. Davis decided to work on some problem solving by asking Jeremy, "Can you think of anything the four of you could do to solve this problem?" Mr. Davis addressed Jeremy because Jeremy's body language indicated he was less upset over the previous recess interaction and therefore could probably reason better. Jeremy stepped back, took a deep breath, and said, "Well, we could make a deal. If we let you play, you have to let us play." Will agreed to that, and Anders and Jeremy were willing to include Will. Henry was holding out, saying, "Not until next recess; this recess we want to play alone." But then Anders whispered to Henry, "This is the last recess of the day." "Oh yeah," acknowledged Henry.

Will saw his chance and piped up, "Come on, Henry. Two against two!" Anders said, "I'll be your partner, it will be us against them." Henry relented and all four boys went back into the box and played ball. At one point Jeremy fell down and Will ran over and pulled him up. He seemed to want to make up for hurting his friends' feelings earlier. ∞

Class discussions, puppet reenactments of class problems, and children's story books can be used to help children consider the viewpoints of others. The process is the same as using these techniques for emotional regulation, but the focus is different. Whereas emotion regulation helps children manage their own feelings, perspective taking helps children tune in to other people's feelings.

When you choose a book to stimulate discussion about feelings, be sure it is a book worth reading rather than just moralistic and simplistic. Look for lively, believable characters, a well-defined dilemma in a powerful plot, and a satisfying conclusion. The value of a story for emotion lessons lies in how well it promotes critical thinking and lends itself to follow-up activities such as role-playing or art (Hansen & Zambo, 2007).

OTHER IMMATURE PERCEPTIONS

Lying, stealing, and even cheating can be caused by children's lack of understanding. Before you decide you have a budding criminal on your hands, work on helping the child understand.

Lying

Young children often get fact and fantasy mixed up (Piaget, 1965). Many adults get very angry when they believe a child is "lying." However, as explained in Chapter 3, the problem may be more a result of being young than one of immorality. Nevertheless, not telling the truth is unacceptable behavior in society. Children still need to learn how to sort out truth from untruth. They also need to learn why the truth is preferable. Effective communication strategies can help us teach both.

∽ Sam constantly bragged about his amazing exploits, patterned after those of cartoon superheroes. Dennis didn't want to call Sam a liar, but his observations of Sam told him that Sam frequently engaged in telling "tall tales." Dennis wanted to help Sam learn the difference between reality and fantasy, so he responded to Sam's tale with an active listening comment that read between the lines: "It sounds like you wish you were big and strong and could do all those things." This response got Sam onto a reality track for the rest of the conversation.

When Sam told these stories to his preschool friends, they weren't so kind. They argued, "You did not!" Sam's reaction was to argue back and defend his incredible statements. Dennis decided Sam needed more specific feedback. He took the child aside and kindly but frankly told him, "Your friends can't believe you when you tell them things they know can't be true." Dennis continued with more information. "If you tell people things that aren't true, they might not believe you when you tell them the truth." Sam needed time to digest this idea, but Dennis was there to assist his growth over time. Dennis's goal was to help Sam sort out the difference between real and pretend without losing his joy in pretending. ∽

Stealing

Almost everyone has an experience with "stealing" as they grow up. Taking what doesn't belong to you is a serious crime in society. Many adults believe they must harshly punish children for stealing to save them from a life of crime. Parents and teachers with more knowledge of young children realize the need for helping them learn about ownership (McElwain & Volling, 2005). Punishment may stop kids from taking something if they think they may get caught, but it won't help them understand why it is unacceptable to take what isn't theirs. Related consequences will help children learn this concept and also increase the likelihood that they will respect others' ownership, even when no one is around to enforce it. A consequence for stealing involves making restitution by replacing what was taken. In the following example, Tory is helped to understand why taking the scissors is a problem, but he is allowed to return them without confrontation.

∞ Naomi complained that there weren't any of the new scissors left. Dennis was surprised. Only two people were cutting, and there should have been three pairs of new scissors. He checked the cubbies and noticed a bunch of cut-paper creations in Tory's. Thinking Tory might have inadvertently scooped up the scissors with his work and stuffed them into his cubby, Dennis picked through the pile. As he moved Tory's backpack aside, Dennis felt a scissors shape pressed against the cloth. A pair of scissors had been stuffed deep into the pack. There was a chance the pair was Tory's own from home, but it wasn't likely. Perhaps he just wanted a good pair of scissors at home.

Rather than putting the boy on the defensive or making him feel guilty by accusing him of stealing, Dennis called a brief class meeting. He announced that one pair of scissors couldn't be found; now there weren't enough for the school. Dennis expressed confidence that they might show up. He concluded, "If anyone finds them, please put them in the lost-and-found basket in the back hallway." Tory looked self-conscious and trapped when Dennis began the meeting. But the final comment brought some relief to his face. No one could see the lost-and-found basket from the classroom. It was back by the cubbies! He could sneak those scissors into it, and no one would see.

An hour later, Dennis glanced in the lost-and-found basket. There were the scissors. He brought them back into the classroom and put them on their tray. Seeing Tory eye them, Dennis offered, "Would you like to use them?" As the child eagerly reached for them, Dennis inquired, "Do you have a good pair of scissors at home?" "Nope," Tory frowned. Dennis replied, "I'll tell your parents where you can buy this kind. Okay?" ∞

Cheating

How often do you hear complaints from your students that another child is cheating? Sometimes the accused isn't following the rules, sometimes the complainer doesn't understand the rules, and sometimes both are confused.

∞ Three boys are playing the Transportation game. The procedure is to roll a die, move your game piece the appropriate number of spaces, land on a picture of a vehicle, and draw a card from the pile. If you land on a vehicle that goes on land and also draw a card that reads "by land," you get to keep the card—having the most cards means winning.

Suddenly Blake calls out, "Teacher, teacher, Jason's cheating!" Mrs. Jensen comes to see and notices that Jason has five "by water" cards. He earnestly defends himself saying, "I'm not cheating." Mrs. Jensen asks Jason what he thinks the game rules are. "I have the boat (game piece), so I get to keep all the 'By water' cards," he explains. Blake is outraged at that explanation and insists, "You don't get to keep the card unless it matches the place where you land." The other child in the game agrees with Blake.

Mrs. Jensen helps the three boys look at the written rules for the game, which confirm Blake's view. She asks the boys if they want to play by the written rules or make up different ones, like Jason's. Jason is outvoted and he also realizes that he had misinterpreted the game. He is disappointed but agrees to play by the written rules. ∞

Mrs. Jensen focuses on clarifying children's perceptions, not on placing blame. She knows that blaming a child for not understanding does no good. Rules are hard for young children, especially if the rules aren't working in their favor. Egocentrism contributes to this problem and is definitely a maturational issue that requires time and adult support (Weber, 2002).

WORKING WITH FAMILIES

This book frequently mentions the importance of getting information from children's families as you try to figure out the causes of behavior problems. Listening to those who know children best is essential to understanding them. The relationships you build with families will play a key role in helping them support their children's development. The NAEYC (2008) recommends that communication with families include an equal sharing of ideas. Asking parents about children's behavior patterns at home can help you to determine how best to work with children. Many parents will welcome discussions about typical preschool behaviors, especially when they focus on successes as well as areas of need. It can be very helpful if schools can help families have a better idea of normal child behaviors; this can put into better perspective some of the frustrations of child rearing. Young children need families that understand and accept them, as well as teachers who appreciate them as they are.

CONCLUSION

This chapter provides only a few examples of the problem situations children encounter simply because they are young. Sometimes the problem requires only your respectful acceptance of the nature of young children, such as when you are dealing with wet pants or spilled juice. If youngsters can be part of fixing the problem, it helps them feel good about themselves. Sometimes the problem requires you to change your expectations to match the abilities of young children, such as adjusting your plans when youngsters can't sit still any longer. At other times you can help children's growth by teaching them a strategy for making friends, or a skill, such as modeling self-expression through I messages. Adults can significantly aid children's social maturation by helping them try to understand another child's viewpoint, which is part of learning to negotiate solutions for interpersonal conflicts. Effective guidance for young children also involves knowing when behavior that looks like lying or stealing is really only a reflection of a child's point of view.

When you are searching for the cause of a discipline problem, be sure to consider lack of maturity as a possibility. Remember, your role as the teacher is to allow youngsters the time they need to grow as well as to provide the experiences they need to learn. It may help you to cope with frustration if you can also remember that it isn't their fault when they are inept.

∞ *FOR FURTHER THOUGHT*

1. A problem to solve: Jason grabs the ball that Tanya and Eric are playing with and runs away laughing. The other two children are hurt and indignant.
   a. Describe the probable cause of the problem.
   b. Describe the guidance approach that addresses that cause.
2. A problem to solve: It is group time at preschool and several children have wandered away to play elsewhere. Most of the children are enjoying the songs and stories in the group, but tend to get distracted by some of the other activities.
   a. Describe the probable cause of the problem.
   b. Describe a guidance approach that helps with that cause.
3. Analyze actual behavior problems and guidance approaches in a setting where you know the children. Cases in which you are the adult providing the guidance will probably prove most instructive.
   a. Describe the situation.
   b. Based on your knowledge of the children involved, state the probable cause.
   c. Describe the adult intervention that addresses that cause.
   d. Describe the children's response to intervention.
   e. If the approach was not helpful, was it unsuccessful because it did not address the actual cause or because one intervention was not enough?
   f. If a different cause is suggested, plan a different strategy for next time.

∞ *RECOMMENDED READINGS*

Bronson, M. B. (2000). Research in review: Recognizing and supporting the development of self-regulation in young children. *Young Children, 55*(2), 32–37.

Landy, S. (2002). *Pathways to competence: Encouraging healthy social and emotional development in young children.* Baltimore: Paul H. Brookes.

SAMPLE CHILDREN'S LITERATURE LINKED TO EMOTION REGULATION

Bang, M. (1999). *When Sophie gets angry, very very very angry.* New York: Scholastic.

Barrett, J. (1988). *Animals should definitely not act like people.* New York: Aladdin.

Henkes, K. (1996). *Lilly's purple plastic purse.* New York: Greenwillow.

Lobel, A. (1982). Tear-water tea. In *Owl at home.* New York: Harper (a division of HarperCollins) Trophy.

Miranda, A., & Emberley, E. (1997). *Glad monster, sad monster: A book about feelings.* New York: Little, Brown.

Parr, T. (2002). *The feel good book.* Boston: Little, Brown.

Viorst, J. (1972). *Alexander and the terrible horrible, no good, very bad day.* New York: Macmillan.

Wojtowycz, D. (2000). *A cuddle for Claude.* New York: Dutton Children's Books.

SAMPLE CHILDREN'S LITERATURE LINKED TO PERSPECTIVE TAKING

Henkes, K. (1988). *Chester's way.* New York: Greenwillow.

Hughes, S. (1988). *Dogger.* New York: Lothrop, Lee & Shepard.

Luttrell, I. (1990). *Three good blankets.* New York: Macmillan Child Group.

Pfister, J. (1992). *The rainbow fish.* Transl., J. Alison James. New York: North-South.

Rosen, M. (1996). *This is our house.* Cambridge, MA: Candlewick.

Zemach, M. (1983). *The little red hen: An old story.* New York: Farrar, Straus, & Giroux.

❧ Chapter **12** ❧
Unmet Needs

NAEYC Standards Addressed in This Chapter

Standard 1a: Promoting Child Development and Learning: Knowing and understanding young children's characteristics and needs.

Standard 1b: Promoting Child Development and Learning: Knowing and understanding the multiple influences on development and learning.

Standard 1c: Promoting Child Development and Learning: Using developmental knowledge to create healthy, respectful, supportive, and challenging learning environments.

GUIDING QUESTIONS

- How do children's needs affect their behavior?
- How can teachers plan to meet children's individual needs?
- How do adult expectations affect children's behavior?

*L*ike a baby's cry, a young child's actions can signal a variety of unmet needs. Although they now have some words, young children may not be articulate enough to communicate their problems. Often they may not even be consciously aware of what they need. What's more, even if they do know what they need and can verbalize it, they may not have any idea of what to do about it. Thus, the adult's role is threefold: to help identify the need(s), to help the child learn to communicate them, and to facilitate problem solving so that the needs can be met. This chapter discusses some typical emotional and physical needs that cause problems if left unmet.

A gardening analogy is useful to explain the importance of dealing with the cause of behavior problems: Discipline that does not focus on the cause of the problem is like weeding your garden without getting the roots of the weeds. The gardening analogy also seems to help explain the importance of meeting children's needs to improve their behavior. Consider the gardener's response to carefully planted seeds that are not growing as expected. Even a novice gardener knows the basic needs of plants—light and water. Checking these needs would be a first step: If the patio table umbrella is shading the plants, move the table. If the roof overhang is keeping rain off, bring the hose over. If you can't figure out the cause of the problem, then you get an expert opinion. But you never "punish" the plants for not growing: You continue to nurture them by meeting their needs to the best of your ability.

Sometimes plants grow, but not the way you wanted. What if you had a trellis for your sweet peas but they were growing along the ground instead? Would you be upset with the sweet peas or would you gently guide the tender shoots onto the trellis? Guiding the growth of children is a lot more complex and demanding than growing plants, but the attitude of the careful gardener can guide the teacher of young children.

DIFFERING NEEDS

Just as different kinds of plants require different treatment, the uniqueness of each child requires different treatment. Differences in gender, physical traits, chemical makeup, personality, and background combine to give each person a distinctive set of needs. If you try to treat each child exactly the same in an effort to be "fair," you are actually being very unfair (Gonzalez-Mena, 2008). Fairness requires that each child has his or her unique needs met. That is why we warn against "one size fits all" discipline programs that tell you how to respond to different behaviors rather than to different children.

Each child has unique life experiences that contribute to different needs and different reactions to circumstances (Gonzalez-Mena, 2008). Your classroom is likely to include a child whose parents are in the middle of a divorce, a child whose beloved grandparent has just died, a child who is having to move due to economic difficulties, and several children dealing with the birth of a new sibling. You may also encounter children dealing with abuse, parental alcoholism, incarcerated parents, and homelessness. Getting help for children coping with serious, long-term problems is discussed in Chapter 14. However, children facing the more common family occurrences usually can be helped through a partnership of supportive teachers and families.

Each child also has a unique temperament and personality: traits that seem to be part of the package at birth, as described in Chapter 2. Fewer behavior problems occur with children who adapt easily to new situations, who have a generally sunny outlook, and whose emotional reactions are fairly mild. However, we all know there are children who do not adapt easily, who expect the worse, and whose emotional reactions are intense (Landy, 2002). These children have greater needs and require more adult assistance in learning to meet them. With individual differences in mind, let's look at some types of behavior problems that are generally linked to unmet needs. Figure 12–1 contains an overview of these needs.

PRIVACY NEEDS

Adults, as well as children, often have difficulty properly identifying their own need for privacy. General grumpiness is frequently a sign of a need to be alone. In the following example, the cause of the child's antisocial behavior should have

- Privacy needs
- Power needs
- Ownership needs
- Attention needs
- Success and challenge needs
- Security needs
- Predictability needs
- Love and acceptance needs
- Teacher recognition needs

FIGURE 12–1 Unmet Needs That Lead to Misbehavior

been recognized sooner. The youngster was finally helped to figure out how to get his need met, however. As we explained in Chapter 4, it is important for the school environment to offer opportunities for privacy.

∾ Shen yelled, "Don't talk! I'm trying to concentrate!" as he sat at a table with three other children who were sounding out words for their daily journal writing. The other children were carefully saying each word aloud in an effort to hear the individual sounds and figure out which letters were in the word. Shen was busy with an intricate drawing in his journal and appeared to be feeling very cross. He repeated his demands for quiet several times and finally crawled under the table to work.

Unfortunately, when Julie got up to show her work to the teacher, she bumped Shen's leg in the process, saying, "Sorry." The bump must have made his pencil move where he didn't want it to. Shen began sobbing and yelling, "She made me mess up! I hate girls! I hate that one girl!"

The tantrum was in full swing when Mrs. Jensen came over and told him, "You can lay under the table and cry for one more minute if you need to, Shen, but then you need to get up and figure out how to solve your problem. I'll help you as soon as you are ready." Then she quietly reassured the other children at the table that Shen was upset but he would get over it. She also acknowledged Julie's bumping Shen as an accident.

It was less than a minute before Shen stopped crying and came out from under the table. As Mrs. Jensen led him away for a private conversation, he again yelled, "I hate girls!" His teacher used reflective listening about his feelings, sympathetically saying such things as: "You were having a really hard time concentrating with other children around." And "You are very upset about making that scribble on your drawing." Mrs. Jensen put Shen in charge of solving his problems. She asked him what he could do if he needed to be alone to work and she asked him what he could do about the scribble.

Having his feelings accepted, Shen was able to think about solutions. He decided that he wanted to work alone at a desk, so Mrs. Jensen helped him find an acceptable one. He also admitted that he could erase the scribble since it was done in pencil. He calmed down and went back to work. ∾

Mrs. Jensen had been collecting observations on Shen's interactions, and this data helped her to recognize that Shen needed some time alone. She berated herself for not intervening sooner and helping him find a spot alone before things escalated to the point they did. She also noted that Shen needed help with emotion regulation, since this wasn't the first time he had fallen apart over a fairly small problem. Shen's temperament made emotion regulation more difficult than normal, since his emotional responses are more intense than most children's. Of course, the unmet need for time alone made it harder for him to control his emotions. As is so often the case, there are interwoven causes for this behavior problem.

POWER NEEDS

Sometimes the more you try to get a child to do something, the more resistance you meet. She won't put her boots on, he won't eat, and nap time is a constant fight. Such behavior is often a symptom of a child's healthy desire to have some control over his or her own life. Arising conflicts can easily turn into fruitless power struggles. If the adult in charge insists, "You have to eat your lunch," the child insists, "I'm not hungry!" A limitation like "No, you can't go outside without your boots. There are puddles under the swings" evokes the response, "I hate those red boots!" To the statement, "Your mother still wants you to take a nap," the child replies, "I'm not tired!"

The problem may not be about hunger or boot color at all, and the child may actually be exhausted. These responses may be expressions of the need for personal power. Recognizing this need, the attending adult can, within reason, give the child as many opportunities for choice as possible (Hyson, 2008). She must eat, but which food does she want to eat first, her apple or her sandwich? How does she want to eat her apple, like a worm nibbling through, or around and around like a circling caterpillar? He must rest, but which nap story would he like: *Rumpelstiltskin* or *Strega Nona*? Does he want a back rub or to be rocked? She must wear her boots to play in the swings with the puddles under them, but if she wants to play in the fort or the playhouse, she can race out to them in her shiny shoes.

These are real choices, both desirable to the child and acceptable to the adult. They give children a chance to satisfy their need for control in a world governed by many rules they don't yet understand. And by allowing them some control at levels appropriate to their age, you will find that children are much more able to allow you to control decisions that must be made by adults. As they experience the desired power, they also develop valuable problem-solving skills. The following situation is an example of a child being allowed some power, choice, and opportunity for problem solving.

∾ The youngsters at the children's center were going outside to play, and they were excited to get out after being cooped up indoors by bad weather. The joyful hustle and bustle of coats and boots was interrupted by Celeste's wail. She threw her boots across the floor and her coat on top of them. Then she sat crying and hitting her heels on the floor. Sheri, the aide in charge of helping everyone get ready, asked another staff person to help with the other youngsters and went over to Celeste to see what the problem was. It turned out that the little girl had new shoes, and she wanted to wear them instead of taking them off and putting on the boots kept at the children's center for muddy days.

Sheri explained carefully to Celeste that her new pink shoes would get ruined if she wore them out in the mud. Celeste continued to cry and say that she wanted to wear her new shoes outside. Sheri tried reasoning with the child while upholding the rule about not going outside without boots, but Celeste kept crying loudly. Suddenly Sheri remembered what she had learned from the head teacher, Dennis, about giving children choices. Sheri changed her tactics and asked Celeste what she thought she might do to protect her shoes if she kept them on.

Celeste's sobs ebbed as she began to talk about some ideas and possible solutions. Sheri stayed with her as the others trooped outdoors with another adult in charge. Finally Celeste decided to wear some big boots from the emergency supply box, which were large enough to fit over her beautiful new shoes. She was pleased with this solution and happily marched outdoors in the giant boots. Later, Celeste asked Sheri for help. She had decided to change into her own boots, explaining that it was hard to run in the other pair. Sheri noticed that Celeste's concern about wearing her new shoes seemed to evaporate once she had an opportunity to make a decision for herself. ∞

Notice that the choices described for children were real ones. Sometimes people give children a "choice" between two undesirable things; that is not a real choice. Other times adults want to be nice, and so they ask children if they would like to do something when there is no other choice. If you say, "Would you like to go on a field trip to the zoo?" be prepared that some children may answer, "no." Similarly, many adults say things like: "Let's all get ready for lunch now, OK?" Unless you are able to accept "no" for an answer, the "OK?" question is not authentic communication.

OWNERSHIP NEEDS

"Naomi won't share!" This cry is familiar to all who spend their days with preschoolers. In Chapter 11, we explored both undeveloped social skills and egocentricity, both of which contribute to sharing problems. However, it is also important to consider whether or not it is necessary for a child to share at this time (Gonzales-Mena, 2008). Adults as well as children have a need for ownership of possessions and territory. Notice that office workers want their own designated spaces, and the contents of each person's desk are personal and private. Adults are not required to share the personal items they bring from home to make work more comfortable. Yet we routinely demand more generosity from young children. The need for ownership must be balanced with social expectations for sharing.

∞ Dennis addressed the problem of personal possessions at preschool by designating a large box as the "precious place." Youngsters who brought things from home that they didn't want others to touch could put their belongings there and be assured that they would be undisturbed. It was a child's decision when and if to bring something out for the group to enjoy.

Mrs. Jensen found that putting a child's name on a personal possession helped children share. She figured out that having the item labeled as their own fulfilled the need for ownership and freed youngsters to be more generous. First graders enjoyed labeling, which became part of their emerging literacy activities. They began using the approach for staking temporary claim to class materials as well. Thus, when Eric was working on a jigsaw puzzle and had to leave it to go out for recess, he placed a sign on it that said, "Do not touch. Eric." The children in the class respect such written notices, which solves many potential conflicts. ∞

Both of these teachers defend children's temporary or permanent ownership rights. Rather than making children selfish, this defense of their rights actually helps them to be more generous. When children have their ownership rights respected, they learn how to respect those of others. When they are not busy defending their rights to an item, they are more likely to give it up voluntarily.

When children compete for limited resources, problems are sure to arise.

ATTENTION NEEDS

Often, behavior labeled as "disruptive" can actually be a plea for attention—a cry for help! It may take some reflection to realize that a child's irritating behavior is a cry for attention. You may know kids who get attention by showing off, and you have probably seen others who seem to deliberately seek a reprimand for misbehavior. Even negative attention, after all, is attention.

⚭ Courtney's daily "owies" are almost microscopic in size, but she insists that they need a band-aid or a cold pack or a kiss. Mrs. Jensen wants to help her find better ways of feeling important and cared for. Courtney is a strong writer, so Mrs. Jensen helps her get attention and approval through sharing her writing with others. Gradually the "owies" diminish.

Mrs. Jensen thinks Ashley's tattling probably comes from a need for attention, too. She knows that Ashley may not get a lot of attention at home in her large family. Mrs. Jensen makes a point of letting Ashley know that she is important: greeting her individually when she arrives, commenting about her activities, and noticing her accomplishments. Mrs. Jensen tries hard to give each child some undivided attention. It's so hard with a large class that she wishes she could clone herself. ⚭

The desire for attention is a legitimate need (National Institute of Child Health and Human Development Early Child Care Research Network, 2008), yet it is often difficult to meet that need adequately in large-group settings. Ratios of 10 or more students to one teacher can make it difficult for even the most conscientious early childhood teacher to give enough personal attention to each individual. Public school classes of 20 or 25 children create an impossible challenge. There is a limit to how many children you can fit into your lap at once! Levels of need vary among children, depending on their personality types and their stages of development. Levels also vary from day to day, and they are often related to the children's rest and stress levels. In addition, sometimes home life can fail to provide adequate attention.

A teacher's awareness of current home factors can provide valuable information, even about children from the best situations. A parent's absence or increased work hours, newborn siblings, or even visiting houseguests can create a need for extra attention. In the following case, teachers combine information from home with observations at school to solve the mystery of Alex's behavior.

∾ Alex was humming loudly and squirming around in his seat. Alicia, sitting next to him, complained that she couldn't hear the reading teacher. The teacher asked Alex if he heard Alicia. Alex was quiet for awhile, but soon began to hum loudly again and wriggle in his seat. The reading teacher became impatient and sent him back to his regular classroom with instructions to tell his teacher why he returned.

After school, Mrs. Jensen talked to the reading teacher and asked about Alex. She said that as soon as she heard the door open, she knew it would be Alex walking through it. She had been having the same problem with him all day. Some checking revealed that Alex's mother was out of town for a meeting again. Mrs. Jensen remembered then that Alex always has this sort of problem when his mom is gone; she should have realized the cause sooner. It definitely would have been helpful to have been informed about the mother's travel.

Mrs. Jensen made a special effort to give Alex individual attention when he came to school the next morning. She asked when his mother was coming home, and said, "I'll bet you really miss her when she's gone, don't you?" When he went to his reading class, the reading teacher invited him to sit beside her and also talked with him about how long before his mom came home. With this support and extra attention from his teachers, Alex was able to cope with his unmet need for his mother's attention. The humming and squirming stopped. ∾

In some cases, disruptive behavior for attention is not a temporary problem. Some youngsters have a well-learned pattern of trying to get attention and status by disrupting class. No doubt you remember these class clowns from your school days. Their behavior is a sad symptom of low self-esteem and a cry for help (Dreikurs, 1966). In addition to work on self-esteem, these children need to unlearn their counterproductive attention-getting strategies; however, as long as their disruptive behavior gets attention, they will continue it (Adams & Baronberg, 2005). We consider behavior modification acceptable when it means ignoring inappropriate behavior. This action helps correct mislearning by extinguishing previously reinforced unacceptable behavior. Chapter 9 describes behavior modification and explains that occasional reinforcement may actually entrench the behavior more firmly than consistent rewards do. But in the following example, a teacher manages to not reinforce negative behavior.

∾ A group of children was listening to a tape recording of a book about birds and following along in their own copies of the book. The children were enjoying the tape and the book; the vibrant and detailed illustrations helped hold their interest. Then Jeffrey quit listening and began to open and close his book loudly.

The other children complained that he was making too much noise and they couldn't hear. Mrs. Jensen went over to Jeffrey and quietly asked him to please stop disturbing the other children. As soon as she walked away, he began the same behavior and got the same complaints from the other youngsters. Refusing to give attention to the behavior this time, Mrs. Jensen said nothing to Jeffrey but instead calmly walked over and turned up the volume on the tape recorder a little so that the others could still hear. Jeffrey's eyes showed his surprise. Because he was no longer getting any attention from his classmates or teacher, he began to follow the text again. Afterward, he had many comments about the birds in the book. ∞

It takes time and patience, but eventually mistaken behavior learned through reinforcement will stop once the reward of attention stops. Mrs. Jensen was able to respond effectively to the cause of Jeffrey's behavior because she had made a special effort to understand him and his problems. She knew that Jeffrey not only needed to have his inappropriate behavior ignored, but also needed to have his desire for attention met in another way. Mrs. Jensen did want to give Jeffrey the attention he craved, but not in response to inappropriate behavior. She had been working with his parents on the problem and was making an effort to notice him when he was working well in school. Rather than make an issue over this minor incident, she appreciated that his inappropriate behavior was happening less and less frequently. They had already survived Jeffrey's initial surge of worse behavior, which Mrs. Jensen had known would be the first result of ignoring his inappropriate behavior. They were through the worst and on the road to recovery.

Although ignoring inappropriate bids for attention may be the best approach for some children's growth, there are many other children who may be inadvertently ignored. It is easy to overlook some very quiet children. The too-quiet ones should cause more serious concern than the too-loud ones because they may have given up. They may have quit trying to get their needs met. They often

Children thrive on activities that make them feel successful.

appear blank or unhappy, uninvolved in activities, and generally unsuccessful. Sometimes these children assume victim roles, but more often they seem to fade into the background. You may find yourself wishing that they would actively disagree with something, get upset, or show some strong emotion—even if it's disruptive! The source of this kind of problem generally lies outside the school and therefore is discussed in Chapter 14.

NEEDS FOR SUCCESS AND CHALLENGE

Youngsters who don't complete school assignments often get into trouble. Children who don't participate in planned activities in preschool worry both teachers and parents. There are reasons for their behaviors. Forcing a child to comply or punishing noncompliance does not address the reasons. The traditional loss of recess for not completing work is a classic example of counterproductive discipline. What should you do instead? The answer depends on the cause of the behavior.

You will get clues to the cause by observing the child's specific behaviors and by noting the circumstances surrounding the problem. Does the child look upset or anxious when confronted with the task? Or does the child appear distracted? Is the child interested in something else instead? If so, what is he or she interested in? What kinds of tasks go uncompleted? Does the child only avoid writing, for example, or does he or she avoid all work? Depending on the answers to these kinds of questions, you may decide that the child lacks the ability to succeed at the task, or you might decide that he or she is not sufficiently challenged by it. You may discover that the child does his or her math just fine but can't read the material to complete the science work. Each of these different findings suggests different responses. The goal is to address the problem in such a way that you help the child find success and satisfaction in his or her work. Treating each child as an individual is an important key in meeting this goal.

∮ If Jacob won't read because the book is too hard, one useful response is to help him find a book at his level. Another response would be to help him improve his reading skills by inviting a volunteer to read to him daily. Perhaps reading in partnership with a friend who is a little more skillful would be more fun as well as more productive.

If Eli is acting up at math time because he is bored, find a more appropriate challenge for him. Help him find material at his level that is related to topics of personal interest. Yes, math can be relevant, too. Many teachers now help their students find math in the real world and use it to solve real problems.

If Madeline never uses the large-muscle equipment at preschool because she is afraid, help her find activities that will increase her confidence in her physical abilities. Perhaps helping her make friends with Kelsey, who is more physically active, would encourage her. Madeline spends a lot of time in the playhouse area; you could suggest large-muscle activities that fit in with her pretend play. ∮

The need for success, coupled with the need for appropriate challenge, continues as the young child matures. Finding the right balance for each child is essential to avoiding the problem behaviors caused by either boredom or frustration

(Hyson, 2008). Protecting children from all failure and frustration is not the goal. A certain amount of frustration is often part of learning and can provide useful lessons in learning to cope with difficulty (Hyson, 2008).

NEED FOR SECURITY

Although adults generally focus on their obligation to keep children physically safe, children's behavior deteriorates if they lack emotional security (Koplow, 2002). Feeling a sense of security is critical to the formation of a healthy personality (Holodynski & Friedlmeier, 2005). Lack of security can be the cause of anti-social behavior and of nonparticipation in school activities.

Predictability

Children feel more safe when they know what to expect and what is expected of them. A predictable schedule for the day is part of this. A place for children to keep their belongings is also important, as is their knowing where to find school materials when needed.

∞ When children arrive for preschool, Dennis is at the door to greet each one warmly. Each child has a cubby for his or her jacket and other personal belongings, so children can put away their things. Then they know that they can choose among a variety of activities and will have enough time to explore them. Many of the activities, such as blocks and the playhouse, are available every day; but something new and different is offered each day too. For instance, foot painting or snack preparation might be set up as a special event.

Lack of emotional security can cause anti-social behavior and nonparticipation in school activities.

Children know that group time comes after choice time and that they have snack after that. They know that outside play time follows snack and that they have story time when they come back inside. If there needs to be a deviation from the schedule, Dennis discusses it with the children and gives them advance notice about the change. ∽

Starting School The routine just described is well known and comfortable to the children after a month of school, but the start of school was a different matter. A child's introduction to the school setting plays a crucial role in feelings of security (Pianta & Rimm-Kaufmann, 2006).

∽ Dennis tries to meet each child and his or her family on an individual basis before the child comes to school for the first time. Some families appreciate his offer of a home visit to get acquainted, while others wait to meet with him during the school visit prior to starting the program. During the initial meeting, Dennis works at making a connection with the child so he will be perceived as a friend when the child comes to school. Dennis also uses the meeting to get an idea of the child's prior experiences and parental expectations.

Family members are encouraged to stay with the child for a while on the first day in the program. Dennis also suggests ideas to help children transition into the new setting. These include bringing pictures of family members and bringing a favorite blanket or toy. Dennis and his assistants offer nurturing support to young children as they adjust to the new setting. ∽

Predictable Limits Another type of predictability involves knowing class guidelines: what behavior is accepted and what is not. Just as they need safety limits set, children need to have clearly communicated and firmly held behavioral expectations. Although they naturally push against their limits, their tests help them find out where the boundaries are and whether those boundaries are flexible.

Teachers who strive for mutual respect with children will involve youngsters in determining appropriate limits and help children understand the reasons for limits. It is wise to have much freedom for individual decisions and choice, but that freedom must have clearly defined limits that protect everyone. Mrs. Jensen, for example, is firm about kindness and safety for all people and animals in her classroom. She also insists on responsible treatment of equipment and materials. Her expectations can be condensed into three easy to remember guidelines: Be kind. Be safe. Be careful. See Figure 12–2 for sample classroom guidelines.

For children to feel secure in a group, they need to know that others will not be allowed to harass, humiliate, or threaten them (Turkel, 2007). When adults observe such behavior, they need to interact to help the perpetrator recognize how the other child's feelings are being affected. It is time for the adult to accept an authority role and set limits (Turkel, 2007).

A child having a tantrum may be a child who needs the security of limits. Children need the emotional security of knowing that someone will help them keep themselves under control. When they experience anger, they can actually terrify

Children need limits as well as freedom. These guidelines are easy for children to remember.
- Be safe
- Be kind
- Be careful

FIGURE 12–2   Classroom Guidelines

themselves with their rage and rapidly escalating emotions. Because they are still learning how to regulate their emotions, they can be overwhelmed by the strength of their feelings and be unable to escape them. Your intervention can actually be a relief, reassuring them not only that you won't let them hurt others, but you also won't let them hurt themselves. Calmly holding a child close and offering comfort will help some youngsters calm down. Others need to be left alone so as not to reinforce the tantrum through attention. However, children must be protected from doing damage to themselves, to others, or to their environment. As they fight to get control of their own actions, children are comforted by the reminder that there are limits outside of themselves.

Teacher Continuity   What if a child gets to school and a stranger is there instead of the teacher? This can be very scary. Knowing that you can count on your teacher to be there is very important to children's sense of security. High staff turnover in child-care programs is a serious threat to children's emotional security (Brown & Bogard, 2007) and academic well-being. Even having a substitute teacher can be a trauma. Being sensitive to the impact of such change on children, schools striving to provide emotional security help children cope. Instead of familiar caregivers disappearing and new ones appearing unexpectedly, proper good-byes are said and new staff members are introduced gradually. If possible, teachers tell children in advance about substitutes and arrange to have someone known to the children be there with them.

NEED FOR LOVE AND ACCEPTANCE

Feeling unloved and rejected can cause some dreadful behaviors. Wouldn't you think that someone wanting to be liked would try to behave in a likeable way? But no, that's not how it is (Landy, 2002).

Feeling loved and expecting others to like you is the result of successful attachment with parents and/or caregivers; attachment is necessary for the development of trust that you can count on other people (National Institute of Child Health and Human Development Early Child Care Research Network, 2008). As explained in Chapter 2, attachment and trust are the earliest developmental tasks for an infant and they provide the foundation for future healthy emotional development.

When teacher–child relationships are weak, children have difficulty with school adjustment, social functioning and learning. In order to develop into fully functioning people, young children desperately need love and acceptance from the significant adults in their lives.

Family Histories

Some children have had experiences that spoil attachment and damage trust. Children's emotional development can be devastated by temporary or permanent loss of a family member due to divorce, military obligation, illness, death, incarceration, or other causes. A young child in child care who has known a caregiver for her entire one year of life can be similarly distressed if that person leaves the job. Some children's temperament is such that birth of a sibling can disrupt attachment and trust. Chapter 14 will help you to better understand how to support children who have experienced these types of unfortunate events.

Teacher Attachment

Children whose attachment and trust have been disrupted need a great deal of your assistance, but all children need to feel loved and accepted by their teachers (Murray, Murray, & Waas, 2008). As explained in Chapter 4, good relationships between teachers and children will prevent many behavior problems and help resolve those that do occur. Time spent making connections with individual children is time well spent.

∞ Dennis circulates among the children during choice time, frequently stopping to chat about a painting, a block construction, or some exciting event outside of school. He smiles acknowledgement to others and gives "high-fives" or a literal pat on the back as children go about their activities. Each child feels the teacher's recognition and affection.

Good relationships between teachers and children will prevent many behavior problems and help resolve those that do occur.

When the children assemble for group time, Dennis often comments on what he observed during choice time, such as the theme of the pretend play or the creations made with playdough. He makes sure that all children know they have been noticed, especially those who need the most reassurance.

Group time often includes songs that help children feel valued and important (Gurian, 2001). One favorite is the familiar "name game" that plays with a child's name:

> Tory, Tory bo bory.
> Fe fi mo mory—Tory.

Another often requested is the "little box" song.

> If I had a little red box
> To put my Sarah in,
> I'd take her out and (kiss, kiss, kiss)
> And put her back in again. ∞

Reasonable Expectations

Asking teachers to truly love all the children in their care may be unrealistic; however, it is reasonable to expect a teacher to have an enthusiastic approach toward children. This enthusiasm can be demonstrated by efforts to create an environment and a program that continually attempt to meet the needs of all the children enrolled. Your efforts are a way of giving love, whether you actually like a particular child or not. What is important is that you accept all children as they are, respecting each child's unique position and potential. The teacher's role is to care for, guide, and encourage all the children as they grow. Some children are just hard to like. Much as you try not to have favorites, you must admit that some kids (and adults, too) are just a lot more pleasant to be around than others.

∞ Bailey was once again yelling at the other children, and Miss Wheeler again wished that Bailey hadn't been placed in her room. What a nuisance she was. She was always getting into fights with the others, and constantly talked out of turn but would never answer a question when called on. As if those difficulties weren't enough, Bailey lost everything. She never had a pencil, never knew where her reading book was, and always lost her lunch box.

Miss Wheeler had tried everything. It seemed that Bailey was constantly given time-out for interrupting or fighting. And Miss Wheeler had finally begun taking everything away from Bailey that she might lose. Bailey's only reaction was to pout and look like she was going to cry, but Miss Wheeler thought it was an act because there were never any tears. Now look at the child! She was crawling under the table instead of sitting on her chair. What next? ∞

Miss Wheeler clearly doesn't like Bailey, and consequently neither do the child's classmates. Her behavior gets constant rejection from others. As a result of this rejection, Bailey has learned that she is a bad girl. The more she believes this lesson, the more she acts accordingly. As strange as it may sound, her reaction is normal and human. People who feel unlovable tend to act unlovable, which makes them feel worse and act worse (Berden, Keane, & Culkins, 2008). What a vicious cycle! The only hope for Bailey is to break the cycle by introducing experiences that teach her good things about herself. It won't be easy to change her self-image. At first, she will be so uncomfortable with positive feedback that she will act even worse. This behavior is the normal reaction of a person with low self-esteem: It is unsettling to be treated in any way incompatible with one's own self-image. Therefore, Bailey's first response to good feedback will be to act worse in order to show others who she really is. It takes dedication and perseverance to help a child unlearn a negative self-image. Planting a positive image in its place is essential to a child's success in life.

Changing Attitudes The following example shows how adults can start the process by gaining a more positive perspective on a child.

> ∞ At one staff meeting of Midway Children's Center, everyone was complaining about Leo, who was exhibiting particularly undesirable behavior. To relieve the negative focus, Caroline, the director, suggested an exercise. She asked everyone to think of just one thing they really liked about Leo. Some were embarrassed to find themselves struggling at first to come up with a positive point.
>
> Gradually, though, they each brought to light one part of the child they could genuinely say they liked. Musical himself, Dennis said he liked Leo's singing. Even though Leo was usually disruptive during music time, at least he was on key! Nancy liked his eyes. Sure, they were constantly darting around, checking to see if anyone was observing his mischief, but Nancy had to admit they were bright, beautiful brown eyes, just like her mother's. Maureen respected his self-assurance. He may have been bossy, but at least he was capable, an attribute Maureen valued.
>
> As the list grew, the teachers felt themselves coming to a new appreciation of the boy they had been complaining about earlier. It didn't erase their irritation with his behavior, but it did put that behavior into a little more positive perspective. They were then in a better frame of mind to brainstorm about ways to help him. ∞

The children who are hardest to like are the ones who need your acceptance the most (Berden et al., 2008). Their unmet needs for love may be acute, causing behavior that is extremely demanding. If you feel unable to meet their needs, they can become an irritation and a drain. Or they can become a challenge! It depends on your attitude.

It can be exciting to work with difficult children; although they may take the most out of you, they are also potentially the most rewarding. You will be delighted when a child who usually hits in anger progresses for the first time to venting that anger verbally. At that important moment, you can see the results of your coaching. A habitually disruptive child who makes it through a whole day, or even a whole hour, without having a negative effect on the group can give you hope for humanity! It also allows you to congratulate yourself on helping that child channel his or her energies more productively.

Peer Acceptance

In addition to needing a close relationship with adults, children need acceptance and friendship from other children. We have previously discussed peer relationships in terms of security and social development. This book has emphasized the importance of helping children understand that other people have feelings and thoughts different from theirs. But sometimes you encounter a child who doesn't seem to care how others feel, and your best efforts at teaching perspective taking have no effect.

∽ By the end of the first week of school, Mrs. Jensen could see that Jason was going to be a challenge. He had been creating problems all week: grabbing things from classmates, pushing and shoving to get in front of others, and showing no remorse for hurting them. Mrs. Jensen had helped Isabel explain to Jason that it hurt when he shoved her, but Jason wasn't interested.

Mrs. Jensen soon realized that Jason's problem wasn't that he didn't understand the impact of his action, but that he didn't care whether the other kids were upset. This was a bigger challenge than a child's lack of knowledge. Her job as a teacher was to figure out why Jason didn't care and then to work on that cause. ∽

Mrs. Jensen found out that such children typically have a history of peer rejection (DeVries & Zan, 1994). They don't have friends and don't expect to have any. This puts them in a position of having nothing to lose by offending other children. As explained in Chapter 3, having a friend is critical to developing social skills. If Jason doesn't think Robert will play with him anyway, he naturally cares more about whether he gets the most clay than whether Robert is mad at him for grabbing it all. Therefore, the cause of disinterest in other children's viewpoints is an unmet need for acceptance from peers. Of course, this is a self-perpetuating problem: the less Jason considers other children's feelings, the less likely they are to accept him in their activities.

∽ Mrs. Jensen decides that what Jason needs most is a friend. She wonders if she can get Beau to take Jason under his wing. Beau is a popular boy with good social skills who would provide a useful role model for Jason. Mrs. Jensen privately asks Beau if he would be willing to play with Jason and teach him how. Beau lives up to her expectations of his compassionate nature and agrees.

Being sought out as a reading buddy and a playground teammate by a highly desirable companion is a major change for Jason. Beau's sponsorship gains Jason's temporary acceptance by others, but Beau reminds him that he has to share the ball if he wants to keep on playing. Now Jason does have something to lose by ignoring how others feel. As a result, Mrs. Jensen has a chance to help Jason learn perspective taking. Jason's whole life just took a turn for the better. ∽

CONCLUSION

When children have behavior problems caused by unmet needs, effective teachers can help them get those needs met in acceptable and productive ways. Accurately determining when a child has an unmet emotional need and responding to that need can eliminate many unproductive discipline efforts. Additionally, you can make a difference in a child's whole future by intervening in the early years and not allowing the problem to escalate.

As you work at helping children get their needs met, you will come to appreciate the obvious "problem children." They are literally crying out for help; you can't ignore them. But they are also generally the survivors. The too-quiet child may have the more serious problem. Consider this child as you read Chapter 14.

∽ *FOR FURTHER THOUGHT*

1. A problem to solve: James refuses to put the race cars away during cleanup time.
   a. What is one possible cause? Describe the guidance approach that addresses it.
   b. What is another possible cause? Describe the guidance approach that addresses it.

2. A problem to solve: Jenny consistently asks for help from her teacher when asked to put her papers into her cubby. She assists with cleanup time without such requests.
   a. What is one possible cause? Describe the guidance approach that addresses it.
   b. What is another possible cause? Describe the guidance approach that addresses it.

3. Analyze actual behavior problems and guidance approaches in a setting where you know the children. Cases in which you are the adult providing the guidance will probably be the most instructive.
   a. Describe the situation.
   b. Based on your knowledge of the children involved, state the probable cause.
   c. Describe the adult intervention that addresses that cause.
   d. Describe the children's response to intervention.
   e. If the approach was not helpful, was it unsuccessful because it did not address the actual cause or because one intervention was not enough?
   f. If a different cause is suggested, plan a different strategy for next time.

∽ *RECOMMENDED READINGS*

Developmental Studies Center. (1998). *Ways we want our class to be: Class meetings that build commitment to kindness and learning.* Oakland, CA: Author.

Howes, C., & Ritchie, S. (2002). *A matter of trust: Connecting teachers and learners in the early childhood classroom.* New York: Teachers College Press.

Hyson, M. (2004). *The emotional development of young children: Building an emotion-centered curriculum.* New York: Teachers College Press.

Koplow, L. (2002). *Creating schools that heal.* New York: Teachers College Press.

∞ Chapter **13** ∞
Diversity

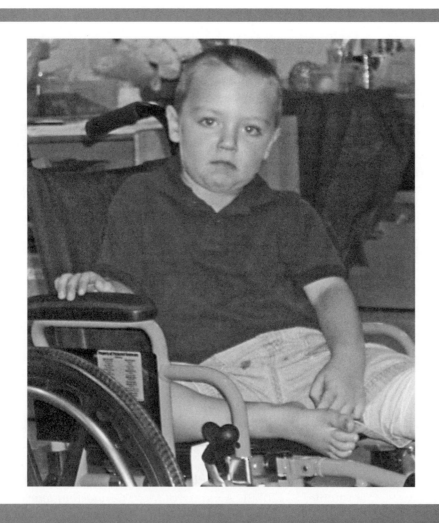

NAEYC Standards Addressed in This Chapter

Standard 1a: Promoting Child Development and Learning: Knowing and understanding young children's characteristics and needs.

Standard 1b: Promoting Child Development and Learning: Knowing and understanding the multiple influences on development and learning.

Standard 2a: Building Family and Community Relationships: Knowing about and understanding family and community characteristics.

Standard 3b: Observing, Documenting, and Assessing to Support Young Children and Families: Knowing about and using observation, documentation, and other appropriate assessment tools and approaches.

Standard 2c: Building Family and Community Relationships: Involving families and communities in their children's development and learning.

Standard 5c: Becoming a Professional: Engaging in continuous, collaborative learning to inform practice.

GUIDING QUESTIONS

- How do children's unique cognitive and social needs affect their behavior?
- What strategies can teachers use to address the needs of children with social and emotional difficulties?
- How do cultural and linguistic diversity influence children's behavior?
- How can teachers support children with diverse backgrounds, languages, and abilities?
- How can the use of family-centered practices support children with diverse backgrounds, languages, and abilities?

Over the course of your career as a teacher you will care for and educate children whose cultures, experiences, and abilities are different from your own or those of people you are familiar with. Meeting the needs of a diverse group of children is one of the most important tasks you will face as an early childhood educator. On any given day, in any given classroom teachers work with children from various cultural backgrounds, children learning English as a second or third language, and or children with special abilities and disabilities. Therefore, it is important for you to consider individual differences when planning to guide children's behavior. To ignore differences in the classroom and expect that every child act in an identical manner is to ignore children—who they are, their uniqueness, beliefs, values, and what they are capable of doing or not doing. Instead you must recognize and respect differences so you can make adjustments in the ways in which you interact with children to meet their unique needs.

In this chapter we discuss how to guide children with diverse academic, social, and linguistic needs. First, we discuss the childhood behaviors that teachers of young children find most difficult to manage. Any child, with or without special needs, may display the behaviors discussed in the first section of this chapter. However, children with attention and communication difficulties, emotional difficulties, or those with learning delays are more likely to resort to these types of behaviors as a means of communicating their frustration or displeasure with classroom expectations. Next, we discuss the cultural considerations of behavior—how teachers' misinterpretations of children's behavior or children's misinterpretation of adult expectations can lead to problems in the classroom. Finally, we look at how to support children learning English as they attempt to interpret classroom routines and expectations while adjusting to an environment where few, if any, other people speak their language.

GUIDING CHILDREN WITH SPECIAL NEEDS

As discussed in Chapter 11, noncompliance, inattention, aggression, and temper tantrums are common behaviors displayed by young children (Wakschlag et al., 2007). Given time and supportive guidance, most young children learn more socially acceptable ways of expressing their wants and needs. There are some children, however, who have identified disabilities or behavioral challenges that make it difficult for them to learn self-regulation. These children require additional support from parents, teachers, and specialists to learn social skills.

As an early childhood educator, you need to be prepared to provide children in your classroom with a continuum of behavioral support (Sugai & Homer, 2008). While most children will learn universal classroom guidelines such as *be kind* or *be respectful* through experience and modeling, some children will need additional support to internalize these guidelines. The Council for Exceptional Children, Division for Early Childhood (CEC/DEC, 2005) and others (Fox, Dunlap, Hemmeter, Hoseph, & Strain, 2003; Stormont, Lewis, & Covington-Smith, 2005) describe three tiers of support that schools can provide to children with social or emotional difficulties to help them become socially competent. They are prevention, intentional instruction, and individualized instruction. We have discussed many preventative strategies in this book. Understanding child development, designing an organized and stimulating classroom, and planning an engaging and meaningful curriculum are strategies known to prevent behavioral difficulties in the classroom. The majority of your students will learn the social skills required to be successful in a school setting through these preventative measures.

About 10% of the children you work with will require intentional instruction (Epstein, 2007) in social skills to help them be successful in the classroom. These children don't respond to preventative guidance strategies or those taught to the whole group. To guide them effectively, you will need to provide more focused instruction, usually delivered in a small-group setting. Teaching specific social skills, such as how to make and keep friends or how to solve peer disputes, involves intentional instruction. You purposefully plan to teach these skills to small groups of children who have limited experience in these areas. Given time and a few reminders, most of these children will internalize the skills and be successful in the classroom.

Sitting on a one-legged stool helps children remain attentive.

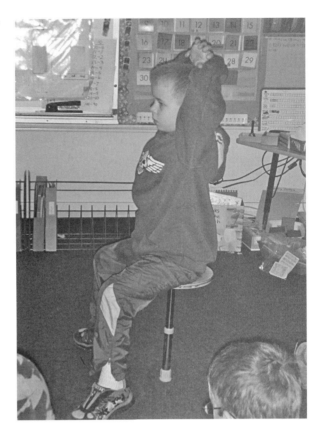

   Another 5% of your students will need intensive individualized instruction before they are able to successfully interact with peers or understand classroom guidelines. They will require one-on-one support to learn how to interact with others in acceptable ways or how to follow classroom guidelines. Generally, a specialist (e.g., special educator, school counselor, etc.) will assist you in planning guidance strategies for these children.

   Children who need intensive instruction in social skills have learned to rely on socially unacceptable ways of meeting their needs. To help these children be successful in the classroom you will need to teach replacement behaviors, another way of meeting their needs that is socially acceptable. For example, if Karla screams to get her needs met, you will have to teach her to ask for help. If Shawn throws a tantrum when he doesn't get his own way, you will have to teach him how to calm himself and how to accept limits. Remember that unlearning one behavior and learning another takes time. Think about a bad habit that you've tried to break—like trying to stop biting your fingernails or quitting smoking. If you've ever tried to stop doing something that wasn't socially acceptable or wasn't good for you, you realize the time, effort, and support needed to do so. When young children attempt to replace one behavior with another, they need unwavering support—you are the person that must provide the consistent encouragement these children need to be successful the classroom.

Labeling Children or Behaviors

While labels for children's disabilities (e.g., autism, attention deficit disorder, etc.) are helpful to medical professionals and families, we believe they are less helpful for teachers who are searching for strategies to address specific behaviors that disrupt children's relationships with others, inhibit their ability to learn new things, or limit their participation in the general life of the classroom. For example, children with a variety of abilities or disabilities might use aggression to get their needs met, and children with any number of disabilities might display "off-task" or inattentive behaviors in the classroom. For this reason, the remainder of this chapter focuses on specific behaviors that teachers have difficulty addressing.

GUIDING CHILDREN WHO ARE "OFF TASK" OR INATTENTIVE

Young children need frequent breaks from demanding academic tasks, even those that are engaging. They signal their need for a mental break by finding something else to do. Teachers usually call children's self-selected breaks "off task" behavior or inattention.

Willis (2008) describes three levels of attention: attention for survival, attention to things of interest, and selective attention. Attention for survival is how we meet our need for security. We take in all of the information from the surrounding environment and determine if we are safe or not—this is also called our fight-or-flight response. Children who feel stressed or confused by activities often work from the attention-for-survival mode. When children work from this mode they cannot filter important information from unimportant information. They have difficulty staying on track and knowing what to focus on. Not much learning takes place when children feel like this.

Attention to things of interest is more focused. In this state of attention children are drawn to a novelty item or surprise. Teachers often use this type of attention to grab students' interest at the beginning of lessons. Most of you have probably seen a teacher begin a lesson by showing children an odd object and asking them what they know about it. We call this type of instructional strategy a "hook." Teachers use hooks to focus children's attention at the beginning of a lesson and to tie the lesson to children's background knowledge. Mrs. Jensen knows that drawing children into a lesson is important to helping them remain on-task.

∞ Mrs. Jensen is holding a flyswatter in her hand. She asks the children, "How might I use this tool?" The children quickly respond, "To kill bugs!" Mrs. Jensen then asks, "Why do we kill bugs?" The children list numerous responses, "They bite!" "They are scary." "They are ugly!" Mrs. Jensen records their answers on the chart paper at the front of the room. She then asks the children "Are there any reasons why we might want to save the bugs, not kill them?" "No!" the children reply. Mrs. Jensen responds, "Well I have a story today that talks about all of the good things that bugs do for us. As we listen to the story, let's see if we can find any reason that we might want to save the bugs." She passes out white boards and markers to the children, noting, "If you hear something good about bugs as I read the story, write it down or draw a picture about it on your white board. When I am finished reading we will share our ideas." ∞

Selective attention allows us to stay focused on a specific task while ignoring other distractions. Mrs. Jensen helps her students build their ability to stay focused on assignments by providing them with engaging activities. She knows that how she plans activities influences whether or not children are able to filter out everything else in the environment so they can remain focused on a specific task. In this case Mrs. Jensen wanted the children to focus on learning about how bugs contribute to the environment. They were able to maintain their concentration because she provided them with a specific task to do while listening to the story.

Prevention

You can prevent inattention by intentionally planning mental breaks or "3-minute vacations" during teacher-directed activities or long work periods (Willis, 2008). You have probably seen adults doodling to remain focused on a phone call or daydreaming during long lectures. These are examples of 3-minute vacations that help us pay attention. You can help children learn these strategies. Many teachers provide children with foam balls to squeeze while they are in circle time or when working on difficult projects. Squeezing the ball for a few moments helps children to refocus their attention on activities without disrupting others. Other types of 3-minute vacations include doing a few short body-stretching activities or singing a quick song between segments of your lessons.

Alternating high and low energy activities throughout the day will help children stay on task.

You might also give the inattentive child a one-legged stool or a small ball to sit on during circle-time activities. Moving to stay balanced on the ball or stool helps the child remain focused (Pfeiffer, Henry, Miller, & Witherall, 2008). Providing children with a private space to collect their thoughts is also effective for children who are unable to attend to activities. Looking at books or completing assignments in a quiet, less stimulating spot is calming to these children. If another adult is available in the classroom, you might have him or her sit near the child during activities that require sustained attention. The adult might hold the child's hand or gently pat the child on the shoulder to help her concentrate.

Balance Activities   As discussed in Chapter 5, having a balanced daily schedule is important for establishing a collaborative classroom climate. Alternating high- and low-energy activities throughout the day will help children stay on task. Plan a mix of large-group, teacher-directed activities, and small-group activities that require teamwork and individual assignments. Keep children in tune with the daily schedule and make sure to provide warnings before an activity ends. Gentle reminders help children with attention difficulties regain focus and maintain some control over the environment.

Movement   Many children with attention difficulties need to move to stay focused. Adults often use this strategy. Have you ever watched adults pace around when they are on the phone or shift back and forth while waiting in line? They are using movement to stay focused on the task they are doing. Think about all of the times that you've felt uncomfortable at a school desk or sitting on the floor when

Use headphones to block out sensory stimuli and promote engagement.

seating was limited. What do you do to get comfortable so you can attend to the task? Chances are you shuffle you feet or adjust the way you are sitting. You might even get up to stretch your legs a bit before getting back to work.

When children are uncomfortable, they have difficulty paying attention. As the teacher, it is your job to help children find a comfortable way to complete assigned tasks. It is okay to let children stand, kneel, or even lay on the floor to complete their assignments. You might need to create a wiggle space in the classroom with a mat or a mini trampoline where children can go to "jump" their wiggles out. Many teachers create invisible boundaries around students' worktables and teach them that they can move about in their own space, but they can't enter other students' spaces during certain times of the day. Again, these types of strategies give students control over their bodies rather than dismissing their need to move.

Intentional Teaching

When working with children who are inattentive, it is important to plan activities that build their attention capacity. Barbara Sher (2006) offers a book of *Attention Games* that help children learn to focus. The games in the book are divided by age group, and are appropriate for use in school. Playing games like *I Spy* or reading books like *Where's Waldo* also help to increase children's attention. Play these games in small groups or while working one-on-one with a child so you can provide individualized support aimed at helping children to focus without becoming frustrated. You might also plan to include an attention game at the beginning of each small-group activity in which the child participates. Many teachers use *Brain Gym* exercises (Cohen & Goldsmith, 2002) to begin their lesson, although any type of movement activity will help improve concentration (Shelton & Wendell, 2005).

Individualized Support

If you still have a few children who have difficulty focusing their attention after you have tried preventative strategies and intentional instruction, you might need to teach specific social skills. Some children with attention difficulties may need help with organization skills (Fei & Timler, 2008). Providing specific steps to activities using visual cues or written directions is extremely helpful for these children. For example, if Aubree is to wash her hands, get a cup and napkin, and take a seat at the snack table, you can take photos of this sequence and make a "reminder card" for her to follow. You can do the same thing for activities in the classroom. In this case you might have a sequence of photos of a child reading a book, getting markers and paper out of his desk, and, finally, writing on the paper. Visual cue cards eliminate the need for constant verbal reminders about how to behave.

You might also provide children with *First Then Boards* (Fox, Lentini, & Dunlap, 2006) to teach the sequence of routines in your daily schedule. *First Then Boards* help children learn to monitor and control their impulses for short segments of time. For example, you might have a picture of children sitting on the rug, you reading a story problem, children writing on white boards, and, finally, children working with manipulatives in the math area. If children get distracted during any step in the sequence, you can point to the board, reminding them of the activity you're doing and of what to expect next.

GUIDING CHILDREN WHO ARE NONCOMPLIANT

We've all experienced a child who is noncompliant from time to time. Not following directions or ignoring requests to clean up are examples of noncompliance that are typical for young children. Complying with requests is all about learning to cooperate with another person. Children begin to learn to balance their needs with the needs of others at a very young age. Parents teach children these helpful behaviors when they ask children to help turn out the lights, make the bed, put clothes into the washer, set the table, or contribute to other family chores. These embedded learning opportunities help children understand that contributing to family and school activities is a pleasant experience. However, some children refuse multiple requests to complete tasks and may become angry or argumentative when required to participate in typical school activities. These children need additional guidance.

Prevention

There are many ways to prevent noncompliance in the classroom. The easiest is to let children assist with creating classroom guidelines. Many teachers are worried about sharing this type of control with children, but it is usually the case that children create more stringent guidelines than adults do. When children help create classroom guidelines they are more likely to understand and follow them. It is also important to teach the guidelines. If children create the guideline *be nice to friends,* it is important for you to teach them what this looks like in the classroom. You might read stories about friends helping one another, act out skits about friends solving problems, or sing friendship songs to make this concept come to life.

It is also important that you provide clear directions about your expectations (Smith & Bondy, 2007). Use short, clear sentences when asking children to complete a required task. Remember that children pay more attention to the last part of a sentence than the beginning. Rather than saying, "It's time to clean up because we have to go to lunch," reverse the sentence and say, "We have to go to lunch; let's clean up our mess." It is also important to use children's names when giving directions. It is often the case that children don't even realize you're speaking to them when you make generalized statements such as *it's time to listen.* It is better to say, *"Jamal, please listen to me."* Some children might need a gentle tap on the shoulder to help them focus on what you're asking them to do. This means getting up and walking over to the child to get his or her attention before stating an expectation.

Sensitivity to Sensory Stimuli   Some children are defiant because they experience stress from sensory overload. These children might feel uncomfortable when exposed to certain sounds, textures, or smells. If you're having difficulty with children who don't comply during large-group activities it may be the noise, lack of space, or even the feel of the carpet that is making them uncomfortable. In these cases it is best to use a process of elimination to determine the cause of the behavior. First, you might try providing the child with another fabric to sit on

Confusion about activities or procedures in daily routines may result in non-compliance.

during circle time. Small squares of cotton fabric are a good, inexpensive alternative to carpet. If this doesn't work, look for other distracters such as sound from an air conditioner or fan. To determine if a particular noise is irritating the child, try holding your meeting in another area of the room.

Many teachers view children who don't follow directions during large-group activities as defiant, but the truth is some children may not even realize that you're speaking to them unless you're in their direct field of vision. It is best if you're eye-to-eye with children when giving directions or asking for their attention. If you sit in a chair during large-group meeting times and children are on the floor, try moving to the floor. If this doesn't work, you may need to move the child so you are in his or her field of vision. Many teachers ask children who are not complying to sit next to them. This is not always the best seating arrangement because the child will have to turn sideways to look at you. Asking the child to sit in the center of the circle facing directly toward you is a better alternative for maintaining eye-to-eye contact. Touching the corner of your eye when asking children to look your direction is a simple prompt that will help children to focus their attention on you.

Managing Workload

When children feel overwhelmed by what you ask them to do, they are more likely to be noncompliant. If you have children who cannot complete a task, break it into parts and ask them to complete one part of the assignment at a time. Rather than asking children to write two paragraphs about their pets, ask for one or two sentences at a time. If children refuse to clean up the block area, ask them to gather all triangle-shaped blocks and hand them to you. Dividing assignments into parts makes them more manageable. Remember that young children tend to focus on one aspect of a task at a time. Tasks with multiple steps can overwhelm them.

Another way to distribute student workload is to design collaborative learning tasks. In these types of activities, children work in small groups to complete

To see an example of how teachers use collaborative learning to help children manage workload, go to MyEducationLab and select the topic "Technology" and watch the video "Social Learning (with Computers)."

investigations. When you provide children with opportunities to work together, they naturally support each other's learning.

Intentional Teaching

Young children are more adept at following simple directions. You can increase children's ability to follow multiple-step directions through intentional teaching. Playing games that require children to follow directions is a fun way to accomplish this goal. Modify simple games like *Simon Says* to teach children to follow multiple-step directions. To do this, give directions such as "*Simon says* touch your head and turn around." As children master one- or two-step directions in the game, gradually increase the number. You can also increase children's ability to follow multiple-step directions during snack time. At the beginning of the year you might ask children to get a napkin from the basket. When they are able to follow this direction, ask them to get a napkin and a cup. Continue to add requests until they are able to collect all of the items needed for snack time.

To see an example of how to teach multi-step directions using music, go to MyEducationLab and select the topic "Transition Strategies" and watch the video "Transitioning: Stand-Up."

Music is another medium you can use to teach children to follow directions. Songs that ask children to do specific tasks, such as Ella Jenkins's, "Play Your Instruments and Make a Pretty Sound," are good for teaching children to follow specific task-related requests. The song directs listeners to select an instrument, wait their turn to play their instrument, and, finally, put their instruments away. Most children enjoy playing with musical instruments and are eager to follow the directions to games that allow them to do so. Use activities like this to keep the learning of social skills meaningful and engaging.

Asking for Help Some children do not know how to ask for help when they need it. Confusion about activities or procedures in the daily routine may result in noncompliance. Make sure that you establish a routine for children to use when asking for help or showing whether they understand your directions or not. A simple thumbs-up/thumbs-down signal is easy to remember. After you give a direction, ask children to indicate their understanding by showing the signal. If one child signals he doesn't understand your request, meet him individually to explain the request again. If several children signal that they misunderstood your directions, you probably need to revisit the instructions with the entire group.

Individualized Support

A few children in your class may need individualized instruction before they will cooperate with requests. For example, you may have a child who runs away from

Use a variety of learning strategies to make learning comprehensible for English language learners.

you when it is time to go inside after recess. Remember that it does little good to chase a child who runs away to avoid a request. Many children run from adults because they are truly engaged in an activity and are fearful that they won't get to do it again. These children need extra reassurance to learn that their favorite activities will be a regular part of the daily routine. To address this type of non-compliance, you may need to work with the child one-on-one.

∞ Mrs. Jensen knows that Mason has difficulty leaving the playground after recess. He runs away from the adults on the playground as soon as the bell rings. To prevent the daily struggle from occurring, Mrs. Jensen positions herself near Mason just before the bell rings. As soon as she hears the signal to go inside she immediately begins working with Mason to clean up his toys. As they work, Mrs. Jensen discusses the afternoon activities and helps Mason plan what he'll work on during project work. ∞

Mrs. Jensen realizes the importance of helping Mason prepare for the next step in the daily routine. She understands that Mason has difficulty complying with requests to change activities and works hard to teach him how to transition from one activity to another by providing individualized attention. Mrs. Jensen has also discovered that providing children with opportunities to assist with tasks that they find interesting increases their desire to comply with requests. Letting children vacuum the classroom or mop the floor when spills occurs is a good way to teach children to help when requested to do so. Providing children with soapy sponges to wash the tables after an art activity is another activity that will encourage cooperation. Asking children who won't stop working on assignments to collect classmates' papers is a good way to help them prepare for the next activity.

While it may seem like individualized strategies such as these serve to reward the noncompliant child, this is not the case. These types of strategies teach children responsibility for contributing to the group. They also teach them that cooperating with others to complete common tasks can be a pleasant experience. It may be the case that these children have not learned this lesson before entering school.

GUIDING CHILDREN WHO USE AGGRESSION TO MEET THEIR NEEDS

It is not surprising that teachers in early childhood classrooms find persistent aggressive behaviors (hitting, biting, throwing, etc.) most problematic for students' development and most disruptive to the classroom community (Nungesser & Watkins, 2005). Some teachers expect children to manage conflict on their own by the time they reach kindergarten (Lane, Faulk & Wehby, 2006). When children aren't able to do this, teachers express concern for the child as well as frustration with their own abilities to address the undesirable behavior.

Occasional use of mild aggression (e.g., a poke, or shouting in response to a perceived wrongdoing) is common in peer disputes, but persistent, intense aggression toward peers is not typical childlike behavior. Frequent hitting, biting, or kicking is cause for concern. Aggressive behavior affects children's friendships, and when children don't have friends they don't do well in school (Hanish, Laura-Martin, Fabes, & Bercelo, 2008). Children who use aggression to meet their needs may do so because they have difficulty with emotion regulation or impulse control. You'll see that these children often act first and think about the consequences of their behavior after they act. Many misinterpret social cues. Children who resort to aggression need help with perspective taking and empathy. They can't imagine how their actions affect others.

Prevention

Daily Check-In   One way to prevent emotional outbursts is to provide children with an opportunity to tell you how they feel each day with a daily check-in. Daily check-in boards for nonreaders should contain pictures of faces showing various emotions (e.g., happy, sad, tired, angry, surprised, etc.). As children enter the classroom, ask them to point to the face that shows how they are feeling. If they are capable of doing so, you might ask them to write a word or phrase indicating their emotional state on your daily attendance sheet. Once you have this information, you can tailor your interactions to meet the needs of individual children. If Lexie says she is sad that day, you can spend a few minutes of private time with her to determine what is causing the upset. If Ryan indicates that he is tired, you'll know that the pace at which he will work won't be as fast as normal. Children who

To see an example of a daily check-in board, go to MyEducationLab and select the topic "Observation and Assessment" and view the artifact "Assessing Emotions Worksheet."

are tired may also be oversensitive, which may mean that you'll need to provide them with extra support during peer interactions.

Feeling word charts offer children another opportunity to discuss their feelings. Provide children with a clothespin with their name printed on it. Ask them to attach their name to the list of feeling words you've posted on a bulletin board. You can do this several times a day, in the morning, after recess or special activities, and at the end of the day. Helping children to monitor their emotions throughout the day is a good way to prevent outbursts. When children learn to acknowledge their feelings they are better able to control the urge to lash out at others.

Being Aware and Acting Calmly   The most important thing for you to know about aggression is how it starts and how it progresses. If you observe carefully, you will see that children usually show specific signs before they resort to using acts of aggression. Sometimes these signs are subtle, such as heavy breathing, pacing, or tapping their feet. Other times the signs are more overt, such as yelling out. Knowing how a child acts before resorting to aggression is important to your prevention efforts. When you witness children trying to control their anger, support them by calmly asking if they need assistance. Dennis knows that it is important to intervene in Jacob's disagreements before the dispute becomes physical.

   ∞ Jacob and Stephen were playing in the sandbox together. Both reached for the blue shovel at the same time. Soon the boys were tugging and screaming. Dennis quickly moved toward the boys and offered them a dump truck. He showed the boys how to fill the dump truck with the shovel and then dump the sand on the hill they were making. He worked with the boys to make a plan about who would hold the shovel and who would drive the dump truck. The boys decided that Jacob would be the dump truck driver and Stephen would shovel the sand. With assistance from Dennis, the boys were able to work cooperatively to build a tall sand hill. ∞

Rather than correcting Jason for screaming and fighting, Dennis helped him find an alternative play plan. Children who've come to rely on aggression to get their needs met have difficulty generating solutions to typical childhood disputes. They need adult assistance to generate possible solutions to their problems.

Prevention is the primary goal for working with children who are aggressive, because once they are enraged there is little you can do to calm them. If a child in your classroom is acting extremely aggressive or throwing a temper tantrum, you must act calmly and limit your interactions with the child. If you do interact with the child, use a matter-of-fact tone of voice and acknowledge the child's feelings. If you raise your voice to the child, you're likely to find that the anger will escalate. Demanding that the child stop misbehaving will most likely get the same results. At this point, it is most important for you to make sure that other children in the classroom are safe. You should never attempt to restrain the child. Instead, you should call for help from another teacher or your administrator.

When the child calms down, talk about the incident. If the child hurt someone or damaged property during the episode, provide an opportunity for restitution, as discussed in Chapter 8. It usually isn't productive to ask why the aggression occurred; instead ask the child what he wanted or was trying to tell you when he was angry. Remember that aggression is a form of communication. It is an expression of a want, need, or feeling. As the teacher, it is your responsibility to uncover the reason behind the aggression. To do this, think about what happened before the outburst. What was happening at the time the behavior occurred, who was with the child, and what was the child trying to accomplish? Was the child trying to avoid an unpleasant task? Was the aggression provoked or unprovoked? If provoked, who was the target of the aggression? Did the child misinterpret the actions of the other child? Having an organized observation plan will help you to answer these questions so you can plan an intervention.

Intentional Teaching

Develop Specific Goals   When planning social skills instruction for children who use aggression to communicate their needs, it is essential that you focus your intervention on teaching replacement behaviors. If these children do not learn other ways in which to meet their needs, the aggressive acts will continue and most likely worsen. It is important to teach one or two behaviors that you know will reduce the tendency to resort to aggression. For example, if you determine that Sascha gets aggressive when frustrated, plan activities that teach her how to ask for help. If Eliana uses aggression to respond to accidental bumps or other unintended physical contact, plan lessons to teach her how to interpret the intentions of other. The goal here is to teach children how to communicate wants, needs, or confusion about social interactions in socially acceptable ways.

Role Play   Drama is a good medium for helping children learn to control their aggressive tendencies. Providing children with situation-specific stories to act out will help them to identify their own feelings and learn about the perspective of others. For example, if a child in your class tends to become aggressive during property disputes, you might develop a script that focuses on how to negotiate turn taking. It is best if you work with small, heterogeneous groups of children when role-playing so that children can serve as models for one another. Act as the narrator of the stories when working with nonreaders. Older children can read scripts on their own.

Remember that children who use aggression often misinterpret social cues. After acting out the scenarios, it is important to talk about the intentions and feelings of all characters and how the plot connects to life in the classroom. This will help children build perspective taking and empathy. It will also help children to generalize the lessons in the skits to real-life situations.

Social Skill Curricula   Conflict resolution programs do reduce instances of aggressive behaviors in children with special needs (Jones & Bodtker, 2001). The *I Can Problem Solve* curriculum by Shure (1992a, 1992b) is appropriate for use with preschool and primary-age children. Conflict resolution programs such as this contain a series of 20 to 40 lessons designed to help children identify their own emotions and those of others, as well as provide lessons aimed at practicing problem-solving skills. If you can't purchase a prepackaged social skill curriculum, you can design your own by embedding social skills instruction into your literacy or social studies curriculum. To do this, select literature and tailor discussions around specific social skills that children need to learn. If teaching social skills during your literacy time, focus on character traits that help children resolve conflicts. When integrating social skills instruction into your social studies curriculum, emphasize the aspects of good citizenship or how the characters in the story work together to help one another solve conflicts. Remember that learning conflict resolution skills takes time, especially for children with learning disabilities. If you're designing your own curriculum, you'll need to plan a series of lessons that build on one another and provide plenty of opportunities to practice newly acquired skills.

Individualized Support

Spending Quality Time Together   Many teachers distance themselves from children who are aggressive (Milner, 2006). While this is understandable, it is the worst thing you can do. These children need more attention, not less. The first thing you can do to teach these children alternatives to aggression is to spend individual time with them each day. You want to do this when the child isn't misbehaving. The goal is to build a relationship with the child so she is motivated to let you help her control her feelings. Spending time with the child during free-choice activities, on the playground, or in the lunchroom will go a long way toward reducing aggressive behaviors.

Social Stories   You can also use social stories to teach children how to control their aggression. Social stories are short, specific stories, written from the perspective of the student, that address specific social skills (More, 2008). Teachers or other adults write the stories using age-appropriate vocabulary and specific sentence structures to address the individual student's needs. The stories state the specific steps to take during social situations. They include descriptive as well as explanatory language. Adding illustrations to the stories will help maintain children's interest in the text. A social story about how to relax when angry might contain the following text.

> ∽ Sometimes I get angry.
> It is okay to get angry, but I cannot hurt others.
> When people get angry, they try to calm down.
> I can calm down by taking a deep breath or going to my cozy spot.
> If I need help calming down, I can ask my teacher.
> She will help me.
> When I calm down, I can play with my friends again.
> They will wait for me. ∽

Relaxation Techniques   Yoga and other gentle exercises help reduce the tension that often leads to aggression. Counting to 10 and taking a deep breath before acting are two easy tension relievers that you can teach young children.

Physical activity also reduces tension. When you notice that a child is agitated or frustrated, send the child on an errand or ask him or her to help complete a task that will release some energy. Doing exercises that tense and release muscles also lessens feelings of stress. Start by having children tighten and relax the muscles in the upper part of the body and then gradually move downward until they have relaxed all of their muscles. Both you and the children will feel more relaxed at the end of the activity.

Painting, sculpting, or drawing also helps children relax, especially when there are no limits put on their creations. Children naturally express their emotions through art. Children also express their emotions through music. Dance is particularly effective because movement releases pent up energy. Remember that learning to relax takes time. In fact, many adults still haven't mastered this skill!

Touch A 5- to 10-minute massage each day at naptime reduces aggressive behavior and inattention in preschool-age children (von Korring, Soderberg, Austin, & Uvnas-Moberg, 2008). Physical contact with aggressive children reduces stress and helps them to know that you are supportive of them. Touching and other playful activities after conflicts decrease aggression and increases co-operation and tolerance (von Korring, Soderberg, Austin, & Uvnas-Moberg, 2008). So, if you're working with older children who do not nap, a gentle pat on the back, a smile, or a bit of relaxing play after a conflict will go a long way toward helping reduce aggression in the classroom.

PROMOTING ACCEPTANCE AND FRIENDSHIP

Children with behavior difficulties are less likely to have friends. In Chapter 3 we discussed how important friendship is to children's social and emotional development. The first step in helping children to make friends is to plan activities aimed at learning the names of classmates. You can do this by singing songs that use children's names or creating games or activities that use children's nametags. For example, you may pull nametags from a basket while taking attendance. As you pull each name from the basket, ask the children whose name is on the nametag and if that child came to school today. If the child is absent that day, discuss the reason for the absence and, if known, when the child will return. Activities like this promote empathy as well as community building.

You can also plan to incorporate opportunities for building friendships into your daily routines. Call children in pairs when asking them to line up, and have them move to the next activity with their friend. When providing materials for activities you can encourage friendship by passing out one piece of equipment for every two children (e.g., one glue stick for two children). Another way to encourage friendships is through activities such as buddy reading or painting—one child reads or paints and the other listens or watches, and then the children reverse roles. Sharing with a partner during *think-share-pair activities* also encourages friendships. In these situations you ask children to turn to their partner and share their thoughts about an activity or discussion. In all of these cases it is important to make sure that children are paired with different friends each day so that each child has an opportunity to engage with every other child in the class at some point in time.

WORKING FROM A STRENGTHS-BASED PERSPECTIVE

It is important for you to discover the types of activities in which children do behave. In Chapter 11 we discussed how to observe children's interactions to determine the cause of behavior. Enlisting input from parents is also important. Ask parents to describe situations when the child is most attentive or most compliant. This is different from telling a parent the child is inattentive or aggressive at school and asking them to provide you with solutions to the problem. If you want to plan your interventions around the child's strengths, you need to discover these strengths and build upon them. If a parent tells you that the child is most attentive while on the computer, make sure to incorporate technology into your activities. If you discover that a child is most compliant in one-on-one situations, be sure to repeat requests you've made to the whole class directly to the child. If you discover that a child is never aggressive to peers when an adult is nearby, you may need to work with the child during small-group activities. The goal is not to "shadow" the child as a means of protecting others; it is to teach the child interaction skills. Watching for aggressive acts and cutting them off does the child little good if you don't teach appropriate ways of interacting or solving conflicts. Remember, the goal is to help children become self-governing, not for you to control their behavior externally.

WORKING WITH FAMILIES AND OTHER PROFESSIONALS

Family-Centered Practice

Working with families is essential to promoting good behavior. When teachers and parents provide children with a consistent set of expectations, children are more successful. To do this, parents and teachers must talk openly and honestly about what is required of children in both the home and school setting. While there are many ways to work collaboratively with parents to support children's behavior, we suggest a few strategies that you may find helpful. First, it is important for parents to know the strategies you're implementing to prevent behavioral issues from occurring. You can share this information with parents in a number of ways. After you and the children create your classroom guidelines, send them home to parents. When you have an open house, invite the children and have them tell their parents about the guidelines they have created. Children can also show parents how they care for the classroom by passing out snacks or materials for an activity and then telling parents what to do when they've finished. Don't forget to review your school's social-emotional standards with parents. Reviewing these guidelines together will open the door for discussion of behavioral expectations at school and home.

If you find that you have a few children who need intentional instruction in social skills, share the lessons you're teaching these students with their parents.

In cases where parents are available to come into the classroom and help, you might ask them to implement the lessons so they become familiar with the language and strategies you are teaching children. If it is not possible for parents to visit the classroom, provide them with materials for the activities so that they can teach the same lessons at home.

In cases when you need to provide individualized instruction to a particular child, involve the parent from the start. Parents can contribute to your attempts to determine the causes of behavior problems by providing information about how children interact with others in out-of-school settings. While many teachers are only concerned about the behaviors that occur in the classroom, it is unwise to think that you can solve persistent behavioral issues by addressing only one aspect of a child's life. Children with persistent behavior problems usually act out in similar ways in all settings. If you intend to teach a child with persistent behavioral issues new strategies that can be generalized to different settings, you will need to discover the cause of these challenges in as many settings as possible.

With a bit of training, most parents will be able to implement the observation strategies discussed in Chapter 11. Having parents look closely at children's behavior in out-of-school settings will help them to assist you in devising strategies that will best meet the needs of the child. If parents are uncomfortable doing this, you might offer to observe the child at home or in another out-of-school setting. It is also important for you to invite the parent to the classroom to observe the child. He or she may see something that occurs before, during, or after the behavior that you have missed in your observations. Working together, parents and teachers can devise developmentally appropriate, consistent ways to help children learn the social skills needed to be successful in school and beyond.

Teaming and Consultation

Managing the intensive support needed by children with persistent behavioral issues while meeting the needs of a classroom full of children is challenging (Heineman, Dunlap, & Kincade, 2005). However, team approaches to addressing children's persistent behavioral issues have proved helpful. The main thing to remember is that how you respond to misbehavior is the key to the social and academic success of all children in your classroom. Sometimes the most appropriate response you can provide to a child who has persistent behavioral issues is to seek outside assistance.

Behavioral specialists such as a school counselor or mental health specialist can support you as you work with children who have behavioral difficulties. Many teachers are reluctant to seek outside assistance when dealing with misbehavior because they fear the others will view them as incapable of managing their classroom. This is not the case. We all need support from time to time, and children benefit from the expertise of all adults in the school setting. Remember that you are not the only "expert" who can help the child. It is a sign of professionalism when you acknowledge that you need an objective set of eyes to help you see what is causing children's misbehavior. Additionally, teachers who seek the assistance of mental health consultants or school counselors have fewer behavior problems in their classrooms (Gilliam & Shabar, 2006), so take advantage of their expertise when you are faced with behavioral issues that you can't manage on your own.

CULTURAL CONSIDERATIONS AND BEHAVIOR

Did you know that children from minority backgrounds are more likely to be referred to the principal or director's office or expelled from school for misbehavior than European American children are (Cartledge, Singh, & Gibson, 2008; Gay, 2006; Gilliam, 2005)? This doesn't occur because children from African American, Latino, Native American, or other non-European American backgrounds misbehave more frequently; it occurs because there is a mismatch between teachers' behavioral expectations, their guidance techniques, and children's cultural backgrounds (Gay, 2006; Weinstein, Tomlinson-Clarke, & Curran, 2004). For example, rough-and-tumble play and verbal sparring are part of African American male culture (Weinstein et al., 2004) but many teachers view this play as unsafe or disrespectful. This mismatch between what children learn at home and what is expected in school often causes conflict between teachers and students (Gay, 2006; Gonzales-Mena, 2008; Rothstein-Fisch & Trumbell, 2008; Weinstein et al., 2004).

So how do you prevent these mismatches from occurring? An important first step to understanding how culture might influence your students' behaviors is to learn about the communication practices of their cultural groups (Gonzales-Mena, 2008). If you're discussing an incident of misbehavior with a child and he smiles at you, what does this mean? Is the child disrespecting you? Does he think that your concern is funny? It may be that he is showing you a sign of respect and offering an apology. If you bend down and get close to a child to help with an assignment and the child pulls back from you, does it mean that she doesn't want your help? Or have you invaded her personal space? What about if you're reading a story or explaining a math activity and a child jumps into the conversation without being invited to speak—does this mean she is impulsive or hasn't been taught to listen, or does it mean that she has been listening intently and has made a connection that she would like to share? What about the child who doesn't ever follow the time constraints inherent in the classroom schedule—the one who always seems to live in the moment and can't tear himself away from one activity to begin another? Is this child being defiant, or has his cultural upbringing made him more "now-oriented" than "future-oriented" (Gonzales-Mena, 2008)?

Culture influences whether you smile or not to express your happiness or remorse, the type of eye contact you make with others, and the ways in which you greet others. Culture also influences decisions about how to speak or respond to adults or others with more power, and it affects your perception about the importance of time. While you can learn about some of these cultural practices from books, it is best to learn them firsthand through observation (Gonzales-Mena, 2008).

It is important for you to watch how the children in your classroom respond to and interact with adults and peers from their own cultural groups. Listen to how adults pose requests to children and how children pose requests to adults. If you tend to phrase requests in the form of a question (e.g., Should we clean-up now so we can eat lunch?), you may confuse students whose parents give direct instructions for activities where there isn't a choice. Pay attention to how parents expect children to behave with one another. Do parents encourage or discourage competition between children? Are older children responsible for monitoring and guiding younger siblings? When children learn to be responsible for one another at home, they may not understand teacher requests to work individually without helping one another.

You should also note how children play and interact with adults. You may witness adult–child interactions where the child is the center of attention. In these situations the adult will stop whatever he or she is doing to tend to the needs of the child. In other instances, you may witness adults who expect children to play or wait quietly until adults are finished with their tasks before they respond to children's requests. Children who learn to wait until adults are finished with their activities before interrupting may be reluctant to ask teachers for help or assistance in the middle of an activity if they see that the teacher is busy. You may need to tell these children that it is okay to ask clarifying questions or to ask for assistance during activities at school. Children need support to learn the interaction patterns of the school, especially if there are substantial differences between adult expectations in the home and school (Espinosa, 2005).

You can also learn about children's communication patterns and family expectations by talking to parents. Parents are in the best position to tell you how their children (a) react to stress, (b) how they show respect, and (c) how they respond to learning a new task. Understanding differences in interaction patterns will go a long way toward helping you understand the causes of children's behavior. Most important, this understanding will help you to avoid misinterpreting children's actions in the classroom.

Listening to Families

Understanding family priorities is essential to understanding children's behavior (Gonzalez-Mena, 2008). Children learn interaction patterns and standards of behavior in the context of families. In some families, collectivism is the norm. Children are taught to help one another for the good of the group, even if this means taking on extra tasks. They are also taught to depend on one another when they need assistance. In other families, individualism is the norm. Children are encouraged to be unique and do their own things. There is less emphasis on responsibility to group members and more on individual responsibility. These children are taught that they are responsible for their own success. While there are certainly exceptions to these broad generalizations, it is important for teachers to understand what families value and what goals they have for their children.

Parents and teachers may have different priorities for children's learning. While schools tend to place great importance on children's cognitive development, many families are more concerned about their children's social development. When families ask more questions about how children are getting along with teachers and peers than how they are doing in reading or math, it does not mean that parents don't value the academic components of the school day. These types of questions most likely mean that families want their children to be respectful of and helpful to their teachers and peers and liked by them. These qualities are important to families with a collectivist outlook.

Other families seem more concerned with children's grades than their social and emotional development. These families equate high levels of academic achievement with success. When these families gloss over social development or behavioral issues, it's not necessarily because they think their children are perfect and don't make mistakes. It is because they see school as a place for learning and want their children to stay on track with academics so they are prepared for future academic pursuits and, eventually, the workplace. Preparing children to take care of themselves is a priority for these families.

It is important for teachers to learn about parents' goals for their children and to address these goals in the classroom. This is not to say that cultural awareness is a one-way street; it isn't (Espinosa, 2005). It is also important for teachers to share the goals and expectations of the school with parents. However, teachers need to be open to families' views about appropriate expectations for education and behavior.

∞ Mrs. Jensen plans her first parent–teacher conference early in the year. She prepares several questions that help her to understand her children's backgrounds. She opens the conference by asking, "What are your goals for Brianna this year?" She follows that question by asking the parents, "In what ways can I or the school help you to meet your goals?" By starting conferences with these types of questions, Mrs. Jensen sends a message to parents that she values their priorities and will work to meet them. After Mrs. Jensen and the parents finish discussing the parents' goals, Mrs. Jensen provides parents with a copy of her school's learning standards and offers them an opportunity to ask questions about the standards. She is careful to point out the social-emotional standards, which are located in the health and social studies standards in her state's standards. She makes sure to ask parents if they work on similar goals with their children at home and what strategies they use to guide their children's behavior. She then shares her discipline philosophy with parents and explains how she will help children to work on the social-emotional standards. Before ending the conference, Mrs. Jensen reminds the parents to contact her if they have any suggestions about how she can better meet Brianna's social or academic needs. ∞

Mrs. Jensen is comfortable sharing control with her students' families. She is well aware that establishing a respectful home–school partnership early in the year will help her students grow socially and academically. Over the years she has also discovered that sharing power with parents makes them comfortable enough to ask her questions about the school program and to offer assistance in the classroom.

CULTURALLY RESPONSIVE GUIDANCE

Imagine entering a classroom where nobody speaks your language. How would you participate? What clues would you look for that would tell you what was expected of you? Would you follow the lead of other students? Would you intently watch the teacher, hoping to decipher her actions? Would you look for clues in the environment that might tell you what to do? Would you listen for words that sound familiar to you? Young English language learners use all of these strategies to make sense of environments that are linguistically and culturally different from their own. You can use several evidence-based instructional strategies to help these children understand classroom routines, interaction patterns, and expectations for activities.

Total Physical Response (TPR)

We all learn through nonverbal communication. Infants learn language from listening and watching parents while they label items and talk about how they are used. When adults are teaching their children to talk, they use what is called parentese—drawn-out speech that places emphasis on nouns and action words. You've probably seen parents do this. They may pick up a teddy bear and say to the child, "Do you want your t-e-d-d-y b-e-a-r?" They are helping children to make connections between the object and the word. Children come to understand the names of many objects and actions long before they can speak. It is important to note that this is not "baby talk." When using parentese you introduce adult vocabulary but use voice intonation to place emphasis on the names of objects and actions. In doing this you call children's attention to the word connected to the object or action.

James Asher (1969) believed that children learn second languages in much the same fashion. Based on this belief, he developed the total physical response (TPR) approach, a method for teaching second language learners. When teachers use TPR they teach children important vocabulary by providing child-friendly definitions and pointing to objects as they are discussed. They also provide children with context clues by using gestures or actions when possible. For example, if you are reading a book and the character is crying, you might make a crying sound and rub your eyes to provide children with a cue about the character's emotional state.

To be effective with English language learners, you should provide children with access to realia or real objects as often as possible. When this is not possible, use visuals and literature to help children make sense of discussions. Children can also act out stories as you read them. This strategy helps children to connect text to self, which builds comprehension.

Making Learning Comprehensible

English language learners (ELLs) may appear off task or inattentive when they don't comprehend the language you're using to explain an activity. To reduce these types of language barriers, slow down your speech and use visuals when giving directions to ELLs. The use of visuals depicting important content vocabulary and drawings of instructions for activities will assist ELLs with comprehension— even stick figures will do the trick. ELLs may also have difficulty processing and answering questions. Make sure you ask a range of questions and provide plenty of wait time before expecting an answer. For children just beginning to learn English, being able to answer lower-level questions (e.g., those requiring a short response) is an opportunity for success. As their English improves, ask higher-level questions that require analysis and synthesis of information and more elaborate responses.

Remember that ELLs need practice speaking, and they are often excited to try out the new vocabulary they are learning. Don't confuse the desire to practice speaking with talking out of turn. To encourage language development, you'll want to make sure that you offer plenty of opportunities for small-group work that encourages interaction between ELLs and children who speak English as their first language.

Song, Chants, and Signs You can also use songs and chants to engage English learners in learning key vocabulary. The rhythmic beat of songs and the actions accompanying chants help children to remember new words. Fingerplays incorporate actions and chants. Connecting actions to words helps ELLs learn new vocabulary and generate meaning. This is particularly important for abstract concepts in science, social studies, and mathematics. Teaching children sign language will help those learning a second language to become more comfortable in the classroom learning (Konishi, 2007). Signs for hello, goodbye, juice or milk, bathroom, and other common words are easily learned by children and provide a common language that everyone in the classroom can speak.

Expectations

Caring is the foundation of culturally responsive teaching and guidance (Weinstein et al., 2004). While warmth and nurturing are the foundation for learning, you must also know your students well enough to set appropriate expectations and opportunities for student success (Gay, 2006). This means creating learning environments and using instructional practices that are responsive to children's ethnic, racial, cultural, social, and linguistic diversity. To be successful at guiding the behavior of English language learners, it is important for you to develop "the ability to think, feel, and act in ways that acknowledge, respect, and build upon ethnic, sociocultural, and linguistic diversity" (Hyson, 2004, p. 50).

CONCLUSION

Wang and Aldridge (2007) suggest that you ask yourself three types of questions before jumping to conclusions about children's behavior or actions. They encourage you to think about how your perception of "normal" child development and children's ways of learning or understanding differ from your own. For example, it is important for you to ask, "How are my expectations for what children of this age group should or shouldn't be able to do influencing my reaction to this behavior?" "How do the ways in which I expect children to use materials affect my perception of how they are actually using them?" "How are my expectations for

PEARSON
myeducationlab

To help you think further about how your attitude and expectations about children's backgrounds and abilities might influence teacher–child interactions, go to MyEducationLab and select the topic "Diverse Learners" and watch the video "Incorporating the Home Experiences of Culturally Diverse Students into the Classroom" parts 1–4.

introducing and completing assignments different from the ways in which children might make sense of the concepts I introduce?"

These are important questions. For example, if you expect all 6-year-olds to able to work quietly and one of your students constantly interrupts his neighbor to share successes or ask for assistance, how will you react? If you expect that children will use a drop of glue to attach a bead to a paper and they cover the entire paper with glue, how might your expectations for material usage influence your reaction to this event? How about if you spend an entire weekend preparing an activity for children, only to receive blank stares and confusion when children try to master the concept without direct guidance from you?

Your perception of children's behavior is important to establishing a positive climate in your classroom. Attempting to understand how children's background experiences affect their interactions in the classroom will prepare you to plan appropriate guidance strategies. When you respect children as individuals with unique needs, you'll be better prepared to plan appropriate guidance strategies for them.

∽ *FOR FURTHER THOUGHT*

1. Interview a parent of a second language learner. Ask the parent about the successes and difficulties the child has had at school. Have there been times when teachers misinterpreted the child's behavior? If so, describe the situation and how it might have been handled differently. Ask the parent about his or her goals for the child. How are the parent's goals different from or similar to the goals that the school might have for the child? If you were this child's teacher, how might you work to embed the parent's goals into your teaching?

2. Observe in a classroom where children with special needs are included. How does the teacher make accommodations to meet the needs of the child? In your

opinion, are the strategies the teacher uses effective in helping the child to be a cooperative, contributing member of the classroom community? If so, what, in your opinion, makes these strategies effective? If not, what other strategies might the teacher implement to help the child be more successful in the classroom?

3. Use one of the strategies mentioned in this chapter to plan a small-group lesson to teach a small group of children a social skill. Implement the lesson plan and reflect on what children learned from the lesson.

4. Create a daily check-in board or emotion word-wall for use in your future classroom.

⬿ *FOR FURTHER READING*

Barnett, D. W., Elliott, N., Wolsing, L., Bunger, C. E., Haske, H., McKissick, C., & Vander Meer, C. D. (2006). Response to intervention of young children with extremely challenging behaviors: What it might look like. *School Psychology Review, 35*(4), 568–582.

Division for Early Childhood. (2005). *Concept paper on the identification of and intervention with challenging behavior.* Missoula, MT: Division for Early Childhood, Council for Exceptional Children. Available online at http://www.dec-sped.org/positionpapers.html.

Kaiser, A. P. (2007). Addressing challenging behavior: Systematic problems, systematic solutions. *Journal of Early Intervention, 29*(2), 114–118.

Serna, L., Nielson, E., Lambros, K., & Forness, S. (2000). Primary prevention with children at risk for emotional or behavioral disorders: Data on a universal intervention for Head Start classrooms. *Behavioral Disorders, 26*(1), 70–84.

Stormont, M., Lewis, T. J., Beckner, R. (2005). Positive behavior support systems: Applying key features in preschool settings. *Teaching Exceptional Children, 37*(6), 24–29.

⚮ *Chapter* **14** ⚮
Vulnerabilities

GUIDING QUESTIONS

- How do social, economic, and family circumstances affect children's social and emotional development?
- How can you support the social and emotional development of children who have experienced adversity?
- How do the guidance principles discussed in this book apply to vulnerable populations?

*A*mong the children you will teach and care for, there may be children whose families are homeless, those who have lost a parent, those who have experienced abuse, and those facing other types of trauma. Millions of children in the United States have experienced adverse social, economic, and family circumstances that make them vulnerable. Abuse, poverty, loss or separation from parents, and living with a chronic illness, among other circumstances, take a toll on children's social and emotional development. While the instability in the lives of these children make them more vulnerable to social and emotional difficulties, it is important to remember that vulnerability does not automatically equate to behavior disorders. It is true that some of these children will experience social and emotional setbacks, but others will overcome the difficulties in their lives and go on to be happy, confident adults.

While many people view children from adverse backgrounds as "at risk," we encourage you to view them as "at promise" (Swadener & Lubbeck, 1995). When we view children from strengths-based perspective, we show them that we believe in their abilities to succeed, even in the face of adversity. *We also lessen the likelihood that we will lower our expectations for these children, and thus lower their self-confidence and social competence.*

In this chapter we discuss how children's life circumstances may affect their social and emotional development. We share guidance strategies, resources, and curricular ideas that will prepare you to provide these children with the additional emotional support that they so desperately need. Because supporting families is one of the best strategies you can use to promote the social and emotional development of children faced with adversity, we also discuss ways in which you can work with families of children in vulnerable situations. Remember that it is your belief in these children and their capabilities that will have the most lasting affect on their lives.

CHILDREN EXPOSED TO VIOLENCE

Child Abuse

You have all heard about instances of child abuse in the news. Unfortunately, these stories are becoming more frequent. According to the U.S. Department of Health and Human Services, approximately 905,000 children were abused in 2006 (U.S. Department of Human Services Administration for Children and Families, 2006). Chances are, you will work with a child who has been abused.

While most of us could never imagine abusing a newborn, infants are more likely to experience abuse than older children (see Figure 14–1). Physical abuse is the most common form of child maltreatment, followed by neglect and emotional abuse. Physical abuse includes things like spanking or slapping, with intent to harm. Parents neglect children by ignoring requests for attention, leaving them unattended, and not attending to their physical needs for food, shelter, and safety. Verbal threats, name-calling, rejection, and isolation are common forms of emotional abuse that young children experience.

Abused children are less likely to form friendships at school. While some will be aggressive in their interactions with peers, a significant number will withdraw from all interactions with classmates (Anthonysamy & Zimmer-Gembeck, 2007). As you might suspect, children who are aggressive or withdrawn have fewer friends at school, which affects their self-esteem.

It is important for you to help children who withdraw from peer interactions to form friendships. Provide these children with many opportunities to work in small-group settings with classmates so they become comfortable interacting in a group. Letting these children play the lead role in one-on-one activities such as buddy reading or peer tutoring will build their self-esteem. You can also show these children how to play with others by helping them to enter playgroups and then modeling how to engage in interactions with others.

Birth to 12 months	24.4 of every 1,000 children
1 year to 3 years old	14.2 of every 1,000 children
4 years old to 7 years old	13.5 of every 1,000 children

FIGURE 14–1 Young Children as Victims of Abuse

Children learn compassion when they experience it in their own lives.

Because children who have been abused are more likely to use aggression to get their needs met, it is especially important for you to teach conflict resolution skills, appropriate methods for expressing emotions, and strategies for dealing with frustration. Remember that these children have learned to be aggressive because they've been abused—for them it is a way of life. You'll need to be patient with these children and show them that no matter what they do or how they act you will not harm them. They also need to know that you won't let them be hurt at school. Once they come to see you as a caring, trusted adult they will become less defensive and more open to learning about how to get their needs met without resorting to violence.

∞ Sheri notices that Crimson is being very aggressive to the "babies" while playing in the home area. She watches the play for a few moments but becomes concerned when Crimson begins spanking the baby and telling her she is a bad girl. Sheri decides to enter the situation as the play leader, taking on the role of the grandmother. Speaking as the grandmother Sheri says, "It looks like I got here just in time to give you some help with the children. I can see that you are angry. What is it that the baby has done to make you so upset?" Crimson tells Sheri that the baby won't stop crying and that is very bad, so she needs a spanking. Sheri replies, "Why don't you let me help you get the baby to stop crying, I'm worried that the spanking will make her cry harder." Sheri gently takes the baby from Crimson and begins singing a soothing song. She then checks to see if the baby needs dry diapers and invites Crimson to help her get the powder for the baby. ∞

It is not uncommon for children who have experienced violence to use violence to solve problems. Sheri realizes this and provided Crimson with a positive alternative to her violent reaction to the baby's misbehavior. As discussed in Chapter 6, children need positive role models. Role models don't have to display extraordinary heroics. In fact, if you think about the people you view as role models, chances are those you remember were kind, compassionate, willing to go the extra mile when you needed help, and, above all, dedicated to their work and their relationship with you. Sheri displays all of these qualities in her interactions with Crimson. In doing so she is modeling how to treat others and how to be a friend.

Just listening to an abused child who wants to talk can be the most helpful thing you can do. As discussed in Chapter 7, listening to children and spending time with them helps them to understand that you are committed to building a positive relationship and will not break the bond that you have established.

Community Violence

Ten million children witness community violence each year. Gang violence, sounds of gunshots, and drive-by shootings all have negative effects on children's social and emotional development. Exposure to violence makes children fearful, anxious, and in some cases causes symptoms of posttraumatic stress disorder (Bussuk, Konnath, & Volk, 2006). Young children experiencing trauma show physical, emotional, academic, and relational difficulties (Bussuk et al., 2006). They often complain of physical illness, such as headaches or stomachaches, and may appear overly nervous at school. Fear of new situations and being crabby during change of routines are common behaviors of children exposed to violence.

Children exposed to violence require extra support to feel safe and comfortable at school. If you have students with such experiences, there are several things you can do (Bussuk et al., 2006). You can be sure to have a soft, calming place in your classroom and help children retreat to it when needed. Additionally, you can help these children find someone to talk to when they feel upset or nervous, being sure that other adults in the environment understand the children's needs. It also helps traumatized children feel safe when you make sure they know what to expect during their school day—this means a predictable routine plus plenty of advance warning about anything new or different.

Many children who experience violence are skeptical about adults, and rightfully so. As discussed in Chapter 2, children who have not had their needs met learn mistrust. Teachers must spend extra time building relationships with these children. One-on-one attention during play times, individual storybook readings, and extra encouragement during peer interactions will help children exposed to violence come to trust you.

CHILDREN EXPERIENCING LOSS AND SEPARATION

Children in Foster Care

There is a good chance that you will teach students who are in foster care. In 2006, there were 510,000 children living in foster care settings (Anne E. Casey Foundation, 2008). These children have experienced a number of hardships: abuse or neglect, family poverty, and/or parental mental health problems. While there is agreement that children in foster care experience more social and emotional problems then do their peers, the direct cause of these problems is unclear (Orme & Buehler, 2001).

When children in foster care have disagreements with peers or adults, they often feel anxiety and fear (Singer, Doornenbal, & Okma, 2004). However, they do not always act on these emotions. In fact, many children in foster care have learned to hide their emotional responses and instead withdraw when faced with unpleasant situations. The unpredictable emotional reactions expressed by children in foster care are related to their earlier experiences of abuse and/or abandonment.

Because these children do not always know how to express their emotions, it is critical that you provide them with experiences aimed at expressing their emotions in appropriate ways. As discussed in Chapter 6, adults should model expression of both positive and negative emotions and provide multiple opportunities for children to discuss their feelings. You can provide children with opportunities to discuss their feelings through songs, children's literature, and class meetings. Jack Hartman's CDs *Follow a Dream* and *Getting Better at Getting Along* contain songs that teach about anger management, keeping the peace, and problem solving.

Children in foster care also benefit from predictable routines. Many children in foster care experience multiple housing changes. Just as they are beginning to know and trust one caregiver, they are moved to another setting. Having a predictable routine at school will help alleviate some of the uncertainties in these children's lives. Mrs. Jensen makes sure her children know when she is going to miss school, and if she has an unplanned absence she leaves a message for the children with the substitute. One such message read:

Dear Children,

I am sorry that I didn't let you know that I would be absent from school today. When I woke up this morning my throat was all scratchy and I have a fever. I am going to visit the doctor this morning to see what she thinks will make me feel better. I hope to be back at school tomorrow. Please help Mrs. Rogers while I'm gone.

Love,
Mrs. Jensen

Informing children about absences helps promote trust and build community. Mrs. Jensen also makes sure that she reports children's absences to the class. In cases of lengthy illnesses, she has the class send get-well cards to the ill child. This practice shows children that they are all valued members of the group and that they are missed during absences.

Class scrapbooks also promote community building. Because children in foster care have so many caregivers, they are less likely to have their accomplishments documented. Taking pictures of children at school, collecting memorabilia of daily life in the classroom, and compiling them in a scrapbook will help children in foster care situations to remember the more pleasant parts of their childhood, rather than only the difficult aspects. Compiling a collection of children's work not only documents learning but also brings about feelings of accomplishment and memories of being part of a community of learners.

Children of Divorced or Separated Parents

It is likely that you know a family that has experienced divorce. You will most certainly work with children in this situation. In the United States, 12.9 million children have experienced divorce (U.S. Census Bureau, 2006). Research shows that divorce has a short-term negative affect on children's well-being (Amato & Cheadle, 2008). However, we are less certain about the long-term affects of divorce on children's development (Amato & Cheadle, 2008).

Children undergo substantial changes when their parents first separate. Moving to a new home, school, or neighborhood, changes in daily routines, and loss of daily contact with one parent causes a significant amount of upheaval in children's lives. These changes cause children to be less secure in their attachment to others. This often results in fear of abandonment.

∞ As the bus pulled out of the driveway, Tyler looked anxious. Dennis gently grabbed Tyler's hand and said, "Remember, your Mom is picking you up in the car today because you are going to your Aunt Julie's house. I bet she had to finish one last job before she could leave work. I have a job that needs to be finished too. I need to clean that guinea pig cage so Pinkey has a clean place to sleep. Will you help me clean the cage while we wait for your Mom? She will be surprised when we tell her that you know how to clean a guinea pig house!" ∞

Young children need help understanding the many possibilities that can cause a change in routines. They also need assistance finding constructive ways to pass time when they feel anxious or impatient. Dennis provided Tyler with both.

Supporting Parent–Child Relationships   We all know how unpleasant the break-up of a relationship can be. We have all heard stories of parents who try to woo children to one side or the other of adult conflicts without thinking about the child's need to have a strong relationship with both parents. Unfortunately, parental disputes often spill over into schools and classrooms. To eliminate potential harm to children, teachers must avoid "parent bashing" with separated or divorced parents, and instead should work to keep everyone focused on the child and his or her needs.

You can use several strategies to keep families focused on their children while in the school setting. First, be sure to provide both parents with information on school events, mailing information if necessary. Keep duplicate copies of children's work or portfolios with equal numbers of originals for each parent. Provide families with specific activities to do during open-house events, such as the following:

1. Ask children to show parents their favorite activity or place in the classroom. Instruct parents to participate in the activity with the child for 5 to 10 minutes.
2. Ask children and parents to complete a shared reading activity where each alternates turns reading pages of the child's favorite book.

3. Ask parents and children to work together to create a section on a family bulletin board or have them co-construct an "all about me" book.

4. Have children tell parents the guidelines for living and learning in the classroom.

5. Collect up-to-date contact information so that you can send emails, letters, or leave messages about children's life in the classroom.

Taking a proactive, neutral stance on the behalf of children sends a clear message to parents that your primary concern is the child, but that you are equally dedicated to supporting them so that they can support their child in the best way possible. While this will take extra time on your part, both children and families will benefit from your efforts.

Children with Incarcerated Parents You may have students whose lives and behavior are impacted by having a parent in prison. On any given day, more than 1.5 million children in the United States are separated from one or both of their parents due to incarceration (LaVinge, Davies, & Brazzel, 2006). The average age of children with a parent in prison is just 8 years old, with one in five being below the age of 5 (LaVinge et al., 2006). The majority of these children are poor and belong to an ethnic minority group (Greenberg, 2006).

Losing a parent under any circumstances causes children to experience uncertainty and emotional distress (Miller, 2006). Children of incarcerated parents tend to have nightmares, be fearful of new situations, and display sadness at unexpected times during the school day (Parke & Clark-Stewart, 2001; Phillips & Gleeson, 2007). These children may also have unexplained aggressive outbreaks and difficulty paying attention in school (Phillips & Gleeson, 2007). Peers often taunt children with incarcerated parents about their parents' wrongdoing. This puts them at greater risk for lower feelings of self-esteem and belongingness at school (Ziebert, 2006).

Teachers can support children of incarcerated parents by listening to them without judging the parent. Young children see their parents in a positive way and are often confused when they are sent to prison for doing something "bad." Discussing the parent's wrongdoing makes the problem worse. It is most helpful for teachers in this situation to acknowledge the child's loss and focus on the parent's love for the child. It is also extremely important for you to provide children in this situation with a consistent routine in the classroom. This offers security to children who have experienced drastic changes in their lives.

The most difficult aspect of working with children whose parents are incarcerated is answering questions about the parent's return. It is best to be as honest as possible in these situations. Because you may not know the answer to these types of questions, it is okay to say you're not sure when the parent will come home.

Supporting Families As you might suspect, children with incarcerated parents also experience drastic changes in living arrangements and difficulty maintaining positive parent–child relationships. Men are more likely to be imprisoned than women are. When fathers go to prison, the mother generally assumes sole responsibility for the care of the children. This causes stress for both mother and

Sometimes just listening to children is the best way to offer support.

child. When a single mother is incarcerated, child custody is less cut and dry (LaVinge et al., 2006). Grandparents or other relatives usually take on parenting responsibilities in these situations (LaVinge et al., 2006). In many cases, children of incarcerated parents are separated from their siblings as well.

One of the most difficult aspects of caring for a child with a parent in prison is maintaining the parent–child relationship. Lack of parent–child contact jeopardizes children's feelings of attachment and their overall well-being. Most children live more than 100 miles from the prison in which their parent is housed (LaVinge et al., 2006). This fact makes regular visitations difficult and expensive. Children who do get to visit their parents in prison often experience trauma when they see their parents behind bars. Complying with the "no-touch" rules that prevent children from physical contact with their parents in the prison setting makes visits particularly difficult for young children (Greenberg, 2006).

Teachers can help support caregivers of children by providing resources such as *Visiting Mom or Dad* (Adalis-Estrin, 2003). This is a booklet designed to help children understand what will happen during prison visits. You can also document children's school activities through pictures and collections of student work so children can share their accomplishments with the parent during visitations. By providing children and parents with something concrete to focus on during visits, you will help to make the experience more pleasurable for both.

Children of Military Families

Over 700,000 children in the United States have parents who are members of the armed services. Almost 500,000 of these children are under the age of 5. Children in military families move frequently. Changes in living arrangements, schools, and the disruption of friendships are difficult for young children. Separation from parents who are deployed is especially difficult. However, it is not only the separation from the deployed parent that is hard on children, it's also the process of preparing for deployment and the readjustment period associated with the military member's return to the home (American Psychological Association [APA], 2007).

You can better help these children if you understand the range of stressors military families face during the deployment cycle. Young children are particularly vulnerable to the added stress and uncertainties associated with preparing for deployment. Preschool and elementary-age children may exhibit the following behaviors during pre-deployment and deployment: confusion, sadness, sleep interruptions, tantrums, separation anxiety, and declines in school performance (APA, 2007).

Children may experience mixed emotions when the military member returns home. Happiness about the parent's return is often accompanied by anger because the parent left in the first place. Fear is also common during the reunion phase; infants and toddlers might not recognize the service member, while older children are fearful that the parent will leave again (APA, 2007). It is important for you to be patient with children during these times. Help them to focus on the fun they are having with the parent while they are home by giving them opportunities to share information about family events or outings. If the child is reluctant to discuss these events, invite family members to the classroom so they can share in school events. The most important thing for you to do during reunions is to support family togetherness.

Several national organizations have prepared materials to support children of military families. Operation Military Kids (http://www.operationmilitarykids.org/public/getinvolved.aspx) distributes *Hero Packs* to children from military families to help them keep in contact with their deployed parent. The backpacks contain stationary sets, journals, and disposable cameras that children can use to maintain contact with their parent. They have also created a training program for teachers and others who work with children called *Ready, Set, Go.* This training provides teachers with information on how to help children and families through the deployment cycle. The National Military Families Association offers free copies of *Coming Home*, a pamphlet that describes how children at various stages of development react during the reunion process. Sesame Workshop, the nonprofit organization behind *Sesame Street*, recently produced *Listen, Talk, Connect: Deployments, Homecomings, and Changes* to help children better understand the deployment process. The videos are available free of charge from the Sesame Street Workshop homepage at http://www.sesameworkshop.org/tlc/.

There are several things you can do in the classroom to support the social and emotional development of children of military families (Allen & Staley, 2007; APA, 2003). First, you should spend extra time in one-on-one activities with the children by playing games or reading with them. Allow them to express their feelings through play, art, writing, or role-playing. Make sure the classroom routine is as consistent as possible and watch for signs of stress such as clinginess or thumb sucking. If you notice changes in children's behavior, be sure to notify parents.

You can also encourage children to bring pictures of the family member to the classroom and ask them to share communications that they have had with the

Provide opportunities for children to express their emotions through art.

parent. If the child asks about the parent's safety or return, be cautious with your answers. Do not offer false hope by saying the parent will be okay, but do acknowledge the child's concern. Children may also ask when their parent will come home. Don't be afraid to say that you don't know.

Finally, it is important for schools and early education programs to form partnerships with other groups supporting military families. Coordinating efforts to support children with parents in the military will provide access to a range of support systems that children may need at any give time (Hoshmand & Hoshmand, 2007).

Death of a Parent

Children do not anticipate death, especially the death of a parent. Yet it is estimated that 3.5% of all children under the age of 18 will experience the death of a parent (Haine, Ayers, Sandler, & Wolchick, 2008). In many cases fictional stories leave children with the erroneous understanding that death is not permanent (Lichten, 2003). In fact, preschool children may take as long as 3 months to realize that the deceased parent isn't coming back (Christ & Christ, 2006).

Children experience a range of emotions when coping with the loss of a loved one, including loneliness, sadness, guilt, anger, and anxiety (Eppler, 2008). Younger children who experience the loss of a parent may experience toileting regression, separation anxiety, irritability, and nightmares (Haine et al., 2008).

Children in the primary and elementary grades often take on parental roles after the death of a parent, which disrupts typical patterns of social interaction (Eppler, 2008). To make sure these children don't miss out on important childhood experiences you can provide families with information on out-of school activities. Engaging children in recreational activities not only gives them a break from the intense feelings associated with the loss of a parent, it also provides the surviving parent with opportunities to enjoy their children in a nonstressful environment.

Many adults are reluctant to talk about death, especially with children. However, young children report feelings of happiness when they talk or think about the parent (Eppler, 2008). Let children talk about their memories of the deceased parent and encourage elaboration by asking questions about such things as the child's favorite time with the parent or a favorite activity that they enjoyed together.

∽ Mrs. Jensen had just read *Napping House* to the class. When she finished she noticed that Ava had tears in her eyes. Miss Jensen quickly released the children to prepare for P.E., strategically making Ava last to be called. Before releasing Ava, Mrs. Jensen asked her if the book had made her sad. Ava indicated that she missed having her dad tuck her in at bedtime. As Mrs. Jensen helped Ava clear her desk in preparation for P.E., she encouraged her to discuss the bedtime rituals she shared with her father. As they walked to P.E., Mrs. Jensen shared how her dad sang funny songs to her before she went to bed at night. The sharing of fond memories made both smile. It also strengthened the bond between the two. ∽

Moments such as the one between Mrs. Jensen and Ava are the hallmark of good teaching. All children, but particularly those with difficult life circumstances, need warm, responsive, caring interactions with their teachers. Having this type of relationship with each of the children in your classroom will go a long way toward eliminating potential behavioral issues. Noticing when children need extra support and making time to provide that support is essential to building positive teacher–child relationships.

Several other strategies will be helpful to you as you work to support children who have lost a parent (Haine et al., 2008). Remember that a positive attitude goes a long way. Make sure you remain upbeat around the child, especially when discussing future events. Provide children with a private space to go when they need to talk or need some privacy. Show children you care about them by spending quality one-on-one time with them each day—even a few minutes will send children the message that you are there if they need you.

It is also important to keep behavioral expectations consistent. We all tend to feel sorry for people who have experienced loss; this is a natural response. However, changing expectations often leads to more confusion for children who have experienced traumatic events. If children have occasional outbursts about their loss, calm them and then provide an alternative activity to help them get their minds off the situation. You can support remaining family members by maintaining frequent contact. It is also important for you to remember that families are overwhelmed immediately following the death of a loved one, so make requests for school projects or paperwork for school activities as easy as possible.

CHILDREN LIVING IN POVERTY

Young children are particularly vulnerable to the effects of poverty (Lareau, 2003). Lack of adequate housing, health care, and social and educational services has a profound affect on children's overall well-being (Wadsworth & Santiago, 2008). According to the National Center for Children in Poverty (2007), 13 million of the 74 million children in the United States live in poverty. When compared to their middle-class peers, children living in poverty have lower levels of academic achievement and social competence at kindergarten entry and beyond (Aiekns & Barbarin, 2008). They are more likely to repeat a grade, be placed in special education, and eventually drop out of school (Schweinhart et al., 2005).

Children living in poverty are also less likely to have access to quality early care and education programs (Aiekns & Barbarin, 2008), experienced, well-trained teachers (Scherer, 2008), appropriate medical care, proper nutrition, and safe neighborhoods in which to play (Lareau, 2003). Sheri and Maureen respond to these needs in ways that don't single out children.

∞ The children's center started the Kids Closet as a way to help parents help one another. Parents and community members donate clothing to the closet and are free to take anything they need. They also have a partnership with the local laundromat and receive free laundry vouchers in exchange for providing the laundromat with free advertising in the center's monthly newsletter—these vouchers are passed along to parents who need them. Most recently, the center entered into a partnership with the community health center and now sponsors Healthy Child Fairs one Saturday per month. Staff and family members donate time to assist with the events. They assist with registration and provide activities for children who are waiting to see the nurse. The playground is open to the community during the event so all children have an opportunity to get some exercise even if they don't participate in the health fair. ∞

Some people believe that we can't change the lives of children living in poverty through educational interventions (Neuman, 2007 p. 21). However, we know that early care and education programs can alleviate the negative effects of poverty on children's lives, *if* they are of high quality and implement evidence-based curricular and instructional practices (Neuman, 2007). High-quality educational programs for children living in poverty must address their social, emotional, physical, and intellectual needs (Santiago, Ferrara, & Blank, 2008). Those programs that give primacy to one domain of development over the other will not meet the needs of our nation's neediest children. Ultimately, we have to stop blaming children for academic and social differences caused by poverty and instead advocate for policies that connect families and their young children to the resources they need to be successful in school (Dryfoos, 2008).

You can serve as an advocate for children and families living in poverty by providing them with access to educational materials, particularly those that support social and emotional development. Provide "family-fun" backpacks filled with literature or games that promote social interaction or discussion of emotions and specific social skills. We have provided examples of children's literature throughout the book that you can use for this purpose. Adding games to the backpacks will provide families with natural opportunities to teach turn taking, sharing, and perspective taking (Perry, Mitchell-Kay, & Brown, 2008). Providing opportunities for parents and children to use the computers in your classroom or school during weekend or evening hours will also promote children's social development. Teaching families to use drawing software to create family drawings, or encouraging them to play online games together, will promote togetherness and strengthen parent–child attachment.

All children have special talents. It's the teacher's responsibility to uncover them.

You can also provide families with information about community-based programs that promote social development. Many community recreation programs provide art and drama programs for little or no cost. These types of programs encourage children to express their ideas, emotions, and feelings through the arts. Sharing information about resources available in your public library is another way you can advocate for children and families living in poverty. Most public libraries offer story hours and family activities that promote appropriate adult–child and child–child interactions. Libraries also provide families with information about other low-cost community events that children and families may enjoy, such as community celebrations or other events that will help children learn how to interact in various group situations.

Myths and Strategies for Family Involvement

Contrary to popular belief, nearly 83% of all children living in poverty have one parent in the workforce. In 60% of the cases, both parents are working (U.S. Census Bureau, 2007). Many work more than one job. These parents care as much about their children's education as their middle-class peers. However, they are less likely to attend school functions or volunteer in the classroom because of their work schedules (Gorski, 2008). Barriers to family involvement including working multiple jobs or working on evenings and weekends make attending school events difficult. Teachers can remove these barriers.

You can provide working families with opportunities to be involved in their children's learning in numerous ways. Create a class newspaper and email or mail it to all families. Offer parents opportunities to contribute to the newsletter or to assist with the publication using a school or home computer. Videotaping school events and placing copies for loan in the classroom library is another useful strategy for keeping parents involved.

You might also ask families to collect useful "junk" such as toilet paper rolls, ribbon, material, wrapping paper, or buttons that can be used in the classroom. Parents might also ask their employers to donate materials for the classroom. These materials can be quite interesting. Leather scraps in all shapes and sizes might come from an auto factory; nuts, bolts, and screws to use for sorting might come from a machine shop; keys in all shapes and sizes might come from a hotel, as well as slightly worn towels and sheets that will make great additions to the art center. Parents who work in restaurants may have access to old menus, interesting-shaped boxes, napkins, aprons, and nametags that might be used in the homemaking area.

Joyce Epstein (2008) recommends making positive phone calls to parents as a way to increase involvement. These calls are designed to let parents know about their child's successes in the classroom. If you can't imagine talking on the phone with 20 or more parents per month, call when you suspect the parent is at work and leave a positive message, or send an email. Receiving positive information about your child after a long day at work is a wonderful way to start an evening. Messages might be as simple as, "I was calling to share a story about Elijah. He is so sensitive to the needs of the younger students in our class. Today he spent 20 minutes teaching Maddie how to build a zoo for her favorite stuffed animals. I really enjoy watching him nurture the younger children. It seems like he was born to teach!"

Forming partnerships with families is one of the best strategies for supporting children living in poverty. When we build respectful relationships with families, we show them that we want them at school, that we respect their position as their child's first teacher, and that we want to work with them to achieve the shared goals that we have for their children.

CHILDREN WITH CHRONIC HEALTH CONDITIONS

Approximately 10.3 million children in the United States have a chronic heath condition (Nabors, Little, Akin-Little, & Iobst, 2008). That is one-third of every 1,000 children. A chronic health condition is described as any illness with symptoms lasting longer than 3 months. They include developmental illnesses (e.g., cystic fibrosis) and chronic diseases (e.g., diabetes, asthma, juvenile rheumatoid arthritis, etc.). When compared to their peers who are healthy, children with chronic health conditions are at higher risk for developing social and emotional difficulties (Guell, 2007; Meijer, Siennema, Bijstra, Mellenbergh, & Wolters, 2000).

Children with chronic illnesses face frequent and often painful medical procedures, side effects from required medications, and high rates of fatigue. When children are faced with weekly doctors visits, shots, surgeries, and a regime of unwanted medication, they experience a great deal of anxiety (Meijer et al., 2000).

This anxiety results from the fact that most children don't like to discuss their illness and often try to cover it up (Guell, 2007).

However, children with a chronic illness learn to manage their health care needs and associated side effects at a very young age. Preschool children with diabetes quickly learn to test their blood sugar, and young children with asthma can sense when they need their medication. These children understand their capabilities and limitations. Therefore, it is important that they be provided with choices in the activities that they can or can't take part in (Guell, 2007).

∞ Out of respect for Aaron, and others in her class who may need a calm activity during recess time, Mrs. Jenkins has created several playground packs. One backpack contains markers and watercolors, construction paper, magnifying glasses, notebooks, and plant and wildlife guides so children can act as botanists on the playground. Another contains board games and craft items for making art constructions. A third contains children's literature and dress-up clothes that offer children opportunities to extend the stories they read through dramatic play. These items are stored in the children's storage shed along with the bikes and other more active toys that are freely accessible to children. This way, no one has to ask for permission for materials or explain why they are choosing one activity over another. ∞

Friendships

Children with chronic illnesses miss school frequently, which lessens their opportunities for peer interaction (Meijer et al., 2000). Friendships are critical for the development of all children, but especially so for children with chronic health conditions. Creating living museums of children's current project work with photographs, art galleries, and videos will help children with extended absences keep up with the happenings of the classroom. You might also provide these children with a traveling classroom mascot during extended illnesses so they have a constant reminder of the love and support from the children and teachers at school.

You can also offer children opportunities to contribute to the life of the classroom by asking them to send drawings, stories, or photographs from home that correspond to topics worked on in class. These contributions can be sent via mail or email. Video conferencing and class Web pages are other ways to keep children with high absenteeism due to illnesses connected to the classroom. If children's health conditions don't permit these types of contributions, keep in contact with the parents and make sure to inform classmates of the child's progress.

Supporting Families of Children with Chronic Health Conditions

Families of children with chronic illnesses experience a great deal of stress as they try to cope with their children's illnesses while managing the demands of everyday life. Thirteen percent of families of children with chronic illnesses do not have health insurance (Szilagyi, 2003). Of those families who do have health insurance, the majority spends between 9% and 12% of their income for medical

Sharing work with other students promotes self-esteem.

procedures not covered by their insurance (Szilagyi, 2003). As you might suspect, these difficult situations cause parents to be anxious about their children's physical *and* emotional health.

Parents of children with chronic illnesses often try to protect their children from peers who might make fun of them, or teachers who might not understand the circumstances surrounding their illnesses (Nabors et al., 2008). This is understandable given the circumstances. Many teachers report feeling ill prepared to support the academic and social need of children with chronic illnesses (Nabors et al., 2008). Most early care and education providers do not have access to school nurses or other health care consultants to support them in meeting the diverse needs of these children.

You can prepare yourself to meet the needs of chronically ill children by taking the following steps. Contact your local medical center to see if they have a pediatric health library for families of children with chronic health conditions. *The Emily House* in Phoenix, Arizona, is one example of this type of resource center. It provides parent- and child-friendly resources that describe health procedures, medications, and information on managing chronic diseases. Local support groups also welcome questions from teachers. Many provide support services for children and parents to meet for the purposes of networking, counseling, and community building. It is important for teachers to take advantage of the information published by these support groups. Most offer short briefs such as *When Your Student Has Arthritis* (Arthritis Foundation, n.d.) or game kits like the *Wisdomkit®* (American Diabetes Association, 2006) that explain diabetes and offer suggestions for supporting children with diabetes in school settings. Gaining a solid understanding of children's chronic health conditions is the first step

PEARSON
myeducationlab

To see an example of how teachers provide activities that build build self-esteem, go to MyEducationLab and select the topic "Guiding Children." Under Activities and Applications, watch the video "Opportunities for Success."

to being able to support families while you strive to enhance children's social and academic development.

PROMOTING RESILIENCE AND SELF-ESTEEM IN VULNERABLE CHILDREN

Teachers have an important role to play in building children's resilience (Miller & Daniel, 2007). Daniel and Wassell (2005) identify several protective factors that help children overcome difficult life situations. Two of the most important protective factors that you can provide in the classroom are strengthening children's attachments and friendships. We discussed how you might accomplish these tasks in Chapters 2 and 3. Here we discuss how you can build on two other protective factors that will promote children's social and emotional development: identifying children's special talents and interests and increasing their self-esteem and self-confidence.

Finding Special Talents

All children have special talents. It is your job as teachers to discover them. One of the best ways to discover children's special talents is to offer choice. Let children select from one of several ways to complete a project or provide opportunities for small groups of children to collaborate on activities. When working collaboratively, children naturally divide tasks according to their strengths. If you observe these types of activities carefully you will pick up on each child's strengths. To help others in the class become aware of children's individual strengths, provide time during the day to acknowledge individual successes. For example, when discussing group projects, make sure to ask how each child helped to complete the project or solve the problem. You might also provide a recall time at the end of the day where children share their work with one another.

Another way to make children's talents visible is by directing children to other children. For example, if a child asks you for help tying his shoe, you might refer him to another child who has mastered this task. Children enjoy sharing their expertise with one another. If you know that you're introducing an activity that might cause some children difficulty, ask for volunteers to help if needed. You can identify volunteer helpers by putting an "I can help" sign in each center in your classroom. When children volunteer to assist in that center for the day, post their picture or name on the "I can help" sign. Children in need of assistance can identify helpers by looking at the sign. By referring children to children, you encourage group cohesion and provide children with opportunities to share their talents with others on their own terms. Providing children with opportunities to serve as a source of support to others helps them to realize that they are valuable members of the group. This improves their self-worth and self-confidence.

Self-Esteem

There are two components of self-esteem (Mruk, 1999). The first is how we feel about ourselves as individuals—our self-worth. The second component of self-esteem deals with how we feel about our ability to do things. This is our self-confidence. In your teaching you will see children with high self-esteem and high self-confidence. They feel good about themselves and their abilities. You will also work with children with low-self esteem and low self-confidence. These children are reluctant to participate in classroom activities and often ask for assistance even for simple tasks.

Of course there are children who display high levels of self-worth and low levels of self-confidence and vise versa. These children have what is called a defensive self-esteem (Mruk, 1999). Children with a low sense of self-worth and a high level of self-competence feel confident in their ability to complete age-appropriate tasks, but don't feel good about themselves as individuals. They will complete simple tasks on their own, but become defensive when they feel someone is attacking their self-worth. These children often say things like, "He's staring at me!" or "They're making fun of me!"

Children with a high sense of self-worth and a low sense of self-competence become defensive when asked to complete age-appropriate tasks on their own. They feel good about themselves, but fear failure. These children will say things like, "I can't do this." They tend to get easily frustrated and give up on tasks that present any challenge. Children who have been abused are more likely to have defensive self-esteem.

It is important for teachers to understand how the self-esteem of vulnerable children may play out in the classroom, especially as peers interact with one another. Mrs. Jensen considers children's self-esteem as she helps them resolve conflicts.

∞ Grace and Emme were working in the art area constructing bird nests. Suddenly, Grace grabbed all of the sticks from the table and headed toward the trashcan. Emme screamed, "Hey, I wasn't finished with those yet!" Mrs. Jensen met Grace at the trashcan and asked, "Did you hear Emme? I think she is speaking to you." "I'm done building those stupid nests," replied Grace. Mrs. Jensen responded, "Okay, if you're finished with your nest, you can help me look at the birds on the computer. But before we do that, we need to give the sticks back to Emme so she can finish her work like you did." When they arrived at the art table, Mrs. Jensen noticed that Grace's bird nest had fallen apart. Rather than offering to fix the nest, Mrs. Jensen said, "When we get to the computer maybe we'll find out what birds do when their nests get broken." ∞

Mrs. Jensen knows that Grace often displays a defensive self-esteem. She gets easily frustrated when she can't complete a task, even one without specific directions or limits. Mrs. Jensen doesn't call attention to Grace's difficulty with the bird nest because she is trying to protect her self-esteem. What she does do is try to show Grace that mishaps do happen and that friends can help you find answers to your problems. Because many children who have experienced trauma

Divorce and Separation	• *Two Homes* (Masurel, 2003) • *Was It the Chocolate Pudding?: A Story About Divorce for Little Kids* (Levins, 2005) • *Amber Was Brave, Essie Was Smart* (Williams, 2001)
Military Deployment	• *Talk, Listen, Connect: Deployments, Homecomings and Changes* (Sesame Workshop, 2007)
Poverty	• *A Day's Work* (Bunting, 1990) • *May'naise Sandwiches & Sunshine Tea* (Belton, 1994) • *The Rag Coat* (Mills, 1997) • *Uncle Willie and the Soup Kitchen* (DiSalvo-Ryan, 1991) • *Something Beautiful* (Wyeth, 1998) • *The Tables Where Rich People Sit* (Baylor, 1994)
Death and Dying	• *A Bunch of Balloons* (Ferguson, 2006) • *I Had a Friend Named Peter* (Cohn, 1987) • *Ragtail Remembers: A Story That Helps Children Understand Feelings of Guilt* (Duckworth, 2003) • *The Wall* (Bunting, 1990) • *The Rise and Fall of Freddie the Leaf* (Buscagila, 1983) • *When Dinosaurs Die: A Children's Guide to Understanding Death* (Kransey-Brown, 1999) • *Samantha Jane's Missing Smile: A Story About Coping with the Loss of a Parent* (Kaplow & Pincus 2007)
Resilience	• *A Good Day* (Henkes, 2007) • *The Streets Are Free* (Kurusa, 1995)

FIGURE 14–2   Strengthening Children's Resilience Through Literature

question their competence and self-worth, it is important for teachers to encourage a "can-do" attitude in the classroom.

In Chapter 6 we discussed the importance of modeling risk taking and caring for others. Both are important skills to teach children who question their self-worth. Throughout this book we have recommended the use of literature to support children's emotional development. Figure 14–2 is a list of children's literature that you can use to support children who have experienced difficult life situations.

CONCLUSION

Outside influences often affect children's lives in negative ways. Children cannot control these situations, and neither can their classroom teachers. Early childhood educators can, however, control what happens inside their classrooms. When we sign on to be teachers, we don't accept responsibility for pieces and parts of children's development; we pledge to care for and educate the whole child. This means considering a child's life circumstances as we plan our curriculum and our interactions with children and families. It also means being flexible enough to change the ways in which we normally conduct business in the classroom to meet children's diverse needs. This is perhaps the most difficult aspect of teaching; it is also the most fulfilling.

∞ *FOR FURTHER THOUGHT*

1. Review the strategies for supporting children's social and emotional development in Chapters 4 through 8. Identify those strategies that you believe will be most useful for supporting children who have experienced violence or loss, have a chronic illness, or live in poverty. Discuss how your implementation of these strategies might differ for vulnerable children and children who have not experienced difficult life situations.

2. Think about how you might feel when interacting with parents who have been incarcerated or those who have previously abused their children. What types of things might you do to make sure that you maintain positive interactions with the parents for the benefit of the child?

3. View several children's movies or cartoons. Document how death is portrayed in each—what are the circumstances surrounding the death? Discuss how the portrayals of death in the media might influence children's thinking about the loss of a loved one.

4. Discuss a time in your life when you experienced a situation that made you feel vulnerable. What support systems (family or community) or inner strengths helped you to overcome the adverse situation?

∞ *RECOMMENDED READINGS*

Algozzine, B., & Yesseldyke, J. (2006). *Teaching students with medical, physical, and multiple disabilities: A practical guide for every teacher.* Thousand Oaks, CA: Corwin Press.

Clay, D. L. (2004). *Helping children with chronic health problems: A practical guide.* New York: Gilford Press.

Frasier, M. (2004). *Risk and resilience in childhood: An ecological perspective.* Washington, DC: National Association of Social Workers Press.

Garbarino, J. (1998). *Children in danger: Coping with the consequences of community violence.* San Francisco, CA: Jossey Bass.

Lareau, A. (2003). *Unequal childhoods: Class, race and family life.* London: California University Press.

Walsh, F. (2006). *Strengthening family resilience.* New York: Gilford Press.

∞ *Chapter* **15** ∞
Analyzing Discipline Problems

You have read about many approaches to discipline and many causes of discipline problems in this book. In case the information is whirling around in your head and you're not sure what to do with it, this final chapter presents guidelines for how to put it all together in a usable fashion. However, it is not a recipe for no-fail discipline, but rather assistance in the difficult task of analyzing discipline problems and matching them with appropriate discipline approaches. Each child and each situation is unique, requiring your professional judgment about discipline.

KEEPING GOALS IN MIND

The first step in exercising your judgment is to examine your goals for discipline. Chapter 1 discusses the importance of keeping long-term goals firmly in mind as you plan discipline strategies. Most early learning standards contain goals for social and emotional development. In the K–3 grades, social and emotional goals are often found in social studies standards (i.e., civic education) or physical education and health standards. This book has emphasized the long-term goals of enhancing self-esteem, self-discipline, and moral autonomy. It is crucial that no discipline approach damage a child's growth in these areas. We attempt to explain how inappropriate forms of discipline counteract progress toward these long-term goals. Rewards, punishment, and other coercive approaches to discipline have become mainstream practices; teachers must understand that these practices work against their long-term goals.

Short-term goals are also important, although meeting them must not conflict with long-term goals. There are certain behaviors that are so disruptive or dangerous that they must be stopped immediately, leaving the teaching aspect of discipline for the next step. If children's actions put them in danger, it is essential to act quickly and decisively. Talking directly to the children involved is much more productive than yelling directions across a room. An emergency situation may require a warning shout, which will be useful if the teacher's voice is usually calm and controlled. However, teachers who routinely raise their voices in an effort to control a group will find that a raised voice quickly loses effectiveness.

FINDING THE CAUSE OF THE PROBLEM

If the situation is not an emergency, or after an emergency situation is over, you are free to think about the most appropriate discipline approach for long-term goals. This step requires a search for the cause or causes of the discipline problem. Many times you will find several interactive causes of a problem. This means you need to address several causes in order to provide effective help. Discipline that deals only with the symptoms rather than the causes of behavior problems is doomed to failure; the problem behavior will continue to surface until the reason for that behavior is addressed. Too often, teachers respond to the behavior instead of the causes (Reeves, 2006). This problem is well demonstrated in schools with posted sets of rules and the preplanned punishments for breaking each rule.

The causes of a problem are not always obvious, and it may take serious study and even some trial and error to get at the root of the matter. The chart in Figure 15–1 may help you in the process of analyzing a discipline problem pattern for an individual child. The organization of this chart follows the organization of the book in moving from the least intrusive to the more intrusive approaches to solving behavior problems. First we consider the possibility that the adult needs to change, and then gradually consider more and more serious needs of the child.

Matching Problem Causes to Solutions

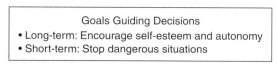

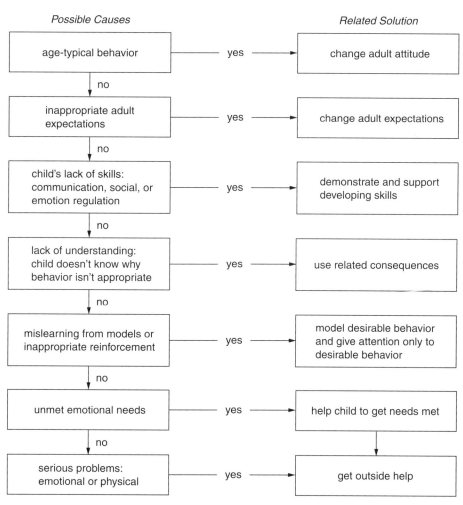

FIGURE 15–1 Matching Problem Causes to Solutions

Age-Typical Behavior

As you start to search for the cause of a child's behavior problem, first ask yourself whether the offending behavior may simply be typical of that child's stage of maturation. Some adults don't realize, for instance, that a 2-year-old is not being naughty when she wets her pants. These adults might punish the child or try bribing her in efforts to change this behavior, unaware that a 2-year-old who isn't potty-trained is exhibiting maturationally normal behavior. The child can't change the behavior until she is older. Chapters 2 and 3, as well as Chapter 11, offer other reminders of age-appropriate child behaviors that may frustrate adults. Your soul-searching may reveal that the "problem" is actually adult intolerance or a misunderstanding of childlike behavior (Landy, 2002). In that case, the cause of the problem is the adult's attitude; therefore, that attitude, not the child's behavior, needs to be changed.

Inappropriate Adult Expectations

The next step in finding the cause of a behavior problem involves examining whether or not inappropriate adult expectations may have created the problem. Inappropriate adult expectations may include those that are incompatible with an individual child's temperament, those that conflict with a family's culture, those that do not reflect gender differences, and those that are a poor match for children's maturational levels.

Chapter 2 summarizes relevant information about child temperament. When we reflect on the unique personalities of children in our care, it is clear that we cannot have the same expectations for all children. Chapter 3 examines behavior-related issues of diversity based on culture, class, and gender. As we become more aware of diverse ways of viewing and responding to experiences, we can better match interactions and expectations to those differences.

Chapters 4 and 5 describe many common ways in which well-meaning teachers and caregivers accidentally cause discipline problems. Adults create problems when they require young children to sit still and be quiet for more than a few minutes, to wait with nothing to do, or to engage in learning activities designed for older youngsters. The National Association for the Education of Young Children and the National Association of Early Childhood Specialists in State Departments of Education (NAEYC/NAECS/SDE) (2003) offer guidelines for appropriate programs and curriculum that teachers can consult to make sure discipline problems are not being caused by an inappropriate environment.

If you suspect that the environment is causing children to react negatively, the solution is to change the situation rather than try to change the children. This preventive discipline approach saves both teachers and children a lot of trouble. The adult response in the following example demonstrates the value of planning to better meet a child's needs.

∞ After eating lunch each day, the children in the child-care program are expected to clear off their table setting and sit back down to wait for a teacher to call them to brush their teeth. Sometimes there is no wait time, but sometimes it can be a couple of minutes, depending on how many children have finished eating. Sheri knows this is not an ideal situation, but it seems to be the only way to handle the tooth brushing with 20 children and only two sinks.

The children don't seem to have a problem with this, with the exception of Sam. Sam sits down for about 10 seconds and then has to get up and move around the room, usually causing a disturbance in the process, or he wanders into the unsupervised kitchen.

Sheri has repeatedly reminded Sam about sitting and waiting his turn. He seems to know what is expected of him but doesn't seem to be able to do it. Sheri decides that this situation just isn't appropriate for Sam and makes a plan to accommodate his needs. The chairs need to be stacked to sweep the floor after lunch. This has usually been done by the staff after the kids leave school, but Sheri asks Sam if he would like to help out and be the chair stacker after lunch. Sam jumps at the chance to do this real and important work—and to get to move around and use his muscles instead of trying to sit still. Now Sam is the proud official chair stacker instead of the kid in trouble every day. What a difference this makes to his self-esteem! ∽

The good news is that most solutions to undesirable behaviors can be found by rethinking adult expectations and overall classroom practices (Hemmeter, Ostrosky, & Fox, 2006).

Missing Skills

Once you have satisfied yourself that you are accepting children at their maturational level and providing an individually appropriate environment and curriculum, you can go on to look for other causes of discipline problems. Young children have a lot to learn about how to get along, how to deal with their emotions, and how to communicate effectively. If you suspect that lack of skill in any of these areas is causing the problem, a discipline approach that works on needed skills is the solution. Most of us work at developing these skills throughout our lives, so it is to be expected that young children will need help with them.

Chapters 3, 6, 7, and 11 present ways of helping children learn social skills and effective communication techniques. Adults can demonstrate and assist in desirable modes of self-expression and interacting with others (DeVries, Hildebrandt, & Zan, 2000). Probably the most important and difficult lesson has to do with perspective taking—understanding other people's viewpoints. This requires a combination of communication and social skills because people need to be able to express their feelings clearly in order to facilitate an exchange of viewpoints. Teachers can help children find words so that they can share their views and feelings with their peers, thus decreasing egocentricity. Helping children learn how to play with others and make friends goes along with teaching them perspective-taking skills. Other useful approaches include the use of I messages and problem-solving techniques to teach children effective conflict resolution (Gordon, 1989).

Emotion regulation, discussed in Chapters 2 and 6, is related to enhanced communication and perspective-taking skills. When children are able to find the words to express their sorrows and frustrations, they have a way of getting support and an acceptable way of letting off steam. When they begin to understand that there may be another side to a situation, they are often comforted. For instance, if children are able to understand that the child who wronged them did so by accident, it often has a calming effect. Similarly, beginning to learn that things don't always go their way because others also want their own way can help children cope with a disappointment. In addition, most children need specific assistance with learning how to comfort themselves and how to delay gratification. Teaching children social skills, perspective taking, effective communication, and emotion regulation are important discipline strategies that promote lifelong, harmonious social interaction.

Lack of Understanding

Perhaps the child has the needed skills but has chosen not to use them. Sometimes children behave in unacceptable ways because they don't understand why they shouldn't. Perhaps the cause of the problem is a lack of knowledge about how to behave or about the results of certain actions. Young children need assistance in learning about cause-and-effect relationships. They need to learn that their behaviors have certain results or consequences (Brady, Forton, Porter, & Wood, 2003).

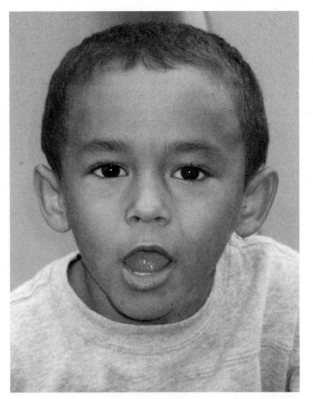

Mislearning causes much undesirable behavior. Sometimes mislearning is caused by accidental reinforcement of inappropriate behavior and sometimes mislearning is due to inappropriate role models.

Chapter 8 explains how natural and related consequences help youngsters to understand why certain behaviors are undesirable or desirable. Adults often have trouble allowing children to learn from experience because of the desire to protect them. Although you do need to keep children away from harm, you don't want to protect them so much that they lose the opportunity to learn. Finding out that you get cold if you don't dress for the weather or that you get hungry if you don't eat are valuable educational lessons. They are examples of natural consequences (Dreikurs, 1964). Related consequences are adult-imposed, but they link the behavior to a result that demonstrates why the behavior needs to be changed. Too often, adults expect children to learn from lectures and forget that experience is the best teacher. Natural and related consequences are effective forms of guidance that help children gain knowledge, which in turn guides youngsters in self-regulating their behavior.

Mislearning

Sometimes children have learned the wrong things. Chapter 12 describes how youngsters often get attention for undesirable behavior and how this attention encourages the behavior to continue. These children have learned to get their emotional needs met in counterproductive ways. In this case, the needed discipline approach involves re-teaching. Children need to unlearn old ways of getting attention and learn new ones. Judicious use of behavior modification techniques guides teachers in ignoring undesirable behaviors and encouraging desirable ones.

Another type of mislearning is a result of undesirable role models. Chapter 6 discusses the problems of media violence and how it impacts the behavior of children and youths. The need to counteract this influence cannot be overstated (Wilson, 2008). Sometimes the undesirable role models are older children, family members, or sports heroes. Additionally, educators frequently employ power tactics that model an undesirable "might makes right" approach.

Whatever the source, positive role models who build trusting relationships with children are desperately needed as the antidote. Teachers must be moral, caring, and socially skilled so they can demonstrate important skills and understandings in word and deed (Nucci, 2006). The most effective models "transparently" model desirable behavior by talking to themselves out loud, demonstrating the thought processes behind their actions (Weber, 2002).

Unmet Emotional Needs

If you are sure that a child knows better and is capable of behaving better, but is still acting out, you need to look deeper for the cause. Sometimes undesirable behavior is motivated by children striving to feel okay in spite of experiences that have left them with emotional deficits (Landy, 2002). Strong survival instincts motivate these youngsters to try to get their needs met, and they frequently act out in extremely disruptive ways that show misguided efforts toward "wholeness." Other youngsters with emotional deficits give up and retreat into their shells. The latter may be easier to deal with but are ultimately an even greater cause for your concern and attention.

Chapter 12 discusses how unmet needs in such areas as trust, pride, love, and power can contribute to discipline problems. If unmet needs are the cause of the problem, a truly effective discipline approach must involve attempts to help children get those needs met. These attempts might be made in conjunction with other approaches that will make the symptoms more manageable, such as related consequences. It is important to keep the cause of the problem in mind, however, and continue to work on helping the child get his or her needs met.

Diversity and Vulnerabilities

Teachers frequently find that a child in their care has unmet needs or other problems that they cannot adequately address by themselves. Chapters 13 and 14 discuss ways to work with children from diverse backgrounds and those children who have experienced traumatic experiences that make them vulnerable for social and emotional difficulties. Many of the practices in this book are applicable to these children. All children need a nurturing teacher, a flexible classroom environment, a challenging curriculum, and friends. Most of the children you encounter will benefit from the universal guidance strategies discussed throughout the text, but some children will need instruction in social skills (Riley, San Juan, Klinkner, & Ramminger, 2008), and a few may need one-on-one assistance from a specialist.

Sometimes teachers find themselves at odds with parental preferences and are torn between what they believe is right for the child and their commitment to honoring families. These are times for consulting the NAEYC Code of Ethics (2005).

Family Communication and Complexity of Causes

This list of possible causes for undesirable behavior (Figure 15–1) may make it appear that there is only one cause for each behavior problem. But, in reality, human beings just aren't that simple, are they? Typically, several different causes are interacting with one another when a child is acting out. Chapter 11 discusses how teachers can use observation to determine the cause of behavior. Chapter 13 discusses the importance of family-centered practices and offers suggestions for how you can form partnerships with families to get at the possible causes of behavioral issues. The following example shows how a teacher and a mother worked together, sharing information about the child to figure out why she had a hard day at school.

∞ Corrie had a terrible, awful, no-good day at preschool. She screamed and cried and clung to her mom at school. Her mother explained that she couldn't stay with her because she had to take Corrie's baby sister home for her nap, but Corrie continued to cry and insisted that her mother stay with her. After her mother finally did leave, Corrie followed the teacher around and wouldn't engage in play with the other children.

Dennis talked to Corrie's mother on the phone that evening in an effort to figure out the cause of her daughter's problem and keep her from having more such bad days. They took into consideration maturational factors: that Corrie was too young to understand other people's needs, so she naturally didn't respond to the explanation of what her mother needed to do. They also acknowledged that preschool-age children still have a long way to go in learning to control their emotions and express them appropriately. Young children can't distinguish between a momentary frustration and a true tragedy; therefore, they tend to respond in the extreme to all upsetting events.

Corrie's teacher and parents had previously discussed her innate temperament: emotionally sensitive and also slow to adapt to change. Because she is more than typically emotionally sensitive, Corrie experiences her feelings deeply, making emotion regulation even more difficult for her. When she gets upset, she has great difficulty getting over it. Corrie's other identified temperament challenge, difficulty in adapting to change, means that disruptions in her schedule upset her. Therefore, it is very significant that this was Corrie's first day back at school after a 2-week family vacation.

As Dennis and Corrie's mother talk, the mother acknowledges that Corrie was pretty tired after their trip and notes that she had been sick most of the time they were gone. In fact, given the day's problems, Corrie's mother now worries that Corrie may still not be feeling well.

Whereas she had previously been frustrated with Corrie, the mother now realizes that Corrie's distressing behavior was probably inevitable, given the combination of factors. The horrible, no-good day was a result of normal maturation limitations interacting with Corrie's individual temperament and compounded by unmet physical needs. ∞

Rather than a list, a set of concentric circles might be a better way of analyzing some behavior problems (Figure 15–2). We could start with the behavior itself

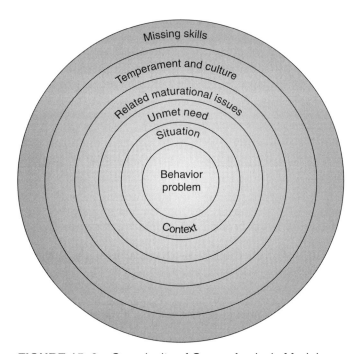

FIGURE 15–2 Complexity of Cause Analysis Model

shown as a tiny circle in the center, and then make surrounding circles that show the context in which the behavior occurred. This way of analyzing a behavior problem may be helpful in connecting multiple, interwoven causes.

The next larger circle can be used to show any unmet physical or emotional needs involved. For instance, is the child tired, hungry, or ill? Could the child be worried, sad, or fearful?

Another larger circle around that one could show the related maturational limitations. Typically, you would expect that young children would not be good at perspective taking, emotion regulation, or any type of logical thinking.

The next circle could be used to show the child's unique characteristics such as temperament and cultural influences. A final, outside circle might look at related learning: What missing skills might be involved? Does the child need help understanding why the behavior is inappropriate? Has the child learned inappropriate behavior due to poor role models and/or reinforcement of misbehavior?

This is just another way of looking at the causes of behavior shown in Figure 15–1. The concentric circle model might help you more easily discover how causes interact with one another.

MATCHING DISCIPLINE APPROACHES TO THE CAUSE

As you try to use the various guidance and discipline approaches described in this book, remember that each is useful only to the extent that it deals with the cause of the problem. Each discipline approach is aimed at a different type of cause. Using all available evidence to discover the cause is the first and most difficult step. The solution is usually fairly evident from there—if you keep in mind that the solution needs to aim at the cause. Too often, people forget that the solution is to treat the cause; they slip back into the old ways of responding to the behavior instead of the cause.

An Example

Perhaps it would be helpful to analyze an actual problem behavior using the chart in Figure 15–1. See how Mrs. Jensen worked as a "detective" to discover the cause of Shayla's problem.

∞ Shayla arrived late this morning and is very quiet during morning circle. When the class begins to work together on writing, Shayla sits alone. Since Shayla usually participates in writing groups, Mrs. Jensen is confused by the girl's behavior.

Given this evidence, do you think that Shayla's behavior is age-typical, or are the expectations inappropriate? Since the others are participating and Shayla usually does, neither of those possibilities seems to be the cause of the problem.

Mrs. Jensen encourages Shayla to find someone to work with, but Shayla insists that the other children don't like her. The teacher decides to leave her alone for the time being. A little bit later, she notices Shayla sitting under the table, looking sad.

Mrs. Jensen thinks back to her previous observations, trying to figure out what is going on. Shayla usually enjoys working with her friends and seems to be well accepted by the other children. Therefore, the teacher doesn't think that missing communication or social skills are the cause of the problem. Mrs. Jensen continues to explore other possibilities. She wonders if Shayla is testing the limits to see if there is any good reason to work on her writing.

Mrs. Jensen reminds Shayla that the class is working on play scripts for Friday Fun Day, when they will act out their plays for one another. Mrs. Jensen expresses concern that Shayla won't get to be in a play. Shayla makes no response.

The teacher decides she is giving Shayla far too much attention for her negative behavior. Mrs. Jensen wonders whether her urging and attention has actually been encouraging Shayla's pouting. She decides to shift her attention to the children who are writing.

After a little while, Shayla brings Mrs. Jensen a picture of a broken heart with a girl crying on it. Next to this picture, she has written her name. She looks so sad that Mrs. Jensen is concerned. She thinks this is starting to look like unmet emotional needs. She decides she must find out what is happening in Shayla's life. She gives Shayla a hug and asks her about her picture. Shayla only says, "That's me feeling sad."

At lunch time, Mrs. Jensen makes some phone calls and discovers that there had been some domestic violence at Shayla's house the night before. The police had been there and Shayla was aware of the trouble.

Mrs. Jensen revises her theory about the cause of the problem from unmet emotional needs to serious emotional needs. She knows that it will be especially important for her to provide a sense of love and security for Shayla at school. ∞

This example explores all the possibilities on the chart, but you will find that most problem analysis stops far short of serious problems. Yes, it may seem like most of your discipline problems have a serious cause because a child with unresolved social and emotional difficulties can take up so much of your time. But in actuality, you have dozens of minor incidents daily that are caused by lack of perspective-taking skills, lack of ability to enter play, or lack of communication skills. We hope you do not have many problems caused by inappropriate expectations. However, if you do, you know what to do about it (Landy, 2002).

Safety First

Discipline approaches aimed at teaching missing skills and understandings are different from your job of keeping children safe.

In an emergency, you must first stop unsafe behaviors or assist an injured child. It is not a "teachable moment" when children are in danger, injured, or upset. However, this does not mean that you should ignore the needed teaching. After the crisis has passed and the children involved are comforted and calmed, you can work on the skills or understandings that can keep the problem from happening again.

EVALUATING GUIDANCE PROGRAMS

Many packaged guidance programs offer a set of discipline approaches. We hope you will use what you have learned from this book to evaluate those approaches. We hope you will not accept ideas that ignore the cause of behavior, use rewards, or that otherwise are not respectful of children.

Much of the current curriculum material for guidance and discipline is in relation to violence prevention, due to recent tragic incidences of school violence. Many violence-prevention guides focus on "managing behavior," which tends to be a focus on symptoms rather than on the causes of inappropriate behavior. The most consistent rule enforcement will not help the child who mistreats others due to unmet attention needs. The most detailed lessons in social skills will not help the child who lashes out due to low self-esteem. Genuine change will come only when the child's needs are met and self-esteem is secure. Superficial change due to a focus on symptoms may submerge the actual problems and allow them to grow more serious over time. These problems will eventually emerge again and be manifested through more serious negative behavior.

Teachers and caregivers working with young children have a unique window of opportunity to make a difference. Children's attitudes about themselves and their world are still malleable during the early childhood years (through age 8). By the time students are adolescents, it is often too late for them to change their views and their behavior.

Analyze discipline problems by asking, "Whose problem is it?"

WHOSE PROBLEM IS IT?

Another way to analyze a discipline problem is to ask yourself, "Whose problem is it?" Gordon (1989) suggests the usefulness of separating those problems that belong to the child from those that belong to you, the adult. You might be amazed at how often you are trying to get a child to solve a problem that is really yours, and by how often you are trying to solve a problem that is the child's to solve. When you know whose problem it is, you have a start on how to solve it (see Figure 15–3). To find out who owns a problem, look at who is bothered by the behavior.

Your Problem

If the child is perfectly content with the situation and you are the unhappy one, the odds are that you own the problem. If you are bothered by children's messiness, exuberance, or lack of logic, you definitely own the problem. These characteristics are part of being young and aren't likely to change until children get a little older. This type of problem leaves you with only one reasonable solution: Change yourself. Perhaps you can increase your understanding of youngsters to the point of increasing your acceptance of them. For some teachers, the solution is to find work with older children.

Other common examples of discipline problems that belong to the teacher include children taking blocks out of the block area, leaving the group at circle time, or talking out of turn. The children exhibiting these behaviors certainly are not bothered by it, and rarely are other children offended by these situations. If the problem is the teacher's, then the teacher is the only one motivated to find a solution.

ADULT'S PROBLEM	CHILD'S PROBLEM
DISCIPLINE APPROACHES	DISCIPLINE APPROACHES
Express "I message"	Reflective listening
Change expectations	Related consequences
Change environment	Coaching in skills
Change curriculum	Help with unmet needs
Remove yourself	Do not reinforce negative behavior

SHARED PROBLEM

Problem-solving negotiations
Conflict resolution steps

FIGURE 15–3 Whose Problem Is It?

Solutions to Your Problem

When you own the problem, you have several options. One is to change your expectations so that you no longer perceive the behavior as unacceptable. For example, you may decide to allow blocks to be used in other centers as long as they are eventually returned to the block storage area. You may also decide to allow children a choice about attending circle time, as long as they don't disturb those who are participating. You might even decide to allow more informal talking and not require raised hands.

Your options also include changing the situation to prevent the problem from recurring. You may decide to locate the block center next to the pretend-play area because the blocks so frequently get taken for use in playhouse scenarios. You may decide to shorten circle time and make it more lively so that the children's attention won't wander. You might decide to encourage more small-group rather than large-group activities, thereby reducing the need for formal turns in discussion. All of these solutions involve creating a more developmentally appropriate learning environment for young children, as discussed in Chapters 4 and 5.

If you cannot overlook the behavior or change it by modifying the situation, you still have other options. If the child is capable of changing the behavior, you might find an I message effective (Gordon, 1989). Matter-of-factly telling a youngster, "I can't read this book when you climb on my back," provides information about the situation and your wishes. It does not suggest that the child is being "bad," nor does it reinforce the behavior with undue attention. If you have established caring relationships with the children around you and have respected their feelings, they are likely to respect your feelings expressed as I messages. Saying "I don't like to be hit" may be the way for you to deal with another problem. This approach also demonstrates to children how they can deal with some of their own interpersonal problems.

If that method doesn't work, you still have options. If you have tried the other approaches without success, you may decide that the behavior has a cause that needs attention. As Lillian Katz suggests, if you have tried the same discipline approach more than two or three times with the same child and it hasn't worked, you can assume it isn't going to be effective for that child (Katz & McClellan, 1997). Perhaps you need to investigate the possibility that the cause of the problem includes mislearned approaches for getting attention, as described in Chapter 12. In that case, the option of walking away from the offending child can not only meet your needs, but also can address the cause. When you withhold attention from inappropriate bids for it, you help the child unlearn the misguided behavior.

There are some behaviors, however, that are too disruptive or dangerous to ignore. When they occur, these instances may be good times for related consequences that teach why certain actions cause problems. These strategies try to make the problem also belong to the child by getting the child involved in a solution. However, remember the cautions in Chapter 8 about imposing consequences; they are dangerously close to punishment.

The Child's Problem

Many times the problem does belong to the child in the first place, but the adult takes it on. We describe this situation in Chapter 8 when we introduce the boy who keeps tipping his chair backwards even though he has been warned that it may hurt him if he falls. Remember that children won't see a need to change behavior that is not causing a problem for them. Therefore, it is crucial that we acknowledge when the problem belongs to the child. Natural and related consequences can get the adults out of the way and let the child experience the problem. These approaches quickly teach youngsters what behavior needs changing. Through natural and related consequences, children experience the problem, understand its cause, and are motivated to solve it.

When a child's problem is of a social/emotional nature, reflective listening (described in Chapter 7) is useful. When you listen carefully and reflect back a child's words, you are not taking over the problem and offering solutions (Gordon, 1989). Rather, you are being a supportive sounding board to help the child arrive at his or her solution. This approach helps children learn to own their problems and demonstrates an effective communication technique for them. Reflective listening respects children's ability to solve their problems, which not only enhances their self-esteem but also provides practice in autonomous decision making.

Mutual Problems

Sometimes a situation arises that makes lots of people unhappy. But even if it only makes two people unhappy, the problem is a shared one. Perhaps a group of youngsters can't start their math game because they can't agree about who should have the first turn. Now mutual problem-solving skills are required: It is important to find a solution that is acceptable to everyone involved. Chapter 7 describes how to brainstorm solutions and look for one that pleases all participants. This process may be a formal and time-consuming operation with a large group, or it may be a quick negotiation between two youngsters or between an adult and a child. Using this process solves many discipline problems, and teaching it to children provides them with a lifetime tool (Levin, 2003).

TAKING TIME FOR DISCIPLINE

Some teachers and parents want solutions too fast. They don't want to take the time to work through problem solving. They provide their adult solutions instead of listening reflectively, and they even force desirable behavior through fear or coerce it through rewards. These adults are short-circuiting the learning process that defines constructive discipline (Watson, 1999). Instead of helping children become autonomous and self-disciplined, this quick-fix attitude makes them dependent, rebellious, and sneaky (Kamii, 1984).

Time for Children to Learn

Teaching desirable behavior is a process of helping children learn a complex set of concepts and skills. Adults need to understand that children's exploration of behavior and social interaction is as natural for them as their exploration and manipulation of a new toy or another interesting object. Children need to try out certain behaviors to see how they work in relation to themselves and others. Given a predictable environment, along with sufficient practice, guidance, and time, youngsters will discover through their explorations that there is a logical pattern or consequence of actions. Children need to experience repeated connections between their behaviors and the results of those behaviors. As they reflect on these experiences, they construct their knowledge of productive behaviors, which eventually allows them to self-direct their actions as morally autonomous people. Such an important process does not happen quickly. Understanding gradually evolves as the child internalizes experiences and information over time. But the results are important enough to be worth waiting for.

Time for Cool-Downs

It is hard to quit rushing. Sometimes teachers hurry to implement effective teaching techniques in a discipline situation. Perhaps two children are fighting. You know that they need to use their words to express their feelings and then negotiate a solution through problem solving. It is tempting to immediately start in on

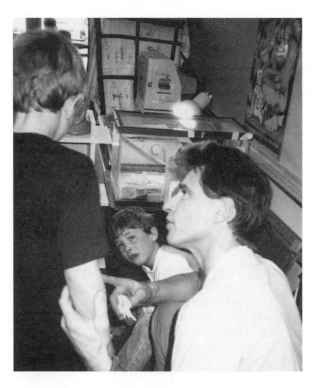

Effective discipline takes time: time to plan for it, time to teach children necessary skills, and time to cool down for clear thinking.

this important teaching as you separate the antagonists, but they are red-faced, short-breathed, and still swinging. Will they hear your voice of reason right now? A wise teacher allows a cool-down time before trying to teach more acceptable social skills. Of course, teachers sometimes need to cool down before they can offer the best guidance.

Time for Adults to Plan

Adults usually don't give themselves time to reflect on behavioral problems or to plan effective discipline. Behavior modification, with its emphasis on immediate feedback, has contributed to the common view that discipline must be instantaneous. Therefore, adults see a child doing something unacceptable and they feel pressured to respond immediately. However, thoughtful, reasoned responses on any subject take time. None of us does our best thinking without reflection time. Many teachers and parents confess to using discipline approaches they don't like simply because they couldn't come up with a better one at the time. It rarely occurs to them to allow sufficient time for effective planning in the area of discipline.

If you discovered a child had a language development problem, you would study the situation and consult others as you carefully planned proper intervention strategies. However, when the subject to be learned has to do with proper behavior, adults tend to act without thinking. Next time you are confronted with a discipline problem that you don't have an immediate answer for, try telling the child or children involved that you need time to think about it. Such a response demonstrates the seriousness of the situation and also models the use of thoughtful reflection in problem solving.

For ongoing and predictable discipline problems, it's possible to plan ahead and have a guidance plan ready to implement. The guides to discovering problem causes that are presented in this chapter will provide useful reflection content. Reflecting on the context of the problem and evaluating your previous responses will help you improve your next response (Hemmeter et al., 2006).

Most of us have learned some highly inappropriate discipline methods from our own childhood role models. When we react quickly instead of thoughtfully, our actions are often influenced by old models. The automatic response generally corresponds with the one our own teachers used. If we want to implement better ideas about effective discipline, then we must make a constant effort to override our automatic responses with rational ones. Be careful and take your time.

FAMILIES AND RESPECT FOR CHILDREN

Few of us experienced discipline with respect in our childhoods and therefore may not know what it means to show respect to children. American mainstream society says it values children but demonstrates little respect for them. Many of us experienced punishment and behavior modification—coercive tactics that damage both character development and intellectual development (DeVries, 1999). Adults in our lives may have also criticized us when they wanted to improve our behavior. Many parents believe that criticism helps people to improve. Yet, in fact, criticism discourages us and it does not improve behavior. When children's efforts result in feedback about their shortcomings, they are discouraged. Discouragement leads to quitting, not to trying harder. Alternatively, encouragement (described as an alternative to praise in Chapter 9) leads to trying harder. Families need to know these things and teachers may be able to communicate them.

Some families may need help realizing that respect accepts the child as a child, not as an imperfect adult. Respecting children means that we provide situations in which they can thrive while still acting their age. It also means that we give them as much choice as possible. When we respect youngsters, we don't force or manipulate them to bend to our will. However, that attitude doesn't mean they are allowed to run wild and be undisciplined. Respect for children guides us in helping them learn effective behaviors and understand the reasons for them. When we respect children, we help them to respect themselves. The resultant self-esteem combines with self-discipline skills to create morally autonomous people—something desperately needed in our society.

CONCLUSION

The teacher with the knowledge and the caring to implement this sophisticated approach to discipline deserves society's highest respect. Few observers realize how much effort and thought goes into a smoothly functioning program for young children. Teachers make hundreds of important initial decisions about the environment and the program, and they must make hundreds more each day as they implement their plans and keep youngsters constructively involved. We hope that this book is helpful to your own professional growth toward implementing the best possible approaches to discipline for young children. We hope that it helps you to envision and create educational relationships in keeping with democracy and human dignity.

∾ FOR FURTHER THOUGHT

1. Think about your goals for guidance and discipline. Do you feel clear about what you hope to accomplish?

2. Analyze an actual, ongoing discipline challenge using the chart in Figure 15–1 and the accompanying explanation as a guide. Does this analysis help you to consider your own possible role as a cause of discipline problems? Have you discovered a cause you had not previously considered? Have you discovered a need for outside help? Does this analysis approach help you to match guidance approaches to the causes of discipline problems?

3. Analyze another discipline situation using the chart in Figure 15–2. Have you been unsuccessfully trying to get children to take responsibility for your problem? Have you been inadvertently taking responsibility for their

problems? Does this analysis help you to match your responses to the situation more effectively?

4. Practice taking your time with responses to undesirable behavior. Give yourself cool-down time and planning time. What are the children's reactions? Do they seem to learn from your example? Are your interventions more effective?

∞ RECOMMENDED READINGS

Anderson, C. A. (2007). *Violent video game effects on children and adolescents: Theory, research, and public policy.* Oxford: Oxford University Press.

Elias, M. J., & Arnold, H. (2006). *The educator's guide to emotional intelligence and academic achievement: Social-emotional learning.* Thousand Oaks, CA: Corwin Press.

Jones, T. S., & Compton, R. (Eds.). (2003). *Kids working it out: Strategies and stories for making peace in our schools.* San Francisco: Jossey-Bass.

Lincoln, M. (2002). *Conflict resolution communication patterns promoting peaceful schools.* Lanham, MD: Scarecrow Press.

Lines, D. (2008). *The bullies: Understanding bullies and bullying.* London: Jessica Kingsley Publishers.

National Association for the Education of Young Children. (2005). *Code of ethical conduct and statement of commitment.* Available online at http://frn.sdstate.edu/CodeofEthicsApril2005.pdf.

Roberts, W. B. (2008). *Working with parents of bullies and victims.* Thousand Oaks, CA: Corwin Press.

Appendix A

Media and Young Children Action Guide • 2008

*T*eachers
*R*esisting
*U*nhealthy
*C*hildren's
*E*ntertainment

TRUCE
Media and Young Children
Action Guide • 2008

TV, DVDs, computers, video games and other electronic media are a powerful force in children's lives. Many children spend more time in front of a screen than in school. Shows, advertisements and the toys and other products linked to the media influence most aspects of children's development, learning and behavior.

Many parents and teachers are concerned about this issue and struggle with what to do.

Our Action Guide will help you to:
- *Promote informed and responsible use of media.*
- *Take action to reduce the harmful impact of media.*

What Do We Know About Children and Electronic Media?

Screen time reinforces the idea of violence as entertainment. It can undermine lessons taught at home and school about how to treat people, solve problems and have fun.

Screen time can undermine children's play. It takes time away from play. When children do play, they often imitate what they see on the screen instead of making their own creative and imaginative play. Toys linked to TV shows and movies further limit creative play. Free-time activities and child-created play can seem boring. Creative play is vital for positive intellectual, social and physical development in the early years; it lays the foundation for academic learning.

Screen time contributes to "problem solving deficit disorder" (PSDD). The more screen time children have, the more involved they will be in a world created by someone else, the more they will come to expect fast-paced action and excitement and be bored when they don't have it, and the harder it will be for them to come up with their own interesting problems to explore, solve and learn from.

Screen time leads to an emphasis on consuming. Children learn to want the products linked to favorite shows—toys, clothes, lunch boxes and food.

In addition, children see 40,000 ads on the screen every year. Young children are victims of marketing because they believe what they see and hear.

Screen time (educational and other kinds of programming) contributes to unhealthy eating habits and childhood obesity. It reduces the amount of physical activity children have and contributes to snacking. The largest category of TV advertising directed at children is unhealthy food.

Screen time teaches children lessons caring adults don't want them to learn. It exposes them to large quantities of violence and anti-social behavior—both pretend and in the news. The violence can lead to increased levels of aggression, fearfulness and play with violence. Also, much of what children see on the screen promotes racial, ethnic and gender stereotypes as well as sexualized appearance and behavior.

Screen time contributes to stress between children and adults. Children watch programs adults find inappropriate. They nag for more and more screen time and nag for the products advertised on the screen. It makes it harder for parents to maintain what they want for their families.

For more information: www.truceteachers.org • truce@truceteachers.org • *TRUCE*, PO Box 441261, W. Somerville, MA 02144
PLEASE COPY AND DISTRIBUTE

341

What You Can Do

Parents and Children

◆ Help children develop thoughtful and responsible media viewing habits.

- Limit screen time. Decide together how much is okay each day or week. (With young children, start with the least amount that can work with your schedule and your child's).

- Set guidelines about what is appropriate viewing in your family. Apply guidelines to all media: TV, cartoons, videos, movies, video games, magazines and comic books. Help children select programs within your family's guidelines.

- Protect children from exposure to inappropriate media as much as possible. Be aware of what you are watching when your child is able to hear or see it.

- Teach your child to ask to watch television before being allowed to turn it on.

- Get TVs, video game systems and computers out of children's bedrooms.

- Make a chart (with simple picture illustrations for non-readers) of shows which your children want to watch and which you can agree are good choices. Check the chart regularly to help you discuss how things are going.

- Watch TV and movies with your children and talk together about what you see. [See box next page]. Aim for a give-and-take discussion rather than a lecture where you give the answers. Listen carefully, find out their ideas and fears, clear up misconceptions and share your ideas and concerns.

- Use media to spark your child's imagination and creativity. You can ask questions like: if you wrote the story, how would you change the ending? Would you add new characters? What would they look or act like?

◆ Encourage and support children's interests and skills beyond electronic media.

- Balance electronic media with playtime - encourage your kids to go outside and be active.

- Promote creative and imaginative play which children control, instead of play that looks like they are imitating what they see on the screen.

- Encourage children's play as a way to help them work out their own ideas and develop a sense of mastery. [Use the TRUCE Toy Action Guide available at www.truceteachers.org].

- Help children resist marketing; choose toys carefully.

- Provide play materials that can be used in many ways over a long period of time, such as blocks, play dough, dress-ups and props for dramatic play.

For more information: www.truceteachers.org • truce@truceteachers.org • *TRUCE*, PO Box 441261, W. Somerville, MA 02144
PLEASE COPY AND DISTRIBUTE

342

- Limit the number of highly realistic toys and other products (such as lunch boxes, tee shirts and breakfast cereals) that are linked to TV programs.

- Avoid media-linked toys, especially those connected to media rated for older children or adults.

- Find appealing non-TV activities for your family.

- Read to your child and go to the library. It's the best way you can build their literacy skills and help them establish a love of books.

- Have art supplies readily available and accessible for your children to use.

- Play age-appropriate board games.

Adults and Children Can Talk Together about TV and Other Media

- **Discuss** each other's reactions (both positive and negative) to what you saw.
  - *What did you think about that show/game?*
  - *Did you like it when _____ happened? Why do you think it happened?*
  - *I didn't like it when _____. I wish they didn't have to hurt each other. What do you think?*

- **Help** them sort out fantasy from reality.
  - *What was pretend and what was real? How could you tell?*
  - *Help clarify confusion by saying things such as, "In real life things don't work that way. I wonder how they made _____ happen on that show."*

- **Help** them develop an understanding of advertising and marketing.
  - *How can we tell the difference between these ads and the show?*
  - *I wonder why they made the ad like that?*
  - *How do you think this product really looks in real life?*
  - *Do you think this toy or product is intended for boys or girls? What makes you think that?*

- **Compare** what they saw to children's own experience.
  - *Could anything like _____ happen to you? When? How could it be the same/different?*
  - *What would you do if you were in that situation?*

- **Talk** about the violence and other mean-spirited behavior that children see on the screen.
  - *What do you think about how _____ solved their problem?*
  - *If you had a problem like that, what could you do? What could you say?*
  - *Can you think of a way to solve that problem where no one gets hurt?*

- **Ask** questions that focus on stereotyped images and behaviors.
  - *I wonder why it's always men with big muscles that go to fight? Did you notice that?*
  - *The women always seem to need to get rescued by men. Have you noticed that? I wonder why?*
  - *I wonder why the "bad guys" have foreign accents? Wear dark colors? Have darker skin?*

  * Adapted from *Remote Control Childhood* (Levin, 1998)

For more information: www.truceteachers.org • truce@truceteachers.org • *TRUCE*, PO Box 441261, W. Somerville, MA 02144
PLEASE COPY AND DISTRIBUTE

343

Parents and Other Parents

◆ Be aware of what children are watching outside your home. Communicate your standards to neighbors, grandparents, child care providers, babysitters, and anyone who may care for your child or children. Ask for their cooperation in limiting media exposure.

◆ Talk about media management with other parents; share tips and provide support for one another.
  • Help each other find solutions to problems media creates for you and your children (how to make good choices about what to watch and buy; how to turn off the TV while you're making dinner).
  • Agree on how you'll deal with TV and other media when your children are at each other's houses for play dates, birthday parties, etc.
  • Use each other to check on appropriateness of TV programs, movies, video and computer games.
  • Support each others' choices to resist media's negative influence.

◆ Challenge those who are still apathetic by sharing information on media's effect on children.
  • Talk about your concerns and approaches to media violence, stereotypical images and behavior, and media-linked toys.
  • Learn some facts to spark conversation and/or advocacy. For example, 61% of babies 1 year or younger watch TV. For more, see *TV and Your Child* on the TRUCE website.

Parents and Community

◆ Raise community awareness about the effects of media on young children.
  • Ask your pediatrician and other health care professionals to become informed and advocate on this issue.
  • Bring TRUCE materials and other information to libraries, clinics, events, family and friends.

◆ Work together to reduce inappropriate content in the media and to create an environment more conducive to children's healthy development.
  • Contact TV stations, movie companies, toy manufacturers and local newspapers to voice your concerns. Urge other adults to do so, too. [See Action Guide Resources, p. 7-8]. Help children write letters. Check our website for letters that can serve as a guide.

Parents and Teachers

◆ Ask your child's school to develop policies and educate parents about the problems created by media violence and how to deal with them.

◆ Work with schools to develop curriculum that incorporates healthy play, media literacy, and conflict resolution and violence prevention programs.

◆ Promote school-wide activities which help create a community of aware parents and teachers.
  • Sponsor school events such as a TV Turn-Off Week or a violent toy trade-in.
  • Create a media resource library to help parents use media wisely.
  • Have the PTA organize workshops and guest speaker events for parents on this topic.
  • Sponsor school-wide activities to involve children in alternative activities such as after school clubs.

For more information: www.truceteachers.org • truce@truceteachers.org • *TRUCE*, PO Box 441261, W. Somerville, MA 02144
PLEASE COPY AND DISTRIBUTE

Teachers and Children

The effects of too much electronic media can reach into the early childhood classroom. Teachers and child care providers can create an environment that counteracts the effects. During indoor and outdoor playtime, small group activities and class meetings teachers can:

◆ Take an active role in creating a peaceful, cooperative community whose values and activities displace those given by the media.

- Set up routines so that children help each other with getting dressed and classroom jobs.

- Introduce stories of people who deal with challenges in powerful and resourceful ways, both real and fictional, for example, Rosa Parks, Sally Ride, the boy in *Abiyoyo*, the characters in *A Chair for My Mother*.

- Work with families to mutually support the values of a peaceful learning environment. For example, create kits with books and activities for families to borrow. At parent/teacher meetings, discuss the effects of media on learning.

- Discuss with children what they need to feel safe. Create a classroom chart with their responses.

◆ Promote creative play that allows children to explore their ideas and use their imaginations.

- Develop curriculum and foster play that encourages creative thinking and problem-solving skills.

- Select open-ended toys and materials (e.g., art and recycled materials, blocks, dolls) that children can use in their own creative ways.

- Resist use of materials that are linked to TV, movies and other electronic media – for example, puzzles, books and games based on characters such as Spiderman and Dora the Explorer. While children are drawn to characters from the media, schools and childcare centers should expand children's experiences and interests.

- In communities where children have access to computers at home, minimize computer use with young children at school.

- Observe for play that imitates popular media and guide children to use more of their own ideas.

- Help children redirect play that includes fighting, such as pretending to be "good guys and bad guys." Often they are stuck. For example, a teacher might say, "The Power Rangers have been very busy.

I wonder if they are hungry and want to go to the dramatic play area and have a picnic."

- Serve as a bridge between children acting out aggressive themes drawn from the media, and other children who are playing peacefully nearby to change the tone of the play.

◆ Promote alternative ways for children to feel powerful other than fighting, excluding, bullying or relying on media images or marketed products.

- Help children redefine power to be the skills and accomplishments they achieve, such as crossing the balance beam, buttoning, opening a friend's thermos, overcoming fears.

- Children's play sometimes deals with monsters. Teachers can extend those ideas by providing props, such as ropes for traps, ingredients for potions, cloth for caves, etc. Children can feel powerful while working creatively and safely on a common goal.

◆ Guide a conversation about superhero play with open-ended questions and comments that invite children to share their thinking. Sometimes children need a prompt; sharing an idea to begin can be helpful.

Some examples:

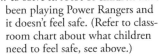

* I have noticed a problem and I need your help figuring out how to solve it. A lot of children have been playing Power Rangers and it doesn't feel safe. (Refer to classroom chart about what children need to feel safe, see above.)

* Can you tell me more about what makes you scared?

* What could Power Rangers do instead of fighting to feel safe and powerful?

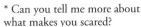

* What can you do to feel powerful?

* What do you think about giving ourselves a name to show that we are powerful? Shall we write your ideas on a list and tally them?

[See TRUCE website for an example of a classroom dialogue.]

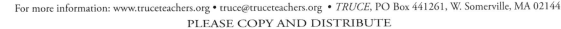

◆ Address racial, gender and other stereotypes promoted in media.

> *Media designed for children often reflect and promote stereotypes that limit children's ideas of who they can be, how they understand others and how they see the world.*

- Respond when children use media stereotypes in their play. For example, a group of white preschool girls who are playing "Princess" tell an African American girl, "You can't be Ariel because you don't look like her." An adult could respond, "What do you think princesses look like?" to help children explore the ideas they are getting about race from the media. Validate for children that they can choose whom they want to be: "Playing pretend means you are using your imagination – you don't have to look like the character in the movie to pretend to be it." This issue is addressed in the children's book *Amazing Grace* – reading the story with the children could create more opportunities to explore it.

- Look for opportunities to expand children's thinking. When a girl brings a Thomas the Tank Engine toy and a boy tells her the toy is for boys, a teacher might say, "Some people think that, but I don't agree. What do you think?"

- Have photos of people in non-traditional roles displayed in the classroom.

◆ Create opportunities for discussion about violence or scary events in the news.

> *These things are often on children's minds, and they worry that they will happen to them. Children need to know that school is a safe place where they can get support processing unsettling information. Honor children's needs by responding honestly while not giving them too much information. Children need to be reassured that adults are working to keep them safe.*

A sample dialogue between children and teachers occurring during free play time:

Sara: *A hurricane came and flooded people's houses.*

Eli: *People are on the roofs!*

Teacher: *Where did you hear about it?*

Sara: *I saw it on the news. A baby was crying.*

Teacher: *I saw that, too. What did you think about it?*

Eli: *I was scared 'cause one time our basement had a little flood.*

Teacher: *A flood is scary, and lots of people are working together to rescue people and bring them to a safe place. Did people work together when the flood happened in your basement?*

Eli: *Yeah. My mom used a vacuum thing and my aunt kept us upstairs where it was dry.*

Teacher: *What do you think people are doing to work together to help with the flood you saw on the news?*

Laura: *They can use a helicopter to get them off the roof. Or a boat!*

Teacher: *What a great idea to use helicopters and boats, Laura.*

A teacher can follow up by bringing in pictures from the newspaper showing people being helped in the ways that the children mentioned and in other ways as well. Avoid pictures that show graphic or scary details. Doing this keeps conversation lines open with children, validates their ideas, and helps them feel more secure knowing that people are helping to make things better.

- When children are experiencing real life violence in their home or community, it becomes even more important to be a keen observer and listener. Children may be working out their own questions and ideas about violence as they play, and caregivers may need to seek support from a counselor, psychologist or from community organizations.

For more information: www.truceteachers.org • truce@truceteachers.org • *TRUCE*, PO Box 441261, W. Somerville, MA 02144.

PLEASE COPY AND DISTRIBUTE

Action Guide Resources

Keep by your phone or computer.

Books

Cantor, J. (1998). *"Mommy, I'm Scared" How TV and Movies Frighten Children and What We Can Do to Protect Them.* San Diego: Harcourt Brace.

Cantor, J. (2004). *Teddy's TV Troubles.* Madison, WI: Goblin Farm Press [Children's book about fears caused by TV.]

Clinton, J. (2003). *The Other Parent: The Inside Story of the Media's Effect on Our Children.* New York: Atria.

De Gaetano, G. (2004). *Parenting Well in the Media Age: Keeping Our Kids Human.* Fawnskin, CA: Personhood Press.

Greenman, J. (2001). *What Happened to the World? Helping Children Cope in Turbulent Times.* Bright Horizons [Download copies at: www.brighthorizons.com/talktochildren; order copies from: www.naeyc.org].

Hoffman, E. (2002). *Changing Channels: Activities Promoting Media Smarts and Creative Problem Solving for Children.* St. Paul, MN: Redleaf Press.

Hoffman, E. (2004). *Magic Capes, Amazing Powers: Transforming Superhero Play in the Classroom.* St. Paul, MN: Redleaf.

Levin, D. (1998). *Remote Control Childhood? Combating the Hazards of Media Culture.* Washington, DC: NAEYC.

Levin, D. & Carlsson-Paige. (2006). *The War Play Dilemma: What Every Parent and Child Needs to Know* (2nd Ed.). New York: Teachers College Press.

Seiter, E. (2005). *The Internet Playground: Children's Access, Entertainment and Mis-education.* New York: Peter Lang.

Videos

[Distributors listed in **Organizations** below]

Game Over: Gender, Race, and Violence in Video Games. Media Education Foundation. Addresses the fastest growing segment of the media and how it exploits gender, race and violence.

Mickey Mouse Monopoly: Disney, Childhood, and Corporate Power. Media Education Foundation. Takes a critical look at Disney's role in shaping childhood and the ideas Disney movies teach about race, gender and ethnicity.

Unplug Your Kids. National Center on Media and the Family. Shows how children learn values, attitudes and behaviors from the mass media and offers suggestions for using media in a healthy way.

National TV Networks

ABC Entertainment
818-460-7477; www.ABC.com
Local Station #_____

CBS Audience Services
212-975-4321; www.CBS.com
Local Station #_____

Cartoon Network
404-827-1500; www.cartoonnetwork.com

Disney Channel
818-569-7500; www.disney.go.com

Fox Broadcast Studios
310-277-2211; www.fox.com
Local Station #_____

NBC Entertainment
212-664-4444; www.NBC.com
Local Station #_____

Nickelodeon
212-258-7579; www.nick.com

PBS
703-739-5000; www.pbs.org
Local Station #_____

Websites

www.kidshealth.org/parent/positive
Helpful one-pagers on dealing with various aspects of the media.

www.mayoclinic.com
Fitness for kids: getting them off the couch.

www.pbs.org/parents/talkingwithkids/news
"Talking with Kids about the News."

www.pbs.org/parents/childrenandmedia/resources.html
List more resources on media and children.

www.tvsmarter.com
Resources to raise consciousness about dangers of rampant advertising and TV and promote action.

For more information: www.truceteachers.org • truce@truceteachers.org • *TRUCE*, PO Box 441261, W. Somerville, MA 02144
PLEASE COPY AND DISTRIBUTE

347

Action Guide Resources

Toy Manufacturers & Retailers

Bandai America, Inc.
310-926-0947; www.bandai.com
Makes Power Rangers.

Hasbro Toy Group
401-431-8697; www.hasbro.com
Makes Transformers, Spiderman & more.

Mattel Toys
310-252-2000; www.mattel.com
Makes Barbie & more.

MGA Entertainment
800-222-4685; www.mgae.com
Makes Bratz dolls.

Saban Entertainment
310-235-5100
Makes Power Rangers media.

Government Officials

Federal Communication Commission
(regulates TV)
888-225-5322; www.fcc.gov

Federal Trade Commission
(oversees marketing)
877-382-4357; www.ftc.gov

President of the United States
202-456-1414; president@whitehouse.gov

US Senator _____
Phone _____ email _____

US Senator _____
Phone _____ email _____

US Rep. _____
Phone _____ email _____

Governor _____
Phone _____ email _____

Keep by your phone or computer.

American Academy of Pediatrics
847-434-4000; www.aap.org
• Prepares position statements and informational pamphlets for pediatricians and the public on media issues.

Campaign for Commercial-Free Childhood
617-278-4172;
www.commercialexploitation.org
• Coalition working to stop marketing practices that harm children.

Organizations

Center for a New American Dream
www.newdream.org
• 32-page booklet: "Tips for Parenting in a Commercial Culture." Download free copy: www.newdream.org/kids

Kaiser Family Foundation
650-854-9400; www.kff.org
• Reports and research on children and families' media use and more.

Media Education Foundation
800-897-0089; www.mediaed.org
• Producers of high quality media literacy videos for educational purposes.

National Institute on Media & the Family
888-672-KIDS; www.mediaandthefamily.org
• Newsletter rating media products' impact on children; produces media literacy materials and advocates for sound policy.

TV-Turnoff Network
202-333-9220; www.tvturnoff.org
• Organizes annual TV turn-off week and materials to support efforts in your community.

TRUCE is a national group of educators deeply concerned about how children's entertainment and toys are affecting the play and behavior of children in our classrooms.

TRUCE's goals are:

➧ To raise public awareness about the negative effects of violent and stereotyped toys and media on children, families, schools and society.

➧ To work to limit the harmful influence of unhealthy children's entertainment.

➧ To provide children with toys and activities that promote healthy play and non-violent behavior at home and school.

➧ To create a broad-based effort to eliminate marketing to children and to reduce the sale of toys of violence.

➧ To support parents' and teachers' efforts to deal with the issues regarding media.

For more information about what you can do and to *make a contribution* **to cover our printing and disseminating costs, contact us: TRUCE, PO Box 441261, Somerville, MA 02144**
truce@truceteachers.org • www.truceteachers.org

TRUCE thanks Matt Damon for his generous support.

For more information: www.truceteachers.org • truce@truceteachers.org • *TRUCE*, PO Box 441261, W. Somerville, MA 02144
PLEASE COPY AND DISTRIBUTE

References

CHAPTER 1

Baumrind, D. (1967). Child care practices anteceding three patterns of preschool behavior. *Genetic Psychology Monographs, 75*, 43–88.

Brady, K., Forton, M. B., Porter, D., & Wood, C. (2003). *Rules in school.* Greenfield, MA: Northeast Foundation for Children.

Bronson, M. B. (2000). Recognizing and supporting the development of self-regulation in young children. *Young Children, 55*(2), 32–37.

Brooks, R., & Goldstein, S. (2007). *Raising a self-disciplined child: Help your child become more responsible, confident and resilient.* New York: McGraw Hill.

Butchart, R. E., & McEwan, B. (1998). *Classroom discipline in American schools: Problems and possibilities for democratic education.* Albany, NY: State University of New York Press.

Canter, L., & Canter, M. (1992). *Assertive discipline. Positive behavior management for today's classroom.* Santa Monica, CA: Lee Canter & Associates.

Charney, R. S. (2002). *Teaching children to care: Classroom management for ethical and academic growth K–8.* Greenfield, MA: Northeast Foundation for Children.

Damon, W., Lerner, R., & Eisenberg, N. (2006). *Handbook of child psychology. Volume 3: Social, emotional and personality development* (6th ed.). New York: Wiley & Sons Inc.

DeVries, R. (1999). Implications of Piaget's constructivist theory for character education. In M. M. Williams & E. Shaps (Eds.), *Character education: The foundation for teacher education* (pp. 33–39). Washington, DC: The Character Education Partnership.

DeVries, R., Hildebrandt, C., & Zan, B. (2000). Constructivist early education for moral development. *Early Education & Development, 11*(1), 10–35.

DeVries, R., & Zan, B. (1994). *Moral classrooms, moral children.* New York: Teachers College Press.

DeVries, R., Zan, B., & Hildebrandt, C. (2002). Issues in constructivist moral education. *Early Education & Development, 13*(3).

Dobson, J. (2007). *The new strong-willed child.* Wheaton, IL: Tyndale House.

Feeney, S., Christensen, D., & Moravick, E. (2006). *Who am I in the lives of children?* (7th ed.). Upper Saddle River, NJ: Merrill/ Prentice Hall.

Garrett, J. (2006). Educating the whole child. *Kappa Delta Pi Record, 42*(4), 154–155.

Greenberg, P. (1992). Why not academic preschool? (Part 2). Autocracy or democracy in the classroom? *Young Children, 47*(3), 54–64.

Gurian, M. (2001). *Boys and girls learn differently.* San Francisco: Jossey-Bass.

Hanish, L., Barcelo, H., Martin, C., Fabes, R., Holmwall, J., & Palermo, F. (2007). Using the Q-connectivity method to study frequency of interaction with multiple peer triads: Do preschoolers' peer group interactions at school relate to academic skills? *New Directions for Child and Adolescent Development, 118*, 9–24.

Howes, D., & Ritchie, S. (2002). *A matter of trust: Connecting teachers and learners in the early childhood classroom.* New York: Teachers College Press.

Jablon, J., Dombro, A., & Dichtelmiller, M. (2007). *The power of observation.* Washington, DC: National Association for the Education of Young Children.

Kaiser, B., & Rasminsky, J. (2006). *Challenging behavior in young children: Understanding, preventing and responding effectively* (2nd ed.). Boston: Allyn & Bacon.

Kamii, C. (1982). Autonomy as the aim of education: Implications of Piaget's theory. In C. Kamii (Ed.), *Number in preschool and kindergarten* (pp. 73–87). Washington, DC: National Association for the Education of Young Children.

Kamii, C. (1984). Obedience is not enough. *Young Children, 39*(4), 11–14.

Kamii, C., & Ewing, J. K. (1996). Basing teaching on Piaget's constructivism. *Childhood Education, 72*(5), 260–264.

Knafo, A., & Plomin, R. (2006). Parental discipline and affection and children's prosocial behavior: Genetic and environmental links. *Journal of Personality and Social Psychology, 90*(1), 147–164.

Kohn, A. (2005). *Unconditional parenting: Moving from rewards and punishment to love and reason.* New York: Atria Books.

Landy, S. (2002). *Pathways to competence: Encouraging healthy social and emotional development in young children.* Baltimore: Paul H. Brookes.

Lapsley, D. (2006). Moral stage theory. In M. Killen & J. Smetana (Eds.), *Handbook of moral development* (pp. 37–66). Mahwah, NJ: Lawrence Erlbaum Associates.

Leman, K. (2005). *Making children mind without losing yours.* Grand Rapids, MI: Baker Publishing.

National Scientific Council on the Developing Child. (2007). The science of early childhood development. Available online at http//www.developingchild.net.

Noddings, N. (2005). *The challenge to care in schools: An alternative approach to education* (2nd ed.). New York: Teachers College Press.

Piaget, J. (1965). *The moral judgment of the child.* New York: Free Press. (Originally published in 1932.)

Smetana, J. (2006). Social-cognitive domain theory: Consistencies and variations in children's moral and social judgments. In M. Killen & J. Smetana (Eds.), *Handbook of moral development* (pp. 119–154). Mahwah, NJ: Lawrence Erlbaum.

Shonkoff, J. P., & Meisels, S. J. (Eds.). (2000). *Handbook of early childhood intervention* (2nd ed.). Cambridge, UK: Cambridge University Press.

Sigsgaard, E. (2005). *Scolding: Why it hurts more than it helps.* New York: Teachers College Press.

Spinrad, T. L., & Eisenberg, N. (in press). Empathy, prosocial behavior, and positive development in the schools. In R. Gilman, E. S. Heubner, & M. Furlong (Eds.), *Handbook of positive psychology in the schools.* Mahwah, New Jersey: Erlbaum.

Swick, K., & Freeman, N. (2004). Nurturing peaceful children to create a caring world: The role of families and communities. *Childhood Education, 80*(1), 2–8.

Turiel, E. (2006). Thought, emotions, and social interactional processes in moral development. In M. Killen & J. Smetana (Eds.), *Handbook of moral development* (pp. 7–36). Mahwah, NJ: Lawrence Erlbaum.

Tzuo, P. (2007). The tension between teacher control and child freedom in a child-centered classroom: Resolving the practical dilemma through a closer look at the related theories. *Early Childhood Education Journal, 35*(1), 33–39.

CHAPTER 2

Adler, A. (1917). *Study of organ inferiority and its psychological compensation.* New York: Nervous Disease Publications.

Ainsworth, M. D. S., Blehar, M. C., Waters, E., & Wall, S. (1978). *Patterns of attachment.* Hillsdale, NJ: Erlbaum.

Berger, K. S. (2007). Update on bullying at school: Science forgotten? *Developmental Review, 27,* 90–126.

Berk, L. E. (2007). *Infants, children, and adolescents.* Boston: Allyn & Bacon.

Bhattacharya, J., & Currie, J. (2001). Youths and nutrition risk: Malnourished or misnourished? In J. Gruber (Ed.), *Risky behavior among youths: An economic analysis* (pp. 438–521). Chicago: National Bureau of Economic Research, University of Chicago Press.

Denham, S. A. (2007). Dealing with feelings: How children negotiate the worlds of emotions and social relationships. *Cognition, Brain, Behaviour, 11*(1), 1–48.

Dreikurs, R. (1964). *Children: The challenge.* New York: Hawthorne Books. (1991 edition published by Plume.)

Eisenberg, N. (2004). Emotion-related regulation: An emerging construct. *Merrill-Palmer Quarterly, 50*(3), 236–259.

Eisenberg, N., Eggum, N. D., & Vaughan-Edwards. (in press). Relations of self-regulatory capacities to maladjustment, social competence, and emotionality. In R. Hoyle (Ed.), *Handbook of personality and self-regulation*. Malden, MA: Blackwell.

Elias, M. J., & Arnold, H. (Eds.). (2006). *The educator's guide to emotional intelligence and academic achievement*. Thousand Oaks, CA: Corwin Press.

Erikson, E. (1963). *Childhood and society* (2nd ed.). New York: Norton.

Flook, L. R., Repetti, R., & Ullman, J. (2005). Classroom social experiences as predictors of academic performance. *Developmental Psychology, 41*(2), 319–327.

Fonagy, P., Twemlow, S. W., Vernberg, E., Sacco, F. C., & Little, T. D. (2005). Creating a peaceful school learning environment: The impact of an antibullying program on educational attainment in elementary schools. *Medical Science Monitor, 11*(7), 317–325.

Gartrell, D., & Sonsteng, K. (2008). Promote physical activity—it's proactive guidance. *Young Children, 63*(2), pp. 51–53.

Gottman, J. (1997). *Raising an emotionally intelligent child*. New York: Fireside.

Gottman, J. M. (2004). *What am I feeling?* Seattle, WA: Parenting Press.

Gurian, M. (2001). *Boys and girls learn differently*. San Francisco: Jossey-Bass.

Hyson, M. C. (2004). *The emotional development of young children: Building an emotion-centered curriculum*. New York: Teachers College Press.

Jelalian, E., & Steele R. G. (Eds.). (2008). *Handbook of childhood and adolescent obesity: Issues in clinical child psychology*. New York: Springer.

Koplow, L. (2002). *Creating schools that heal: Real-life solutions*. New York: Teachers College Press.

Landy, S. (2002). *Pathways to competence: Encouraging healthy social and emotional development in young children*. Baltimore: Paul H. Brookes.

Levin, D. E. (2004). Beyond banning war and superhero play: Meeting children's needs in violent times. In D. Koralek (Ed.), *Spotlight on young children and play*. Washington, DC: National Association for the Education of Young Children.

Macklem, G. L. (2008). *Practitioner's guide to emotion regulation in school-aged children*. New York: Springer Science.

NAEYC. (2008). *NAEYC position statement on developmentally appropriate practice in early childhood programs serving children birth through age 8*. Washington, DC: Author.

Riley, D., San Juan, R., Klinkner, J., & Ramminger, A. (2008). *Social and emotional development: Connecting science and practice in early childhood settings*. St. Paul, MN: Redleaf Press.

Rothbart, M. K., & Bates, J. E. (2006). Temperament. In W. Damon, R. L. Lerner (Series Eds.), & N. Eisenberg (Vol. Ed.), *Handbook of child psychology: Vol. 3: Social, emotional, and personality development* (6th ed., pp. 99–166). New York: Wiley.

Watson, M. (2003, July). Attachment theory and challenging behaviors: Reconstructing the nature of relationships. *Young Children*, 12–20.

CHAPTER 3

Ashiabi, G. (2007). Play in the preschool classroom: Its socioemotional significance and the teacher's role in play. *Early Childhood Education Journal, 35*(2), 199–207.

Barrera, I., & Corso, R. M., with D. Macpherson. (2003). *Skilled dialogue: Strategies for responding to cultural diversity in early childhood*. Baltimore, MD: Paul H. Brookes.

Berk, L. E. (2002). *Infants, children, and Adolescents*. Boston: Allyn & Bacon.

Bloom, A. (2007, September 7). Insight into the minds of 5-year-olds. *The Times Educational Supplement, 4753*, p. 12.

Bodrova, E., & Leong, D. J. (2007). *Tools of the mind: The Vygotskian approach to early childhood education* (2nd ed.). Upper Saddle River, NJ: Merrill/Prentice Hall.

Corso, W. A. (2003). *We're friends, right? Inside kids'culture*. Washington, DC: Joseph Henry Press.

Denham, S., Mason, T., Caverly, S., Schmidt, M., Hackney, R., Cameron, C., & DeMulder, E. (2001). Preschoolers at play: Co-socialisers of emotional and social competence. *International Journal of Behavioral Development, 25*(4), 290–301.

DeVries, R., Hildebrandt, C., & Zan, B. (2000). Constructivist early education for moral development. *Early Education & Development, 11*(1), 10–35.

DeVries, R., & Zan, B. (1994). *Moral classrooms, moral children.* New York: Teachers College Press.

deWaal, F. (2008). Putting the altruism back into altruism: The evolution of empathy. *Annual Review of Psychology, 59,* 279–300.

Dunn, J. (2006). Moral development in early childhood and social interaction in the family. In M. Killen & J. Smetana (Eds.), *Handbook of moral development* (pp. 331–350). Mahwah, NJ: Lawrence Erlbaum.

Eisenberg, N., & Eggum, N. D. (2007). Empathy-related and prosocial responding: Conceptions and correlates during development. In B. A. Sullivan, M. Snyder, & J. L. Sullivan (Eds.), *Cooperation: The political psychology of effective human interaction* (pp. 53–74). Malden, MA: Blackwell.

Flavell, J. H., & Hartman, B. M. (2004). Research in review: What children know about mental experiences. *Young Children, 59*(2).

Flicker, E. S., & Hoffman, J. A. (2002). Developmental discipline in the early childhood classroom. *Young Children, 57*(5).

Flicker, E. S., & Hoffman, J. A. (2002). Developmental discipline in the early childhood classroom. New York: Teachers College Press.

Gonzalez-Mena, J. (2008). *Diversity in early care and education: Honoring differences.* New York: McGraw-Hill.

Gredler, M., & Shields, C. (2008). *Vygotsky's legacy: A foundation for research and practice.* New York: Guilford Press.

Gurian, M. (2001). *Boys and girls learn differently.* San Francisco: Jossey-Bass.

Hanish, L., Barcelo, H., Martin, C., Fabes, R., Holmwall, J., & Palermo, F. (2007). Using the Q-connectivity method to study frequency of interaction with multiple peer triads: Do preschoolers' peer group interactions at school relate to academic skills? *New Directions for Child and Adolescent Development, 118,* 9–24.

Haskett, J., & Willoughby, M. (2007). Paths to child social adjustment: Parenting duality and children's processing of social information. *Child: Care, Health and Development, 33*(1), 67–77.

Hoffman, M., & Powlishta, K. (2001). Gender segregation in childhood: A test of the interaction style theory. *Journal of Genetic Psychology, 162*(3), 298–313.

Howes, C. (1988). Same- and cross-sex friends: Implications for interaction and social skills. *Early Childhood Research Quarterly, 3,* 21–37.

Howes, D., & Ritchie, S. (2002). *A matter of trust: Connecting teachers and learners in the early childhood classroom.* New York: Teachers College Press.

Hyson, M. C. (2004). *The emotional development of young children: Building an emotion-centered curriculum.* New York: Teachers College Press.

Jablon, J., Dombro, A., & Dichtelmiller, M. (2007). *The power of observation.* Washington, DC: National Association for the Education of Young Children.

Jalongo, M. R., & Isenberg, J. P. (2004). *Exploring your role: A practitioner's introduction to early childhood education.* Columbus, OH: Merrill/Prentice Hall.

Johnson, C., Ironsmith, M., Snow, C. W., & Poteat, G. M. (2000). Peer acceptance and social adjustment in preschool and kindergarten. *Early Childhood Education Journal, 27*(4), 207–212.

Kaiser, B., & Rasminsky, J. S. (2003). Opening the culture door. *Young Children, 58*(4), 53–56.

Kemple, K. (2004). *Let's be friends: Peer competencies and social inclusion in early childhood programs.* New York: Teachers College Press.

King, M., & Gartrell, D. (2003). Building an encouraging classroom with boys in mind. *Young Children, 58*(4), 33–36.

Kohn, A. (2005). *Unconditional parenting: Moving from rewards and punishment to love and reason.* New York: Atria Books.

Koplow, L. (2002). *Creating schools that heal: Real-life solutions.* New York: Teachers College Press.

Landy, S. (2002). *Pathways to competence: Encouraging healthy social and emotional development in young children.* Baltimore: Paul H. Brookes.

Lapsley, D. (2006). Moral stage theory. In M. Killen & J. Smetana (Eds.), *Handbook of moral development* (pp. 37–66). Mahwah, NJ: Lawrence Erlbaum Associates.

Lillard, A., & Curenton, S. (1999). Do young children understand what others feel, want, and know? *Young Children, 554*(5), 52–57.

National Association for the Education of Young Children. (2005). Code of Ethical Conduct & Statement of Commitment. Washington, DC: NAEYC.

Noddings, N. (2005). *The challenge to care in schools: An alternative approach to education* (2nd ed.). New York: Teachers College Press.

Noddings, N. (2008). All our students thinking. *Educational Leadership, 65*(5), 8–13.

Paley, V. G. (1999). *The kindness of children.* Cambridge, MA: Harvard University Press.

Pass, S. (2004). *Parallel paths to constructivism: Jean Piaget and Lev Vygotsky.* Greenwich, CT: Information Age Publishing.

Pettit, R. W., & Sugawara, A. I. (2002). Age, gender, socioeconomic status, race/ethnicity, temperament, and actual social cognitive competence as factors contributing to preservice teachers' perceptions of preschool children's social and cognitive competence. *Journal of Early Childhood Teacher Education, 23*(2), 125–136.

Piaget, J. (1960). *The child's conception of the world.* Totowa, NJ: Littlefield, Adams. (Original work published in 1929.)

Piaget, J. (1964). *Judgment and reasoning in the child.* Totowa, NJ: Littlefield, Adams. (Originally published in 1928.)

Piaget, J. (1965). *The moral judgment of the child.* New York: Free Press. (Originally published in 1932.)

Powlishta, K. K. (1995). Gender segregation among children: Understanding the "Cootie phenomenon." *Young Children, 50*(4), 61–69.

Ramsey, P. G. (1991). Making friends in school: *Promoting peer relationships in early childhood.* New York: Teachers College Press.

Riley, D., San Juan, R., Klinkner, J., & Ramminger, A. (2008). *Social and emotional development: Connecting science and practice in early childhood settings.* St. Paul, MN: Redleaf Press.

Russell, A., Hart, C. H., Robinson, C. C., & Olsen, S. F. (2003). Children's sociable and aggressive behavior with peers: A comparison of the U.S. and Australia, and contributions of temperament and parenting styles.

International Journal of Behavioral Development, 27, 74–86.

Selman, R. L. (1980). *The growth of interpersonal understanding.* New York: Academic Press.

Selman, R., & Schultz, L. (1990). *Making a friend in Youth: Developmental theory and pair therapy.* Chicago: University of Chicago Press.

Siccone, F., & Lopez, L. (2000). *Educating the heart: Lessons to build respect and responsibility.* Boston: Allyn & Bacon.

Smetana, J. (2006). Social-cognitive domain theory: Consistencies and variations in children's moral and social judgments. In M. Killen & J. Smetana (Eds.), *Handbook of moral development* (pp. 119–154). Mahwah, NJ: Lawrence Erlbaum.

Spinrad, T. L., & Eisenberg, N. (in press). Empathy, prosocial behavior, and positive development in the schools. In R. Gilman, E. S. Heubner, & M. Furlong (Eds.), *Handbook of positive psychology in the schools.* Mahwah, New Jersey: Erlbaum.

Valiente, C., Eisenberg, N., Fabes, R., Shepard, S., Cumberland, A., & Losoya, S. (2004). Prediction of children's empathy related responding from their effortful control and parents' expressivity. *Developmental Psychology, 40*(6), 911–926.

Vygotsky, L. S. (1962). *Thought and language* (E. Hanfmann & G. Vokar, trans.). Cambridge, MA: MIT Press. (Original work published in 1934.)

Vygotsky, L. S. (1978). Mind and society: The development of higher mental processes. Cambridge, MA: Harvard University Press.

Wadsworth, B. (2004). *Piaget's theory of cognitive and affective development: Foundations of constructivism* (5th ed.). Allyn & Bacon.

Wall, E. (2008). Teaching to the testosterone. *The New York Times Magazine,* March 2, 2008. p. 28.

Wheeler, E. J. (2004). *Conflict resolution in early childhood: Helping children understand and resolve conflicts.* Columbus, OH: Merrill/Prentice Hall.

Yanghee, A. K. (2003). Necessary social skills related to peer acceptance. *Childhood Education, 79*(4), 234–238.

CHAPTER 4

Arbeau, K., & Coplan, R. J. (2007). Kindergarten teachers' beliefs and responses to hypothetical prosocial, asocial, and antisocial children. *Merrill-Palmer Quarterly, 53*(2), 291–318.

Barry, E. (2006). Children's memory: A primer for understanding behavior. *Early Childhood Education Journal, 33*(6), 405–411.

Bransford, J. D., Brown, A., & Cocking, R. (Eds.). (2000). *How people learn: Mind, brain, experience and school.* Washington, DC: National Academy Press.

Brumbaugh, E. (2008). DAP in ECE: Respect. *Kappa Delta Pi Record, 44*(4), 170–175.

Conrad, D. J. (2008). An early start: Skill grouping and unequal reading gains in the elementary years. *Sociological Quarterly, 49*(2), 363–394.

Copple, C. (Ed.). (2003). *A world of difference: Readings on teaching young children in a diverse society.* Washington, DC: NAEYC.

Derman-Sparks, L., & Ramsey, P. (2006). *What if all the kids are white? Anti-bias multicultural education with young children and families.* New York: Teachers College Press.

DeVries, R., Hildebrandt, C., & Zan, B. (2000). Constructivist early education for moral development. *Early Education & Development, 11*(1), 10–35.

DeVries, R., & Zan, B. (1994). *Moral classrooms, moral children.* New York: Teachers College Press.

Downer, J. T., Rimm-Kaufman, S. E., & Pianta, R. C. (2007). How do classroom conditions and children's risk for school problems contribute to children's behavioral engagement in learning? *School Psychology Review, 36*(3), 413–432.

Dyson, L. L. (2005). Kindergarten children's understanding of and attitudes toward people with disabilities. *Topics in Early Childhood Special Education, 25*(2), 95–104.

Feeney, S., Christensen, D., & Moravick, E. (2006). *Who am I in the lives of children?* (7th ed.). Upper Saddle River, NJ: Merrill/Prentice Hall.

Fox, L., & Lentini, R. H. (2006). You got it! Teaching social and emotional skills. *Young Children, 61*(6), 36–4.

Greenman, J. (2005). *Caring spaces, learning places: Children's environments that work.* Redmond, WA: Exchange Press, Inc.

Hansen, C., & Zambo, D. (2007). Loving and learning with Wemberly and David: Fostering emotional development in early childhood education. *Early Childhood Education Journal, 34*(4), 273–278.

Hatherly, A. (2006). The stories we share. Using narrative assessment to build communities of literacy participants in early childhood centers. *Australian Journal of Early Childhood, 31*(1), 27–34.

Honig, A. S. (2004, March/April). How to create an environment that counteracts stereotyping. *Child Care Information Exchange, 156.*

Howes, D., & Ritchie, S. (2002). *A matter of trust: Connecting teachers and learners in the early childhood classroom.* New York: Teachers College Press.

Kantrowitz, E. J., & Evans, G. W. (2004). The relation between the ratio of children per activity area and off-task behavior and type of play in day care centers. *Environment and Behavior, 36*(4), 541–557.

Kirmani, M. H. (2007). Empowering culturally and linguistically diverse children and families. *Young Children, 62*(6), 94–98.

Koplow, L. (2002). *Creating schools that heal: Real-life solutions.* New York: Teachers College Press.

Lehman, B. J., & Repetti, R. L. (2007). Bad days don't end when the school bell rings: The lingering effects of negative school events on children mood, self esteem and perceptions of parent-child interaction. *Social Development, 16*(3), 506–618.

LoCasale-Crouch, J., Konold, T., Pianta, R., Howes, C., Burchinal, M., Bryant, D., Clifford, R., Early, D., & Barbarin, O. (2007). Profiles of observed classroom quality in state-funded pre-kindergarten programs and associations with teacher, program, and classroom characteristics. *Early Childhood Research Quarterly, 22*(1), 3–17.

Long, S., Volk, D., & Gregory, E. (2007). Intentionality and expertise: Learning from observations of children at play in multilingual, multicultural context. *Anthropology & Education Quarterly, 38*(3), 239–259.

Maxwell, L. E. (2007). Competency in child care settings: The role of the physical environment. *Environment and Behavior, 39*(2), 229–245.

Maxwell, L. E., & Chmielewski, E. J. (2008). Environmental personalization and elementary school children's self-esteem. *Journal of Environmental Psychology, 28*(2), 143–153.

Miller, R., & Pedro, J. (2006). Creating respectful classroom environments. *Early Childhood Education Journal, 33*(5), 293–299.

Noddings, N. (2005). *The challenge to care in schools: An alternative approach to education* (2nd ed.). New York: Teachers College Press.

Reynolds, E. (2000). *Guiding young children: A problem-solving approach.* New York: McGraw-Hill.

Rightmyer, E. C. (2003). Democratic discipline: Children creating solutions. *Young Children, 58*(4), 38–45.

Seefeldt, C. (2002). *Creating rooms of wonder: Valuing and displaying children's work to enhance the learning process.* Beltsville, MD: Gryphon House, Inc.

Sink, C. A., Edwards, C. N., & Weir, S. J. (2007). Helping children transition from kindergarten to first grade. *Professional School Counseling, 10*(3), 233–237.

Styles, D. (2001). *Class meetings: Building leadership, problem-solving, and decision making in the respectful classroom.* Markam, Ontario: Pembroke. (Distributed in the U.S. by Stenhouse.)

Szente, J. (2007). Empowering young children for success in school and in life. *Early Childhood Education Journal, 34*(6), 449–453.

Tabors, P. O. (1998). What early childhood educators need to know: Developing effective programs for linguistically and culturally diverse children and families. *Young Children, 53*(6), 20–26.

Tomlinson, C. (2003). Deciding to teach them all. *Educational Leadership, 61*(2), 5–11.

Vance, E., & Weaver, P. (2002). *Class meetings: Young children solving problems together.* Washington, DC: NAEYC.

Volante, L. (2008). Equity in multicultural student assessment. *Journal of Educational Thought, 42*(1), 11–26.

Wasik, B. (2008). When fewer is more: Small groups in early childhood classrooms. *Early Childhood Education Journal, 35*(6), 515–521.

Watson, M., & Battistich, V. (2006). *Building and sustaining caring communities.* In C. M. Evertson & C. S. Weinstein (Eds.), *Handbook of classroom management: Research practice and contemporary issues* (pp. 253–280). Mahwah, NJ: Lawrence Erlbaum Associates.

Wilson, K. H., Pianta, R. C., & Stuhlman, M. (2007). Typical classroom experience in first grade: The role of classroom climate and functional risk in the development of social competencies. *The Elementary School Journal, 108*(5), 461–465.

Zan, B., & Hildebrant, C. (2003). First graders understanding during cooperative and competitive games. *Early Education and Development, 14*(4), 397–410.

CHAPTER 5

Bartel, V. B. (2005). Learning communities: Beliefs embedded in content-based rituals. *Early Childhood Education Journal, 33*(3), 151–154.

Beneke, S. J., Ostrosky, M. M., & Katz, L. (2008). Calendar time for young children: Good intentions gone awry. *YC Young Children, 63*(3), 12–16.

Bodrova, E., & Leong, D. J. (2007). *Tools of the mind: The Vygotskian approach to early childhood education* (2nd ed.). Upper Saddle River, NJ: Merrill/Prentice Hall.

Boyd, J., Barnett, S. W., Bodrova, E., Leong, D. J., & Gomby, D. (2005). *Promoting children's social and emotional development through preschool education.* National Institute for Early Education Research.

Christie, J., Enz, B. J., & Vukelich, C. (2006). *Teaching language and literacy: Pre-school through the elementary grades* (3rd ed.). New York: Allyn & Bacon (Addison-Wesley-Longman).

Cohen, C., Onunaku, N., Clothier, S., & Poppe, J. (2005). *Helping young children succeed: Strategies to promote early childhood social and emotional development.* (Research and Policy Report). Washington, DC: National Conference of State Legislatures.

Dark, D. (2007, October). Making "cute" count. *Teaching Children Mathematics,* 153–159.

DeVries, R. (2001). Constructivist education in preschool and elementary school: The sociomoral atmosphere as the first educational goal. In S. L. Golbeck (Ed.), *Psychological perspectives on early childhood education: Reframing dilemmas in research and practice* (pp. 153–180). Mahwah, NJ: Erlbaum.

DeVries, R., & Zan, B. (1994). *Moral classrooms, moral children.* New York: Teachers College Press.

Epstein, A. S. (2008). An early start on thinking. *Educational Leadership, 65*(5), 38–42.

Feeney, S., Christensen, D., & Moravick, E. (2006). *Who am I in the lives of children?* (7th ed.). Upper Saddle River, NJ: Merrill/Prentice Hall.

Fields, M., Groth, L., & Spangler, K. (2008). *Let's begin reading right: A developmental approach to emergent literacy.* Columbus, OH: Merrill/Prentice Hall.

Hemmeter, M. L., Ostrosky, M. M., Artman, K. M., & Kinder, K. A. (2008). Moving right along: Planning transitions to prevent challenging behavior. *YC Young Children, 63*(3), 18–25.

Hyson, M. C. (2004). *The emotional development of young children: Building an emotion centered curriculum.* New York: Teachers College Press.

Jalongo, M. R. (2007). Beyond benchmarks and scores: Reasserting the role of motivation and interest in children's academic achievement. An ACEI position paper. *Childhood Education,* International Focus Issue, Association of Children's Education International.

Jalongo, M. R., & Isenberg, J. P. (2004). *Exploring your role: A practitioner's introduction to early childhood education.* Columbus, OH: Merrill/Prentice Hall.

Jenson, E. (2006). *Enriching the brain: How to maximize every learner's potential.* San Francisco: Jossey-Bass.

Justice, L. M., Pence, K., Bowles, R. B., & Wiggins, A. (2006). An investigation of four hypotheses concerning the order by which 4-year-old children learn the alphabet letter. *Early Childhood Research Quarterly, 21*(3), 374–389.

Kagan, S. L., & Scott-Little, C. (2004). Early learning standards: Changing the parlance and practice of early childhood education. *Phi Delta Kappan, 85*(5), 388–396.

Kamii, C. (2000). *Young children reinvent arithmetic: Implications of Piaget's theory.* New York: Teachers College Press.

Katz, L. G., & Chard, S. C. (1989/2000). *Engaging children's minds: The project approach.* Norwood, NJ: Ablex.

Koplow, L. (2002). *Creating schools that heal: Real-life solutions.* New York: Teachers College Press.

Loughran, S. B. (2005). Thematic teaching in action. *Kappa Delta Pi Record, 41*(3), 112–117.

Marcon, R. A. (2002). Moving up the grades: Relationship between preschool model and later school success. *Early Childhood Research and Practice, 4*(1). Available online at http://ecrp.uiuc.edu/v4n1/marcon.html.

Michaels, S., Shouse, A. W., & Schweingruber, H. A. (2008). *Ready, set, science! Putting research to work in K–8 science classrooms.* Board on Science Education, Center for Education, Division of Behavioral and Social Sciences and Education. Washington, DC: The National Academies Press.

National Association for the Education of Young Children. (2006). *Accreditation standards for early childhood programs.* Washington, DC: Author.

National Association for the Education Young Children/National Association Early Childhood Specialists in State Departments of Education. (2003). *Early childhood curriculum, assessment, and program evaluation: Building an effective accountability system in programs birth through age 8.* Washington, DC: Author.

National Council of Teachers of Mathematics. (2000). *Principles and standards for school mathematics.* Reston, VA: Author.

National Research Council. (2005). *How students learn: History, mathematics, and science in the classroom.* Washington, DC: National Academies Press.

Nelson, K. (2007). *Young minds in social worlds: Experience, meaning and memory.* Cambridge, MA: Harvard University Press.

Noddings, N. (2005). *The challenge to care in schools: An alternative approach to education* (2nd ed.). New York: Teachers College Press.

Piaget, J. (1970, c1969). *The child's conception of time.* (A. J. Pomerans, Trans.). New York: Basic Books.

Riggins-Newby, C. (2005). They're not just playing. *Principal Magazine, 85*(1), 8.

Ruckman, A. Y., Burts, D. C., & Pierce, S. H. (1999). Observed stress behaviors of 1st-grade children participating in more and less developmentally appropriate activities in a computer-based literacy laboratory. *Journal of Research in Childhood Education, 14*(1), 36–46.

Shan, L. S., & Reichel, A. G. (2008). Read all about it! A classroom newspaper integrates the curriculum. *YC Young Children, 63*(2), 12–18.

Tishman, S. (2008). The object of their attention. *Educational Leadership, 65*(5), 44–46.

Vespo, J. E., Capece, D., & Behforooz, B. (2006). Effects of a nurturing curriculum on social, emotional, and academic behaviors in kindergarten classrooms. *Journal of Research in Childhood Education, 20*(4), 275–285.

Vygotsky, L. S. (1978). *Mind and society: The development of higher mental processes.* Cambridge, MA: Harvard University Press. (Original work published in 1933.)

Weber, E. (2002). Rules, right and wrong and children. *Early Childhood Education Journal, 30*(2), 107–111.

Wilson, K. H., Pianta, R. C., & Stuhlman, M. (2007). Typical classroom experience in first grade: The role of classroom climate and functional risk in the development of social competencies. *The Elementary School Journal, 108*(5), 461–465.

Zaslow, M., & Martinex-Beck, I. (2006). *Critical issues in early childhood professional development.* Baltimore: Paul H. Brooks.

CHAPTER 6

Bandura, A. (1986). *Social foundations of thought and action: A social cognitive theory.* Englewood Cliffs, NJ: Prentice Hall.

Barrera, I., & Corso, R. M., with D. Macpherson. (2003). *Skilled dialogue: Strategies for responding to cultural diversity in early childhood.* Baltimore, MD: Paul H. Brookes.

Berger, K. S. (2007). Update on bullying at school: Science forgotten? *Developmental Review, 27*, 90–126.

Betts, L. R., & Rottenberg, K. J. (2007). Trustworthiness, friendships and self-control: Factors that contribute to young children's school adjustment. *Infant and Child Development, 16*, 491–508.

Brady, K., Forton, M. B., Porter, D., & Wood, C. (2003). *Rules in school.* Greenfield, MA: Northeast Foundation for Children.

Brazelton, T. B., & Greenspan, S. I. (2000). *The irreducible needs of children: What every child must have to grow, learn, and flourish.* Cambridge, MA: Perseus Books.

Byrne, R. W. (2005). Social cognition: Imitation, imitation, imitation. *Current Biology, 15*(13), 498–500.

Committee for Children. (2003). *Second step: A violence-prevention curriculum.* Seattle, WA: Committee for Children.

De Schipper, E. J., Riksen-Walraven, J. M. A., Geurts, S. A. E., & Derksen, J. (2008). General mood of professional caregivers in child care centers and the quality of caregiver-child interactions. *Journal of Research in Personality, 42*(3), 515–526.

DeVries, R., & Zan, B. (1994). *Moral classrooms, moral children.* New York: Teachers College Press.

Dweck, C. S. (2007). The perils and promises of praise. *Educational Leadership, 65*(2), 34–39.

Erikson, E. (1963). *Childhood and society* (2nd ed.). New York: Norton.

Fields, M., Groth, L., & Spangler, K. (2008). *Let's begin reading right: A developmental approach to emergent literacy.* Columbus, OH: Merrill/Prentice Hall.

Gibbs, J. (2001). *Tribes: A new way of learning and being together.* Sausalito, CA: Centersource Systems, LLC.

Gurian, M. (2001). *Boys and girls learn differently.* San Francisco: Jossey-Bass.

Hansen, C., & Zambo, D. (2007). Loving and learning with Wemberly and David: Fostering emotional development in early childhood education. *Early Childhood Education Journal, 34*(4), 273–278.

Hesse, P., & Lane, F. (2003). Media literacy starts young: An integrated curriculum approach. *Young Children, 58*(6), 20–26.

Hyson, M. C. (2004). *The emotional development of young children: Building an emotion centered curriculum.* New York: Teachers College Press.

Hyson, M. C. (2008). *Enthusiastic and engaged learners: Approaches to learning in the early childhood classroom.* New York: Teachers College Press.

Hyson, M. C., & Molinaro, J. (2001). Learning through feeling: Children's development, teachers' beliefs and relationships, and classroom practices. In S. L. Golbeck (Ed.),

Psychological perspectives on early childhood education: Reframing dilemmas in research and practice (pp. 107–130). Mahwah, NJ: Erlbaum.

Kamii, C., Long, R., & Manning, M. (2001). Kindergartners' development toward "invented" spelling and a glottographic theory. *Linguistics & Education, 12*(2), 195–210.

Kochenderfer-Ladd, B., & Pelletier, E. M. (2008). Teachers' views and beliefs about bullying: Influences on classroom management strategies and students' coping with peer victimization. *Journal of School Psychology, 46*(4), 431–453.

The Lancet. (2002, September 28). Selling to— and selling out—children. *The Lancet, 360*(9338), 959.

Landy, S. (2002). *Pathways to competence: Encouraging healthy social and emotional development in young children.* Baltimore: Paul H. Brookes.

Lantieri, L. (2003). Waging peace in our schools: The resolving conflict creatively program. In M. J. Elias, H. Arnold, & C. S. Hussey (Eds.), *Best leadership practices for caring and successful schools* (pp. 76–88). Thousand Oaks, CA: Corwin Press.

Levin, D. E. (2004). Beyond banning war and superhero play: Meeting children's needs in violent times. In D. Koralek (Ed.), *Spotlight on young children and play.* Washington, DC: National Association for the Education of Young Children.

Linn, S. (2004). *Consuming Kids: The Hostile Takeover of Childhood.* New York: The New Press.

McKay, G. D., & Maybelle, S. (2004). *Calming the Family Storm.* Atascadero, CA: Impact Publishers.

Meltzoff, A. N. (2007). "Like me": A foundation for social cognition. *Developmental Science, 10*(1), 126–134.

Nielson, M., & Christie, T. (2008). Adult modeling facilitates young children's generation of novel pretend acts. *Infant and Child Development, 17*, 151–162.

Osofsky, J. D. (1997). *Children in a violent society.* New York: Guildford Publishers.

Paley, V. G. (1999). *The kindness of children.* Cambridge, MA: Harvard University Press.

Pfeifer, J. H., Iacoboni, M., Mazziotta, J. C., & Dapretto, M. (2008). Mirroring others' emotions relates to empathy and interpersonal competence in children. *NeuroImage, 39*(4), 2076–2085.

Plattner, I. E. (2003). Granting children their emotions. *Child Care Information Exchange, 152,* 34–36.

Rimm-Kaufman, S. E., Fan, X., Chiu, Y., & You, W. (2007). The contributions of the responsive classroom approach on children's academic achievement: Results for a three year longitudinal study. *Journal of School Psychology, 45*(4), 401–421.

Sanders, M. R., Pidgeon, A., Gravestock, F., Connors, M. D., Brown, S., & Young, R. (2004). Does parental attributional retraining and anger management enhance the effects of the Triple P-Positive Parenting Program with parents at-risk of child maltreatment? *Behavior Therapy, 35*(3), 513–535.

Shayla-Holub, C., Tisak, M., & Mullins, D. (2008). Gender differences in children's hero attributions: Personal hero choices and evaluations of typical male and female heroes. *Sex Roles, 58*(7), 567–578.

Shore, J. B. (2004). *Born to buy: The commercialized child and the new consumer culture.* New York: Scribner.

Siccone, F., & Lopez, L. (2000). *Educating the heart: Lessons to build respect and responsibility.* Boston: Allyn & Bacon.

Sinclair, S., Dunn, E., & Lowery, B. (2005). The relationship between parental racial attitudes and children's implicit prejudice. *Journal of Experimental Social Psychology, 41*(3), 283–289.

Teaching Tolerance. (1997). *Starting small: Teaching tolerance in preschool and the early grades.* Montgomery, AL: The Southern Poverty Law Center.

Weber, E. (2002). Rules, right and wrong and children. *Early Childhood Education Journal, 30*(2), 107–111.

Wheeler, E. J. (2004). *Conflict resolution in early childhood: Helping children understand and resolve conflicts.* Columbus, OH: Merrill/Prentice Hall.

Wilson, B. J. (2008). Media and children's aggression, fear, and altruism. *Future of Children, 18*(1), 87–118.

Children's Literature—Chapter 6

Alexander, M. G. (2005). *Nobody asked me if I wanted a baby sister.* Watertown, MA: Charlesbridge.

Aliki. (1995). *Best friends together again.* New York: Greenwillow.

Armstrong, J. (2006). *Once upon a banana.* New York: Simon & Schuster.

Arnold, T. (2006). *Hi! Fly guy.* New York: Scholastic.

Bang, M. (1999). *When Sophie gets angry . . . really, really angry.* New York: Scholastic.

Beaumont, J. K. (2006). *Move over rover.* Orlando, Florida: Harcourt, Inc.

Beaumont, K. (2005). *I ain't gonna paint no more!* San Diego: Harcourt.

Carle, E. (1977). *The grouchy ladybug.* New York: HarperCollins.

Corey, D. (1992). *Will there be a lap for me?* Morton Grove, IL: Albert Whitman.

Cosby, B. (1997). *The meanest thing to say.* New York: Scholastic Inc.

Curtis, J. (1998). *Today I feel silly: And other moods that make my day.* New York: HarperCollins.

dePaola, T. (1979). *Oliver Button is a sissy.* San Diego: Voyager/Harcourt Brace Jovanovich.

Falconer, I. (2000). *Olivia.* New York: Simon & Schuster.

Havill, J. (1987). *Jamaica's find.* Boston, MA: Houghton.

Henkes, K. (1987). *Sheila Ray, the brave.* New York: Greenwillow Books.

Henkes, K. (1991). *Chrysanthemum.* New York: Greenwillow.

Henkes, K. (1996). *Lilly's purple plastic purse.* New York: Greenwillow Books.

Hoff, S. (1985). *Who will be my friends?* New York: HarperCollins.

Howe, J. (2003). *Horace and Morris but mostly Dolores.* New York: Aladdin Library.

Interater, R. G. (2000). *Two eyes a nose and a mouth.* New York: Scholastic.

Keats, E. J. (2004). *Louie.* USA: Puffin.

Krasny-Brown, L. (2001). *How to be a friend: A guide to making friends and keeping them.* New York: Little Brown.

Lester, H. (1999). *Hooway for Woodney Wat.* New York: Houghton Mifflin Company.

Leventhal-Belfer, L. (2008). *Do I have to? A book for children who find themselves frustrated by everyday rules.* London: Jessica Kingsley.

Muldoon, K. M. (1989). *Princess Pooh.* Niles, IL: Albert Whitman & Company.

Parish, P. (2003). *Good work, Amelia Bedelia.* New York: Harper Collins.

Parr, J. (2001). *It's okay to be different.* Boston: Little & Brown.

Parr, T. (2005). *The feelings book.* Boston: Little, Brown & Company.

Pfister, M. (1992). *Rainbow fish.* New York: North-South Books.

Portis, A. (2006). *Not a box.* New York Harper Collins.

Spinelli, E. (1998). *Lizzie Logan wears purple sunglasses.* New York: Simon & Schuster.

Steig, W. (1988). *Spinky sulks.* New York: Scholastic.

Steptoe, J. (1987). *Mufaro's beautiful daughter.* New York: Lathrop, Lee, & Shepard.

Vail, R. (2002). *Sometimes I'm a bombaloo.* New York: Scholastic.

Verdick, E. (2000). *Hands are not for hitting.* Minnesota: Free Spirit Publishing.

Verdick, E. (2003). *Teeth are not for biting.* Minnesota: Free Spirit Publishing.

Viorst, J. (1972). *Alexander and the terrible, horrible, no good, very bad day.* New York: Scholastic.

Wells, R. (2002). *Max cleans up.* New York: Viking.

Yashima, T. (1976). *Crow boy.* New York: Puffin/Penguin.

CHAPTER 7

Adams, S. K., & Wittmer, D. S. (2001). I had it first: Teaching young children to solve problems peacefully. *Childhood Education, 78*(1), 10–17.

Arcavi, A., & Isoda, M. (2007). Learning to listen: From historical sources to classroom practice. *Educational Studies in Mathematics, 66,* 111–129.

Bailey, B. (2002). *Easy to love, difficult to discipline: The 7 basic skills for turning conflict into cooperation.* New York: HarperCollins.

Curwin, R. L., & Mendler, A. N. (1999). *Discipline with dignity.* Alexandria, VA: Association for Supervision and Curriculum Development.

Faber, A., & Mazlish, E. (1996). *How to talk so kids can learn at home and in school.* New York: Fireside/Simon & Schuster.

Ginott, H. (1965). *Between parent and child: New solutions to old problems.* New York: Macmillan.

Gordon, T. (1970). *Parent effectiveness training.* New York: Wyden.

Gordon, T. (1974). *T.E.T.: Teacher effectiveness training.* New York: Wyden.

Gordon, T. (1989). *Teaching children self-discipline: At home and at school.* New York: Random House.

Gordon, T., & Sands, J. S. (1976). *P.E.T. in action.* New York: Bantam.

Koplow, L. (2002). *Creating schools that heal: Real-life solutions.* New York: Teachers College Press.

Kreidler, W. J. (1999). *Teaching conflict resolution through children's literature.* New York: Scholastic.

Landy, S. (2002). *Pathways to competence: Encouraging healthy social and emotional development in young children.* Baltimore: Paul H. Brookes.

Lantieri, L. (2003). Waging peace in our schools: The resolving conflict creatively program. In M. J. Elias, H. Arnold, & C. S. Hussey (Eds.), *Best leadership practices for caring and successful schools* (pp. 76–88). Thousand Oaks, CA: Corwin Press.

Levin. D. E. (2003). *Teaching young children in violent times: Building a peaceable classroom* (2nd ed.). Washington, DC: National Association for the Education of Young Children.

Piaget, J. (1965). *The moral judgment of the child.* New York: Free Press. (Originally published in 1932.)

Porter, L. (2000). *Young children's behavior: Practical approaches for caregivers and teachers* (2nd ed.). Baltimore, MD: Paul H. Brookes.

Rightmyer, E. C. (2003). Democratic discipline: Children creating solutions. *Young Children, 58*(4), 38–45.

Rogers, C. (1951). *Client-centered counseling.* Boston: Houghton-Mifflin.

Schmidt, F., & Friedman, A. (1992). *Peacemaking skills for little kids.* Fresno, CA: Peace Works Inc.

Siccone, F., & Lopez, L. (2000). *Educating the heart: Lessons to build respect and responsibility.* Boston: Allyn & Bacon.

Trawick-Smith, J. (2006). Early childhood development: A multicultural perspective. Upper Saddle River, NJ: Merrill/Prentice Hall.

Vance, E., & Weaver, P. (2002). *Class meetings: Young children solving problems together.* Washington, DC: National Association for the Education of Young Children.

Watson, M. (1999). The child development project: Building character by building community. In M. M. Williams & E. Shaps (Eds.), *Character education: The foundation for teacher education* (pp. 24–32). Washington, DC: The Character Education Partnership.

Wheeler, E. J. (2004). *Conflict resolution in early childhood: Helping children understand and resolve conflicts.* Columbus, OH: Merrill/Prentice Hall.

CHAPTER 8

Brady, K., Forton, M. B., Porter, D., & Wood, C. (2003). *Rules in school.* Greenfield, MA: Northeast Foundation for Children.

Charney, R. S. (2002). *Teaching children to care: Classroom management for ethical and academic growth K–8.* Greenfield, MA: Northeast Foundation for Children.

DeVries, R., & Zan, B. (1994). *Moral classrooms, moral children.* New York: Teachers College Press.

Dreikurs, R. (1964). *Children: The challenge.* New York: Hawthorne Books. (1991 edition published by Plume.)

Dreikurs, R. (1966). *Psychology in the classroom.* New York: Harper and Row.

Dreikurs, R., Cassel, P., & Ferguson, E. D. (2004) *Discipline without tears: How to reduce conflict and establish cooperation in the classroom.* Hoboken, NJ: John Wiley & Sons.

Dreikurs, R., Grunwald, B., & Pepper, F. C. (1998). *Maintaining sanity in the classroom: Classroom management techniques.* Philadelphia: Taylor and Francis.

Goodman, J. F. (2006). School discipline in moral disarray. *Journal of Moral Education, 35*(2), 213–230.

Kamii, C. (1982). Autonomy as the aim of education: Implications of Piaget's theory. In C. Kamii (Ed.), *Number in preschool and kindergarten* (pp. 73–87). Washington, DC: National Association for the Education of Young Children.

Piaget, J. (1965). *The moral judgment of the child.* New York: Free Press. (Originally published in 1932.)

Riley, D., San Juan, R., Klinkner, J., & Ramminger, A. (2008). *Social & emotional development: Connecting science and practice in early childhood settings.* St. Paul, MN: Redleaf Press.

Thronberg, R. (2008). School children's reasoning about school rules. *Research Papers in Education, 23*(1), 37–52.

Children's Literature—Chapter 8

Geisel, T. (Dr. Seuss). (1954). *Horton hears a who.* New York: Random House.

CHAPTER 9

Algozzine, K., & Algozzine, B. (2007). Classroom instructional ecology and school-wide positive behavior support. *Journal of Applied School Psychology, 24*(1), 29–47.

Brady, K., Forton, M. B., Porter, D., & Wood, C. (2003). *Rules in school.* Greenfield, MA: Northeast Foundation for Children.

Canter, L. (1976). *Assertive discipline: A take charge approach for today's educators.* Los Angeles: Lee Canter and Associates.

Canter, L., & Canter, M. (1992). *Assertive discipline. Positive behavior management for today's classroom.* Santa Monica, CA: Lee Canter & Associates.

Carr, J. E., Fraizer, T. J., & Roland, J. P. (2005). Token economy. *Encyclopedia of behavior modification and cognitive behavior therapy.* Thousand Oaks, CA: Sage Publications. Retrieved June 30, 2008, from http://sage-ereference.com/cbt/Article_n2132.html.

Charney, R. S. (2002). *Teaching children to care: Classroom management for ethical and academic growth K–8.* Greenfield, MA: Northeast Foundation for Children.

DeVries, R. (1999). Implications of Piaget's constructivist theory for character education. In M. M. Williams & E. Shaps (Eds.), *Character education: The foundation for teacher education* (pp. 33–39). Washington, DC: The Character Education Partnership.

DeVries, R., Hildebrandt, C., & Zan, B. (2000). Constructivist early education for moral development. *Early Education & Development, 11*(1), 10–35.

Dweck, C. S. (2007). The perils and promises of praise. *Educational Leadership, 65*(2), 34–39.

Feinberg, T., Lewis, V. E., & Williams, B. B. (2005). Ethical issues regarding behavior management in the schools. *Encyclopedia of behavior modification and cognitive behavior therapy.* Thousand Oaks, CA: Sage Publications. Retrieved July 30, 2008, from http://sage-ereference.com/cbt/Article_n3061.html.

Gartrell, D. (2004). *The power of guidance: Teaching social-emotional skills in early childhood classrooms.* Clifton Park, NY: Thomson/Delmar Learning.

Goodman, J. F. (2006). School discipline in moral disarray. *Journal of Moral Education, 35*(2), 213–230.

Gordon, T. (1970). *Parent effectiveness training.* New York: Wyden.

Gordon, T. (1989). *Teaching children self-discipline: At home and at school.* New York: Random House.

Hemmeter, M. L., Ostrosky, M., & Fox, L. (2006). Social and emotional foundations for early learning: A conceptual model for intervention. *School Psychology Journal, 35*(4), 583–601.

Henderlong, J., & Lepper, M. R. (2002). The effects of praise on children's intrinsic motivation: A review and synthesis. *Psychological Bulletin, 128,* 774–795.

Henshey, (2004). Consider the fact that corporal punishment is still permissible in 23 states.

Hitz, R., & Driscoll, A. (1988). Praise or encouragement? New insights into praise: Implications for early childhood teachers. *Young Children, 43*(5), 6–13.

Human Rights Watch. (2008). A violent education: Corporal punishment of children in U.S. public schools. Retrieved August 13, 2008, from http://www.hrw.org/reports/2008/us0808/index.htm.

Kamii, C. (1982). Autonomy as the aim of education: Implications of Piaget's theory. In C. Kamii (Ed.), *Number in preschool and kindergarten* (pp. 73–87). Washington, DC: National Association for the Education of Young Children.

Katz, L. G., & McClellan, D. E. (1997). *Fostering children's social competence: The teacher's role.* Washington, DC: National Association for the Education of Young Children.

Kohn, A. (1996). *Beyond discipline: From compliance to community.* Reston, VA: Association for Supervision and Curriculum Development.

Kohn, A. (2005). *Unconditional parenting: Moving from rewards and punishment to love and reason.* New York: Atria Books.

Landrum, T. J., & Kauffman, J. M. (2006). Behavioral approaches to classroom management. In C. M. Evertson & C. S. Weinstein (Eds.), *Handbook of classroom management: Research practice and contemporary issues.* (pp. 47–72). Mahwah, NJ: Lawrence Erlbaum Associates.

Landy, S. (2002). *Pathways to competence: Encouraging healthy social and emotional development in young children.* Baltimore: Paul H. Brookes.

Martin, E. J., & Tobin, T. J. (2005). "Time-out." Group contingency. *Encyclopedia of behavior modification and cognitive behavior therapy.* Thousand Oaks, CA: Sage Publications. Retrieved July 30, 2008, from http://sage-ereference.com/cbt/Article_n3143.html.

Massetti, G. M., & Fabiano, G. A. (2005). Group contingency. *Encyclopedia of behavior modification and cognitive behavior therapy.* Thousand Oaks, CA: Sage Publications. Retrieved July 30, 2008, from http://sage-ereference.com/cbt/Article_n2064.html.

Noddings, N. (2005). *The challenge to care in schools: An alternative approach to education* (2nd ed.). New York: Teachers College Press.

Nucci, L. (2006). Classroom management for moral and social development. In C. M. Evertson & C. S. Weinstein (Eds.), *Handbook of classroom management: Research practice and contemporary issues* (pp. 645–664), Mahwah, NJ: Lawrence Erlbaum Associates.

Piaget, J. (1965). *The moral judgment of the child.* New York: Free Press. (Originally published in 1932.)

Piaget, J. (1980). In J.-C. Bringuier (Ed.), *Conversations with Jean Piaget.* University of Chicago Press. (Original work published 1977.)

Pianta, R. (2006). Classroom management and relationships between children and teachers: Implication for research and practice. In C. M. Evertson & C. S. Weinstein (Eds.) *Handbook of classroom management: Research practice and contemporary issues*

(pp. 685–710). Mahwah, NJ: Lawrence Erlbaum Associates.

Reeve, J. (2006). Extrinsic rewards and inner motivation. In C. M. Evertson & C. S. Weinstein (Eds.), *Handbook of classroom management: Research practice and contemporary issues* (pp. 645–664). Mahwah, NJ: Lawrence Erlbaum Associates.

Reynolds, E. (2000). *Guiding young children: A problem-solving approach.* New York City: McGraw-Hill.

Simpson, R. L., & Sasso, G. M. (2005). Punishment. *Encyclopedia of behavior modification and cognitive behavior therapy.* Thousand Oaks, CA: Sage Publications. Retrieved July 30, 2008, from http://sagepereference.com/cbt/Article_n3110.html.

Skinner, B. F. (1971). *Beyond freedom and dignity.* New York: Knopf.

Thronberg, R. (2008). School children's reasoning about school rules. *Research Papers in Education, 23*(1), 37–52.

Weiss, N. R., & Knoster, T. (2008). It may be nonaversive, but is it a positive approach? Relevant questions to ask throughout the process of behavioral assessment and intervention. *Journal of Positive Behavior Interventions, 10*(72), 72–78.

CHAPTER 10

Brady, K., Forton, M. B., Porter, D., & Wood, C. (2003). *Rules in school.* Greenfield, MA: Northeast Foundation for Children.

Bredekamp, S., & Copple, C. (Eds.). (1997). *Developmentally appropriate practice in early childhood programs.* Washington, DC: National Association for the Education of Young Children.

Broderick, C. B. (2005). The structure of family rules about hitting: A family-systems perspective. In M. Donnelly & M. A. Straus (Eds.), *Corporal punishment of children in theoretical perspective* (pp. 287–298). New Haven, CT: Yale University Press.

Butchart, R. E., & McEwan, B. (1998). *Classroom discipline in American schools: Problems and possibilities for democratic education.* Albany: State University of New York Press.

Concerned Educators Allied for a Safe Environment (CEASE). (2004, Spring).

Corporal punishment in America—2004.
25(1), 6. Cambridge, MA: Author.

Daro, D., Abrahams, N., & Robson, K. (1988, May). *Reducing child abuse 20% by 1990: 1983–86 baseline data.* Chicago: National Center on Child Abuse Prevention Research.

DeVries, R. (1999). Implications of Piaget's constructivist theory for character education. In M. M. Williams & E. Shaps (Eds.), *Character education: The foundation for teacher education* (pp. 33–39). Washington, DC: The Character Education Partnership.

DeVries, R., Hildebrandt, C., & Zan, B. (2000). Constructivist early education for moral development. *Early Education & Development, 11*(1), 10–35.

Dodge, K. A., Bates, J. E., & Pettit, G. S. (1990). Mechanisms in the cycle of violence. *Science, 250,* 1678–1683.

Donnelly, M. (2005). Putting corporal punishment of children in historical perspective. In M. Donnelly & M. A. Straus (Eds.), *Corporal punishment of children in theoretical perspective* (pp. 41–54). New Haven, CT: Yale University Press.

Feld, S. (2005). Difficulties of making rational choices concerning corporal punishment of children. In M. Donnelly & M. A. Straus (Eds.), *Corporal punishment of children in theoretical perspective* (pp. 152–164). New Haven, CT: Yale University Press.

Garbaino, J. (2005). Corporal punishment in ecological perspective. In M. Donnelly & M. A. Straus (Eds.), *Corporal punishment of children in theoretical perspective* (pp. 8–18). New Haven, CT: Yale University Press.

Gathercoal, F. (1998). Judicious discipline. In R. E. Butchart & B. McEwan (Eds.), *Classroom discipline in American schools: Problems and possibilities for democratic education* (pp. 197–216). Albany: State University of New York Press.

Hart, C. H., Olsen, S. F., Robinson, C. C., & Mandleco, B. L. (1997). The development of social and communicative competence in childhood: Review and a model of personal, familial, and extrafamilial processes. *Communication Yearbook, 20,* 305–373.

Jenson, E. (2006). *Enriching the brain: How to maximize every learner's potential.* San Francisco, CA: Jossey-Bass.

Kamii, C. (1982). Autonomy as the aim of education: Implications of Piaget's theory. In C. Kamii (Ed.), *Number in preschool and kindergarten* (pp. 73–87). Washington, DC: National Association for the Education of Young Children.

Kochanska, G. (1991). Socialization and temperament in the development of guilt and conscience. *Child Development, 62,* 1379–1392.

Kohlberg, L. (1984). *Essays in moral development. Volume 2: The psychology of moral development.* New York: Harper & Row.

Landrum, T. J., & Kauffman, J. M. (2006). Behavioral approaches to classroom management. In C. M. Evertson & C. S. Weinstein (Eds.), *Handbook of classroom management: Research practice and contemporary issues* (pp. 47–72). Mahwah, NJ: Lawrence Erlbaum Associates.

McCord, J. M. (2005). *Unintended consequences of punishment.* In M. Donnelly & M. A. Straus (Eds.), *Corporal punishment of children in theoretical perspective* (pp. 165–170). New Haven, CT: Yale University Press.

McEwan, B. (1998). Contradiction, paradox, and irony. In R. E. Butchart & B. McEwan (Eds.), *Classroom discipline in American schools: Problems and possibilities for democratic education* (pp. 135–156). Albany: State University of New York Press.

Miller, D. F. (2004). *Positive child guidance* (4th ed.). Albany, NY: Delmar.

National Association for the Education of Young Children. (1996). *Prevention of Child Abuse in Early Childhood Programs and the Responsibilities of Early Childhood Professionals to Prevent Child Abuse: A position statement of the National Association for the Education of Young Children.* Washington, DC: Author.

Papatheodorou, T. (2005). *Behaviour problems in the early years. A guide for understanding and support.* London; New York: Routledge Falmer.

Paintal, S. (2007). Banning corporal punishment of children: An ACEI position paper. *Childhood Education, 83*(6), 410–413.

Piaget, J. (1965). *The moral judgment of the child.* New York: Free Press. (Originally published in 1932.)

Polakow, V. (2007). *Who cares for our children? The child care crisis in the other America.* New York: Teachers College Press.

Powell, B., Cooper, G., Hoffman, K., & Marvin, R. (2007). Circle of security project: A case study—"It hurts to give that what you did not receive." In D. Oppenheim & D. F. Goldsmith (Eds.), *Attachment theory in clinical work with children: Bridging the gap between research and practice* (pp. 172–202). New York: Guilford Press.

Reynolds, E. (2000). *Guiding young children: A problem-solving approach.* New York City: McGraw-Hill.

Rich, J. M. (2005). Moral development and corporal punishment. In M. Donnelly and M. A. Straus (Eds.) *Corporal punishment of children in theoretical perspective* (pp. 170–182). New Haven; London: Yale University Press.

Roffey, S. (2005). Helping with behaviour: Establishing the positive and addressing the difficult in the early years. Retrieved July 13, 2008, from http://www.myilibrary.com/Browse/open.asp?ID=24467&loc=81.

Sabatino, D. (1991). *A fine line: When discipline becomes child abuse.* Summit, PA: TAB Books/McGraw-Hill.

Scheff, T. J. (2005). Punishment, child development and crime: A theory of the social bond. In M. Donnelly & M. A. Straus (Eds.), *Corporal punishment of children in theoretical perspective* (pp. 233–243). New Haven, CT: Yale University Press.

Springen, K. (2000, October 16). Family: On spanking. *Newsweek, CXXXVI* (16), p. 64.

Thompson, R. A. (1998). Early sociopersonality development. In Damon & Eisenberg (Eds.), *Handbook of child psychology* (pp. 25–104). New York: John Wiley & Sons, Inc.

Turner, H. (2005). Corporal punishment and the stress process. In M. Donnelly & M. A. Straus (Eds.), *Corporal punishment of children in theoretical perspective* (pp. 255–276). New Haven, CT: Yale University Press.

United States Department of Justice. (2004). Prevalence of imprisonment in the United States. Available online at http://www.ojp.usdoj.gov/bjs/crimoff.htm.

Vissing, V. M., Straus, M. A., Gelles, R. J., & Harrop, J. W. (1991). Verbal aggression by parents and psychosocial problems of children. *Child Abuse and Neglect, 15,* 223–238.

CHAPTER 11

Bredekamp, S. (Ed.). (1997). *Developmentally appropriate practice in early childhood programs serving children from birth through age 8* (expanded ed.). Washington, DC: National Association for the Education of Young Children.

Curwin, R. L., & Mendler, A. N. (1999). *Discipline with dignity.* Alexandria, VA: Association for Supervision and Curriculum Development.

DeVries, R., & Kohlberg, L. (1987). *Constructivist early education: Overview and comparison with other programs.* Washington, DC: National Association for the Education of Young Children.

DeVries, R., & Zan, B. (1994). *Moral classrooms, moral children.* New York: Teachers College Press.

Fleisher, D. (2004). Understanding toilet training difficulties. *Pediatrics, 113,* 1809–1810.

Gottman, J. (1997). *Raising an emotionally intelligent child.* New York: Fireside.

Hansen, C., & Zambo, D. (2007). Loving and learning with Wemberly and David: Fostering emotional development in early childhood education. *Early Childhood Education Journal, 34*(4), 273–278.

Horowitz, A., Westlund, K., & Tomas, L. (2007). Aggression and withdrawal related behavior within conflict management progression in preschool boys with language impairment. *Child Psychiatry and Human Development, 38*(3), 237–253.

Hyson, M. C. (2004). *The emotional development of young children: Building an emotion-centered curriculum.* New York: Teachers College Press.

Hyson, M. C., & Molinaro, J. (2001). Learning through feeling: Children's development, teachers' beliefs and relationships, and classroom practices. In S. L. Golbeck (Ed.), *Psychological perspectives on early childhood education: Reframing dilemmas in research and practice* (pp. 107–130). Mahwah, NJ: Erlbaum.

Kamii, C. (1982). Autonomy as the aim of education: Implications of Piaget's theory. In C. Kamii (Ed.), *Number in preschool and kindergarten* (pp. 73–87). Washington, DC: National Association for the Education of Young Children.

King, M., & Gartrell, D. (2003). Building an encouraging classroom with boys in mind. *Young Children, 58*(4), 33–36.

Koc, K., & Buzzelli, C. A. (2004). The moral of the story is . . . Using children's literature in moral education. *Young Children, 59*(1), 92–97.

Landy, S. (2002). *Pathways to competence: Encouraging healthy social and emotional development in young children.* Baltimore: Paul H. Brookes.

McCord, J. M. (2005). *Unintended consequences of punishment.* In M. Donnelly & M. A. Straus (Eds.), *Corporal punishment of children in theoretical perspective* (pp. 165–170). New Haven, CT: Yale University Press.

McElwain, N. L., & Volling, B. L. (2005). Preschool children's interactions with friends and other siblings: Relationship specificity and joint contributions to problem behavior. *Journal of Family Psychology, 19,* 486–496.

NAEYC (2008). NAEYC position statement on developmentally appropriate practice in early childhood programs serving children birth through age 8. Washington, DC: Author.

Paintal, S. (2007). Banning corporal punishment of children: An ACEI position paper. *Childhood Education, 83*(6), 410–413.

Piaget, J. (1965). *The moral judgment of the child.* New York: Free Press. (Originally published in 1932.)

Ramsey, P. G. (1991). *Making friends in school: Promoting peer relationships in early childhood.* New York: Teachers College Press.

Riley, D., San Juan, R., Klinker, J., & Ramminger, A. (2008). *Social & emotional development: Connecting science and practice in early childhood settings.* St. Paul, MN: Redleaf Press.

Stork, S., & Sanders, S. W. (2008). Physical education in early childhood. *Elementary School Journal, 108*(3), 197–206.

Vygotsky, L. S. (1962). *Thought and language* (E. Hanfmann & G. Vokar, trans.) Cambridge, MA: MIT Press. (Original work published in 1934.)

Weber, E. (2002). Rules, right and wrong and children. *Early Childhood Education Journal, 30*(2), 107–111.

Children's Literature—Chapter 11

Bang, M. (1999). *When Sophie gets angry, very very very angry.* New York: Scholastic.

Barrett, J. (1988). *Animals should definitely not act like people.* New York: Aladdin.

Henkes, K. (1988). *Chester's way.* New York: Greenwillow.

Henkes, K. (1996). *Lilly's purple plastic purse.* New York: Greenwillow.

Hughes, S. (1988). *Dogger.* New York: Lothrop, Lee & Shepard.

Lobel, A. (1982). Tear-water tea. In *Owl at home.* New York: Harper (a division of HarperCollins) Trophy.

Luttrell, I. (1990). *Three good blankets.* New York: Macmillan Child Group.

Miranda, A., & Emberley, E. (1997). *Glad monster, sad monster: A book about feelings.* New York: Little, Brown.

Parr, T. (2002). *The feel good book.* Boston: Little, Brown.

Pfister, J. (1992). *The rainbow fish.* J. Alison James, trans. New York: North-South.

Rosen, M. (1996). *This is our house.* Cambridge, MA: Candlewick.

Steig, W. (1988). *Spinky Sulks:* New York: Scholastic.

Viorst, J. (1972). *Alexander and the terrible horrible, no good, very bad day.* New York: Macmillan.

Wojtowycz, D. (2000). *A cuddle for Claude.* New York: Dutton Children's Books.

Zemach, M. (1983). *The little red hen: An old story.* New York: Farrar, Straus, & Giroux.

CHAPTER 12

Adams, S. K., & Baronberg, J. (2005). *Promoting positive behavior: Guidance strategies for early childhood settings.* Upper Saddle River, NJ: Merrill/Prentice Hall.

Berden, L. E., Keane, S. P., & Calkins, S. D. (2008). Temperament and externalizing behavior: Social preference and perceived acceptance as protective factors. *Developmental Psychology, 44*(4), 957–968.

Brown, B., & Bogard, K. (2007). Pre-kindergarten to 3rd grade (PK-3) school-based resources and third grade outcomes. CrossCurrents, 5. Washington, DC: Child Trends. http://www.childtrendsdatabank.org/PDF/PKtoThree.pdf.

DeVries, R., & Zan, B. (1994). *Moral classrooms, moral children.* New York: Teachers College Press.

Dreikurs, R. (1966). *Psychology in the classroom.* New York: Harper and Row.

Gonzalez-Mena, J. (2008). *Diversity in early care and education: Honoring differences.* Washington, DC: National Association for the Education of Young Children.

Gurian, M. (2001). *Boys and girls learn differently.* San Francisco: Jossey-Bass.

Holodynksi, M., & Friedlmeier, W. (2005). *Development of Emotions and Emotion Regulation.* Springer-Verlag New York Inc.

Howes, D., & Ritchie, S. (2002). *A matter of trust: Connecting teachers and learners in the early childhood classroom.* New York: Teachers College Press.

Hyson, M. C. (2004). *The emotional development of young children: Building an emotion-centered curriculum.* New York: Teachers College Press.

Hyson, M. (2008). *Enthusiastic and engaged learners: Approaches to learning in the early childhood classroom.* New York: Teachers College Press.

Katz, L. G., & Chard, S. C. (1989/2000). *Engaging children's minds: The project approach.* Norwood, NJ: Ablex.

Katz, L. G., & McClellan, D. E. (1997). *Fostering children's social competence: The teacher's role.* Washington, DC: National Association for the Education of Young Children.

Koplow, L. (2002). *Creating schools that heal: Real-life solutions.* New York: Teachers College Press.

Landy, S. (2002). *Pathways to competence: Encouraging healthy social and emotional development in young children.* Baltimore: Paul H. Brookes.

Murray, C., Murray, K. M., & Waas, G. A. (2008). Child and teacher reports of teacher-student relationships: Concordance of perspectives and associations with school adjustment in urban kindergarten classrooms. *Journal of Applied Developmental Psychology, 29*(1), 49–61.

National Institute of Child Health and Human Development Early Child Care Research Network. (2008). Mothers' and fathers' support for child autonomy and early school achievement. *Developmental Psychology, 44*(4), July 2008, pp. 895–907.

Pianta, R. C., & Rimm-Kaufman, S. (2006). The social ecology of the transition to school: Classrooms, families, and children. In K. McCartney & D. Phillips (Eds.), *Blackwell handbook of early childhood development* (pp. 490–507). Oxford, England: Blackwell.

Rabiner, D., & Cole, J. (1989). Effect of expectancy inductions on rejected children's acceptance by unfamiliar peers. *Developmental Psychology, 25*(3), 450–457.

Turkel, A. R. (2007). Sugar and Spice and Puppy Dogs' Tails: The Psychodynamics of Bullying. *Journal of American Academy of Psychoanalysis and Dynamic Psychiatry, 35:* 243–258.

CHAPTER 13

Asher, J. (1969). The total physical response approach to second language learning. *The Modern Language Journal, 53*(1), 3–17.

Cartledge, G., Singh, A., & Gibson, L. (2008). Practical behavior-management techniques to close the accessibility gap for students who are culturally and linguistically diverse. *Preventing School Failure, 52*(3), 29–38.

Cohen, I., & Goldsmith, M. (2002). *Hands on: How to use brain gym in the classroom.* Ventura, CA: Edu Kinesthetics.

Council for Exceptional Children, Division for Early Childhood (CEC/DEC). (2005). *Concept paper on identification of and intervention with challenging behavior.* Author.

Epstein, A. S. (2007). *The intentional teacher: Choosing the best strategies for young children's learning.* Washington, DC: National Association for the Education of Young Children.

Espinosa, L. M. (2005). Curriculum and assessment considerations for young children from culturally, linguistically, and economically diverse backgrounds. *Psychology in the Schools, 42*(8), 837–853.

Fei, L., & Timler, G. R. (2008). Narrative organization skills in children with attention deficit hyperactivity disorder and language impairment: Application of the causal network model. *Clinical Linguistics & Phonetics, 22*(1), 25–46.

Fox, L., Dunlap, G., Hemmeter, M. L., Joseph, G., & Strain, P. (2003). The teaching pyramid:

A model for supporting social competence and preventing challenging behavior in young children. *Young Children, 58*(4), 48–52.

Fox, L., Lentini, R., & Dunlap, G. (2006). Individualized intensive interventions: Developing a behavior support plan. Vanderbilt University: The Center on the Social and Emotional Foundations for Early Learning. Retrieved July 13, 2008, from http://www.vanderbilt.edu/csefel/modules/module3b/script.pdf.

Gay, G. (2006). Connections between classroom management and culturally responsive teaching. In C. M. Evertson & C. S. Weinstein (Eds.), *Handbook of classroom management: Research, practice, and contemporary issues* (pp. 343–370). Mahwah, NJ: Erlbaum.

Gilliam, W. S. (2005). *Prekindergartners left behind: Expulsion rates in state prekindergarten programs.* New Haven, CT: Yale Child Development Center.

Gilliam, W. S., & Shabar, G. (2006). Preschool and Child Care Expulsion and Suspension: Rates and Predictors in One State. *Infants & Young Children: An Interdisciplinary Journal of Special Care Practices, 19*(3), 228–245.

Gonzalez-Mena, J. (2008). *Diversity in early care and education: Honoring differences.* Washington, DC: National Association for the Education of Young Children.

Hanish, D., Laura-Martin, C. L., Fabes, R. A., & Bercelo, H. (2008). The breadth of peer relationships among preschoolers: An application of the connectivity method to externalizing Behavior. *Child Development, 79*(4), 1119–1136.

Heineman, M., Dunlap, G., & Kincaid, D. (2005). Positive support strategies for students with behavioral disorders in regular classrooms. *Psychology in the Schools, 42*(8), 779–794.

Hyson, M. (2004). *The emotional development of young children: Building an emotion-centered curriculum.* New York: Teachers College Press.

Jenkins, E. (1995). *Play your instruments and make a pretty sound.* Smithsonian Folkways Recordings.

Jones, T. S., & Bodtker, A. (2001). Mediating with heart in mind: Addressing emotion in mediation practice. *Negotiation Journal, 17*(3), 217–244.

Konishi, C. (2007). Learning English as a second language: A case study of a Chinese girl in an American preschool. *Childhood Education, 83*(5), 267–272.

Lane, K., Falk, K., & Wehby, J. (2006). Classroom management in special education classrooms and resource rooms. In C. M. Evertson & C. S. Weinstein (Eds.), *Handbook of classroom management: Research, practice, and contemporary issues* (pp. 439–460). Mahwah, NJ: Erlbaum.

Milner, H. R. (2006). Classroom management in urban classrooms. In C. M. Evertson & C. S. Weinstein (Eds.), *Handbook of classroom management: Research, practice, and contemporary issues* (pp. 491–522). Mahwah, NJ: Erlbaum.

More, C. (2008). Digital stories targeting social skills for children with disabilities: Multidimensional learning. *Intervention in School and Clinic, 43*, 168–177.

Nungesser, N. R., & Watkins, R. W. (2005). Preschool teachers' perceptions and reactions to challenging classroom behavior: Implications for speech-language pathologists. *Language, Speech, and Hearing Services in Schools, 36*(2), 139–151.

Pfeiffer, B., Henry, A., Miller, S., & Witherell, S. (2008). The effectiveness of Disc 'O' Sit cushions on attention to task in second-grade students with attention difficulties. *American Journal of Occupational Therapy, 62*, 274–281.

Rothstein-Fisch, C., & Trumbull, E. (2008). *Managing diverse classrooms: How to build on students' cultural strengths.* Alexandria, VA: ASCD.

Shelton, L., & Wendell, Z. (2005). *Natural Health, 35*(3), 46–48.

Sher, B. (2006). *Attention games: 101 fun, easy games that help kids learn to focus.* San Francisco: Jossey-Bass.

Shure, M. B. (1992a). *I can problem solve: An interpersonal cognitive problem-solving program. Preschool.* Champaign, IL: Research Press.

Shure, M. B. (1992b). *I can problem solve: An interpersonal cognitive problem-solving program. Kindergarten and primary grades.* Champaign, IL: Research Press.

Smith, A., & Bondy, E. (2007). "No! I won't!": Understanding and responding to student defiance. *Childhood Education, 83*(3), 151–157.

Stormont, M., Lewis, T. J., & Covington-Smith S. (2005). Behavior support strategies in early childhood settings: Teacher's importance and feasibility ratings. *Journal of Positive Behavior Interventions.* Vol 7. 131–139.

Strain, S. S., & Joseph, G. E. (2004). Engaged supervision to support recommended practices for young children with challenging behaviors. *Topics in Early Childhood Special Education, 24*(1), 39–50.

Sugai, G., & Homer, R. H. (2008). What we know and need to know about preventing problem behavior in schools. *Exceptionality, 16*(2), 67–77.

von Korring, A., Soderberg, A., Austin, L., & Uvnas-Moberg, K. (2008). Massage decreases aggression in preschool children: A long-term study. *Acta Paediatrica, 97*(9), 1265–1269.

Wakschlag, L. S., Briggs-Gowan, M. J., Carter, A. C., Hill, C., Danis, B., Keenan, K., McCarthy, K. J., & Leventhal, B. L. (2007). A developmental framework for distinguishing disruptive behavior from normative misbehavior in preschool children. *Journal of Child Psychology and Psychiatry, 48*(10), 976–987.

Wang, D. X., & Aldridge, J. (2007). Re-examining diversity issues in childhood education. *Childhood Education, 83*(5), 250–260.

Weinstein, C. S., Tomlinson-Clarke, S., & Curran, M. (2004). Toward a conception of culturally responsive classroom management. *Journal of Teacher Education, 55*(1), 25–38.

Willis, J. (2008). *Brain-friendly strategies for the inclusion classroom: Insights from a neurologist and classroom teacher.* Alexandria, VA: Association for Supervision and Curriculum Development.

CHAPTER 14

Adalis-Estrin, A. (2003). *Visiting mom or dad.* Palmyra, VA: Children of Prisoners Library.

Aiekns, N. L., & Barbarin, O. (2008). Socioeconomic differences in reading trajectories: The contribution of family, neighborhood, and school contexts. *Journal of Educational Psychology, 100*(2), 235–251.

Allen, M. & Staley, L. (2007). Helping children to cope when a loved one is on military deployment. *Beyond the Journal: Young Children on the Web.* Available online at

http://journal.naeyc.org/btj/200701/pdf/BTJAllen.pdf.

Amato, P. R., & Cheadle, J. E. (2008). Parental divorce, marital conflict and children's behavioral problems: A comparison of adopted and biological children. *Social Forces, 86*(3), 1139–1161.

American Diabetes Association. (2006). *Wizdomkit®.* Author.

American Psychological Association (APA). (2003). *Resilience in a time of war. Tips for parents and day-care providers of preschool children.* Washington, DC: Author.

American Psychological Association (APA). (2007). *The psychological needs of U.S. military service members and their families: A preliminary report.* Washington, DC: Author.

Anne E. Casey Foundation. (2008). *2008 KIDS COUNT data book.* Baltimore, MD: Author.

Anthonysamy, A., & Zimmer-Gembeck, M. J. (2007). Peer status and behaviors of maltreated children and their classmates in the early years of school. *Child Abuse & Neglect, 31,* 871–991.

Arthritis Foundation. (n.d.). *When your student has arthritis.* Author.

Bussuk, E. L., Konnath, D., & Volk, K. T. (2006). *Understanding traumatic stress in children.* The National Center on Family Homelessness.

Christ, A. & Christ, G. (2006). Current practices to helping children cope with a parent's terminal illness. *CA—A Cancer Journal for Clinicians, 56,* 197–212.

Daniel, B., & Wassell, S. (2005). Resilience: A framework for positive practice. Scottish Executive Education Department. Available online at http://www.scotland.gov.uk/Publications/2005/05/18120009/00103.

Dryfoos, J. G. (2008). Centers of hope. *Educational Leadership, 65*(7), 38–43.

Epstein, J. L. (2008). *School, family, and community partnerships: Your handbook for action* (3rd ed.). Thousand Oaks, CA: Corwin Press.

Eppler, C. (2008). Exploring themes of resiliency in children after the death of a parent. *Professional School Counseling, 11*(3), 189–196.

Gorski, P. (2008). The myth of the "culture of poverty." *Educational Leadership, 65*(7), 32–37.

Greenberg, R. (2006). Children and families: Mothers who are incarcerated. *Woman & Therapy, 29*(3/4), 165–179.

Guell, C. (2007). Painful childhood: Living with juvenile arthritis. *Qualitative Health Research, 17*(7), 884–892.

Haine, R. A., Ayers, T. S., Sandler, I. N., & Wolchick, S. A. (2008). Evidence-based practices for parentally bereaved children and their families. *Professional Psychology Review and Practice, 39*(2), 113–121.

Hartman, J. (1996). *Follow a dream.* Saint Petersburg, FL: Hop 2-It Music. Available online at http://www.jackhartmann.com/contactjack.htm.

Hartman, J. (n.d.). *Getting better at getting along.* Saint Petersburg, FL: Hop 2-It Music. Available online at http://www.jackhartmann.com/contactjack.htm.

Hoshmand, L. T., & Hoshmand, A. L. (2007). Support for military families and their communities: Policy, research and practice. *Journal of Community Psychology, 35*(2), 171–180.

Lareau, A. (2003). *Unequal childhood: The importance of social class in family life.* Ewing, NJ: University of California Press.

LaVinge, N. G., Davies, E., & Brazzel, D. (2006). *Broken bonds: Understanding the needs of incarcerated parents.* Washington, DC: Urban Institute Justice Policy Center.

Lichten, E. (2003). *Children and the death of a parent. Handbook of death and dying.* Sage Publications. Available online at http://sage-ereference.com/death/Article_n87.html.

Meijer, S. A., Siennema, G., Bijstra, J. O., Mellenbergh, G. J., & Wolters, W. H. (2000). Social functioning of children with chronic illness. *The Journal of Child Psychology and Psychiatry, 41*(3), 309–317.

Miller, D., & Daniel, B. (2007). Competent to cope, worthy of happiness? How the duality of self-esteem can inform a resilience-based classroom environment. *School Psychology International, 28*(5), 605–622.

Miller, K. M. (2006). The impact of parental incarceration on children: An emerging need for effective interventions. *Child and Adolescent Social Work Journal, 23*(4), 472–486.

Mruk, C. (1999). *Self-esteem: Research, theory, and practice.* London: Free Association Press.

Nabors, L. A., Little, S. G., Akin-Little A., & Iobst, E. A. (2008). Teacher knowledge and confidence in meeting the needs of children with chronic medical conditions: Pediatric psychology's contribution to education. *Psychology in the Schools, 45*(3), 217–226.

National Center for Children in Poverty. (2007). *Low-income children in the United States— national and state trend data, 1996–2006.*

National Military Families Association. (n.d.). Coming home: A guide for service members returning from mobilization/deployment. Available online at http://www.nmfa.org/site/DocServer?docID=160.

Neuman, S. (2007). Changing the odds. *Educational Leadership, 65*(2), 16–21.

Operation Military Kids. Hero packs. Available online at http://www.operationmilitarykids.org/public/getinvolved.aspx.

Operation Military Kids. Ready, set, go training. Available online at http://www.operationmilitarykids.org/public/getinvolved.aspx.

Orme J. G., & Buehler, C. (2001). Foster family characteristics and behavioral and emotional problems of foster children: A narrative review. *Family Relations, 50*(3), 3–15.

Ortege, S., Beauchemin, A., & Kaniskan, R. B. (2008). Building resiliency in families with young children exposed to violence. The safe start initiative pilot study. *Best Practices in Mental Health, 4*(1), 48–64.

Parke, R. D. & Clarke-Stewart, K. A. (2001). *Effects of Parental Incarceration on Young Children. U.S. Department of Health and Human Services.* The Urban Institute. National Policy Conference. January, 2002. From Prison to Home: The Effect of Incarceration and Reentry on Children, Families, and Communities.

Perry, N. J., Mitchell-Kay, S., & Brown, A. (2008). Continuity and change in the home literacy practices of Hispanic families with preschool children. *178*(1), 99–113.

Phillips, S. D., & Gleeson, J. P. (2007). *What we know now that we didn't know then about the criminal justice system's involvement in families with whom child welfare agencies have contact.* Chicago: Jane Addams Center for Social Policy and Research, Jane Addams College of Social Work, University of Illinois at Chicago.

Santiago, E., Ferrara, J., & Blank, M. (2008). A full-service school fulfills its promise. *Educational Leadership, 65*(7), 44–47.

Scherer, M. (2008). Harnessing our power. *Educational Leadership, 65*(7), 7.

Schweinhart, L. J., Montie, J., Xiang, Z., Barnett, W. S., Belfield, C. R., & Nores, M. (2005). *Lifetime effects: The High/Scope Perry Preschool Study through age 40.* Ypsilanti, MI: High/Scope Press.

Singer, E., Doornenbal, J., & Okma, K. (2004). Why do children resist or obey their foster parents? The inner logic of children's behavior during discipline. *Child Welfare, 83*(6), 582–610.

Swadener, B. B., & Lubbeck, S. (Eds.). (1995). *Children and families "at promise." Deconstructing the discourse of risk.* Albany: State University of New York Press.

Szilagyi, P. G. (2003). Care of children with special health care needs. *Future of Children, 13*(1), 137–151.

U.S. Census Bureau. (2007). *Income, poverty, and health insurance coverage in the United States: 2006.* Washington, DC: Author.

U.S. Department of Health and Human Services, Administration on Children, Youth and Families. (2008). *Child maltreatment 2006.* Washington, DC: U.S. Government Printing Office.

Wadsworth, C. D., & Santiago, M. E. (2008). Risk and resiliency processes in ethnically diverse families in poverty. *Journal of Family Psychology, 22*(3), 399–410.

Ziebert, R. (2006). *No easy answers: The effects of parental incarceration on children.* Milwaukee, WI: Alliance for Children and Families.

Children's Literature—Chapter 14

Baylor, B. (1994). *The tables where rich people sit.* New York: Macmillan.

Belton, S. (1994). *May'naise sandwiches and sunshine tea.* New York: Four Winds Press.

Bunting, E. (1990). *A day's work.* New York: Clarion.

Bunting, E. (1990). *The wall.* New York: Clarion.

Buscagila, L. (1983). *The rise and fall of Freddie the leaf.* New Jersey: Charles B. Slack, Inc.

Cohn, J. (1987). *I had a friend named Peter.* New York: William Morrow.

DiSalvo-Ryan, D. (1991). *Uncle Willie and the soup kitchen.* New York: Mulberry.

Duckworth, L. (2003). *Ragtail remembers: A story that helps children understand feelings of guilt.* Omaha, NE: Centering Corp.

Ferguson, D. (2006). *A bunch of balloons.* Omaha, NE: Centering Corp.

Henkes, K. (2007). *A good day.* New York: Greenwillow Books.

Kaplow, J., & Pincus, D. (2007). *Samantha Jane's missing smile: A story about coping with the loss of a parent.* Washington, DC: Magination Press.

Kransey-Brown, L. (1999). *When dinosaurs die: A children's guide to understanding death.* New York: Hachette Book Group.

Kurusa, D. (1995). *The streets are free.* Toronto, ON: Annick Press.

Levins, S. (2005). *Was it the chocolate pudding?: A story about divorce for little kids.* Washington, DC: APA.

Masurel, C. (2003). *Two homes.* Massachusetts: Candlewood Press.

Mills, L. (1997). *The rag coat.* Boston: Little Brown.

Sesame Workshop. (2007). *Talk, listen, connect: Deployments, homecomings and changes.*

Williams, V. B. (2001). *Amber was brave, Essie was smart.* New York: Greenwillow Books.

Wyeth, S. D. (1998). *Something beautiful.* Prince Fredrick, MD: Doubleday.

CHAPTER 15

Brady, K., Forton, M. B., Porter, D., & Wood, C. (2003). *Rules in school.* Greenfield, MA: Northeast Foundation for Children.

DeVries, R. (1999). Implications of Piaget's constructivist theory for character education. In M. M. Williams & E. Shaps (Eds.), *Character education: The foundation for teacher education* (pp. 33–39). Washington, DC: The Character Education Partnership.

DeVries, R., Zan, B., & Hildebrandt. (2002). Issues in constructivist moral education. *Early Education & Development, 13*(3).

Dreikurs, R. (1964). *Children: The challenge.* New York: Hawthorne Books. (1991 edition published by Plume.)

Gordon, T. (1989). *Teaching children self-discipline: At home and at school.* New York: Random House.

Hemmeter, M. L., Ostrosky, M. M., Artman, K. M., & Kinder, K. A. (2008). Moving right along: Planning transitions to prevent challenging behavior. *YC Young Children,* 63(3), 18–25.

Kamii, C. (1984). Obedience is not enough. *Young Children, 39*(4), 11–14.

Katz, L. G., & McClellan, D. E. (1997). *Fostering children's social competence: The teacher's role.* Washington, DC: National Association for the Education of Young Children.

Landy, S. (2002). *Pathways to competence: Encouraging healthy social and emotional development in young children.* Baltimore: Paul H. Brookes.

Levin, D. E. (2003). *Teaching young children in violent times: Building a peaceable classroom* (2nd ed.). Washington, DC: National Association for the Education of Young Children.

National Association for the Education of Young Children. (2005). Code of Ethical Conduct & Statement of Commitment. Washington, DC: NAEYC.

National Association for the Education of Young Children/National Association of Early Childhood Specialists in State Departments of Education. (2003). *Early childhood curriculum, assessment, and program evaluation: Building an effective accountability system in programs birth through age 8.* Washington, DC: Author.

Nucci, L. (2006). Classroom management for moral and social development. In C. M. Evertson & C. S. Weinstein (Eds.), *Handbook of classroom management: Research, practice, and contemporary issues* (pp. 645–664). Mahwah, NJ: Lawrence Erlbaum Associates.

Riley, D., San Juan, R., Klinkner, J., & Ramminger, A. (2008). *Social and emotional development: Connecting science and practice in early childhood settings.* St. Paul, MN: Redleaf Press.

Watson, M. (1999). The child development project: Building character by building community. In M. M. Williams & E. Shaps (Eds.), *Character education: The foundation for teacher education* (pp. 24–32). Washington, DC: The Character Education Partnership.

Weber, E. (2002). Rules, right and wrong and children. *Early Childhood Education Journal, 30*(2), 107–111.

Wilson, B. J. (2008). Media and children's aggression, fear, and altruism. *Future of Children, 18*(1), 87–118.

Author Index

Subject Index